'ENOUGH TO KEEP THEM ALIVE'
INDIAN WELFARE IN CANADA, 1873–1965

Far from reflecting humanitarian concern or enlightened political thinking, Indian welfare policy in Canada was formulated and applied deliberately to oppress and marginalize First Nations peoples and to foster their assimilation into the dominant society. *'Enough to Keep Them Alive'* explores the development and administration of social assistance policies targeting First Nations peoples in Canada from Confederation to the 1960s, demonstrating a continuity with earlier practices that originated with pre-Confederation fur-trading companies.

Extensive archival evidence from the Indian Affairs record group at the National Archives of Canada is supplemented for the post–Second World War era by interviews with some of the key federal players. More than just an historical narrative, the book presents a critical analysis with a clear theoretical focus drawing on colonial and post-colonial theory, social theory, and critiques of liberalism and liberal democracy.

HUGH SHEWELL is an associate professor in the School of Social Work at York University.

'Enough to Keep Them Alive'

Indian Welfare in Canada, 1873–1965

HUGH SHEWELL

UNIVERSITY OF TORONTO PRESS
Toronto Buffalo London

© University of Toronto Press Incorporated 2004
Toronto Buffalo London
Printed in Canada

ISBN 0-8020-8838-4 (cloth)
ISBN 0-8020-8610-1 (paper)

Printed on acid-free paper

National Library of Canada Cataloguing in Publication

Shewell, Hugh, 1947–
    'Enough to keep them alive' : Indian welfare in Canada, 1873–
1965 / Hugh Shewell.

    Includes bibliographical references and index.
    ISBN 0-8020-8838-4 (bound)   ISBN 0-8020-8610-1 (pbk.)

    1. Indians of North America – Public welfare – Canada – History.
    2. Indian reservations – Canada – History.   I. Title

    E78.C2S52 2004   362.84'97071   C2003-902927-1

University of Toronto Press acknowledges the financial assistance to its publishing program of the Canada Council for the Arts and the Ontario Arts Council.

This book has been published with the help of a grant from the Canadian Federation for the Humanities and Social Sciences, through the Aid to Scholarly Publications Programme, using funds provided by the Social Sciences and Humanities Research Council of Canada.

University of Toronto Press acknowledges the financial support for its publishing activities of the Government of Canada through the Book Publishing Industry Development Program (BPIDP).

To Karin and Eliana

and

to my mother and in memory of my father

Contents

Preface

Several years ago an acquaintance told me there would be no interest in a book about Indian welfare. 'What could be written that wasn't already known? Isn't welfare a relatively straightforward matter relating to lack of jobs and economic dependence?' At first I thought that perhaps this person was right, that once I embarked on the task I would soon see there was no material of any academic importance or popular appeal, that there was no argument to be made that would shed greater light on the problems facing First Nations peoples within Canada's borders. Nevertheless, I felt compelled to explore the material that existed. I was troubled by my own work experience with the federal Indian Affairs department and by the disdain for the welfare program expressed by most Indian social workers. That disdain went beyond mere antipathy towards the fact of welfare and the attitudes commonly associated with it: it reached to the heart of the relationship between First Nations and both the Canadian government and the Canadian people. It is a relationship that, in Canada's postcolonial period especially, has so corrupted and destroyed Native people's economic and social fabrics that their traditional capacities to foster collective well-being have been practically destroyed.

In this book I argue that welfare – relief, social assistance – has been used by the state as a weapon to undermine First Nations cultures and to induce their assimilation and hence disappearance into the dominant Canadian economic and social order. In my analysis of government archival materials from as early as 1873, a clear pattern emerges: federal administrations were determined to subdue Indians and to teach them lessons in liberal economic theory and individual survival in the marketplace. In developing and executing Indian policy – particularly Indian *welfare* policy – politicians and public servants alike willingly wore the mantle of civilization and modern progress. Although the language of the 'white man's burden' became somewhat more muted after the Second World War, the underlying ideology of Euro-Canadian superiority remained wholly intact, and it continues to inform the essential approach to Indian social welfare.

The period covered in this book, 1873 to 1965, represents the essential time frame during which the federal Indian administration developed what is still the central tenet of Indian welfare: that there be no distinction between Indians and other Canadians. On the surface this may seem a reasonable policy objective, but as I will show, it was misguided and fraught with assumptions about what was best for First Nations peoples. I offer no solutions *per se*; that said, I believe the answers to the questions posed by Indian marginalization and poverty must come from the First Nations themselves and from a far greater willingness on the part of the Canadian state to listen to and act on their wishes. It is no small irony that Canada and its colonial past have created these problems and completely failed to solve them. That the oppressor now contends to be the liberator simply highlights the arrogance of the Western worldview.

My bibliography reveals, I hope, the rich scholastic sources from which I have been able to draw in developing my arguments. As I began to write this book I was influenced especially by the theoretical work of other scholars, some of whose names have since fallen out of the manuscript. For my critique of liberalism, liberal democracy, and liberal capitalism, I owe much to the work of Anthony Arblaster, Noam Chomsky, and C.B. Macpherson. My understanding of the nature and history of the encounter between First Nations and the emerging forces of Western capitalism has been heavily influenced by Eric R. Wolf's superb book, *Europe and the People without History*, as well as by Arthur J. Ray's two great works, *Indians in the Fur Trade* and *The Canadian Fur Trade in the Industrial Age*. As well, I have drawn on Marxist thought and dependency theory in contextualizing my overall approach. Here I am thinking mainly of the works of André Gunder Frank and Immanuel Wallerstein. Finally, I could not have developed my style of analysis and consideration of discourse without consulting the works of Albert Memmi, Edward Said, Sara Mills, and Lise Noël.

I could not have written this book alone. It reflects the guidance, support, and patience of many friends and colleagues. I thank Professor Allan Irving for his wonderful support, scholarly advice, wit, and wisdom

over many years. Professors Don Bellamy, Adrienne Chambon, Jim Struthers, and Mel Watkins offered important advice, insights, and criticisms,
all of which helped shape the final form and content of this book. James
Milloy, Peter Kulchyski, and Frank Tester all contributed needed ideas
and criticisms. I am grateful as well to the anonymous readers from the
University of Toronto Press and the Humanities and Social Science Federation of Canada for their enthusiastic responses and suggestions,
which helped strengthen the manuscript. While I was on sabbatical
leave, John Dixon and the University of Plymouth, England, provided
the perspective of distance, as well as much support and a quiet space to
work. Without these I would not have been able to complete the often
daunting task of refining the manuscript. Professor Ken Moffatt, my
friend and colleague at York University, was a constant support throughout the process, offering many helpful suggestions and helping me
appreciate Foucault! Finally, thank you to Jessa Chupik-Hall whose
enthusiasm for the original manuscript encouraged me to continue.

I am most grateful for the support and assistance I received at the
National Archives of Canada, where I conducted the bulk of the primary research. As well, I wish to acknowledge the grants I received from
the former National Welfare Grants program and the Atkinson Faculty
of Liberal and Professional Studies at York University. These grants
enabled me to spend time in Ottawa, to complete critical phases of the
research, and to edit and transcribe the manuscript. Virginia Rose
Smith initially edited the manuscript, making it infinitely more readable
and approachable. Thanks are also due to Kristen Adlhoch and Christopher Galloway, who toiled many hours committing an earlier revised
copy to computer files. Their work was invaluable.

I am especially grateful to the Aid to Scholarly Publications Program
of the Humanities and Social Sciences Federation, without whose financial support this book could not have been published. Special thanks to
Dr George F. Davidson, Jerry Gambill, Claude Isbister, Charles N.C.
Roberts, and Walter Rudnicki, who all agreed to be interviewed and
whose comments have given many parts of the book added life and
dimension. I am also very grateful to my editor, Len Husband at the
University of Toronto Press, who has supported me every step of the way
from the moment I deposited the voluminous manuscript on his desk.

Many thanks as well to Robert and Bob in Ottawa, whose bed-and-
breakfast house was a true home, and to my friends Hugh and Jean
Millar and Annabella Spagnut in Vancouver. My family in Ottawa, Vancouver, and Toronto has been a source of strength and inspiration

throughout. My partner, Karin Adlhoch, contributed much valuable advice, as well as assistance in transcribing the earlier work from DOS to Windows. She has been a model of patience and moral support in bearing with a crotchety academic through thick and thin. I could never thank her enough. Finally, my daughter Eliana has made sure that her father remembers the important things in life – caring, love, respect, and time for each other. She reminds me constantly that the world can and must become a better place.

'ENOUGH TO KEEP THEM ALIVE'

1

Themes and Issues

In came the nice fat dividends, up rose the lofty thoughts, and we did not realize that all the time we were exploiting the poor of our own country and the backward races abroad ...

E.M. Forster, 'The Challenge of Our Time'

The quest for truth is always the establishment of power.

Bryan S. Turner, 'Periodization and Politics in the Postmodern'

What's real and what's true aren't necessarily the same.

Salman Rushdie, *Midnight's Children*

The Complexity of the Issue

Indian welfare: in Canada this phrase occasions much opinion, mostly pejorative. Canadians as a rule have much to say and lament about Indian welfare dependency but little to offer in the way of solutions. Most rely on stock answers: Indians are lazy, welfare has made them lazy, they have to stop drinking, they should get a job, they should leave the reserve – in short, they should be like us. There is an abundant literature on issues related to Indian self-government, health, land claims, economies and education, yet there is scarcely any on Indian welfare. This is ironic, because welfare is, arguably, the issue that motivates most discussion within and outside Indian communities and is clearly one of the most significant budget items within Indian and Northern Affairs Canada, the federal department charged with administrating those communities.

This book examines the history of welfare policy on reserves in Canada. In doing so, it explores the history of Indian–Canadian relations, especially since Confederation. This book was inspired by my work in British Columbia during the 1980s. At that time I was the regional supervisor of income maintenance services – a euphemism for welfare – for Indian and Northern Affairs Canada. I was responsible for the overall policy and administration of social assistance programs on BC reserves. British Columbia, like all Canadian provinces except Ontario, does not extend its welfare services to the reserves. This position is based on the provinces' belief that Indian welfare is a federal responsibility. For at least the past half-century, the federal government has argued that the provinces ought to be responsible for Indian welfare because Indians are citizens of their respective provinces. Given provincial intransigence on the matter, Ottawa resolved in 1964 to provide social assistance in a manner comparable to each provincial jurisdiction. Thus, in my position I was dealing with and interpreting provincial policy in British Columbia and trying to make it palatable and responsive to the many Indian bands in that province.

Believing myself to be a good and fair public servant, I was struck by the level of hostility directed toward the program by the bands. They fundamentally rejected it, citing cultural incompatibility and irrelevance. In the end, I came to understand that First Nations in British Columbia and Canada could not be treated like other Canadians in need. For First Nations social welfare was a touchstone that symbolized everything that was wrong with the relationship between Canada and themselves. It was what liberal civilization had wrought upon them in thanks for two-and-a-half centuries of mutual trade and nation building. In *First Nations? Second Thoughts*, Flanagan challenges what he calls contemporary aboriginal orthodoxy with respect to self-determination and the adverse effects of European civilization. Sounding more like a late-nineteenth-century political philosopher trumpeting the glories of Western civilization, he essentially uses arguments of the Enlightenment to rationalize Euro-Canadian superiority over First Nations. The only way out for Indians in Canada is upward and onward.[1] In this book I reject Flanagan's position and argue that Euro-Canadian civilization – liberal democratic capitalism – has laid waste to aboriginal peoples and their cultures. The study of welfare provision on reserves illuminates how this has happened; it also puts under the microscope the complex relationship between the Canadian state and First Nation peoples.

The depth of poverty on reserves is not the simple outcome of a lack of work; nor is the modern provision of social welfare (relief assistance) the simple outcome of benevolent state intervention in the face of need and hardship. Indians have been economically marginalized because Europeans have stolen their lands. But whatever people think, their extreme poverty and dependency is not a direct result of their inability to be wage labourers or to engage in the dominant economy. Rather, it is the inevitable result of both the history of Indian–European[2] encounter in Canada and the ultimate domination of Western liberal capitalism and ideology.[3]

Until recently, data about the extent of on-reserve welfare dependency were difficult to obtain and not always reliable. Only in the past twenty years or so has the Department of Indian Affairs and Northern Development systematically begun to collect, organize, and analyse these data on a consistent basis. Before then, dependency rates were estimated only from time to time, usually during the preparation of specific reports. For example, in 1972–3 and 1973–4 – the earliest years for which estimated figures are available – the dependency rates were 57 per cent and 55 per cent respectively. By 1980–1, the rate was estimated at 59 per cent. These rates compared with general Canadian dependency rates of 6 to 7 per cent for provincial social assistance programs funded under the former Canada Assistance Plan. More recently, on-reserve Indian dependency rates have declined to about 42 per cent (1990–1) and 41 per cent (1998–9). These rates compare to the general Canadian rate of about 7.6 per cent reported on 31 March 1999. Some of the recent decline in on-reserve dependency may be attributable to the phenomenal growth and administrative devolution of Indian Affairs programs, which has resulted in more employment on reserves.[4]

Indians' sometimes overt but more often silent resistance to the efforts of colonial and Canadian governments to subjugate them, and to integrate them into mainstream society has contributed greatly to the form and extent of welfare dependency on Indian reserves. More exactly, welfare dependency on reserves is as much an outcome of policies to suppress Indians' cultural and political sovereignty as it is a result of economic deprivation and high unemployment. But this is not to say that government policies created welfare dependency. It is easy to concede how oppressed Indian peoples have been, but having conceded as much, we still haven't come to grips with all that statement entails.

Trigger alludes to the issue's complexity. Indian dependency can be better understood, he writes, 'by many further detailed investigations of the economic, social, and political history of native peoples under European control as well as more systematic historical studies of the policies that colonial, provincial, and federal governments formulated for dealing with these peoples and how these policies were administered.'[5] The questions at hand, then, are these: How are we to formulate such studies? How are we to determine what needs to be studied? And how are we to develop an appropriate and explanatory framework of analysis? To begin to address these questions and to develop that explanatory framework, we must review some early Canadian history with respect to settlement and the origins of Indian policy.

Settlement and the Development of British Colonial and Canadian Indian Assimilation Policy

Regarding the character of European literature at the beginning of the twentieth century, Said writes:

> At the apex of high imperialism early in this century ... we have a conjunctural fusion between, on the one hand, the historicizing codes of discursive writing in Europe, positing a world universally available to transnational impersonal scrutiny, and on the other hand, a massively colonized world. The object of this consolidated vision is always either a victim or a highly constrained character, permanently threatened with severe punishment, despite his or her many virtues, services, or achievements, excluded ontologically for having few of the merits of the conquering, surveying, and civilizing outsider. For the colonizer the incorporative apparatus requires unremitting effort to maintain. For the victim, imperialism offers these alternatives: serve or be destroyed.[6]

In the colonial social systems described by Memmi, the colonized were invariably judged to be inferior to the colonizers. This was reflected in a social infrastructure that not only enforced physical separation between colonizers and colonized but also offered inferior services, such as in education, to the colonized. The colonizing power was held up as a superior civilization to which the indigenous peoples should aspire, even though, in practice, systemic racism precluded that possibility. Nevertheless, the choice to assimilate or to resist ultimately lay with the colonized.[7] Generally speaking, colonial governments did not actively pursue policies to assimilate indigenous peoples. Because the colonized usually far outnumbered the colonizers, assimilation simply was not a practical possibility. As a principle, however, the need for

assimilation was constantly justified on the basis of the colonizers' superiority; at the same time, the failure of the colonized to assimilate was
conveniently ascribed to their inferior and primitive status.

This pattern arose when England's imperial purpose became one of
colonizing British North America. The relatively accommodating views
of the fur traders toward the First Nations gradually gave way to the
much less respectful ones of the colonists.[8] The Royal Proclamation of
1763 declared that settlement was a fact, but also recognized the dangers that settlement posed to the Indian way of life. The proclamation
declared that the lands described in its text that had not already been
ceded to or purchased by the Crown could be surrendered only
through a representative of the Crown, and only with the clear and public consent of representatives of the appropriate First Nation.[9] One purpose of the proclamation was to protect and minimize disruption to
traditional Indian societies. Even so, the strategy for dealing with Indians and their lands, as articulated by the Crown, assumed a *de facto*
sovereign-subject relationship. This assumption carried with it two
implications. First, Indians were not considered self-determining
peoples; instead, they owed their continued existence to the Crown's
pleasure. Second, the First Nations' own history as independent peoples
was moribund; their future now lay within Western civilization, however
that history unfolded.

The issue of protection of Indian lands raised two important questions: What was to be the relationship between the First Nations and the
growing numbers of European settlers? And how was that relationship
to be addressed in pragmatic terms? In the first half of the nineteenth
century, the British Colonial Office struggled with these questions as it
sought to create a policy that would satisfy the requirements of settlement while protecting Indians from exploitation and destruction. The
proclamation, its implications, and the questions it raised thus represent
the beginning of modern Indian administration in Canada. At the same
time, the operation of Foucault's schema of domination–repression[10]
through processes of state legitimation became increasingly apparent.

After the American War of Independence and the War of 1812, the
British settlement of the Maritimes and of Upper and Lower Canada
greatly intensified. This created considerable conflict among the settlers, their colonial governments, and the First Nations. These conflicts,
which centred mainly on land and land use, placed the British Colonial
Office in a difficult position. On the one hand, the office's policies had
to support the consolidation of economic interests without unduly

thwarting the colonial legislatures. Permitting the continued acquisition of land for settlement could accomplish this objective. On the other hand, the Royal Proclamation required the office to find ways to ease the relentless pressure for land and 'manage' the displacement of the Indians.[11]

By the mid-nineteenth century, the office had arrived at a compromise solution. Having considered four alternatives, including the extermination and enslavement of Indians, it decided to take measures to 'insulate' or 'remove' them from colonial society. At the same time, the Indians would be civilized and actively but gradually assimilated into the mainstream. The term 'assimilation' was originally 'amalgamation.' McNab describes amalgamation as a 'consciously assimilative policy, [which] entailed in the long term the complete or partial loss of the native culture and economy.' Furthermore, according to McNab, assimilation policy was to be implemented differently across the continent. The principle of protection (insulation) was to be emphasized more in the Maritime colonies; in the United Canadas, to which the responsibility for Indian administration was soon to be transferred, more emphasis was to be placed on assimilation. In Rupert's Land, where settlement was still not a significant issue in the 1840s, responsibility for the treatment of Indians was left mainly to the judgment of the Hudson's Bay Company, though the HBC would still be subject to these general principles. Policy for Vancouver Island was left largely to the discretion of its governor, James Douglas, a former HBC trader.[12]

The policy of insulation followed by assimilation had several advantages. It allowed for the peaceful and economical acquisition of land by the colonial governments, while reserving enough land to protect the Indians and ensure their humane treatment. In addition, the monies received by Indians from land surrenders and sales would increase the funds available for their administration and support. This last point was especially critical in the United Canadas. Beginning in 1818, cash payments to First Nations for land surrendered or sold for settlement were made by annual instalments called annuities. As of 1830, annuity payments could also be made 'in kind' in the form of housing, equipment, and provisions. In 1842, after the Bagot Commission presented its report, Indians were encouraged to subdivide their lands and sell them off as individual freeholders.[13]

The pattern that emerged became increasingly significant after 1867. The funds derived from land sales were held in account for each band, and sometimes for each individual band member. The Crown used these funds for Indian administration and services. This government control of Indian monies, which involved tight restrictions on Indians' access to them, exemplified the paternalism that was the worst aspect of Indian protection. The government spent the monies in the 'best interests' of Indians; in the government's view, this meant for the project of civilizing and assimilating them. Assimilation was a substitute for outright extermination. The administration of Indian matters became a silent war against the First Nations; its objective was to pacify, dominate, and repress those nations. Assimilation policy and its euphemistically named successors thus provided the overarching principle for every form of Indian administration to follow, including welfare relief.

An active assimilation policy (in contrast to passive espousal of the principle) was only a slight twist on usual colonial practice. This policy was still driven by imperial assumptions about the inferiority of 'backward races.' A key part of assimilation policy – which was also an outgrowth of typical colonialist thinking – was the creation of reserves as laboratories for teaching Indians the ways of European civilization. The reserve system was precisely the type of enforced exclusion that Memmi has more recently described as a dominant trait of the colonizing process. Because settlers quickly outnumbered the First Nations, Indians could be isolated and contained geographically with relative ease. The reserve system was comparable to the practice of separate quarters employed by the English and colonizing powers elsewhere; it differed mainly in scale.

True, the reserves flowed from the idea of protection for First Nations peoples as reflected in the 1763 proclamation. That said, the reserves ultimately served to exclude and discriminate against Indians and simultaneously protect settlers. Contact between the groups was minimized. Colonial legislation and its post-Confederation counterpart, the Indian Act, defined (as it still does) who was an Indian, for the purpose of clarifying to which people the policies of civilization and assimilation applied. The Indian legislation set out the criteria for successful assimilation and allowed the task of settlement to continue apace. It also provided justification – moral and other – for the cruel business of dispossession.[14]

Assimilation policy was linked to the idea of protecting Indians from the corrupting influences of commercial society; but it was also intended as preparation for participation in that society. For the colonial office, the policy's chief advantage was that it offered a way to subdue Indians and minimize the potential for conflict. It was also a complement to Indian land policy. As Indian land was acquired through purchase or surrender, protection and assimilation came to be seen as the Indians' only alternative. Later, after Confederation, land surrender and assimilation came to be seen as a key aspect of nation building.

Nation building was seen as the embodiment of Western progress and modernism; Indian peoples were retrograde forces if their traditional land tenure impeded the development of the nation. In nineteenth-century bourgeois liberalism, the achievement of statehood was a key indicator of a society's maturity. A liberal state provided the foundation for a market society, that is, a society of choice in which people were free to pursue private self-interest. Such states were emblematic of liberal ideology. According to Hobsbawm, there are two reasons why this world view developed. Both are especially pertinent to how indigenous peoples came to be perceived and treated within the context of nationhood. The nation-state came to be associated with liberal ideology because, first of all, it was seen as a phase of human development:

> From the small group to the larger, from family to tribe to region, to nation and, in the last instance, to the unified world of the future in which, to quote the superficial ... G. Lowes Dickinson, 'the barriers of nationality which belong to the infancy of the race will melt and dissolve in the sunshine of science and art' ...
> ... in the perspective of liberal ideology, the nation (i.e. the viable large nation) was the stage of evolution reached in the mid-nineteenth century ... The other face of the coin 'nation as progress' was therefore, logically, the assimilation of smaller communities and peoples to larger ones.[15]

From this perspective, the Indian peoples of Canada were, by virtue of their band and tribal groupings, understood to be primitive. Not only that, but it was inconceivable that they should wish to remain so. Their only hope for survival and advancement lay in casting off their past and accepting the progress embodied in the expanse and embrace of the nation-state.

Second, the nation-state represented the triumph of the 'people' over monarchic or despotic rule. The idea that the people had a right to govern themselves according to constitutional law instead of being governed by those who claimed a natural right to govern through birth was quite new, and gained its most inspired expression in the French Revolution. The 'people' really meant the bourgeoisie; it certainly did not apply to the working and peasant classes, although for a time the French Revolution championed their cause and relied on their support in the struggle to overthrow the monarchy. My point here is that *nation* came to mean an entity governed by the people, and because of that 'it was opposed by conservatives and traditionalists, and therefore attracted their opponents.'[16] It follows that Indian peoples, who governed themselves by status and custom, were seen as hopelessly mired in their own past and traditions. They represented the antithesis of liberalism, which was of the present. The past was to be discarded and the future embraced.

Yet we cannot separate nation building and other, more practical bases of assimilation policy from the perceptions of the Indian 'other' that prevailed in colonial and post-Confederation times. These perceptions were held by settlers, by their colonial governments, and in less virulent form by the colonial office in London. These perceptions were racist, but they were also more than that; they reflected and expressed the imperial materialism and liberal culture that supported racism. Liberal culture and values, in all their glory, emphasized property, individualism, and the virtues of work, science, and progress. English perceptions about Indians revealed more about European liberal bias than they did about the true nature of First Nations peoples.

Herman Merivale, a classical political economist and a follower of Edward Gibbon Wakefield, was permanent undersecretary at the Colonial Office from 1847 to 1860. At that post, he did much to influence land and assimilation policies and to shape Indian administration in Canada. Merivale's general views of Indians are of special interest:

> They seem possessed of a higher moral elevation than any other uncivilized race of mankind, with less natural readiness and ingenuity than some but greater depth and force of character; more native generosity of spirit, and manliness of disposition; more of the religious element; and yet, on the other hand, if not with less capacity for improvement, certainly less readiness to receive it; a more thorough wildness of temperament; less curiosity; inferior excitability; greater reluctance to associate with civilized men; a more ingovernable impatience of control. And their primitive condition of hunters, and aversion from every other, greatly increases the difficulty of including them in the arrangements of a regular community.[17]

In fact, Merivale believed that Indians 'would not be very easy to absorb by amalgamation, for except for their religiosity, they were usually regarded as "barbarians" or "savages."' Here, Merivale was alluding to the attitudes and perceptions of the colonists and of the colonial administrations. It seems that the general hostility toward the First Nations expressed in British North America at the time, coupled with the pressure for responsible government, caused Merivale eventually to despair that assimilation would ever work as a 'humane' solution. McNab writes that in 1841, Merivale inclined toward amalgamation 'as the "only possible Euthanasia of savage communities." Later, Merivale recognized that neither insulation nor amalgamation would provide satisfactory solutions to the native question in British North America.'[18]

What were the racist perceptions that infused the thinking of the colonial office? The dominant European perception of Indians in the mid-nineteenth century was that they were primitive. This perception accords with McGrane's analysis of European formulations over time of the non-European 'other.' During the nineteenth century these formulations were based on both evolutionary theory and changing ideas about time and history.[19] The perception that Indians were primitive was further affected by negative or at best romantic nineteenth-century attitudes. Fisher[20] captures the nature of European–Indian relations in British Columbia during this period. His history of the fur trade and settlement in British Columbia shows in microcosm the change in perceptions of the Indian as the European purpose shifted gradually from trade to settlement. Central to Fisher's analysis is Europeans' ambivalence about Indians. On the one hand, many perceived the Indian in ways that expanded on nearly all of McGrane's formulations! These were, in one sense, the most profoundly racist. Indians were ignorant and without religious belief and 'acted more from instinct than from reason.' In appearance and habits they were repulsive, untrustworthy, 'lazy and unsuited to manual labour.' Their ceremonies were 'disgusting' and 'grotesque,' and their homes and bodies 'filthy.' They had no concept of land's value and use for accumulation of wealth. Indeed, Fisher observes, there was hardly an aspect of Indian society that did not confirm the settlers' preconceived notions of Indian inferiority.[21] The settler majority held this perspective, seeing Indians as standing in the way of progress. 'So the disappearance of the Indians was regarded as inevitable as the influx of European settlers. It was widely held both in Britain and North America that colonization by definition involved the extermination of the "inferior" indigenous peoples. The inevitability of the Indians' doom was said by some to be a law of nature.'[22]

Another, less common view, which carried considerable influence in London, saw European settlement as inevitable but lamented the doom of the 'noble savage.' With this view came two further perceptions. A distinctly romantic one pictured the Indian as degraded and corrupted by commerce and progress, and to be despised for succumbing to European ways.[23] The other, which reflected race and evolutionary theory, saw the Indian as an endangered species that should be protected from, but not permitted to hinder the necessary progress of, the superior English civilization.[24] Members of various humanitarian movements such as the Aborigines Protection Society especially held this latter view. The noble savage was a romantic notion, one most likely to be held by the bourgeois at home, and rarely entertained by settlers.

The settlers' various, ambivalent perceptions of Indians found expression in the colonial policy of the late 1840s and 1850s. The colonial policy of protection (i.e., isolation from settlement) and eventual assimilation succeeded in pacifying both the majority and the less popular points of view.[25] Chamberlin's analysis of how these apparently opposing views found expression in the same policy is especially telling. He writes of middle to late nineteenth century thought that

> some form of arbitrary separation has always been an aspect of attempts to integrate the natives with the majority society ... Behind all of this are some implicit assumptions: that to be an Indian is to be something different; that to change an Indian into a white man is to do something important; and that to remain an Indian is to remain unreconstructed. From time to time, being unreconstructed has been fashionable, but not often, nor for long.[26]

After Confederation, the moderating influence of the colonial office was lost. The treatment of First Nations was left in the hands of the former colonists, whose economic rapaciousness was generally contrary to the Indians' interests. Although protection remained a salient feature of new Canadian Indian policy and law, greater emphasis was placed on subjugating Indians and preparing them for assimilation into Canadian society and nationhood.[27] Green, for example, persuasively argues that treaty making after Confederation was the fourth – usually unacknowledged – component of Macdonald's National Policy, which was formally adopted in 1878. For the National Policy to work, the Indians would have to be controlled and subjugated, so that their lands could be secured for immigrant settlement and for railway building.[28] Macdonald saw this issue as so important that in 1878 he retained the portfolio of Minister of the Interior. In doing so, he controlled the department initially responsible for Indian matters.[29] The Indian Act of 1876 consolidated past colonial and federal pieces of legislation relating to the status and treatment of Indians and set out the framework for assimilation policy. Tobias writes that 'the new legislation incorporated all the protective features of the earlier legislation, and established more stringent requirements for non-Indian use of Indian lands and for their alienation ... What becomes ... clearer is the Government's determination to make the Indians into imitation Europeans ... to eradicate the old Indian values through education, religion, new economic and political systems, and a new concept of property.'[30] Indians thus retained their previous colonial status. They remained disenfranchised wards of the federal government, confined to their reserves and subject to increasingly coercive and restrictive administrative authority.[31]

The subsequent creation of the Department of Indian Affairs in 1880 institutionalized the relationship between Canada and the First Nations, creating a subculture within the civil service that Hawthorn later described as quasi-colonial, isolated, and functioning like a 'miniature government.'[32] After Confederation, and well into the first half of the twentieth century, departmental personnel reflected the prevailing belief in the superiority of white civilization. Many were unabashed British imperialists, 'faithful and obedient' civil servants unswerving in their dedication to the task, which was to subjugate Indians and assimilate them into Canadian society.[33]

Duncan Campbell Scott was typical of the civil servants the department attracted during this period. He joined the department in 1880, became deputy superintendent – that is, deputy minister – in 1913, and held that position until his retirement in 1932. Scott presided over or was involved in the final great land surrenders – the four numbered treaties after 1880 and the Williams Treaties of 1923. Titley writes:

Scott firmly believed in the great civilizing mission of the British Empire, and he saw Canada's international role as an integral component of that entity ...

If the Indian in the past had been prone to savagery and superstition, what of his future? Scott was convinced that aboriginal economic activities such as hunting, trapping, fishing, and food-gathering would have to be abandoned. The Indian should learn how to cultivate the soil or prepare himself for employment in the 'industrial or mercantile community.' This economic transformation would have to be accompanied by 'the substitution of Christian ideals of conduct and morals for aboriginal concepts of both.'

Passing on the advantages of white civilization to the Indians would be a slow and tedious process. This was inevitable since they harboured primitive instincts that would take generations to eradicate. Education would be a key element in the cultural transformation. While still young and impressionable, the Indian child would be introduced by the school to a superior set of behaviours and values. One outcome would be Indian adults who had internalized the work ethic and a sense of civic responsibility ... If the savage impulses ... were deep-rooted in their collective psyche – primeval instincts that were somehow genetically transmitted – it followed that ... advancement could only take place through the injection of a superior strain of blood. Intermarriage with the more advanced caucasian race would provide the Indians with the best prospect for progress.

But the task was an onerous one for the state. Scott once observed that the British North America Act had given to the federal government 'the burden of the Indian,' and the acquisition of the western territories had 'largely increased the burden.' Here was an unmistakable echo of the rhetoric of nineteenth century imperialism.[34]

The government banned religious and cultural rites such as potlatching, dancing, and traditional funerals and burials. New forms of political organization were imposed on bands; these supplanted traditional decision making with liberal, parliamentary rules of conduct.[35] Very often, bands were formed by uniting unrelated and even hostile peoples. Criminal and civil law were declared applicable on reserves. Indian children were removed from their homes, placed in residential schools, forbidden to speak their native language, and systematically taught white ways. Industrial training schools were established to teach young Indians basic labouring skills. Housing was built according to European design, and individuals were encouraged to earn certificates of possession, thereby alienating their property from the reserve. Indian political activity was first discouraged, then effectively curtailed.[36]

Not only that, but the superintendent and his delegates could enfranchise Indians on application or even against their will. Enfranchisement, which bestowed on Indians – usually men – full rights of citizenship, signified final assimilation, since enfranchised Indians lost their status and protection under the Indian Act. In effect, they were no longer recognized as 'being Indian.' Enfranchisement was thought to be a goal worth reaching, but it became as much a weapon of the state as a prize. The idea was to encourage Indians to 'earn' and apply for the franchise, but the state did not hesitate to threaten it as punishment for rebellious or politically active Indians.[37] Enfranchisement and assimilation became an insoluble dilemma. To enfranchise an Indian, the state first had to know who an Indian was, and it did this through registration under the Indian Act. By establishing a legal class of persons called Indians, the state excluded from Canadian society a specific group of people in order to have them prove their worth to be included.[38] Ultimately, the Indian Act and an entire department devoted to its administration provided the First Nations with a common, visible enemy as well as a confirmation of their distinctiveness. The department's existence focused Indian resistance and provided a broad basis for their solidarity.

Another factor that strongly impinged on the history of Indians in Canada was the modern perception of the individual and individualism. By the eighteenth century, Western thought had come to define the individual in terms of a Natural Law, a direct relationship with God. The common constitution of all individuals – that is, their orderly and reasonable behaviour – was understood to emanate from this relationship, since God was the source of reason and order. The idea of a universal human nature derived from this understanding; variations were simply peculiar to the individual.[39] Seligman contends that this understanding slowly changed during the eighteenth century as it came to be understood that the individual possessed metaphysical and moral value. This revised view of the individual led to the modern reformulation of the universal. According to modern notions, society as universal 'is so only as a derivative of the individual; that is of the growing recognition of the individual as subject and society as the amalgamation of these 'universally' constituted subjects. What becomes a universal in the individualism ethic is thus the individual him/herself. That the particular becomes the universal is the reigning ethic of individualistic societies – hence equality (of individuals/ particulars).[40]

This depiction of the individual in relation to the universal helps explain the official thinking about assimilation and nationhood. Modernism tried to effect the loss of differences among people and peoples. The Indian individual could become the universal, civilized individual. According to this liberal vision, Indian survival lay in embracing Western civilization and progress, in the loss of indigenous culture, in the loss of difference.

Domination and Repression: The Ideology of Liberal Democracy

By the time of Confederation, the fundamental approaches toward civilizing and assimilating the Indians had been established by the colonial office and enacted by the colonial assemblies.[41] Thus, attitudes and policies directed at aboriginal peoples in the emergent Canadian context were embedded in English colonial imperialism, which itself was an extension of English political and economic thought and of English liberalism. The development of English liberalism from the seventeenth century onwards, which culminated in the emergence of contemporary liberal democracy, especially influenced the relationship between Indian peoples and the incoming English traders and settlers. Liberalism involved more than a new economic order; it was a way of thinking and behaving rooted in new ideas about individualism, property, and the politics of free choice. It redefined the relationship between the individual and society, and it propelled the emergence of the modern, secular state.[42] Moreover, liberalism, which is at the heart of North American and English cultures, became the sustaining ideology of Capitalism.[43]

In evolving from a rudimentary bourgeois democracy concerned solely with the protection of private property and capital toward its more sophisticated, contemporary form, the liberal capitalist state developed a particular ethos, its liberal democratic ideology. One way to identify the characteristics of this ethos – which has over time done so much to destroy the social integrity and cultural autonomy of First Nations – is to review Macpherson's three models of liberal democracy.[44]

The earliest model of the liberal democratic state is described by Macpherson as 'protective democracy.' It developed in the eighteenth and early nineteenth centuries during England's Industrial Revolution. It was really more of an 'arrangement,' under which competing private interests could argue and resolve their differences through the auspices of the state. The state was arbiter, regulator, and provider for a class of competing elites. This model developed as a means to protect the new industrial society and the propertied, capitalist class. About this model, Macpherson writes:

There is no enthusiasm for democracy, no idea that it could be a morally transformative force; it is nothing but a logical requirement for the governance of inherently self-interested conflicting individuals who are assumed to be infinite desirers of their own private benefits. Its advocacy is based on the assumption that man is an infinite consumer, that his overriding motivation is to maximize the flow of satisfactions, or utilities, to himself from society, and that a national society is simply a collection of such individuals. Responsible government, even to the extent of responsibility to a democratic electorate, was needed for the protection of individuals and the promotion of the Gross National Product, and for nothing more.[45]

Protective democracy was the model under which nineteenth-century laissez-faire capitalism flourished. This model was transformed during the twentieth century, but it did not vanish. Indeed, the raison d'être of the liberal state – the protection of private property and capital – remains fundamental to our contemporary system.

Developmental democracy, the second model, arose in response to the social ills produced by the first and to the real threat of socialist revolution that existed during the latter half of the nineteenth century. Its chief proponent, liberal philosopher John Stuart Mill, saw in the first model a denial of the fullness of human nature, the result of which was desperation among the English working classes, who lacked any meaningful stake in society. Mill, a long-time employee of the East India Company, did not take issue with capitalism nor did he equate the great distress of the working classes solely with class exploitation. Instead, he envisioned a liberal society in which liberalism's promise of full and equal development for all individuals would be possible. He advocated public state education, the enfranchisement of the working class, and the development of measures that would allow working class individuals to aspire to greater participation in the political process and in society as a whole. In Mill we see the vision of liberal democracy as an agent of moral purpose and the rights of citizenship. Mill thought that equal citizenship and opportunity for individual development would lead to a classless society, and would do so without any need to alter the basic nature of market society or of capitalism.

According to Macpherson, developmental democracy was first and foremost a moral model that was naive in its understanding of the necessary relationship between the classes in a capitalist economy.[46] Mill became convinced that the full development of democracy within capitalism would dispel the inequalities arriving from the exploitation of the working classes. He saw the interests of both classes as lying in a democratic system that had the full and equal development of the individual as its goal. To achieve this end, it was not necessary to impose measures to establish structural equality; rather, 'the people [would] reach the goal themselves, improving themselves by participating actively in the political process, every instalment of participation leading to an improvement in their political capacity, as well as their all-round development, and making them capable of more participation and more self-development.'[47]

For this to happen, the working classes had to aspire to the elite's level of education and informed participation in social affairs. The working classes required the opportunity for individual self-development and needed to learn about society and how to participate in it. They could reach this point not only through enfranchisement and a system of public education, but also through co-operative enterprises through which the working classes could begin to compete in the marketplace. Mill continued to champion market society, but erroneously assumed that equal opportunity for individual development within the society could lead to equal participation in it. Mill erred, Macpherson asserts, because he failed to understand that market society *needed* exploitative class relationships in order to function. By their very nature, these relationships resulted in unequal participation.[48]

The importance of this model as an idea was that it fostered the notion of democracy as the vehicle for individual equality and self-development. Social reforms, including public health and education, the extension of the franchise, and attempts to regulate and redistribute wealth, promoted the idea that the democratization of the political process and limited state intervention in the market could result in the maximization of individual equality. Mill's vision contributed to a popular image of the benign, benevolent, disinterested state in which individual political equality and the absence of class were at least possible. This vision of developmental democracy flourished and provided the ideological justification that capitalism urgently required, since it could be harnessed to the ideal of human betterment.

The third model, equilibrium democracy, which represents the current form of liberal democracy, can be seen as an amalgam of protective and developmental democracy. This could be an effective mix, because in some respects developmental democracy performs an ideological function that sustains protective democracy with the illusion of equality and social justice. Macpherson contends that developmental democracy failed to transform protective democracy because theorists of the early and mid-twentieth century either ignored or did not understand that a capitalist economy needs class relations. This failure did not, however, erase the second model's promise of equality, which of necessity produced the third model. This is essentially the argument of George and Wilding, who contend that the welfare state as it emerged in England amounted to a compromise among the capitalist classes over how to resolve the gulf between rich and poor – between the wealth capitalism produced and the profound inequalities it created.[49]

Equilibrium democracy has two important features: the democratic party system, and the welfare state. The former has allowed the realities of class division to be 'apparently' dispersed by providing plural interests with a forum that presumably transcends inequalities in the marketplace. The individual is free to express his or her interests through a preferred party, and through the ballot box empowers the state to act as an impartial arbiter of all individual interests. This is the exercise of equal citizenship.

The welfare state – which Macpherson argues would have evolved with or without democracy, in order to avert class conflict – provides the individual with some benefits of citizenship. The welfare state concedes that there is inequality in the marketplace and seeks to promote citizenship as the most important feature of democracy. In a sense, welfare state benefits are a progression from Mill's notion of developmental democracy, in that they attempt to offer a more level playing field. Welfare state measures try to reduce inequality of opportunity and to provide a level of social security that increases the stake the individual feels in society. The welfare state thus serves forcefully both as an agent of state legitimation and as an organizing principle for the development of consent.

An important feature of both of these structures, the party system and the welfare state, is that they ostensibly serve individual rather than collective or class interests. Both spring from the heart of liberal democracy's ideology and ethos – that is, the concepts of individual freedom and equality of citizenship. These are the concepts that provided – and still provide – liberal democracy with its moral purpose, and with its self-acquired image as the fountainhead of progress, civilization, and individual rights.[50]

It should not be too surprising that proposals for assimilating Indians in Canada were similar to those made by Mill for 'solving' working-class alienation in England. Both took their form in the ideological and social context of nineteenth-century England. Principles that pertained to the ill-developed and morally inferior working classes at home could just as easily apply abroad. Mill came from a class and a long line of thought that regarded the poor and working classes by nature as practically sub-human and without any substantial social or political rights.[51] From his liberal belief in human progress, Mill articulated a vision of the working classes as capable of transformation and of aspiring to the civilized culture of the upper classes. They could raise themselves through individual self-development – that is, through education and by studying the workings of politics and government. The same thinking governed Indian assimilation policy. If Indians were ill-developed 'brown White men,' it stood to reason that they could advance only if they aspired to the superior civilization of the English colonizers.[52]

The assimilation policies expounded by politicians and civil servants were fully supported by the attitudes of the liberal society that they served. Liberal society, where Indians now found themselves, did not 'see' Indian peoples. It saw only the 'other' – that is, beings who lacked liberal consciousness and liberal values. The liberal view of the world was the way the world was meant to be. Arblaster suggests that the hegemony of liberal ideas in the West was (and is) so dominant as to escape everyday consciousness: 'They are so widely accepted that they lurk concealed and undiscussed beneath the surface of our ordinary, apparently non-ideological language.'[53] The First Nations lacked the attributes and skills of the liberal world, and this 'fact' defined the 'Indian Problem' in a manner that suggested its solution. Dyck writes that 'discussions of the Indian "problem" revolve around a deep-rooted belief that perceived differences between Indians and other Canadians constitute a regrettable situation that needs to be remedied ... the phrase "what is the Indian problem" is not so much a question as an assertion that a "problem" exists.'[54] Thus, in the late nineteenth and twentieth centuries, the Indian 'other' lacked the attributes of liberalism: a sense of being a possessive, autonomous, rational individual, free to seek his or her welfare in the market society and to acquire and utilize property for his or her own self-interest and wealth. In short, the Indian was a Hobbesian savage who had yet to become civilized, who was not yet governed by a superior sovereign, and who was not yet inspired by progress.[55]

Policies were needed that would compel Indians to adopt liberal values and behaviour. However, by the mid-nineteenth century it was considered uncivilized to impose social order by force of arms. A modern nation should bring about subjugation through administrative surveillance sanctioned by constitutional law. According to Sir Henry Maine in his 1861 study, *Ancient Law*, primitive peoples could only begin to become modern if they were transformed, or transformed themselves, from societies of 'fixed' status to ones based on contractual arrangements. In effect, they would have to learn to adhere to the bourgeois principle of individual property rights. Maine, according to Said, 'outlined a theory amazingly like Marx's: that feudalism in India, challenged by British colonialism, was a necessary development; in time, he argued, a feudal lord would establish the basis for individual ownership and allow a prototype bourgeoisie to emerge.'[56] Maine's thinking, as interpreted by Said, contained two principles applicable to the development of Canadian Indian policy. First, if Indians were to become civilized, the method of their domination would have to offer a civil example. In other words, domination would have to be brought about through lawfully sanctioned administrative surveillance. Their progress would be measured as a function of their willingness and ability to accept and adopt administrative surveillance as a means of internal control. Second, policies would have to be aimed at undermining those cultural practices which reinforced 'fixed' status. In tandem with this, liberal behaviour based on individual property rights would have to be encouraged. Progress would be measured by the co-operation of indigenous leaders, by conversion of collectively held lands to individual possession, and by behaviour conducive to participation in a liberal, market society.

Within this framework, Indian policy in Canada has had two distinct phases. The first, lasting from Confederation until the Second World War, amounted to a continuation of English colonial policy within a national framework. During this period the focus of policy was on the subjugation of Indians and their preparation for white civilization. Both the law and its administration emphasized Indian education, moral improvement, and self-development; the imposition of new forms of band government; and the principle of individual freehold on reserves. At the same time, Indian cultural practices were repressed either by outright ban or by forms of limitation and control. The administration of welfare relief was intended to complement measures the goal of which was to prepare Indians for entry into liberal society. To that end, these measures emphasized individual family responsibility, work, self-reliance, and thrift. The value of a wage, no matter how small, was consistently stressed; only certain worthy groups – the aged, the infirm, widows, and children – were considered eligible for relief. Policy was administered mainly by the church, which dominated Indian education, and by the Department of Indian Affairs. The trading companies – predominantly the Hudson's Bay Company – assisted these two in matters affecting Indian economy, especially in the provision of relief.[57]

The second phase, which began after the Second World War, saw an increasing emphasis on actual integration through the extension of citizenship rights, although some preparatory work for entry into Canadian society was still deemed necessary. During the first phase, Indians had been thought generally to *be* the problem. After the war, Indians were more thought of as having problems, which scientifically conceived programs could address and resolve. Policy governing relief administration began to reflect distinctly modern approaches to needs and eligibility testing.[58] Moreover, relief policy increasingly focused on how Indians could be integrated into the labour force. Related to this was the idea of social work intervention to help Indian individuals and families overcome problems thought to be associated with welfare dependence. These problems were seen as impediments to the search for gainful employment.

During this second phase, Indian administration became exclusively secular. This was reflected in the increasingly complex organization and administration of Indian Affairs, which gradually mirrored the institutions of the modern state. The department assisted Indians in the integration process by replicating on the reserves some of the institutions and services of the mainstream society. These included local government, economic development, education, housing and social welfare. These were consistent with the principles and benefits of good citizenship and were intended to encourage Indians to make the transition from their reserves to the broader community, or else to make aspects of reserve life more similar to what was seen as the Canadian way of life.

Conclusion

Indian welfare dependency has been a manifestation of the loss of First Nations' political and economic autonomy and of the impact of the processes of state legitimation on their communities. Thus, Indian dependence on welfare is not simply an episode in the history of their dispossession; it is an integral aspect of the continuing history of relations between First Nations and Europeans. Indian welfare policy evolved as a feature of the continuing subjugation and domination of First Nations by the Canadian state, and it has been a consistent part of state attempts to assimilate Indians into Canadian society. During both the subjugation period and the citizenship period that followed it, assimilation was seen as a product of community-based programs – programs that reflected liberal values and principles. Indians were expected to adopt behaviour that conformed to liberal thinking.

In the rest of this book, I tell the history of relief assistance for reserve Indians in Canada. I explore the bias of government officials who, as they developed and administered assimilation and welfare policies, honestly believed themselves to be doing good and to be bringing progress, advancement, and modern citizenship to Indian peoples. Most of this history is gleaned from federal government archival documents and correspondence. Some of these are internal to the Indian Affairs administration; others reflect the department's communications and relationships with other federal and provincial government departments, outside bodies, and interested citizens. In constructing this history, I annotate the documentary evidence, using relevant literature and other sources to highlight or critique its meaning, to clarify its historical importance, or simply to enrich the text.

The documents reviewed from the post-Confederation period of subjugation reveal a department isolated and unswerving in its task and methods. Relatively little non-government correspondence or outside interest impinged on the department's work, and the physical 'presence' of Indians was barely apparent. Indians were merely objects of an administrative mission; in keeping with their status as wards of the government, they simply were not heard. Indian resistance, as in the case of F.O. Loft and the pan-Canadian Indian movement, was undermined, discredited, and made difficult through constraining legislation. During the citizenship period, the department continued to exert firm control over the general direction of its policies, but it became more open to interest expressed by mainstream society. It responded to and even initiated consultation and research, and it attempted – with some success – to develop support for its policies within reputable, somewhat elitist voluntary organizations and university bodies. Beginning with the Jules Sioui affair in 1943, there also emerged a revival of active resistance expressed by and through Indian organizations, publications, and press reports. Although the department either managed or dismissed this resistance, it certainly remained aware of it. Thus, while the citizenship period represented a continuing, unremitting effort to assimilate Indians, it also marked the transition to a new political context and culture to which the department would have to adapt.

2

The Context of Relief Policy Development at the Time of Confederation

Dependence upon the central administration – and in this case, on the charity of the government – replaced an independence which was surely one of the wonders of environmental adaptation, but which was becoming less and less possible.

J.E. Chamberlin, *The Harrowing of Eden*

The Situation of First Nations in 1867

At the time of Confederation in 1867, Indian matters were divided among several administrations. The colonial office in London had transferred legislative authority for Indian policy to the Province of Canada (Canada East and Canada West) in 1860, but had retained final authority over these matters in the Maritime colonies and in British Columbia.[1] Indian policy in Rupert's Land – from which the Northwest Territories were created and subsequently the three prairie provinces – was overseen by London, but left largely to the administration of the Hudson's Bay Company, which retained its complete control and trading monopoly over this vast area.[2] Indians in Rupert's Land were not colonized; they continued to trade with the company as independent peoples – a fact that became important for Indian policy after Confederation.

According to Siggner, Indian population figures before 1867 are not highly reliable. However, more accurate census methods introduced shortly after Confederation indicated an Indian population in 1871 of roughly 102,000 in the whole area of present-day Canada.[3] This figure represented about 2.8 per cent of the general Canadian population of 3.69 million.[4] Warfare between the competing nations during the fur trade had taken a heavy toll of Indian life. However, the greatest reduction of the Indian population in the period subsequent to contact with non-natives resulted from the introduction of alcohol and epidemic diseases by the Europeans.[5] Throughout the nineteenth century, loss of life through smallpox epidemics was exacerbated by widespread food shortages and famines on the prairies, intertribal wars for survival, and the decline of Indian economies, which was hastened by the destruction of the buffalo populations and the changed prairie ecology.[6]

By 1867, Indians in the Maritimes and in the Province of Canada were well acquainted with colonial administration. In those places, waves of settlement and the establishment of a market economy engulfed Indian populations. In turn, these developments were supported and enforced by new administrative structures. Except in Quebec and the district of Ungava, Indians had been treated with varying degrees of formality and settled on reserves.[7] In the pre-Confederation period, treaty activity in the Maritime colonies took the form of informal or hastily written documents of 'peace and friendship.' These treaties, most of which predated the 1763 proclamation, essentially amounted to assurances of peaceful coexistence; they did not, however, address the issues of land title and surrender. Their failure to address land rights became a source of dispute between the Colonial Office and the colonial legislatures, which ignored Indian land claims while encouraging settlement and turning a 'blind eye' to squatters. Indians were displaced from their lands; reserves were created only as an afterthought and often after the Indians themselves petitioned for them. Thus, compensation either in lump sum or in the form of annuity payments was not a factor in the Maritimes.

In Canada West (Ontario), most of the treaties postdated the proclamation. As in the Maritimes, however, the reserve system was not immediately established; thus for many bands, reserves had to be instituted retroactively. Nevertheless, the question of title was more clearly acknowledged in Ontario, because of the force of the proclamation, the strength of white humanitarian organizations, and the growing resistance of Indians to wholesale land grabs. Most of the Ontario treaties included compensation, although in widely disparate amounts and usually after little or no negotiation.

Canada East (Quebec) had been excluded from the conditions of the proclamation. It was thought that aboriginal title had been extinguished by prior French occupation and that questions of land surrender and compensation were therefore irrelevant. A reserve system was instituted in the original Quebec, but just as in the Maritimes, it represented an accommodation of aboriginal needs rather than a recognition of their rights. In the eyes of the new federal government, the First Nations of Ontario and Quebec (especially in the southern areas) and those of the Maritimes were relatively advanced in their adaptation to market society. With respect to the First Nations in eastern Canada, the government's main goal was to finish the task of civilization that had been begun by its colonial predecessors. This meant concerted efforts to have First Nations abandon their traditional methods of government in favour of constitutional and parliamentary forms at the band level, and to bring about their unconditional acceptance of the authority of the federal and provincial governments. First Nations were also supposed to abandon communal concepts of land rights and to adopt the liberal principles of individual land tenure and privacy. These measures were intended to foster individual self-reliance and wage-dependent labour.[8]

Programs in western Canada were different, although the overall goal of assimilation remained the same. After the transfer of Rupert's Land from the Hudson's Bay Company to the Dominion of Canada in 1870 and the entry of British Columbia into Confederation in 1871, Macdonald's Conservative government was able to pursue vigorously its policy of one nation *a mari usque ad mare*. The agricultural development of the Northwest Territories and the completion of the transcontinental railway were important goals, which could be achieved only through a rapid land surrender and treaty process and by confining First Nations to reserves.[9] Because these peoples were still independent and had not previously been subjected to colonial administration and the rule of liberal law, they were considered less advanced than Indians in eastern Canada and probably more hostile to European immigration. For this reason, the federal government instituted rigorous policies to civilize them and at the same time to minimize any threat they might pose to settlers.[10]

The case of British Columbia was unique. Until 1871, when it joined Confederation, it had followed a somewhat independent course in Indian administration. It had not experienced a mercantile period comparable to the one in eastern Canada. Instead, the relatively brief, quasi-mercantile exploitation by the Hudson's Bay Company was followed quickly by a rush of miners and fortune seekers. This induced rapid pressure for settlement and a free market economy.[11] British Columbia never considered itself subject to the Royal Proclamation.[12] Instead, questions of access and title to land were considered in terms of English settlement law, which was based on occupancy and use.[13] When colonial

legislators saw 'unoccupied' land, they counted it fair to enact legislation by which that land could be acquired and settled. Indigenous law
respecting title did not apply.[14] These principles of English settlement
law were exercised with great enthusiasm in British Columbia before
and immediately after Confederation.

The first governor of British Columbia, James Douglas, made several
early treaties with small bands near Victoria, Nanaimo, and Fort Rupert.
Further treaty-making efforts in the early 1860s collapsed as a result of
wrangling over responsibility between the colonial office in London and
the colonial legislature. After the treaty process failed, Douglas permitted Indian bands to define their land needs and set aside reserves based
roughly on these definitions.[15] Douglas's policies were significant for
two reasons. First, they conceded the inevitability of settlement while
also accepting that First Nations would require some protection. Second, there were attempts to place Indians on an equal footing with
whites. Indians constituted a majority in British Columbia, and Douglas
saw them becoming full and equal citizens. Given their greater numbers, they might even come to dominate the colony politically.[16]

Douglas's successors, Joseph Trutch and his brother-in-law Peter
O'Reilly, were much less accommodating toward First Nations. The colonial office was unable or unwilling to protect aboriginal interests or to
interfere in the colony's government, and this cleared the way for British
Columbia's rapacious land policies. Fisher describes Trutch as the 'arche-
typal colonialist.' A thorough racist when it came to Indians, Trutch was
obsessed with the notion that they were obstructing the colony's development.[17] Trutch's land policies from 1864 to 1871 – and O'Reilly's after his
– promoted the interests of settlers to the complete detriment of First
Nations. Most of Douglas's reserve allocations were reduced, and the
more fertile and resource-rich lands so reacquired were sold or made
available to European settlers. New reserves were created, under the
application of a strict formula of ten acres per family.[18] In contrast, federal treaties on the prairies were based on a minimum of 160 acres per
family. Trutch was acting with the full support of the colonial legislature.
The reallocation of Indian lands to white settlers was fuelled and, in a
purely ethnocentric sense, morally justified by popular perceptions that
Indians were lazy, backward, and intellectually inferior savages.[19]

Indians in British Columbia complained bitterly of their treatment at
the hands of Trutch. Indeed, the final terms of union included a clause
ostensibly introduced by Trutch ensuring the continuation by the
Dominion government of Indian policy 'as liberal as that hitherto pur-

sued by the British Columbia Government.'[20] Thus, British Columbia entered Confederation with the understanding that aboriginal title, even if it had existed, was extinguished. As well, since the British Columbia government took the position that Indian title did not exist, federal Indian treaty making effectively stopped at the Alberta–British Columbia boundary. For a considerable time after British Columbia's entry into Confederation, Indian land remained a source of bitter contention between that province, the federal government, and the First Nations.[21] Tennant's comments on this period leave little doubt that it was a thoroughly bleak one for the province's First Nations: 'Under the Trutch regime, Indians became a residual category with fewer rights than aliens. Segregation and inequality would ... be the hallmarks of ... provincial Indian policy.'[22]

Trutch's policies opened a long period of mistrust between the First Nations of British Columbia and the provincial government. Clearly, the provincial government was determined to ensure that First Nations submitted to white domination[23] and to leave them economically marginalized. Their best hopes for survival lay in maintaining subsistence economies where possible, in gaining access to menial wage labour, and in political action to redress the injustices wrought by the meanness of the province and the personal indifference of Sir John A. Macdonald.[24]

The Administration of Relief: Fears of Dependency and Indian Uprising

Confederation and the twenty years or so following presented the federal government – to paraphrase Dickason – with a complex front of matters relating to the Indian 'question.'[25] In terms of the nation as a whole, the Indian 'question' focused on three main issues: land, civilization, and assimilation. However, these issues were handled differently in each region, with the differences relating to the government's perception of how advanced in a given region the Indians were. All of this helps explain why the Department of Indian Affairs created two administrative filing systems: the Red Series for eastern Canada, and the Black Series for western Canada. Fundamental to the issues of land and assimilation – in the European mind, at least – was the need for Indians to make the transition to an agricultural and wage economy without becoming dependent on the government for subsistence. The fear that Indians would become dependent on state charity was a continuing obsession with the federal government; in fact, this fear became a constant theme in policy statements and case examples of Indian relief. Relief would be more than a drain on the federal treasury;[26] it would be a failure of progress and civilization and a challenge to the inherent and manifest merits of self-interest, individual thrift, and industry. Chamberlin captures this succinctly:

> Increasing rations to pacify the Indians, was in fact *the* issue of Indian affairs throughout the nineteenth century and up to the present day. How does one encourage habits of industry and thrift and at the same time maintain a measure of stability and continuity among the Indians themselves, and provide reasonably for their welfare and protection? Putting them on the dole, while humane and in many cases absolutely necessary, was scarcely conducive to the inculcation of habits of self-sufficient enterprise. The giving of alms may be government's most compelling function, but it is seldom its most constructive – unless, of course, one takes a radical approach and assumes that at the base of it all it is the *only* function of a central government, whatever the masks it puts on. Whatever the case, the patterns of social coherence and economic reward upon which the non-native civil *and* religious orthodoxies were founded were foreign to most, though not all, of the Indian cultures.[27]

Chamberlin is right to a point. Welfare relief, however, was not a readily accepted function of the state in the middle to late nineteenth century, especially in North America. Only in industrialized England, in the wake of the miserable social conditions wrought by unrestrained capitalism, had the state begun to involve itself in small measure in the provision of relief.

Indians were inextricably involved in Canada's economic structure and hence in its system of government. As a result, potential and existing dependence was unavoidably influenced by two main issues – access to land and labour, and credit advances in the fur trade. In the populous southern regions of eastern Canada and British Columbia, land and its use were central to whether Indians would be able to participate meaningfully in the economy. Contradictory dynamics regarding land use placed Indians in an untenable situation. First Nations were under constant pressure to surrender lands, either to accommodate the needs of new or growing municipalities or to allow for the development of agriculture and emerging resource industries by whites. Yet at the same time, policies carried forward from the colonial administrations continued to exhort Indians to become farmers and gardeners and to remain self-

sufficient. Thus, desirable Indian lands were surrendered or acquired
for white exploitation, while smaller tracts – usually less fertile – were left
to Indian bands. On these, they were expected to maintain a meagre subsistence.[28] Schmalz writes a compelling account of the Ojibwa land surrenders in southern Ontario and of the repeated attempts by colonial
and federal administrations to civilize the Ojibwa through the encouragement of 'gentleman farming.' Ojibwa men resisted involvement in
agriculture because 'traditionally, the men were hunters and fishermen
and the women produced the crops.' Yet these agricultural policies were
directed at the men. Their resistance to agriculture combined with the
substandard quality of the land left to them resulted in the general failure of the agricultural policy of both the colonial administration and the
Department of Indian Affairs.[29]

Policies regarding work contained similar contradictions. The colonial administrations – especially in the Province of Canada – and the
federal administration that followed these pursued policies of Indian
education designed to prepare Indians for simple, nuclear family life as
well as for menial wage labour. For boys, this meant learning trades necessary for agriculture or mechanics; for girls, it meant training in
domestic work such as sewing and cooking.[30] Even for those who could
work and who wanted to, a livelihood was by no means assured. As mentioned, Indians were quickly being displaced from their lands, and agriculture was increasingly less available to them. The alternative – wage
dependency, either in agriculture as an agricultural labourer or in
industry – was constrained by limited access to jobs.[31] For Indians, this
limited access was often the result of geographic isolation. Moreover,
the Canadian economy was simply too underdeveloped to provide
enough jobs for working people. Kierans describes Canada from 1860
until about 1900 as 'not a land of hope and immigration, but a land of
frustrated ambition and emigration.'[32]

Competition for scarce jobs between existing Indian and new, non-
Indian labour pools had arisen as a result of the mid-nineteenth-century
emigrations of British 'surplus populations' and the limited success of
post-Confederation government immigration policies generally. One
result was that non-Indians were hired in preference to Indians.[33] The
significant exceptions were in northern areas, where Indians secured
wage employment, such as guiding and trapping, associated with traditional Indian economies.[34] In the south, however, the federal government's vigorous efforts to train Indians in vocations rarely resulted in
consistent or enduring employment.

These patterns with respect to both land and labour were quickly repeated on the prairies.[35] Buckley points out that in the West, settlers showed little tolerance for Indian participation in the economy; she contrasts this with the more tolerant attitudes in eastern Canada, based on the years of contact. She notes quite accurately that the Mohawk were in strong demand as high-steel workers; otherwise, however, she seems to overestimate the degree to which eastern First Nations were welcome in Canada's economy. In the end, federal policies to encourage Indians to adapt to the wage economy, and to become self-sufficient individuals with European attitudes,[36] were met by collective resistance (which non-Indians interpreted as backwardness, laziness, or stupidity),[37] by countervailing policies of immigration and settlement, by limited access to jobs, or by all three.

The Pattern of Credit Advances in the Fur Trade

A second early factor affecting Indian dependence for subsistence was the credit advance practices of the fur-trading companies, notably the Hudson's Bay Company. In the 'off-season,' the company would foster the loyalty of those bands with whom it traded by offering credit, in the form of goods, in advance of the next season's furs. This pattern was common in the northern areas of all provinces where the fur trade was still important to the economy, especially Ontario, the Northwest Territories, and British Columbia. This pattern of trade dependency and credit advances was probably the strongest influence on federal government attitudes toward Indian relief, and on the methods of providing it.

To appreciate how this pattern evolved, it will help to understand how the original Hudson's Bay Company used to assign monetary value to furs. Indian economies did not use money as a standard means of valuation, so the company had to devise a method of barter and exchange by which furs could be equated with European goods. The system devised was called the *made beaver rate*, or the MB standard. The MB 'was equivalent to the value of a prime beaver skin and the prices of all trade goods, other furs, and country produce were expressed in terms of MB ... Trade goods coming from Europe were assigned these values according to the *official standard of trade*, while the furs received from the Indians were evaluated according to the *comparative standard of trade*.'[38] The system later became more complex than this because the company had to account for inflation, changing markets, and economic conditions in Europe, whereas Indians essentially held firm to the idea of a fixed

Table 2.1
Hudson's Bay Company standard of trade goods by selected years (valued in terms of made beaver [MB])

Goods	1720–1	1742–3	1760–1
Kettles	1½ per lb.	1	
1 pint			
2 quart			
3 quart			16
1 gallon			18
Gun powder	1 per lb.	1 per lb.	1 per lb.
Tobacco			
Brazil	2 per lb.	1 per lb.	1 per ¾ lb.
English roll	1 per lb.	1 per 1½ lbs.	1 per lb.
Virg. leaf		1 per 1½ lbs.	
Beads			
large	4 per lb.		
small	2 per lb.		
Guns	14 each		
4 ft		12 each	14 each
Gun flints	1 per 16	1 per 20	
Hatchets	1 per 1	1 per 2	1 per 1
Awl blades	1 per 8	1 per 12	1 per 8
Twine	1 per sk.	1 per sk.	1 per 1
Blankets	7 per 1	6 per 1	7 per 1
Cloth			
broad	3 per yd	2 per yd	
corded			3 per yd
flannel	1½ per yd	1½ per yd	1½ per yd
Brandy	4 per gal.	4 per gal.	4 per gal.
Knives		1 per 8	1 per 4

Source: Adapted from Arthur J. Ray, *Indians in the Fur Trade* (Toronto, 1998), 66–7.

price.[39] For our purposes, the basic principle of MB is what is important: furs were exchanged for goods rather than money, and the value of the furs was systematically equated with the value of the European goods.

Table 2.1 provides some typical valuations from Hudson's Bay Company trading post records during the eighteenth century. Considerable emphasis was placed on items required for hunting and trapping. Luxury items were usually offered as gifts and varied with the success of the fur season. The MB system of trade valuation was gradually adapted as a method of advancing credit both to Indian middlemen and to the hunters and trappers themselves.

After the American War of Independence the Hudson's Bay Company faced increased competition both from the Nor'westers and from individual entrepreneurs. This competition created problems of 'customer loyalty' and placed ecological pressure on the fur resource and the entire environment that sustained it. To counter the possible loss of trading loyalty, and to provide relief from hardship as environmental conditions made it more and more difficult for the Indians to survive, the company began advancing credit to Indians based on the projected MB return of furs.[40] This practice eventually led to abuses (from the company's perspective!), at which point the method of advances was modified, though the basic format did not change. By the middle of the nineteenth century, environmental conditions, combined with company trading and credit policies, were placing restrictions on Indian territorial movement and habitation. The economic policies introduced after 1828 by the HBC's governor, George Simpson, were intended to promote more effective management of the fur resource by restricting nomadic patterns of existence and by encouraging community life closer to the posts.[41]

The use of the credit advance and the encouragement of settlement near the posts altered the economic precepts on which the fur trade was based, by encouraging greater individualization and differentiation among Indians within the trade, and by turning Indians into largely dependent wage labourers. Chamberlin points out that the policy was not just economic; it represented a distinct ideological point of view about the future of First Nations in Canada and North America:

> The traders differed in their suggestions as to what might be done about or with the Indian ... but they generally agreed that there was a need to work towards the transforming of the Indian so that he might better be able to cope with the new order which was encroaching upon his domain ... The Indian should be, to the greatest degree possible, exposed to the economic activities which sustained the fur trade, on the assumption that trade was a fairly basic instrument of civilization – something like the assumptions surrounding wage employment during the middle decades of the twentieth century; or that the Indian should be encouraged, and if necessary forced, to turn to agriculture.[42]

By the mid-nineteenth century, food relief had begun to supplement the credit advance because of severe winter hardship, the depletion of game, and the complete disruption of traditional, seasonal movement patterns.

> At Fort Pelly, one of the principal Hudson's Bay Company posts in the Swan River District ... economic considerations appear to have been the leading motivation behind the traders' practice of feeding the Indian bands in the department. Moderate fur resources still remained ... but to tap them it was necessary to support the more reliable Indian hunters. One of these was an Indian called 'The Rattlesnake.' On 16 November 1853, he came to the post to trade his furs and he was given 'gratis' ammunition, meat and barley.[43]

Eventually, the European traders began dispensing food relief, accounting for it in a manner comparable to the credit advance. Although humanitarian considerations were a factor in this, the principal reason for providing relief was economic: if the Indians weren't given food, they would spend valuable time hunting scarce game instead of trapping, and the company would lose some fur revenue. Indeed, according to Ray, the provision of food relief and the establishment of more sophisticated methods of transporting food to the posts hastened the demise of seasonal movements for subsistence hunting; it also ensured the total dependence of Indians on the company and on the trade itself. These changes

> made the Indians dependent on the company not only for clothing, as had been the case for nearly fifty years by 1870, but also for food – and not just pemmican, but so-called 'store food' as well, such as flour and biscuits. In effect, to a large extent the woodland Indians had virtually become company employees. They trapped for the company and were provided with nearly all their requirements at the company store on credit.[44]

By the 1870s, nearly all the prairie Indians involved in or affected by the fur trade were ready to take treaty and settle on reserves.[45] The credit advance system had slowly succeeded in incorporating Indians into the activities of commerce and labour; it had also created a method for determining and relieving need – a method that could be employed by other Indian agencies, including church missions and the government itself. It also prepared the ground for later conflict between the Hudson's Bay Company and the federal government over responsibility for

Indian welfare. The resolution of this conflict would further entrench Indians as objects of ideology, public policy, and administration.

The Guiding Philosophy and Organization of the Department of Indian Affairs

In 1876 the Deputy Superintendent General of Indian Affairs, Lawrence Vankoughnet, drafted a reply to an inquiry about Canada's Indians from W.P. Ross, the editor of the American newspaper the *Indian Journal.* He wrote:

> The improvement and elevation of the Indian Race, socially and morally ... engages the earnest attention of the Government. With this object in view, religious, educational and industrial ideas are promulgated; and the machinery for carrying the same into effect is systematically kept in motion among such of the Bands as the circumstances ... will warrant the same being done with any fair possibility of success.
>
> The legal status of the Indians of Canada is that of *minors* with the Government as their guardians; and laws are in force prescribing how this responsibility ... shall be discharged – the same being from time to time amended with a view to their adaptation, as far as possible, to present circumstances, and to the progress towards civilization attained by the Indian race ...
>
> Their moral welfare is carefully looked after by the prevention of vice among them ...
>
> Inducements are moreover held out to the Indians to take advantage of the provisions in the law for their elevation from the position of tutelage to that of Citizens ...
>
> The law also prescribes regulations for the internal economy of resident Indian Bands or Tribes, including among other essentials to the general weal, keeping in repair of Roads, ditches, fences, School and Council houses, and other public buildings and works – providing for their sick and disabled – election of their Chiefs – penalty for family desertion – the descent of property of deceased Indians – the prevention of intemperance &c&c.
>
> With regard to Indians with whom no treaties have been made or who are not settled on any Reserves, the Government also exercises a paternal supervision by prohibiting the sale of intoxicants to them – protecting their property from seizure for debt – affording relief to their sick and aged – and, when it can be done with any prospect of success, providing their children with the means of education.[46]

The pacification and subjugation of First Nations were essential to the early·nation-building objectives of the federal government, especially in Western Canada, where it most mattered. Vankoughnet's letter makes it clear that this was to be a paternalistic exercise, accomplished through the ceaseless promotion of liberal values and the zealous inculcation of ideas about progress, civil order, and culture.

His remarks represent the quintessential statement of federal government policy in the early period, 1873–1912; they also embody two critical principles – tutelage and patronage. These two concepts were important to the extent that they reflected the difference between white Canadians (personified by their government) and the First Nations as perceived by the former. As principles, tutelage and patronage suggest an inherent condescension and timelessness. Dyck describes the insidiousness of tutelage in the context of Indian policy:

> Tutelage comprises a form of restraint or care exercised by one party over another as well as the condition of being subjected to such protection or guardianship ...
>
> What is unusual about the particular form of tutelage experienced by aboriginal peoples in Canada is [that it] has been based neither upon a contractual agreement nor a negotiated understanding but upon the power of one side to regulate the behaviour of the other in accordance with a set of unilaterally selected purposes ... Contrary to relationships between parents and ... children ... the form of tutelage that has held Indians captive for so long has not been [a] stage in the life cycle but a permanent condition. The involuntary tutelage that Canada's Indians have endured has been imposed upon an entire people virtually in perpetuity.
>
> The control exercised by various tutors or tutelage agents over Indians has been founded upon one unshakeable premise – the presumed moral and cultural 'superiority' of, first, European and, then, Euro-Canadian society over native peoples.[47]

Perhaps more powerfully stated, because the oppressive ideological purpose is so artfully woven into the explanation, is Chamberlin's treatment of the same theme:

> As the native people were ushered into the stadium of late nineteenth-century enthusiasms, and as the banners of self-sufficiency and individual enterprise were waved before them, somebody forgot to mention that the

rules of the game had changed. For so long in native affairs, an heroically 'authoritarian tradition' had prevailed, in which the indigenous inhabitants were encouraged to pay respect to the Great Mother or the Great Father who supposedly ruled the society that was being established in their midst. All of a sudden this situation was altered; quite different skills from those of obedience or unquestioned respect were called for, and a quite different concept of self-interest and mutual responsibility was expected. The exercise of choices and of responsibilities was urgently demanded; and when it was not forthcoming, the illusion was fostered that choices had been made and responsibilities accepted. But it was nothing more than an illusion; and when the illusion was shattered, a deep disillusion set in, which in many cases continues still. For those who were in authority over the Indians never stopped reigning, and never began to govern.[48]

Chamberlin comments on the wholly conscious level at which patronage emerged from the European mind as the desired relationship between Indians and whites. He is commenting on American Indian policy, but he intends us to understand that patronage was every bit as present in Canadian thought – which, as evidenced by Vankoughnet's remarks, it was:

The tradition of patronizing philanthropy was already a long one and had as its early spokesman Thomas L. McKenney, the energetic and humane superintendent of Indian trade from 1816 to 1822 and (under Secretary of War John C. Calhoun) first head of the Bureau of Indian Affairs from 1824 to 1832. 'Our Indians,' wrote McKenney in 1821, 'Stand pretty much in the relation to the Government as our children do to us. They are equally dependent, and need, not infrequently, the exercise of parental authority to detach them from those ways which might involve both their peace and their lives.' This was the thesis that informed the entire 'wardship' theory which had been popularized by G.W. Manypenny and which was so generally accepted in the latter part of the century.[49]

Early relief administration must be considered in the context of these guiding principles, because the philosophy of relief posed an underlying, unperceived contradiction: How could peoples seen as primitive, childlike wards of the state at the same time be expected to be self-reliant, independent adults? The patronage of Indians induced an organizational culture that required Indians to be perceived as collectively dependent. Their independence, which was defined in individual terms, became a perpetual goal never to be attained because it was never correctly conceived.

At the beginning of Canadian federal government administration, the former Indian Department of the united Canadas became a branch of the Department of the Secretary of State. Its internal organization and administrative structure, and its governing colonial statutes, policies, and objectives, were all carried forward and reaffirmed by the new regime. The first Deputy Superintendent General of Indian Affairs, William Spragge, continued in the post he had held since 1862 in the former Indian Department.[50] (The title, Deputy Superintendent General of Indian Affairs, was used until 1936 and was accorded to the highest-ranking public servant in charge of Indian Affairs.) The new Indian Affairs branch, with its colonial core intact, faced the challenge of developing and extending a uniform administration to the West and to the Maritimes.

Quebec and Ontario were each divided into seven superintendencies. Each of these superintendencies comprised several reserves and was headed by a full-time superintendent or agent. The Maritime provinces were similarly divided; the sole exception was that in Nova Scotia, nineteen administrative units were established, each headed by a part-time agent – usually a local farmer, doctor, or clergyman. British Columbia's Indian administration was established in 1872 as a single superintendency headquartered in Victoria. Shortly after, in 1874, a second one was formed with offices in New Westminster. This arrangement eventually proved inefficient, and in 1880 a single superintendency was reestablished, which oversaw six new agencies.[51]

The prairie region proved to be the most difficult to organize, yet strategically, this was the region where it mattered most to subjugate the Indian nations. How could the federal government develop an effective organizational presence at the same time as the numbered treaties were being negotiated and signed and Indians were being confined to reserves? Several forms of organization were tried; eventually, in 1879, a single office was created in Winnipeg headed by a commissioner of Indian affairs. This commissioner was a powerful man. He reported directly to Ottawa and was responsible for an extensive bureaucracy of inspectors, agents, and agencies scattered throughout Manitoba, the Northwest Territories, and the district of Keewatin.[52]

The Indian Affairs Branch remained under the wing of the Department of the Secretary of State until 1873, when it was transferred to the Department of the Interior.[53] In 1876, existing legislation with respect to Indians was consolidated and streamlined under the new Indian Act, which was to apply to all Indians across the country. Finally, pursuant to an amendment to the Indian Act in 1880, the branch was accorded full departmental status. Overall responsibility for the department, however, remained with the Department of the Interior. Consequently, the Superintendent General of Indian Affairs was also the minister for the Department of the Interior. Since 1878, Prime Minister John A. Macdonald had been the department's minister.[54] That Macdonald himself carried the portfolio demonstrated the importance he attached to ensuring the subjugation of Indians. Only having done so could he achieve the main objectives of the National Policy. In 1874, Macdonald appointed his close personal friend, Lawrence Vankoughnet, as Deputy Superintendent General of Indian Affairs. Vankoughnet's family was Loyalist and unwaveringly Tory. He himself was a conscientious administrator who embraced economy and restraint, as well as a stickler for detail.[55] He held the post until 1893, which made him the longest-serving Deputy Superintendent General of the post-Confederation era. Arguably, it was his administration that created the department's peculiar, enduring culture, which set it apart from the rest of the federal civil service and made it, until well into the twentieth century, an inward-looking, isolated colonial oddity consumed by its mission and barely answerable to its handful of critics.[56]

In theory, the policy of civilization and assimilation was to be applied with deliberate inconsistency, as a function of the perceived advancement of the Indians in central and eastern Canada relative to those in the West. In practice, centralized bureaucracies do not generally make these kinds of differentiations very well. Indian Affairs was no exception, especially with respect to the administration of relief, which was dispensed with depressing uniformity. In addition, although the department was structurally decentralized for administrative purposes, it was highly centralized in regard to policy, decision making, and procedures for approving nearly all agency matters, including the provision of relief.[57] By 1890 the department had about five hundred employees. Of these, forty were located in the 'inside' service in Ottawa; the rest were in the 'outside' service, which consisted mainly of the various offices and agencies across the country.

3

The Development of Rudimentary Relief Administration during the Initial Period of Subjugation, 1873–1912

We do not propose to expend large sums of money to give [the Indians] food from the first day of the year to the last. We must give them enough to keep them alive; but the Indians must, under the regulations that have been sanctioned by Parliament, go to their reservations and cultivate their land. They must provide partially for their wants. And therefore, if, by accident, an Indian should starve, it is not the fault of the Government nor the wish of the Government.

Sir Hector Langevin, MP, House of Commons, *Debates*, 15 April 1886

The early policy governing relief reflected prevailing European attitudes about deservedness, self-reliance, thrift, and the moral virtue of work. It was neither complexly formulated nor well articulated. As such it sprang from charitable and residual responses to need. The former derived from a humanitarian concern for suffering; the latter from a need to promote work, cultivation, and industry, rather than reliance on the state for support. The wonder, as Ray points out, was that there was any policy at all, given the reluctance of the state at the time to interfere with the 'natural laws' of economics.[1] Especially on the prairies and in the more remote areas of the country, relief for Indians was initially seen only as a means to ease distress – usually caused by starvation – and to ensure their pacification and loyalty.[2] As Indians became settled on reserves and annuity trusts were established based on surrender settlements and land sales, the department allowed limited and carefully controlled expenditures from either these funds or from special parliamentary appropriations for the provision of relief. Analysis of instances of relief from different regions of the country during this early period provides insight into the changing Indian social landscape and the government's determination to convert First Nations to liberal views of the individual in market society.

The Early Administration of Relief in Quebec

The Montagnais Incident of 1873

One of the earliest documented cases of government relief, from the winter of 1873, involved the Montagnais Indians of Mingan, Quebec, on the north shore of the St Lawrence River. Indians in Quebec were not treatied; for that reason, a special welfare fund called the Lower Canada Indian Fund had been established by Parliament in 1872 to prevent the recurrence of hardship among the province's Indians. The fund was to allocate relief from the interest it earned on its initial capital. A committee of the Privy Council made the first appropriations on 6 May 1872.[3] The fund's total value at the end of December 1872 was $115,727.37, which included $5,873.16 in interest. The committee approved the following distribution of funds for the department to administer:

1.	For purchase of seed grain and Agricultural implements	$2,500.00
2.	For relief to aged and destitute Indians	1,150.00
3.	For Medical Attendance	180.00
4.	For aid to Missionaries (North Shore St. Lawrence)	500.00
5.	Permanent salaries of Missionaries and	
	Salaries of School Teachers and aid to School Buildings	1,620.00
		$5,950.00[4]

About one year after the committee's distribution, on 10 July 1873, W. Whitcher of the Department of Marine and Fisheries forwarded to E.A. Meredith, deputy minister of the Department of the Interior, the following extract from a report dated 1 July 1873. The report's author was D. Lavoie, commanding officer of the government schooner *La Canadienne*: 'The "mission" being over at Mingan, there remained but a few Indians at the settlement. They all looked thin and wore the signs of long privation. The Missionary, Father Arnaud, assured me that they suffered terribly through last winter's privations: forty-seven of them died from hunger and exposure! Fur they had plenty of, but were unable to shoot a single caribou, not one having been seen even as far as 900 miles in the interior.'[5] Lavoie's report raised very serious concerns.

What had happened to the funds allocated in May 1872, ostensibly to prevent such a tragedy?

In a brief memo to Meredith, Spragge noted that $500 was allocated annually to Bishop Langevin of St. Germain-de-Rimouski for the benefit of the Mingan Indians and that no report had ever been received about its disbursement. Spragge suggested writing a letter to the bishop, requesting an account of the items purchased from the funds and how they had been distributed. Enclosed with the letter should be a copy of Lavoie's report.[6] Meredith concurred. So Spragge wrote to the bishop, who soon enough wrote the following reply:

> In answer, I have the honor to refer you to a letter sent to me, on the 8th May, 1872 by the Hon. the Secretary of State for the Provinces, transmitting me ... a cheque, no. 3805 for the Indians of Moisie, Mingan &c.&c. You will be made aware by that letter, that the whole sum sent, amounting to $250.00 was destined to the purchase of seed grain and of Agricultural Implements. – You will also see, by a letter I sent to the Hon. Mr. Howe, on the 20th July, that the intention of the Government concerning that amount and others, had been communicated to the Rev.[d] Father Arnaud by letter ... but the Rev.[d] Father, foreseeing that it would be necessary to employ a portion of that Sum, in the purchase of provisions for the Indians of Mingan, did buy some, among which were 250 Bushels of potatoes ...
>
> The Missionaries have done all in their power to prevent the Indians from suffering; – but the cause which has brought them to the reduced state mentioned in M. Lavoie's report is also therein indicated. The assistance granted by the Government is altogether inadequate and the Indians have to rely for their further maintenance, upon hunting game during the winter season; – but M. the Commandant informs you that the unfortunate Indians 'have not killed a Single Caribou nor have they seen any within 900 miles in the Interior.' I must say that the Indians have no other means to obtain food for their families and themselves especially since they are more strictly prohibited from fishing in the ... rivers, as they were in the habit of doing prior to that prohibition. – According to the last census the Indian population numbered 1309 souls and the total amount granted in 1872 was $1025, which gives the sum of $0.78¢ per capita for the year ... as I am called upon to give explanations, I think it right, to give them as complete as possible, leaving to the wisdom of the administration to remedy for the state of destitution prevailing amongst the Indians, and which seems to engross their [minds] with so much solicitude.[7]

The bishop attached additional, unattributable comments he had received from either the commander of *La Canadienne* or Father Arnaud. Two criticisms had been made concerning government relief efforts. First, the distributions had been approved and transmitted too late. It was recommended that the allocations for the summer and fall distributions be made not in May but rather in March, so that suppliers in Quebec City would receive the funds in time to stock the vessels sailing from Quebec at the end of April and early autumn. A second bit of advice – and it is not clear from the following quote whether it was a statement of practice or a recommendation – was that 'the Missionaries, in order to protect themselves from suspicion of dishonesty – or of partiality, entrust the chiefs themselves with distributions.'[8]

Spragge accepted the bishop's explanations and notified the minister that future allocations would be transmitted in September. This would enable the missionaries to purchase the necessary supplies and transport them to the Mingan mission before the winter freeze. Spragge also pointed out to the minister that the Lower Canada Indian Fund was undercapitalized. He referred the minister to the department's own numbers, which projected that an additional $400 in excess of the interest yielded would be required. He suggested that this amount be increased to $1,000 in the future so that the interest from the fund plus the extra amount 'would admit of increased assistance where it is needed.'[9]

The Montagnais case is instructive for several reasons. First and most obvious was the problem of logistics. A centralized, psychologically isolated bureaucracy was finding it hard to provide timely relief to peoples living in geographically remote and climatically severe locations. Also, the method of approving and transmitting the funds was cumbersome; it involved not only the Privy Council and the department but also the bishopric, the missionaries, private suppliers, the Canadian government's supply ship, and other private shippers. Furthermore, in planning the annual disbursements, Ottawa had not considered that winter arrived earlier in more northern regions.

A second factor in this case was the remote location of the Mingan reserve. The department lacked administrative capacity, and as a result it was the missionaries, rather than the North Shore Indian agents, who were responsible for distributing relief to the reserve. This arrangement raised doubts in Ottawa about the missionaries' reliability and honesty.[10] This issue was further complicated by the department's ambivalence about relief. If the department was too often seen as the primary relief agent, Indians might feel encouraged to become dependent upon the state; whereas if the church – or even better, the Hudson's Bay Company – provided relief, this would encourage the Indians to maintain their independence. So ran the government's thinking.[11] The issue of honesty and the department's overriding concern about strict adherence to its policies contributed to the development of a system consumed with accountability and attention to the tiniest details.

A third feature of the case is that it indicates the difficulties experienced by First Nations caught in the transition from traditional subsistence modes to market economies. The Montagnais had been assigned a reserve and were becoming more and more dependent on the church mission. The provision of seed grain as relief was linked to government attempts to promote Indian agriculture. In remote areas such as Mingan, where settlement and resource exploitation still had not necessitated strict confinement or rigorous implementation of assimilation policies, Indians were encouraged to remain dependent on traditional survival modes. Coates refers to this treatment as the 'best left as Indians policy' and attributes it partly to the mandate of Indian protection – a mandate clearly acknowledged by Bishop Langevin.[12] Yet the severe scarcity of game that plagued much of northern North America in the latter half of the nineteenth century rendered traditional subsistence increasingly difficult, as the Montagnais case illustrates. The Montagnais could not find any caribou, and according to the missionaries, government conservation policies and restrictions on fishing further contributed to their dreadful hardship. The question of conservation and government regulation of hunting and fishing was an important issue in post-Confederation Canada. Rapid settlement and the virtual extinction of some species had contributed to significant changes in game, bird, and fish populations and distributions. Ray observes that government conservation measures were at first rather welcomed by the First Nations, since they were seen as curbing the destructive and rapacious practices of white hunters, trappers, and settlers. Yet problems soon arose as Indians were increasingly subjected to new game laws and restrictions, which they saw as interfering with their traditional and guaranteed treaty rights.[13]

Finally, the Montagnais case provides an example of the collective relief measures that prevailed in this early period. In its estimates, the government regularly made provision for this form of relief. Collective relief – that is, relief allocated to the band as a whole to prevent hardship – was extended mainly in remote areas and in the West. This form of relief was not seen as support *per se*, but rather as a way to tide Indians over from one season to the next and also as a way to introduce them to agricultural forms of self-sufficiency. In this sense, relief vaguely resembled the Hudson's Bay Company's credit advance system. The distribution of seed and some staple foods was made at most twice a year. The dollar values were extremely small and entirely inadequate, as Langevin noted so derisively in his letter. Nevertheless, Spragge's concern about their actual disbursement served as a warning of what was to come. Once the department began seeking greater accountability for allocations, it was only a matter of time before more complex administrative procedures were introduced, ceiling amounts were set, and benefits were tied to individuals and their families.

The Distribution of Funds for the Benefit of Indians of Quebec, 1877

In 1874, Vankoughnet succeeded Spragge as deputy superintendent general. Soon after, in 1877, he implemented the more rigorous accounting mechanisms called for by his predecessor. Under these mechanisms, every expenditure had to be backed by explicit reasons. As one result, the department's relief policies became more sharply defined and more clearly articulated. Because the Quebec fund was unique, the Department of Indian Affairs had to engage in a fiscal planning and reporting exercise there – one that was different from the other regions. This annual exercise demonstrated the department's early thinking about Indian relief, not only in Quebec but elsewhere. The process for accessing funds from the Quebec allocation is well documented for 1877 and is known to have continued until at least 1891.[14]

In February 1877 the department submitted an itemized estimate of relief expenditures to the Privy Council for approval. The submission listed every band in Quebec along with a proposed allocation for each and a detailed statement of its projected use. For example, the department requested approval of funds 'to the Micmacs of the Township of Maria for purchase of Seed Grain and Agricultural implements. Cheque 3407, $150.00.'[15] A total of forty-two similar entries appeared, which included amounts for medical fees, maintenance of school buildings, salaries of teachers, and so on. The Privy Council approved a total of $7,090 on 13 March 1877.

More important, however, was the administration of the total allocation. In mid-March, Meredith, the deputy minister of the Department of the Interior, advised one Mr McNeill[16] to write to several organizations and persons, advising them of the approved amounts and authorizing the specific distribution of supplies (e.g., eighteen bushels of flour, six buckets of lard) to various agencies and missions. (McNeill's position in the Department of Indian Affairs was not identified. Most likely he was the secretary – a powerful position that entailed co-ordinating, preparing, and sending out all departmental correspondence and instructions.) Among these persons and organizations were James Bissett, an officer of the Hudson's Bay Company in Montreal, and A. Fraser & Co., a general supply firm in Quebec City. In addition, on Meredith's instructions, McNeill was to write to John Holliday, captain of a Canadian government schooner harboured at Quebec City, asking him to take certain supplies – to be provided by A. Fraser & Co. – and to ensure their distribution to the Indians, 'who are in actual want and unable to attain their own subsistence. The supplies should be given them at such times as they be most serviceable to them.'[17] This statement reflects a basic principle of residual relief – that is, that state relief is to be provided as a last resort. Such relief was based entirely on demonstrated need and was only to be offered at the time the need was obvious.

On the advice of the minister, David Mills, McNeill also asked Holliday 'to furnish the Dep^t with a statement showing the granting and description of the articles given in each case.' McNeill also wrote to James Bissett at the Hudson's Bay Company: 'I have the honour to request that you will have the goodness to instruct the HBC° Officer at Mingan to supply each of the Indians of that place as are unable to procure their own living, with articles absolutely necessary for their subsistence to an amount not exceeding $125 and to forward to the Dept the Apc for the same for payment.'[18] Bissett immediately acknowledged McNeill's letter and informed him that his officers at Mingan had been so advised.[19]

Cheques were mailed directly to each Indian agency, mission, responsible parish, or supplier. The sole exception to this procedure was the Hudson's Bay Company, which submitted a detailed account and request for reimbursement. Distributions were made in the form of goods; the administrator then recorded their money value. After this, the agents sent to the department either detailed explanations of the distributions or requests for further advice. Typical of the latter was correspondence from Father Boucher relating to the $75 that had been allocated to the Hurons of Lorette (known today as Loretteville) near Quebec City.

I have the hon. to ack. receipt of cheque no. 3414 for the purchase of seed grain for the Indians here. I pray you to tell me how you wish me to make the distribution. Do you require receipts from the Chiefs and those who receive aid? In this case I shall have to divide the money among all the families of the Village, in presence of the Chiefs, who will give receipts as well as those who got the money.

Very few persons sow – they have neither land nor manure. Some put in a few potatoes, beans, peas – three sow oats. I will do what you prescribe, and will retain the money till I hear from you.

There has been less misery this year than last – still there are many very poor families and who continually want help – many widow and sick are under the impression that I always have money from the Department to assist them; and nearly every day children come asking me for bread, in their mothers' names.[20]

What is implied in Father Boucher's letter is as revealing as what is directly stated. He was assuring the department that distribution would be done in the chiefs' presence; this would assuage any doubts as to how it was done. He was suggesting that the chiefs knew more about the community's needs and that their decisions would carry greater credibility. Even more important, he was trying to convey that no one would be able to impugn his own integrity in the matter. His letter also constituted an appraisal of the department's agricultural policy; he left little doubt that its success was minimal at best, and that it was somewhat unrealistic, given both the lack of access to land and the poor quality of what had been made available. Still, he neither criticized or mocked the merits of the policy, in which Vankoughnet had placed such great store.[21] Father Boucher's statement that there 'has been less misery this year than last' was cold comfort in an unhappy and impoverished situation, one that left many Hurons in need of government assistance, contrary to the government's explicit objectives. Unfortunately, there is no record of any reply to Father Boucher.

A record of relief disbursement in the Gaspé provides deeper insight into the system's accountability procedures and how benefits were linked to specific individuals and families. The curé of the Gaspé reported to the department on 17 June 1877:

I had to distribute some provisions to those Indians to enable them to sow their land, otherwise they would have to work for their living during the time most favorable for sowing. I generally distribute according to the number of souls in each family, except in the case of widows, to whom I give more than to other families, as they have no one to work for them. There are here 17 families comprising 71 souls.

I have distributed: –

3 bbls flour,	@ $9.50	$ 28.50
100 lb pork,	@ 14¢	14.00
61 bbls Potatoes	@ $1.40	85.40
10 " Oats	@ $2.00	20.00
Cartage		1.75
Postage and Other Expenses		.35
Total		$150.00

List of Distribution

	Number of Souls	Pounds of Flour	Pounds of Lard	Quarts of Potatoes	Quarts of Oats
1. Peter Jacques	9	72	12	6	1
2. John Lambert	7	56	9	5½	1
3. Baptiste Samson	5	40	8	3½	1
4. John Basque	4	32	6	3	1
5. Baptiste Basque	5	40	7	3½	1
Etc., to 17.					

I bought the grain and provisions here – the former from farmers in the neighbourhood the latter from the merchants.

I have the pleasure of stating that the Micmacs have made greater efforts to sow this spring than ever before.

Some talk of leaving on account of the high price of provisions and the scarcity of work. I give your Honorable govm't unbounded thanks for generosity to these poor Micmacs.[22]

This form of reporting was one of the first examples of a systematic relief allocation method. To some degree it replicated the format used by the Hudson's Bay Company for itemizing its credit advances. The curé truly appreciated government relief – though the Micmacs may have been less enthusiastic – and he seemed to support efforts to transform Indians into independent farmers. He also recognized the positive impact of the government monies on the local economy. Clearly, the white community benefited when Indians relied on government purchases of supplies.

Other 1877 correspondence pertaining to the Quebec fund consisted mostly of submissions by Holliday and Bissett regarding their distributions. Invoices for payment always accompanied Bissett's distribution lists. A common theme in many submissions was the hardship experienced by Indians arising from the loss of game, the absence of seals and seabirds, and government prohibitions on fishing.

The Threat of Starvation from Nabaskowan to Bonne Espérance, 1878

An exchange between Bishop Langevin of St-Germain-de-Rimouski and Vankoughnet further highlights the transitional situation of Quebec's North Shore Indians and the government's increasing concern about how much relief to provide for them, what conditions to attach to it, and how to distribute it. Langevin wrote to Vankoughnet on 27 October 1878 to bring to his attention correspondence he had received from one of his priests:

> I cannot do otherwise says the good priest than show you the extreme poverty of the Indians scattered about the part of the coast from Nabaskowan to Bonne Espérance a distance of about 90 leagues. These Indians together with a certain number of families of mixed race will perish from hunger this winter if someone does not come to their assistance ...
>
> They are truly in isolation and in a very critical position from all accounts. There are about *forty families* of these Indians scattered about on this part of the coast.
>
> These Indians as you know have never participated in the aid given to those of Bersimi and Godbout which are already insufficient for them. The soil of this barren coast ... is not arable; besides all efforts on behalf of the Indians, even those more favorably placed for agriculture have always failed. The causes of their greatest poverty are known, these are the prohibition to fish in several of the large rivers, the absolute refusal of the HBC to make advances to them as formerly and the scarcity of game. The consequence is that the poor Indians are reduced to starvation.
>
> I request then ... that these forty Indian families be not abandoned that they be granted an annual allowance. Ten dollars a family would be a slight aid and nevertheless they would be content and would be very grateful to the government.
>
> Since 1874 I have received nothing from your Dept. For the Indians of Mingan, Moisie and Seven Islands.[23]

Vankoughnet waited nearly a month to respond. In his apology to the Bishop, he attributed the delay to the recent change of government in Ottawa. Macdonald's Conservatives had returned to power – a return that likely pleased Vankoughnet. Still, the delay revealed a callousness that reflected the central government's removal from the condition of Indians and its increasingly mean and antipathetic attitude toward relief measures. This attitude – heightened by a dwindling federal treasury – is revealed in Vankoughnet's response. He wrote that the department would

> sanction the extension by the Missionary at that place [Nabaskowan] of relief to an amount not to exceed altogether two hundred dollars to the Indians between Nabaskowan and Bonne Espérance; but this grant must be considered as altogether exceptional being necessitated by the ... position in which these Indians are this year placed owing to the circumstances described in your letter and which may not occur again for years. The Indians to whom relief is given should therefore be made to understand that this grant is not necessarily to be repeated another year.[24]

These relief measures were eventually exercised through the missionary, who authorized the local merchant at Nabaskowan to issue food and clothing. The total value of the goods was $255. Indians were able to contribute $100 of the total. The government reimbursed the merchant for the balance.[25]

Langevin's correspondence contains important information about the situation of the North Shore Indians. The land was barren, so the federal government's policies for encouraging Indians to lead a settled, pastoral life had not met with any success. Game continued to be scarce, and the government had not lifted its ban on fishing. As a result, the Indians' ability to provide for themselves was seriously impaired. All of this was compounded, the Bishop noted, by the Hudson's Bay Company's refusal to advance credit as it had in the past. Here we can see the first stages of a developing conflict between the government and the company. However, Langevin offered no insight as to why the company was refusing credit. Finally, Langevin observed in his letter that he had received no funds for relief since 1874. From the cases already described in this chapter, it is clear that since the 1873 Montagnais incident, the government had been turning to the company to administer relief along the North Shore. Evidently the government was still unsure of the integrity of missionaries, or it had doubts about their ability to determine whether the need actually existed, or both. This was a period of crisis for the company, however. The HBC had lost its monopoly, and the market for its furs was considerably weaker. In fact, around this time it was considering closing down the trade altogether.[26]

Vankoughnet's delayed reply showed no concern for the Indians' distress. Earnestly bureaucratic, he was mainly concerned about how the funds were to be administered, and he framed his response tightly around the emerging relief policy. He simply ignored the problem's continuing nature (which had been known to the department since at least 1873), choosing instead to describe the situation as unusual. He cautioned the bishop to make sure the Indians understood that the grant was temporary and exceptional. To underscore this point, he reduced Langevin's request by half. The case does more than illustrate Vankoughnet's parsimony; it also offers a vivid example of how First Nations became objects of administration and of the government's fiscal and political objectives.

The Early Administration of Relief in Ontario

Relief in Ontario was administered differently than in Quebec. In Quebec, there was an annual appropriation, which was accessed not only by Indian agents but also by the Hudson's Bay Company and the various church missions. In Ontario, relief typically was paid from individual band funds that had been established through treaty annuities and land sales and that were held in trust in Ottawa. Most often, the Indian agent, acting on written instructions from the department, and/or at the request of the band council, applied to Ottawa for permission to pay relief funds from the trust on behalf of identified members of the band. The trust funds were technically a band asset, yet the department placed rigid controls on them. This part of the process of Indian tutelage focused on the bands' acquisition of fiscal management skills, their development of self-governance (with municipal government as a rough model), and, with respect to relief, on their adherence to strict guidelines – guidelines that reflected largely liberal ideas about individualism, self-reliance, and the capacity to work.[27]

A key element of the Ontario system, and one that soon spread to other regions where Indian agents worked closely with bands, was that the agent at hand acted as an intermediary between the band and the government. In much the same manner as a parent represents the interests of a child, the Indian agent represented the band to the government, and the government to the band.[28] It is worth noting here the similarity of roles and functions between the district officers of the British Raj in India and of the Canadian Indian agents. Paul Scott in *The Towers of Silence*, one of the novels in the *The Raj Quartet*, described the role of the district officer as *man-bap*: 'It meant Mother-Father, the relationship of the *raj* to India, ... of a district officer to the people of his district ... I am your father and your mother.' Robin Moore writes that Scott's treatment of *man-bap* was among the key elements in his work. According to Moore, Scott was interested in this relationship not simply because it masked economic exploitation, but because it sought 'not to unite Indians' under the raj 'but to attach them to itself.'[29]

The Indian agent facilitated much the same relationship between the Canadian state and the First Nations; he was first and foremost an agent of the government and of the systems in place to foster Indians' complete attachment to Canada and to Canadian culture. Consider the following excerpts from the file copy of correspondence to Joseph Perillard, Indian agent at Oka, Quebec:

> With reference to my letter ... informing you that you would be further communicated with in regard to your duties as Indian Agent, I beg to inform you that it will be your duty to encourage the Indians to make progress in the arts of civilization. To this end you should assist them as far as possible by advice and practical instruction. You should accordingly encourage the Indians by every means in your power to cultivate the soil and, where practicable, you should instruct them with regard to seeding the land and reaping their crops; in fencing and building, and in the keeping of their premises in good order with a view to cleanliness and good health. I beg to emphasize the desire of the Department that a special effort be made by you to induce the Indians to look to the soil to yield them a return for their labour, and to convince them that there is no way in which they can become so independent and prosperous as by farming ...
>
> You should also use your utmost endeavours to effect the prevention of intemperance among the Indians by advising them constantly against the use of intoxicants and bring in to justice any person who may be credibly reported as having furnished ... liquor to the reserve, or who may have had any Indian possession thereof ...
>
> The education of the Indian children, for which the Department has afforded facilities, should form the subject of constant advice to the Indians and you should bring all the influence you can to bear on them to send their children regularly to school.[30]

In this same vein, the agent was critical to the administration of relief. To bring consistency to communications about relief and to place stringent controls on its provision, the inside service in Ottawa issued periodic policy circulars to its agents regarding eligibility for relief and how to apply to Ottawa for it. One of these early circulars was found in a general policy file from 1893.

> Sir,
>
> I have to request that you will be good enough, from personal observation, to inform me of any cases of actual distress among the Indians of your [*agency name*] which, in your opinion, should receive periodical assistance from the funds of the Band during the ensuing winter.
>
> You should state the date upon which you visited and acquainted yourself with the circumstances of each case, and what amount should, in your opinion, be allowed and at what intervals the relief should be afforded, giving full particulars as to the age, number in family, why he or she cannot support himself or herself, &c. If provision has already been made for any such cases through pensions voted by the Band, you should state the names of the pensioners, amount of pension for each, and whether it is sufficient to provide the actual necessities of life.[31]

Thus, in Ontario, all requests for relief gradually were framed around increasingly explicit circumstances and conditions. In most cases, the band met in council and voted the payment of pensions from their funds, subject to the recommendation of the agent and to Ottawa's approval. Occasionally, however, in cases of acute distress, the agent would issue relief through a local merchant and seek retroactive approval. In some other instances, the agent would apply for relief funds without a prior resolution from the band council. As in Quebec, funds were rarely if ever issued in cash. Instead, relief was provided by local suppliers in kind up to the amount approved. In this way, Ottawa was able to control what goods were actually provided.

The most striking aspect of Indian relief in Ontario during this early period, even in the more remote areas, was the way it and thus Indian poverty had already been individualized. Very often, the language encountered in the Ontario documents suggests that the Indians had happily settled down. They hadn't; the reality was grimmer than the documents so often try to suggest. Yet because relief cases so often focused on individuals, these cases sound exceptional. The result is a false image of overall Indian progress, especially in the realm of culture.

'Periodical' and Pension Relief

In December 1878, Superintendent Phipps of the Manitowaning Agency requested relief on behalf of Chief Edowekezis of the French River Band near Georgian Bay. Phipps was asking for $10 to support the chief until the following summer, at which time 'I have every expectation that he will be able to support himself.'[32] In making the request, Phipps was required to substantiate that relief was necessary (Chief Edowekezis was ill) and to assure Ottawa that the chief would soon be well again.

A second case, from the Six Nations Reserve near Brantford, highlights the roles of the band council and the Indian agent. Here, the term 'pension' is used rather than relief. A. Dingman, the Indian agent for the Six Nations, wrote to Vankoughnet on 8 February 1889:

> Sir,
> I beg to enclose decisions and applications of the Chiefs of the Six Nations Council to place Mrs. Christian Walker, widow of the late Chief Moses Walker; Chief George Elliott; Susannah Powless; and Sampson Fish on the pension list at the rate of twenty-five each per annum to be paid quarterly. From a personal visit to one of the parties, and from inquiry respecting the condition of the others I think there is a necessity for the assistance proposed to be given.[33]

Accompanying Dingman's letter was a Band Council Resolution (BCR) for each applicant. An example follows:

> Oshweken Council House
> January 17, 1889.
>
> With reference to the application of one Sampson Fish through George Gibson who is said to be blind and very poor and no relation to support him. After the Council was satisfied that the above statement was true decided to put him on the pension list at the rate of twenty five dollars per annum to begin from the first of the current years.
>
> Josiah Hill
> Secy. S.N.C.[34]

Apparently distinctions were made between people who were old or infirm and unable to work and those who were temporarily incapacitated or able bodied but without funds. For the former, an annual pension could be approved; for the latter, only periodical relief was possible.

This distinction is clear in the sad case of Edward Atthill, a Mississauga, and his wife, a Chippewa. George McDermot, the Indian agent for the Mississaugas of Scucog Island near Port Perry, wrote to Vankoughnet on behalf of both, even though Mrs Atthill had returned to live with her mother on the Rama Reserve near Barrie.

> I beg to acknowledge receipt of Department Circular of 11th Dec. last No. 101348 asking for any cases of actual distress existent among any of the Indians of my agency and in reply I would report that I consider that Edward Atthill and his wife should receive periodical during the winter from the funds of the Band. I visited Atthill yesterday and he is looking very ill and not able to work. His wife is I am afraid now on her death bed at her mothers house on the Rama Reserve and agent McPhee writes me that her parents are very poor and not able to do anything for her I think. Atthill and his wife should be allowed $3.00 pr. month payable each month apiece during the winter months. I don't think Mrs. Atthill will live until spring but I hope Atthill will get strong enough to work again in course of two or three months. Consumption is their complaint.[35]

Vankoughnet approved McDermot's request at the end of January 1890. In the Atthill case we see the department making a distinction between interim relief (periodical) for temporary distress and permanent relief (pension) for age and disability. McDermot in his letter to the department conveyed some sympathy for the Atthills, yet he was also mindful of the department's policy and its longstanding fear of Indian dependency. Thus, he assured Vankoughnet of Atthill's probable fitness for work by summertime, even though the man had tuberculosis.

In McDermot's letter we also see the diligence and attention to protocol so typical of Indian agents. McDermot's sympathy for the Atthills existed in the context of his function: it was he who decided which cases would satisfy Ottawa's criteria for relief. What the file does not tell us is whether McDermot assessed others to determine whether they were in 'actual distress' and found that they were not. McDermot could represent the Atthills' situation to Ottawa as one that fulfilled the requirements of 'actual distress,' and thus do them some good by recommending relief. But he could equally decide that others failed the test – others whose names and situations simply were not recorded. First and foremost, McDermot was an agent of the state. As an agent and intermediary, he spoke the state's language; thus, even the interests of the Atthills, which he presented to the state, were interests carefully circumscribed by what the state was predisposed to hear. In this exchange McDermot appeared kindly – and perhaps he was – but his kindness was also defined by his relationship with First Nations, which revolved around patronage and dominance on his part, and humility and gratitude on theirs.

One final observation should be made about the distinction between periodical and pension relief. Agents' recommendations to Ottawa were guided in part by their knowledge of the band's ability to pay. So it may well be that this factor helped determine an agent's recommendations about periodical or pension relief, whatever the actual situation. If a band was extremely poor, relief might not be possible in any circumstances. Much later, the ability of bands to pay relief became central to the issue of welfare provision on reserves. The same question would later drive debates over federal versus provincial responsibility under the British North America Act.

The Ojibwa of the Port Arthur Agency, Northwestern Ontario:
From Humble Gratitude to Pauperization, 1890–1896

The plight of the Ojibwa Nation bands served by the Port Arthur agency captures the essence of the evolving social and economic nightmare of First Nations caught in the expanding grip of government policy and administration. These bands, which were signatories to the Robinson-Superior Treaty of 1850, were the Fort William Band near present-day Thunder Bay; the Pic Band located on Heron Bay, Lake Superior, and at Mobert, near White River; and the Pays Plat Band near Schreiber. The Robinson-Superior Treaty, in tandem with the Robinson-Huron Treaty of the same year, ceded title to 'all the land north of Lakes Superior and Huron to the height of land separating Rupert's Land from Canada.'[36] The land involved was twice the amount already ceded in all of Upper Canada, and it was known to be rich in mineral resources. In return for this land the Ojibwa Nation was provided with reserve lands, annuity payments, and the unlimited right to hunt and fish in the surrendered territories 'with the exception of such portions as might "from time to time be sold or leased to individuals or companies of individuals and occupied by them with the consent of the provincial government."'[37]

After 1850 the Ojibwa continued to combine their traditional ways with trapping and trading, although clearly the fur trade was no longer as successful an enterprise for them.[38] The fur trade was in decline relative to the rest of the economy. In absolute terms it would enjoy some of its peak years in the late nineteenth and early twentieth centuries. That being said, it was no longer consistently lucrative, and success often varied from region to region and from band to band, depending on the availability and price of the two most popular furs, muskrat and beaver. The incursion of whites seeking mineral wealth, the building of the Canadian Pacific Railway, the contraction of game populations, and outbreaks of tuberculosis and influenza in the end undermined the Indians' economy and severely limited their ability to negotiate the demands of the market economy. The government's response to the deteriorating circumstances of the Pic and Fort William bands exemplifies the increasing complexity of Indians' lives, including their absorption into a bureaucratic, organizational matrix. This matrix included the state and all its allies: the Hudson's Bay Company, the CPR, and the church. The story of the Ojibway bands' difficulties highlights above all the state's expectations: loyalty, effort, and obedience.

The period 1890 to 1896 was one of administrative change in the department, prompted partly by the decline of the governing Conservative Party. The 1885 Riel Rebellion and Indians' unexpected sympathy for it had shaken the federal government. Criticism of the Indian administration in the House of Commons was focused on the department's failure to treat Indians humanely and hasten their advancement and civilization. This public criticism of Indian Affairs hardened the federal government's resolve to assimilate Indians into the Canadian mainstream, with the goal of preventing more Indian uprisings.[39]

Criticism of the department also arose within its own ranks. Most of this criticism was aimed at Vankoughnet, who was seen as increasingly out of touch and insensitive to the needs of his field agents. After Macdonald's death in 1891, his critics became even more vocal; by 1893, the new Minister of the Interior, T. Mayne Daly, had forced him into early retirement.[40] Duncan Campbell Scott, the department's chief clerk and accountant, filled his position on an interim basis until the permanent appointment of Hayter Reed later the same year. Reed, an Indian agent in Battleford until 1888 and the Indian commissioner for Manitoba and the Northwest Territories since then, had been one of Vankoughnet's biggest detractors and part of the movement to depose him. Still, the appointment of someone from the outside service like Reed was a token gesture rather than a harbinger of policy change and administrative renewal. Like his predecessor, Reed was a card-carrying Conservative, and, in his brief tenure before that party fell from power, he showed himself to be every bit as parsimonious and authoritarian as Vankoughnet. In fact, he prided himself on his reputation for hard-heartedness. In correspondence with Edgar Dewdney, the Indian commissioner for the Northwest Territories, he wrote: 'I have but little doubt, Sir, but that your ears will be greeted, on setting foot in this Agency, with sorrowful tales as to my hardheartedness [sic] as it is, I am now called the "Iron Heart."'[41]

Toward the end of Vankoughnet's tenure as deputy superintendent general of Indian affairs, the chiefs of the Pic and Pays Plat bands wrote to him thanking him for his kindness and attention and presenting him and his wife with 'two fine stones' as a New Year's gift. The letter is a classic of imperial homage; the image of Vankoughnet as sovereign is inescapable.

> Sir,
> Permit us the chiefs of the Pic and Pays Plat Bands, to present you through our Agent as a New Years gift two fine stones, one is for your good Lady Mrs. Vankoughnet, as a small token of our regards towards you, for the kindness and attention we have always received from your Department, in many ways more than we could demand according to our Treaty, and to mention also to you that within the past few years we have prospered on our new Reserves, and can afford to make this small presentation, if you will accept it from us, and hoping you may see many more New Years is the wish of your faithful Indian Servants.[42]

It is unlikely that the chiefs wrote the letter, which seems to have been penned and signed by one hand, in a style contrived for the purpose. More likely, J.P. Donnelly, the Indian agent for Port Arthur, wrote the letter at the chiefs' request, embellishing it so as to please Vankoughnet and protect or enhance his own stature.[43] Vankoughnet was not especially popular among his agents, according to Leighton. He was perceived as out of touch and as insensitive to the needs of his staff. Yet his manner demanded deference, and those agents who knew how to show it could presumably benefit from doing so. It hardly mattered whether the bands had actually prospered on their reserves; Vankoughnet wanted to be told that they had, and wanted to believe those who told him so. And perhaps there was some truth to agents' claims that they had, in situations where the Indians' alternative was utter destitution. Whatever the truth, Vankoughnet was wonderfully grateful to 'his' Indians, and wrote to them forthwith with a certain *noblesse oblige*:

> I have received your kindly worded letter of the 6th inst, as well as the two fine stones which you forwarded as a New Year's gift to myself and wife. Believe me, I appreciate your remembrance of me as evidenced by the token of regard, and while valuing the beautiful agates which you forwarded, nevertheless the letter which accompanied it, is appreciated by me much more, showing as it does, the gratitude which you have in your hearts toward the Dept for favours wh. have been shown you in your advancing welfare as an industrial people. It has also been a pleasure to me to forward your interests in any reasonable manner, when it lay in my power to do so, provided I was assured that what you requested would be to your advantage to receive, and also avoiding as I have endeavoured to do in y[r]. case as that of all other Indians, making you too dependent on the government for articles which you might fairly be expected to procure for yourselves. I am pleased to learn from your agent M[r]. Donnelly, who has done so much to advance you in material prosperity that you are doing so well, and making profitable use of the articles that have been given to you by the Dept.
>
> Hoping that you will continue in this laudable course, and wish you many returns of the New Year
> Believe me to remain,
> Your sincere friend[44]

Ever mindful of duty, Vankoughnet could not resist this opportunity to remind the chiefs that their material welfare could only have resulted from the department's efforts to advance them as an industrial people. By implication, the onus was on the First Nations to maintain their prosperity through continued hard work and self-reliance. Conversely, using this line of thought, the department could always attribute a decline in their fortunes to the Indians' failure to remain diligent.

The period of 'prosperity' for the Pic Band was short. In early 1894, Donnelly wrote to Hayter Reed, the new deputy superintendent general, requesting permission to grant relief to certain Indian individuals and families of the Pic Band:

> I have to ask the Dept. to permit me to furnish No. 67. 11. 70. 51. 8 & 15 with each one and a half Bushels of Corn, the freight is the same on 100 pounds as upon one bushel and each in Separate Bags addressed to them

in Care of the H.B. Co. Agent – Cost is $1^{00} per Bushel and about 70 Cents
per 100 pounds freight. One Bushel of Corn is equal to about one Barrel of
Flour in feeding a family, these Indians belong to the Pic Band and live at
Montazambert 40 miles east of the Pic Reserve & 240 East of here, the La
Gripp is all through this portion of the Country, and more Deadly than the
La Gripp of last year or before, a great Many Deaths particularly among the
Indians, as they often go out too soon after the illness get a relapse and die,
I enclose a letter from the H.B. Co. Officer at this place, who is very chari-
table to the sick Indians, so much so that the Company have noticed it, and
forbid any more advances.[45]

Reed replied three days later:

I have to acknowledge the receipt of your letter of the 17th instant, from the
Officer of the Hudson's Bay Company at Montizambert, together with a list
of the names of the Indians of the Pic Band who he states are in need of assistance; and in reply I beg to inform you that you may furnish Nos 67, 11, 70,
51, 8, and 15, the Indians in question, each with one and a half bushels of
corn the cost of which must not exceed $1.^{00} per bushel. The corn should be
sent to the Indians in care of the Hudson's Bay Officer at Montizambert, and
the Indians should be told to be economical in the use of it.[46]

In this correspondence we see again the problems associated with
increased competition in the fur trade and the company's refusal to
advance credit for goods, upon which the First Nations were now dependent. Reed's admonition that the Indians be economical suggests that
Ottawa distrusted Indians' capacity to grasp the concept of monetary
value. There was always suspicion that relief allocations would lead to
spendthrift behaviour. At any rate, Donnelly acknowledged Reed's
instructions in early February; at the same time, he made a request concerning additional reported distress among the Pic at Mobert. 'I
received a letter from White River still further East on the C.P.R. asking
for assistance for No.10 and 55 Indian families of the same Pic Band
who were also in distressed circumstances, and I took it upon myself to
send them also a Bag of Corn 2 Bushels; they asked for an order on a
stove, to be taken out of their Annuity Money which I declined giving
for 10^{00/00}$, this Corn will Carry them over this winter.[47] Reed con-
curred, but in keeping with the policy initiated by Spragge, he asked
Donnelly to send a list of the recipients' names signed by them and witnessed by the Hudson's Bay Company officer.[48]

Two months later, Donnelly again wrote to Reed, this time requesting relief for Antoine Desmoulin of the Pic Band, who

> about a year past ... accidentally Shot himself through his lungs with a Ball. Dr. Pringle attended him for which he was paid by the Dep.ᵗ, Since that time his wife and only child died, I visited him while at the Reserve last Month, has been in Bed all the time since the accident, and is gradually recovering and is supported by the Charity of the Indians, somedays had something to eat and other days nothing, and is almost transparent, and I have been asked for a bag of Corn One and a half Bushels 1^{50/100}$ and the freight about 65 Cents.[49]

This request was approved. However, in the meantime Donnelly was still awaiting approval to provide relief to members of the Fort William Band. The band council had met 15 January and had passed a resolution requesting

> the Department to furnish the following Indigent Indians on our Reserve the following supplies & Charge the same to our account – Mrs. Monchu-wiskin, widow – John [   ], sick with consumption, Peter Kolkolkida infirm by La Gripp – Old Indian Margaret, Old Marian Piska, Whisky Jack a Crip-ple – []ishwalick Old and sickly, Old Mrs Busha – Old Widow Shabba, []anette White, Indian girl with only one leg – Old Messobie – Old Mrs Peelow, widow – Old Luc Duchamp sick with Rhumatism, Mrs Edward Gordon No husband and a family to each allowed 50 pounds Oat Meal @ 5.¢ equal $2.^{50} – in all $35.^{00}.[50]

On 23 April, Donnelly wrote to Ottawa asking for the disposition of this request. It is not clear why he took so long to follow up. He had been visiting the Pic reserve in March and possibly had been visiting others as well. His absence from his office might be the reason; more likely, though, he was simply fearful of seeming impudent to Reed. In reminders to Ottawa, he noted that 'the chiefs asked me several times for the expected supply' and that the indigent band members had 'been fed by Charity this past winter, principally by the sisters of St Josephs Orphanage and the R.C. Missionary, and other Charitable assistance.'[51] Five days later, Ottawa issued a cheque for $40, five dollars less than the band had requested. The discrepancy was not explained. When Reed received Donnelly's accounting of the allocation, he wrote to the agent, asking him to 'kindly furnish receipted accounts from the merchants from whom the purchases were made, showing in detail the quantity and prices of articles supplied.' He added, 'I would be glad if you would also explain why a uniform amount ($2.86) was allowed to each individual.'[52]

Reed's diligent, somewhat supercilious attention to detail was greater even than Vankoughnet's. This reflected Ottawa's growing suspicion that the Indians of the Port Arthur agency had come to expect relief and were depending on it too much. Furthermore, they were not progressing in their adoption of white ways, and Donnelly himself was not being attentive enough to his primary duty, which was to teach and advance the Indians. This heightening expectation that every detail of relief be explained probably reflected not only Reed's authoritarian manner, but also the growing influence of Duncan Campbell Scott, the future deputy superintendent. Besides this, there was already an abiding belief in Ottawa and in the outside service that Indians were prone to misrepresent or overstate their circumstances in order to procure relief rations. Reed made this clear in January 1895, when the Fort William Band submitted yet another band council resolution. The resolution requested 'six hundred ... dollars to be taken from our fund ... that comes to ten dollars to ever family which articles are mentioned as follows ... 3 bags of flour and Pork on Balance which are 62 families on the Reserve.'[53] Reed immediately expressed his displeasure:

I am in receipt of your letter of the 8th instant, enclosing a copy of a resolution of Council passed by the Fort William Indians, asking the Department to grant the sum of $600.[00] wherewith to purchase provisions for sixty families on the Reserve, together with a letter from the Revd W.F. Gagnier in the matter; and in reply I beg to inform you that even if it were considered advisable to comply with the request of the Indians the state of their interest etc. would not admit of its being done, and I might remind you that the Department only furnishes relief in cases of absolute distress arising from sickness, old age or other infirmity, If there are any such among the Fort William Band you might furnish me with a statement shewing the circumstances which appear to you warrant the intervention of the Department, that is to say the age, cause of destitution, and the smallest amount which you think would be sufficient to relieve want, and upon receipt of this the question of making advances to such will be considered. I might add that where those who are in indigent circumstances have friends or relatives able to assist them, it is expected that they will do so. The Department is strongly averse to the granting of indiscriminate aid, believing as it does that such action tends to pauperize the Indians, and thus negative the main feature of its policy in regard to them vis: to educate them up to the status of self-supporting Whites.[54]

The department's moralizing about relief is ironic, because the funds in question were technically the band's, derived from treaty right. Nothing illustrates better the humiliation of First Nations under the Indian Act than this paternal guardianship of their assets. Even though First Nations paid for their relief from the interest on their own trust accounts, Ottawa managed the monies as if they were directly derived from parliamentary appropriation. This practice can be traced to the department's political masters from both sides of the House, who in the latter part of the nineteenth century hotly debated the merits and amounts of the annuity payments that the government was required to make through the treaty process.[55] The federal government, caught in its own philosophical quandary about the nature of the treaty versus the nature of the treated, chose to see treaty payments as a never-ending handout rather than as just compensation. In effect, the policy had transformed all Indians into beggars of their own monies.

The government's perception of the moral impact of relief was closely linked to this dislike of annuity payments and their use for relief. This is illustrated well in Reed's letter to Donnelly, which provided the first clear departmental statement about how the provision of relief related to the goal of assimilation. If relief was granted indiscriminately, it would surely undermine the department's central task, which was to civilize and advance the Indians. No greater evidence of Indian advancement could be adduced than their individual ability to be self-supporting. In setting up this expectation, the department grossly idealized the realities of Canadian society and the population as a whole. By 1895, the ability of Canada's non-Indians to be self-supporting was under considerable strain. Reform movements during the 1890s, especially in the urbanized, newly industrialized areas of eastern Canada, were demanding better working conditions, public health, housing, and a modicum of social security; at the same time, provincial social welfare expenditures – including those directed toward relief – were rising significantly.[56]

Even members of the British Poor Law Commission of 1832–4 could not have expressed Reed's view better. Woven into the text of Reed's letter was the principle of 'less eligibility' – the idea that a trade-off must be made between the ill effects of pauperization and the requirement for people to earn their living on even the meanest of wages. How else could the 'progressive' ideas of liberal individualism and the pursuit of self-interest in the marketplace be inculcated if not by this trade-off? The poor law commission used the less eligibility principle in its efforts to distinguish the working poor from paupers. Commission members considered the condition of the independent wage labourer to be morally superior to that of the dependent pauper, even though 'the independent labourers are commonly maintained upon less money.' 'The whole purpose of the reform [enacted in 1834],' writes Himmelfarb, 'was not so much to redeem the pauper as to rescue the poor from the fate of pauperism, to prevent the independent labourer from succumbing to the dependency that brought with it all the vices of pauperism.'[57]

It is difficult to assess the impact of the principle of less eligibility on peoples who had never been materially acquisitive and for whom the idea of subsistence living was not necessarily a bleak proposition. Clearly Ottawa held contradictory expectations of Indians. One expectation would have them behave as childlike wards of the state who had to be brought under the civilizing influence of wage labour – a supposition that ignored Indians' abilities as fur traders, soldiers, and guides. Simultaneously, another expectation would have them immediately grasp the principle of less eligibility and wage dependence when it was placed before them.

The problem was that Ottawa never really defined what activity might satisfy the requirement for self-support. All we can glean from the available evidence is that 'earning' a living wage was considered superior to traditional, subsistence forms of 'maintaining' an existence. Paradoxically, as the Quebec examples reveal, and as Coates stated in his study of the Yukon, the department often thought it 'best to leave them as Indians.'[58] From the Reed–Donnelly correspondence and elsewhere, it is clear that the federal government was so caught up in the ideological platitudes of the day that it failed to recognize the contradictions in what it was trying to achieve.

Early in 1896, in the waning months of the Conservative Party's time in office, Donnelly wrote again to Reed, describing the increasingly desperate circumstances of the Pic River Band and requesting authorization for further relief:

> Enclosed is a list of poor Indians of the Pic River Band who always winter about White River, their Hunting Ground, and each year as the Fur and fish grow more scarce they get more poor ...
> Widow TobKisa & Daughter, Widow Weseean & family of 4 – Widow Janice

& family of 4 – Widow Shoes & Boy – Widow Shonette & 3 small children – Nicolas & Sick wife cut his hand and is Mortifying I asked the Doctor to Call and See them last week and I think will both die, with a Baby 3 – Tussant Weseean with a cut foot wife & child 3 – twenty one persons in all. this time of year until fish time in the spring is their hardest time to live, and in my opinion 10 Bushels Corn at 80 Cents – 10 Bags at Cents – 10 pounds fat Bacon (grease) to each family 70 at 10 Cents – freight on same $2. $\frac{45}{100}$ in all = $18 $\frac{45}{100}$ Cents, and I could visit them about 300 miles East of here, and see they get this supply if granted at a cost of about $1 $\frac{50}{100}$ per day & would take about 3 days –[59]

Reed apparently granted the request. In later correspondence, Donnelly described the Pic Band as his 'poorest band and getting poorer every year.'[60] He attributed its poverty to growing numbers of whites invading the trap line territories, where they competed with the Indians and with each other. According to Donnelly, these incursions were disrupting the Indians' seasonal movements as well as their hunting and trapping, and were forcing them to be more sedentary and to confine themselves to their reserves. Donnelly, in some despair, ultimately suggested more funds for buildings on all the reserves, including the construction of a poor house for the Fort William Band. Donnelly's observation is important. Ray attributes the decline of Indian participation in the fur trade to increased incursion by whites into First Nations' northern trapping territories during the bull market that the fur industry enjoyed in the 1920s. This incursion was linked to economic hard times and high unemployment in the cities. If Donnelly's observation is accurate, the decline had already set in farther south and can be explained by the impact of the railway. Ray made this point in his earlier article, 'Periodic Shortages'; however, he does not make it again in his later work. Rather, in *The Canadian Fur Trade*, he pinpoints the 1920s as the time when these incursions had their strongest impact.[61]

The early administration of Indian relief in Ontario typified the principles and policies that the department had begun to apply uniformly across the country. Relief was defined two ways: first, as a periodic, temporary measure to relieve distress perceived to have been caused by unusual circumstances; and second, as a more ongoing payment to compensate for the loss of a male breadwinner or for a person's chronic incapacity because of sickness or old age. In the latter situations, the term 'pension' was sometimes used. In fact, although there were two types of relief, the actual amount and the category under which it was granted were determined entirely by the Indian agent and his functional relationship with Ottawa. Equally important in determining the amount and category of relief was the state of a band's trust account and the interest it yielded. Furthermore, in order to determine the existence and extent of need, the agent often had to rely on information from Hudson's Bay Company officers or from parish priests and missionaries on the reserves.

The building of the CPR and, later, the National Transcontinental made many of the reserves more accessible to the Indian agents. The railways also enabled faster movement of relief items to those in distress. As well, they made policy easier to enforce, because agents could more readily establish a physical presence. The railways also increased white incursions into native hunting and trapping grounds, and the displacement of Indians from those territories. This led to more sedentary lifestyles and even greater reliance on government relief. In addition, faced with greater competition in the fur trade, the Hudson's Bay Company began questioning its role as an intermediary for First Nations and as a conduit for government policy. As it had in Quebec, the company began cutting back on its credit advances. The government was failing to intervene to protect Indians' economic independence; at the same time, it was establishing a hidebound relief administration. All of this created a situation in which the government's dominance increased, and Indians' subjugation became even more marked.

Early Relief in the Northwest Territories

In contrast to the relatively settled situation of the First Nations in Ontario, the image conveyed by government files of First Nations in the Northwest Territories was of peoples in upheaval, who were being displaced and dispersed as the frontier of settlement steadily advanced. They were refugees within their own land. Despite the stories of hardship and despair that reached Ottawa, the administration of relief there was not fundamentally different from that in Ontario or Quebec. The southern parts of the territories – that is, those parts which were predominantly the prairies – had been treatied by the mid-1870s. However, the First Nations' acceptance of life on the reserves was by no means clear, as the Riel Rebellion later demonstrated. Farther north, a melting pot of Metis, treaty, and non-treaty Indians presented the department with a confused, ill-defined mandate.

The confusion about the department's responsibilities toward non-treaty Indians and the Metis was most crucially evident in matters concerning relief. The following exchanges between Indian agent N.L. Orde of the Battleford Agency and Deputy Superintendent General Vankoughnet evoke both the human dilemma and the sense of rising chaos. This correspondence must be understood in the context of Treaty Six. Signed in 1876, this was the only treaty that gave a First Nation (i.e., the Cree) assurances of government assistance in times of famine.[62] Orde wrote to Vankoughnet in November 1879 requesting 'that you will be good enough to inform me, at your convenience, whether I am to give destitute, non-treaty Indians food, or not.'[63] Vankoughnet replied: 'I have to refer you to your general instructions in which you were informed that no provisions were to be given to able-bodied Indians unless work for the same had been done by them. The circumstances should however be very exceptional indeed under which relief is extended to non-treaty Indians. In respect to sick and aged Indians whether they come within the Treaty or not moderate assistance should be extended to them.'[64] Before Orde received this reply, he had already written again to Vankoughnet regarding assistance for the Metis, whose situation in Canada since the Manitoba Act of 1870 had become increasingly insecure and perilous.[65] In the federal government's view, Manitoba was needed as a province mainly to secure Euro-white domination of the Northwest and to head off the possibility of a distinct Metis province. With the creation of Manitoba, the Metis, although they had been promised a land base, were effectively dispersed into what is now northern Saskatchewan and Alberta. Orde wrote to Vankoughnet that some Metis women in the Battleford area were receiving treaty money. 'In one or two instances these women are employed by Whitemen as domestic servants: these men come to me for rations for their servants. I refused to give provisions to a Mr. Dufferin a day or two ago, so he turned the poor creature out, he could not afford to keep her as he is a poor man and has a wife and family to support ... I am giving her rations & would be glad to get instructions on the point.'[66]

Vankoughnet replied two months later:

I reply to your letter of the 15 Nov. last relative to relieving half Breed (Indian & French) women who are on the Indian paylist and some of whom are widows and others cast off I have to inform you that provided these women come under the class of sick and aged, limited assistance can be given them and is done to others of that class: but if they are able to work and support themselves there appears to be no reason why the Dept should contribute towards their support without receiving some value in the shape of labor for what may be given them.[67]

Vankoughnet referred Orde to his instructions; from this it is apparent that general directions were given to the agents with respect to relief provision. No clear difference in policy from either Quebec or Ontario can be gleaned from this correspondence; however, a difference in tone and in the use of certain qualifiers can be detected. The tone was meaner: Ottawa was determined to deter Indians from relief, and there would not simply be the standard differentiation between the able-bodied and the old or infirm. Also, distinctions were being made among treaty Indians, non-treaty Indians, and the Metis. For the non-treatied and able bodied, relief was to be on an exceptional basis, and under this rubric were widowed Metis women. Although this correspondence did not specify how all widows were to be treated, this was the first time they had been named as not necessarily eligible. In contrast, in Ontario, besides those widows who were old or infirm, those who were sole-support mothers could also be assisted.[68]

More important were the conditions attached to all relief. First, when provided for the able bodied, it was to be granted only in exchange for labour, regardless of treaty status. In this way, the principle of the work test was quickly established; it emerged from a distinctly artful interpretation of Treaty Six.[69] Moreover, standard relief for the sick and infirm was to be provided in moderation – the first such limitation placed on 'deserving' poor Indians. Unless the term 'moderate' had been defined in the general instructions[70] to all agents, there was no indication in Vankoughnet's 21 December correspondence to Orde what this might mean and whether it referred to duration as well as to amount.

Beyond the nineteenth-century liberal, laissez-faire aversion to relief, how are we to understand this meaner attitude? Three related considerations were in play: the continuing threat of Indian unrest, the state of the federal treasury, and the obsessive fear of Indian dependency should assimilation policy fail. At a time of acute game shortages and continuing famine among the First Nations on the prairies, the government had decided to use food strategically as a means both to encourage treatied Indians to stay on their reserves and to entice non-treatied Indians to take treaty. Food relief was thus a lever to force settlement and begin the task of 'civilizing' the Indians.[71] The general public was being led to believe that Indian policy humanely afforded Indians protection from the expanding frontier. Yet according to Chamberlin, parliamentary debates after the 1885 Riel Rebellion revealed a 'policy of starvation' that 'attempted to force Indians onto their reserves ... out of frustration and impatience at their stubborn reluctance to embrace a new social and economic order.'[72] Relief had become a tool for subjugating Indians. The government was using it to force the treatied back onto the reserves and to make the taking of treaty seem a choice better than hunger.

In all this, the government was motivated by desperation to secure the land and ensure the success of the National Policy. The country was in dire economic straits; the federal purse was almost empty. The severity of the recession combined with the very rapid decline of the buffalo herds was forcing a steep climb in relief expenditures. Both the opposition and members of the governing Conservatives expressed varying degrees of alarm and outrage at these increases, and they blamed the Indian commissioners responsible for Treaty Six for setting a precedent that had probably created a permanent drain on public funds. Macdonald defended the expenditures as a temporary, humanitarian measure. They were, he argued, necessary for the survival of the country. In his now infamous comment, he proclaimed, 'It is cheaper to feed them than to fight them.'[73] Although federal expenditures on relief rose sharply from the late 1870s to the late 1880s, the per capita amounts received by Indians remained deliberately small and grossly inadequate.[74] Despite the political acrimony that surrounded it, the rise in relief expenditures was in fact a restrained, carefully measured response to the seven numbered treaties and to increasing unrest among all First Nations in the Northwest Territories.

The fear of dependency was clearly fuelled by market ideology and by beliefs about individualism. Relief was seen as a disincentive to industrious enterprise.[75] Cost was the primary concern, but the link was inevitably made between cost and dependency. If relief fostered dependency, then Indians were likely to become permanent wards of the state and costs would therefore continue to rise.[76] In the case of the Northwest, it was important therefore to nip dependency in the bud. Relief had to be made singularly unattractive and was to be offered only in the direst circumstances. In the words of the agent-general[77] of Indian Affairs, speaking in 1880, 'it was a dangerous thing to commence the system of feeding the Indians. So long as they know they can rely, on any source whatever for their food they make no effort to support themselves. We have to guard against this, and the only way to guard against it is by being rigid, even stingy in the distribution of food, and require absolute proof of starvation before distributing it.'[78]

To minimize the possibility of unconditional relief, the department applied the idea of work for rations in conjunction with its home farm program.[79] This program, instituted in 1879, was based on English tenant farming principles, adapted to the agency system and its reserves. Essentially, agency farms – including nine in Treaty Six – were established as the focal point of agricultural instruction. On them, Indians were to learn how to develop and operate their own farms on reserves. This was to be the key step in helping *individual* Indians and their families settle and become self-reliant and independent of traditional nomadic modes of survival. Additionally, two 'non-instructional' farms were to become a source of food production and relief supplies for the Indians.

The home farm program was disbanded in 1884, having failed for several reasons. Besides being underpaid and poorly equipped by Ottawa, many of the instructors were incompetent and had no understanding of the vagaries of prairie farming. The program was undercapitalized, and as a result, although many of the Indians had excellent farming skills, adequate farming technology wasn't available to them. There was limited access to gristmills, which reduced the Indian farmers' capacity to turn grain into flour. Thus they were denied the opportunity to be self-sufficient or to market their surplus. Poor infrastructure and planning, low-quality seed and temperamental prairie weather also contributed to the demise of the program.

Ottawa encouraged the instructors to do most of the labour on agency farms, to ensure (in the logic of Locke) that the Indians did not lay claim to the farms and their produce through the performance of labour. Thus, Indians were to be encouraged to labour, but only enough to earn rations. Work for rations to support the farms was also introduced; tasks included clearing and fencing land and constructing roads and trails. The rations 'earned' were usually insufficient; furthermore, there was not enough work for the numbers who wanted it, and no account was taken of family size. Other needs such as clothing and utensils simply were not included. Consequently, the work for rations policy often forced Indians off their reserves to look for wage labour. Carter sarcastically observes: 'The Indians did not always see the work they performed for rations as their course of study in the mysteries of self-help and industry.'[80]

The home farm program was one of the first, most publicly visible failures of assimilation policy. To save face, the government attributed the failure to the Indians and to their 'inherent, restless disposition' and 'idleness.'[81] This was precisely the position taken by Hayter Reed, who succeeded Orde at the Battleford Agency. By blaming the Indians for the continuing failure of the farm program, the government was able to justify harsher policies and to strengthen its resolve to link work with welfare. In even stricter terms, Reed determined that the Indian agent was to act as a moral educator and policeman. According to Carter, he was to 'compel obedience, and "when moral suasion failed the only means of coercion was to stop their rations and try and establish the apostle's law that if a man would not work he should not eat" ... Reed took the success of the work for rations policy as his special mission ... the misery and suffering that it created could be viewed as a necessary stage in a training program.'[82]

Shortly after succeeding Orde at Battleford in 1881, Reed wrote to Indian Commissioner Dewdney at Winnipeg, stating exactly what he and Ottawa wanted to hear:

> considering that there have been a number of disturbing elements among them the Indians have on the whole worked fairly well. Where it was found feasible daily rations were issued and the system so far as I could enforce it, of no work no pay was carried out – and I am happy to say to advantage – Very few Indians are now on the Reserves adjacent to Pitt – they having gone off – that is the most industrious – fishing – the balance coming to Battleford expecting to be fed for nothing – on which point they were sorely disappointed as they received no provisions unless a fair amount of work was performed notwithstanding several days parleying.[83]

The 'disturbing elements' to which Reed referred were probably the Metis, whom Reed blamed for most other problems that he could not attribute directly to the Indians.[84]

Reed may have been partly right in his assigning of blame; if so, it was for all the wrong reasons. He was incapable of any insight into the effects of the meanness and narrow-mindedness of government policy toward both First Nations and the Metis. He was an ideologue and a willing oppressor who viewed government assimilation policy in Macdonald's terms, as a means of subduing Indians and promoting stability for white settlement.[85] The Indian and Metis uprisings in the 1880s only strengthened his and Ottawa's resolve to subjugate the First Nations according to Canada's wishes.[86] In this context, one government apologist during the debates following the 1885 uprising, a Mr O'Brien, rose to the defence of continuing work-for-relief policy:

In dealing with Indians hereafter, the great trouble will be to feed them just exactly in that proportion which will stimulate them to work, and, at the same time, will be sufficient to keep them from suffering from want of food. I may have expressed myself clumsily, but I think the honourable gentlemen understand the difficulty, and that it is in endeavouring to hit that happy medium that the Indian officials have failed and have not supplied them as far as they ought.[87]

This was a distinctly eighteenth-century, functional view of poverty, and one that conformed precisely with the government's project of turning Indians into menial peasants or a working class within the structure of Canadian society. Indians were to aspire to a humble life of agriculture or industry; they were to enjoy the benefits of citizenship and contribute to the overall wealth of the community through their labour. However, their reward for that labour should not be so great as to lead them into idle debauchery or to encourage them to aspire to anything greater than the virtue of the labour itself. For without their labour, how would the community survive?[88]

The Indians were being abandoned by the very policies that had induced them to farm in the first place. It is a bitter irony that it was they who had performed much of the early farming in the Northwest Territories. First Nations' work for rations had laid the foundations for waves of successful settlers, who benefited from their pioneering labour and then displaced them.

Distress among the Beaver Indians Near Fort Vermilion, and the Threat of Conflict with the Encroaching Cree

Fort Vermilion in 1880 was an isolated Hudson's Bay Company trading post on the Peace River about 350 miles north of Edmonton. The Beaver First Nation – an Athapaskan people – were the principal inhabitants of the territory along the Peace River in what is now northwestern Alberta and northeastern British Columbia. For many years prior to European contact, the Beaver had inhabited a far greater territory to the south and east; however, the advance of the fur trade brought with it the Cree, who, as agents of the traders, were armed. The Cree pushed the Beaver farther north and west. The Cree and Beaver called a truce in their conflict near the Peace River, apparently named by the traders to mark the event.[89] In the late nineteenth century, the Beaver still maintained a traditional lifestyle, one that depended largely on hunting, with fishing only a last resort. They were also active in the fur trade; in this, they found themselves competing with the Cree and with independent whites.

Early in 1880, H.D. Moberly, the Hudson's Bay Company officer at Fort Vermilion, wrote a letter of desperation and warning to David Laird, the new lieutenant governor of the Northwest Territories, who had previously been the Indian commissioner. In that letter, Moberly expressed his distress at the starvation of the Beaver Indians, whose hunting grounds – so he asserted – were being encroached upon by the Cree. Moberly feared that war might break out between the two nations; although the Beaver had not yet resisted the Cree advance, 'they had greatly resented it.'[90] According to Moberly, the problem was that the company could do nothing to stop the Cree. As well, there had been a great increase in the number of independent traders at the post, and if the company did interfere, they would all 'go over to the Cree and hunt the country as they liked.'[91] To protect its interests and somewhat those of the Beaver, he said, it was best for the company to do nothing at present. He continued, as though troubled by his own conclusion,

> but what can we do in case of one Band going into the other's hunting grounds, which will happen more and more unless some steps are taken soon to assist Indians when starving. The game on which they entirely depend is almost gone, and times are getting worse & worse, deaths from starvation have happened thro' Peace river every winter for the last 3 winters and during last winter some 13 Indians died within 60 miles of this place, literally starved to death, and the prospect ahead is, of course worse as the game is decreasing ...
>
> In the meantime, I will keep, if possible, war from being commenced between the two nations.[92]

This vivid correspondence from Moberly tells us much about Indian dislocations in the Northwest at the time. Moberly was describing just one example of the havoc that resulted when the highly competitive fur trade clashed with the pressures of settlement. As settlement continued to expand in the south, those bands that refused to take treaty found themselves forced more and more to the north; in the process, old rivalries, such as the one between the Beaver and the Cree, resurfaced as part of a final struggle to continue a way of life. In this example can be seen the company's new dilemma. On the one hand, it wanted to maintain the trading loyalty of the local Beaver without alienating the Cree, who were also a reliable source of fur. But how could it satisfy both nations? Moberly knew the company could not, so for help he looked instead to the federal government. In doing this, he became one of many voices on a question that was to become central to a prolonged conflict between the government and the company: Who was responsible for the welfare of Indians? Fundamental to the conflict were two issues: Who could best bring about the Indian transition to self-reliance in the marketplace? And whose interests were really at stake?[93] Parliamentarians were concerned about the drain on the public treasury caused by relief, yet at the same time, they were anxious to ensure that their friends and companies gained from the lucrative contracts to be had in providing the goods for relief. The Hudson's Bay Company and the I.G. Baker Company of Montana had benefited enormously from such contracts in the 1870s and 1880s. From the company's perspective then, it was now more important to be a supplier than an administrator of relief.

Starvation at Ungava Bay: A Critical Turning Point

The growing conflict over responsibility for Indian welfare was nowhere better illustrated than in many incidents of starvation at Fort Chimo, a Hudson's Bay Company post on Ungava Bay on the coast of the Northwest Territories east of Hudson Bay. These incidents were part of the widespread pattern of Indian famine from the north shore of the St Lawrence to the entire trading area around James Bay and as far west as Fort Vermilion. An important feature of the Ungava incidents, besides the disputes they provoked between the company and the department, was the department's discomfort at finding itself subjected to more outside observation than it wished. The Ungava incidents present us with early examples of this outside interest in the department's work (including reports from another government department and offers of help from a French philanthropist) and of its resentment of outside interference.

The problem of famine at Ungava Bay must first be placed in the context of correspondence between Sir Donald Smith, who was both Conservative MP for Montreal West and chief governor of the Hudson's Bay Company in Canada, and T. Mayne Daly, the new superintendent general of Indian Affairs. Daly was writing to Smith in response to a letter from Smith to Sir John Abbott in early November 1892, just before Abbott's retirement as prime minister. Daly and Smith were both members of the ruling side of the House, and the problems between the company and the government were very much understood as a 'family problem.' From the early part of Daly's letter, we can ascertain that Smith had shared with Abbott reports from company officers relating to incidents of distress during the previous winter among the Indians of the Rupert's River and Fort Good Hope trading districts. This distress was attributed to the scarcity of game. Smith was apparently trying to determine from Abbott whether Parliament had made provision for these Indians in its current appropriations and was thus prepared to accept ongoing responsibility for their relief. Daly's reply was based on a letter of briefing from his deputy, Vankoughnet. Daly wrote:

> No doubt you are aware that these portions of the Dominion are outside Treaty limits, and ... the Government is under no obligation except on humanitarian grounds, to supply Indians with food or other necessaries. Relief has ... been given to non-Treaty Indians from charitable motives, when their circumstances were such as to render the same advisable.
>
> Last year the Department received reports of a similar nature regarding the Indians of the Athabaska and McKenzie River Districts, but subsequent information shewed ... that the ... accounts ... had been greatly exaggerated. Without doubting the accuracy of the reports ... so far as the Company's officers are concerned, still their information may have been magnified ... I have no doubt but that your experience coincides with that of the Department, that Indians are prone to greatly exaggerate their condition at times. The Department had not contemplated being called upon to provide anything for these Indians, and consequently no provision was made by Parliament this year.[94]

Vankoughnet's briefing letter to Daly, however, was decidedly more pointed with respect to the company. Vankoughnet was probably no friend of Smith, who had fallen out with Macdonald during the Pacific Scandal of 1873.[95] At any rate, Vankoughnet took a dim view of the Hudson's Bay Company's expectations concerning the government provision of Indian relief:

> I respectfully submit that, in the consideration of the relief to be afforded to Indians situated ... outside of treaty limits, and the benefit of whose labour in hunting the Hudson's Bay Co. for the most part enjoys, in times of distress such as are represented it might fairly be expected that the ... Co. should come to the relief of the Indians as the heads of these families

and their young men are simply hunters in the employ of the Hudson's Bay Co. It is, no doubt, a great saving to that Company for the Government in such times to come to the relief of the Indians and thereby save them the expense of doing so, which obligation ... fairly rests upon the Company. The Government derives no benefit whatever from the land, and it has not been considered worth while up to the present to ask the Indians to surrender it.[96]

Vankoughnet was no favourite of Daly, and it is clear that his views of the company were considered too harsh and politically naive to send to Smith. Daly massaged Vankoughnet's opinions into a form acceptable to Smith, but he did not altogether discount what his deputy was saying. His letter included a suggestion that Indian independence would be better promoted by maintaining the link of responsibility between the employer (i.e., the company) and the Indian employee and his family. This position included the idea that the employer should provide relief as a paternalistic, ersatz employment insurance scheme. In sum, the government was declining responsibility for non-treated Indians and for the costs of the company's business. Indeed, since the government had no interest in acquiring the land, the Indians were 'best left as Indians.'[97]

The company's point of view was precisely the opposite. According to Ray, by 1880 the issue of responsibility for relief had begun to surface directly in internal company correspondence. Before Confederation, and certainly well afterwards, the company had used the credit advance as one method of maintaining trading loyalty – albeit an increasingly unreliable one. After Confederation, with competition intensifying, it had supplemented the credit advance by providing relief to sick and destitute Indians. For this, the company sought reimbursement from the federal government, with mixed success. The company believed that since it no longer enjoyed a trading monopoly, Ottawa should not expect it to accept the major responsibility for Indian relief. Some company officers began to argue that it would be better to encourage non-treated Indians to take treaty; the government would then be responsible for their welfare. The company would then administer relief funds on the government's behalf and remain to all appearances the benefactor, Indians' trading loyalty could in this way be maintained.[98] This was a neat solution to the losses associated with the credit advance; it was also the position subsequently adopted by C.C. Chipman, the company's chief commissioner in Winnipeg.

In early November of 1893, Dr George M. Dawson, then assistant director of the Geological Survey of Canada, wrote a covering letter to T. Mayne Daly, who was also Minister of the Interior, highlighting an attached, preliminary report from one of his leading field geologists, A.P. Low. The first paragraph of his letter, which presumably was considered the most important, concerned the discovery of significant, accessible iron ore deposits in the Labrador interior, that *terra incognita* which was now *known*.[99] On the second page of the letter, he drew Daly's attention to a profoundly distressing situation as described by Low:

> At Fort Chimo we were hospitably received by Mr. Duncan Mathewson, and there learned that a great famine during the past winter had killed more than two thirds of the indians belonging to this post. Of nineteen families in one party only one man and woman survived, another party of six families have not been heard from since last fall and are given up as dead. Besides these several scattered bands are also missing and of the survivors, almost every family lost one or more of its members from starvation during the winter. Among the Esquimaux five families also starved to death along with several other single instances in other parties. This disaster was due to the cariboo travelling to the northward in the Fall instead of going south as they have ... [been] accustomed to do.[100]

Low, describing incidents typical of that time, further told how the Indians – probably Naskapi – had traditionally hunted the caribou near river crossings. When the hunt failed, they tried instead to fish, but they had been unable to catch enough before freeze-up:

> Then the stronger ones tried to reach the Post in search of succor but the greater number died from weakness and exposure before reaching it.
> Mr Mathewson estimates that upwards of one hundred and sixty indians and twenty-five esquimaux died. There remain less than one hundred indians counting men, women and children and they are all in a state of abject poverty, as they made no fur hunt last year, and in consequence were unable to buy food or clothing except what they earned working about the Post. If the deer fail to come south this Fall, and at present there are no signs of them, the remainder of these poor people will surely die, as they are starting from here almost naked and very poorly supplied with ammunition owing to lack of means to purchase it. A collection was taken up among the white people here and the officers of the Company's ship Erie, and sufficient was obtained to partly clothe the naked children and widows

whose husbands died last year. Owing to the lack of deer's meat ... the extra supply of salted meat at the Hudson's Bay Post was used up, and the new supply is only sufficient for the use of the post.[101]

Low's description of the Naskapi's plight contains the unmistakable implication that the Indians must fend for themselves on the market. From Bishop Langevin's 27 October 1878 correspondence (discussed earlier in this chapter), we know that the company either had curtailed or no longer employed the credit advance in the eastern sub-Arctic. Low certainly did not mention an advance; instead he referred to the Indians' inability to purchase goods because they had no furs to sell. He noted that white charity was being extended only to widowed women and children. Other Indians were left without the means to purchase necessities.

Dawson suggested to Daly that government help be provided to the Indians, although he knew that it was already too late in the year to deliver provisions by sea. Perhaps, he thought, if the government promised the accessory funds, the company would be able to authorize Fort Chimo overland from Rigolette to provide rations from its own stores.[102] Daly, through his new deputy, Hayter Reed, acted swiftly; by 10 November 1893 the department had informed the Hudson's Bay Company in Montreal that it was willing to reimburse the company for provisions issued to the Naskapi near Fort Chimo. The following day, McKenzie, an officer at the company's Montreal office, wrote to Duncan Campbell Scott, then the department's chief clerk, expressing deep regret for the 'sad state of affairs.' McKenzie continued: 'I regret very much that it is ... out of the question to communicate with Fort Chimo till next summer by the steamer going from London ... We never send a Winter Packet to that District, the distance is too great, it would not reach there till the end of April or beginning of May when assistance would be of no avail – it is in the Fall & Middle of Winter that these disasters occur.'[103] Thus, the possibility existed for a repeat of the previous winter's tragedy. Despite the lessons drawn from Mingan some twenty years earlier, the department still had no procedures in play to prepare for these eventualities in remote regions. In fact, as subsequent correspondence revealed, it continued to offer, *de facto*, one-time sums on the understanding that such incidents were considered unusual and unlikely to repeat themselves.

Amidst the flurry of correspondence concerning Ungava Bay arrived a letter forwarded from Her Majesty's embassy in Paris by way of the governor general's secretary in Ottawa. Enclosed in the letter from a M.

Henri Rousseau was a 50-franc note with this explanation: 'For distribution among the Canadian Indians who are suffering from famine.'[104] Within days a reply letter was sent to Arthur Gordon, the governor general's secretary, thanking Rousseau for his thoughtfulness, and continuing:

> The Superintendent General is ... in a position to contradict the report which it appears has been widely circulated in Europe to the effect that great destitution exists among our Canadian Indians from Labrador to British Columbia. This report is without foundation in so far as the Indians of Canada are concerned for they never were more contented and prosperous than they are at present. Such being the case the money so kindly donated by Mons. Rousseau cannot be used ... and I am to request that you cause it to be returned.[105]

This was a bold statement by the department, especially since destitution among Indians, both registered and non-registered, while difficult to assess statistically, was clearly frequent – and on the prairies almost endemic – during the entire post-Confederation period. Their contentment was similarly doubtful, especially in the wake of the Metis uprisings scarcely eight years earlier. The letter was an excellent example of the state's power to interpret the condition of native peoples to the world in such a way as to support and justify its policies. The letter thus demonstrated the gate-keeping power the federal government exercised by being both protector and subjugator of the First Nations. In later years – in fact, well into the middle of the twentieth century – this power to speak for the native peoples, would remain central to the project of subjugating First Nations and of maintaining public acceptance of assimilation policies.

Still, the department was not through in its reply to Rousseau. Though it denied his claims, it went on to suggest that he might wish to assist in relieving the extraordinary plight of the Ungava Bay Indians. This was an ideal opportunity for the department to do what it was so good at doing – saving the government some money without appearing to be begging or negligent. Having described the unfortunate circumstances at Ungava Bay, the letter writer continued:

> Immediately I received news of the calamity which had befallen the inhabitants ... I communicated with the Hudson's Bay Company, although no funds have been provided for such a purpose, and requested them to

instruct the officer in charge of the post at Fort Chimo to afford relief to those in want before the setting in of winter.

I promptly received a reply which I regret to say shows the utter impossibility of rendering any assistance until next summer ...

I would suggest that if ... Rousseau feels so disposed he might forward his donation to the Head Office of the Hudson's Bay Company in London, with a view to its being used for the relief of those unfortunate people, should destitution be found to exist amongst them when the steamer arrives ... next summer.[106]

The potential for further disaster at Fort Chimo still existed. Early in June 1894, Reed nervously brought to Dawson's attention an article in the *Brandon Mail* dated 31 May 1894,[107] which reported Low's account of starvation at Ungava Bay. Reed surmised that the article was about a further occurrence of famine, which was his worst fear after the failure to provide relief through Fort Chimo. Dawson assured Reed that given Low's movements during the recent winter, 1893–4, the article must be referring to the 1892–3 famine, which had probably become public through the release of Low's private correspondence.[108] Dawson shrewdly proposed – and committed to public record – the plan that 'in case of further famine in the Ungava Bay region next winter, & referring to a conversation which we had before on the subject, it might I think be well to arrange with the H.B. Co. in good time as to what could be done for the Indians in case of necessity.'[109]

Reed, perhaps somewhat uneasy about this increased visibility, decided to follow up Dawson's suggestion. On 9 June he wrote to Daly, bringing to his attention the continued dilemma at Ungava Bay and recommending that the department act on Dawson's idea. Reed, who still did not wish to appear to be the agent of unrestrained benevolence, tempered his recommendation with the government position that 'the scarcity of food which was experienced in the winter of 1892–93 is not likely to be experienced again for some considerable time. I submit ... for your decision the question as to whether arrangements should be made with the Hudson's Bay Company ... in order to guard against possible starvation.'[110] Daly scrawled his response in the margin of Reed's original text: 'I think we should arrange this matter with the H.B.Co. & write them at once. Indn. relief only to be given in case of absolute necessity.'[111] Important here is that Daly authorized the arrangement for Fort Chimo only. Nevertheless, it was the opening that C.C. Chipman, the company commissioner in Winnipeg, was seeking.

Reed wrote to Chipman with the department's proposal and specifically couched it in the context of the famine at Ungava Bay: 'The Superintendent General has decided to authorize your Company to give assistance to the Indians of that country ... in extreme cases of need and to have such expenditures ... repayed on the presentation of an account supported by vouchers in detail. Would you Kindly, therefore, arrange to have supplies given to any ... Indians who may be in actual destitution during next winter.'[112] Chipman replied within the week. He began by acknowledging 'the government's desire to prevent further hardship in the Ungava Bay area,'[113] but then noted that the opportunity for communicating with Fort Chimo had already gone by for the season. He indicated, however, that he would still endeavour to inform the post so that assistance might be given according to the department's instructions. Then he raised a more important matter:

> This may be an opportune time for ... consideration the question of the Government giving relief in anticipation of destitution among Indians who do not receive Treaty Allowances in other parts of the Country. The Department may rest assured that the policy of the Company is to make the Indians as self-supporting as possible, and that this matter is again only urged on the ground that when starvation occurs, there is no opportunity of bringing it to the notice of the Government until it is too late to render assistance.
> I feel sure you will recognize the spirit in which this suggestion is made.[114]

Chipman, a wily strategist, was trying to plant the seed of public embarrassment in Reed's mind by indicating that the time to notify Fort Chimo had already passed. The logistics of relief, he was implying, were more complex than Ottawa seemed able to appreciate. Given that both the government and the company shared the objective of promoting Indian self-reliance, would it not make more sense to institute a general system of relief so that local instances of Indian destitution could be responded to quickly?

Reed, who like Vankoughnet saw a plot by the company, was not easily convinced. His reply was terse: 'It is hoped that other Indians outside treaty will not require aid and if they do that sufficient time will be given to alleviate any pressing wants.'[115] Chipman pressed his point; after all, the company stood to gain much business from such an arrangement. He wrote Reed on 4 July 1894 that he now hoped the instructions would reach Fort Chimo in time. This was fortunate, but the same conditions exist in other parts of the country and ... when starvation occurs, it prevents travelling and thus conveying the information which the Government desires, and ... the distances are so great that even were it possible to obtain information it would often be too late to render assistance. The Government may rest assured that the Company will do all possible to see that assistance is given in cases of extreme necessity only.

It is sincerely hoped ... that you may see your way to recommending that provision for other parts of the Country may be made in the same manner as for Ungava Bay.[116]

Reed, at a loss for a reply, sought the advice of his chief clerk, D.C. Scott. Scott wrote Reed the following memo, which Reed adopted nearly word for word when he replied to Chipman on 16 July.[117] The memo, which exuded Scott's manipulative penny-pinching,[118] was a sign of things to come: 'Ack. & say we are glad to hear that he has every hope that etc. etc. – Say that owing to the smallness of the vote for Dest. Indians Dept. does not see its way clear to give the general order for relief wch he recommends but that in such cases ... everything that can be done will be to ensure that no avoidable suffering be permitted.'[119]

Reed's letter of 16 July crossed with another letter from Chipman dated 12 July. In this letter Chipman appealed, on the one hand, to the government's potential to be humanitarian, and on the other, to its shame if it should seem unnecessarily callous. This letter was carefully drafted to corner the government into a decision favourable to the Company:

I have just received information by way of Esquimaux Bay, Labrador, that there are bad accounts from Ungava, and that it is feared there may have been a repetition of the starvation of the previous winter. Beyond this there is no news, and I merely mention it as possibly being of some interest, and as showing how opportune has been the late [i.e., recent] action of the Government in providing means of assistance in anticipation of such an event, though of course, any help now furnished will be of no avail for the past if the news should unfortunately be true.

I regret to add that I have also had news that there has been much privation among some of the Indians to the north of the railway on Lake Superior.[120]

This letter propelled Reed to consult with Daly; he was at a loss about how to respond to the company's pressure. He knew the company was not looking to spend money on relief and that it stood to gain handsomely if the government reimbursed it for goods provided. The department did not wish to spend money on Indian relief either. With these restrictions in mind, Reed wrote to Daly:

> I felt it necessary to limit the authority granted to the Ungava Bay District. It would be, I think, impolitic to give the Hudson Bay Company *carte blanche* in the relief of distress amongst Indians outside Treaty limits. It is unfortunately, very often the case that suffering does follow the disappearance of game, but the natural protector of these hunters in such a time ... is the Hudson Bay Company, and it is a duty ... the Company seems to have charged itself that any destitution which it is in their power to relieve should be relieved; although the Department should, I think, be ready to extend a helping hand in extreme cases, I could not ... recommend such a general order as would permit the Hudson Bay Company to look to this Department for the relief of any but very extreme and widely prevalent distress.[121]

Reed's argument to Daly against establishing a regular system of relief continued that of Vankoughnet – that is, the relationship between the company and its Indian traders was something of a trust, rooted in mercantile era traditions of employer–employee responsibilities. Reed conceded that *ex post facto* relief was useless. His final comments suggest discomfort with even the limited permission given at Ungava Bay: 'In all these cases, it is ... true that the relief cannot be provided when it is required. We are only now getting the reports of suffering last winter, and next winter may pass without the necessity of using the permit now given for relief.'[122] The records would later show that Fort Chimo issued relief in the form of blankets, flour, shot, powder and percussion caps to sixty Indian families for a total of $120.17.[123] Someone – probably Scott – noted in an internal memo that the amount was too large and that in the future, the department 'will pay for provisions such as flour & meat supplied in small quantities to Indians who are unable to provide for themselves.'[124]

The department's limited concession at Ungava Bay by no means constituted an acceptance of a general relief system. That being said, over the same period the department also reimbursed the company for relief provided at Rupert House and Moose Factory. Unlike the arrangement at Fort Chimo, these reimbursements were not authorized in advance; rather, they were made on a case-by-case basis at the company's request after relief had already been granted.[125] To qualify for reimbursement from the department, the company had to report its expenditures systematically and prove that the need existed. This was in keeping with the increased sophistication of relief dispensation by the Indian agents in the south. Thus, the department was not directly involved; instead, its relief policies were implemented *through* the company. In this way, Indians increasingly became subject to public policy and its ideology. For example, the usual eligibility standards of age, infirmity, and disability were reflected in the following sampling from a record submitted by Moose Factory:

Date	Name	Supplies	Value	Reason why given
1895				
June 1	Arischapick	6 lbs. flour	3.51	Anile imbecile and unable to do anything for herself
	Pesquotch	2 lb. pork	.34	Infirm, supported by friends during hunting season
	Ap.AaKeeschow	2 lb. beef	.34	Consumptive, unfit for any exertion
	Chum	3/4 tea	.24	Old & failing, manages to keep himself spring & autumn[126]

The record was many pages in length. For several pages the company officer did not enter any reason – perhaps because the litany of suffering was repetitious: 'old,' 'infirm,' 'widowed with several children,' 'sick and destitute,' blind,' 'consumptive,' and often, simply 'destitute.' Regular issues included sugar, suet, tobacco, oatmeal, and bacon, and in the autumn, parchment, druggets, and thread for preparing winter necessities. A special entry simply recorded: 'Christmas Dole.' The total value of all supplies issued over the year was $513.51.[127] At Rupert House, a similar report for the same year was submitted by the company officer; there, gunpowder and shot were provided in addition to the standard food supplies, deerskin, 'Eskimo boots,' and cotton. Reasons given for providing relief included 'crippled, unable to hunt ... An old widow with orphan children ... Orphans having no one to provide for them ... An old, helpless Indian ... A miserable Indian with a young family.'[128]

On 23 June 1896, Laurier and the Liberal Party won a convincing majority in the federal election. Daly was replaced as superintendent general briefly by Hugh Macdonald, then by Clifford Sifton. Reed's days were numbered.[129] Chipman, however, continued his efforts to broaden the authority established at Ungava Bay so that all remote company posts could issue assistance with departmental permission. On 5 and 10 November 1896, he wrote to Reed to confirm reports that famine was continuing along the coast of Labrador. In these letters, Chipman pursued his argument that it was futile to provide relief after the fact.[130] Reed did not reply until 18 December, but when he did, he struck a generally more co-operative tone. 'With reference to ... your letter of the 5th ultimo, I beg to inform you that the Department recognizes the necessity for some provision being made with a view to affording relief to sick and destitute Indians of Ungava Bay, and other remote points, and the matter will be brought before the Superintendent General when the Estimates are being prepared.'[131] Chipman replied quickly to Reed, indicating his pleasure with the department's apparent commitment to resolving the problem. To dispel any fears about opening the government floodgates, he added that 'in the interests of the Department ... if such an appropriation can be obtained, its specific purpose should not be publicly announced. The knowledge that any Fund exists is apt, as those acquainted with the Indians are aware, to create a demand for relief.'[132]

Early in 1897, Chipman again sought clarification regarding the government's intention to seek parliamentary appropriation for Indian relief in remote areas. He reminded Reed of the issues and concluded: 'The ... necessity for [relief] is constantly existent and increasing ... In previous correspondence I have pointed out the probability of this distress not diminishing, and that its relief should devolve upon the Department, rather than upon the Hudson's Bay Company.'[133] Finally, in the fall of 1897, Chipman received the approval he had been seeking. The new superintendent general, Clifford Sifton, on the advice of Reed, authorized the company to provide relief in remote areas. Reed, however, in conveying the decision to Chipman, added the following cautionary proviso: 'We do not wish to establish a general system of relief, nor do we desire to have it understood that the government intends in any way to provide for distressed Indians, otherwise, as you yourself have pointed out to me, they might go in for a larger quantity than they really need.'[134]

The company wasted no time taking advantage of the decision. By

1905 it was billing the department regularly for relief costs in Ontario, Ungava, Quebec, and Keewatin.[135] The practice soon involved other trading companies, including Revillon Frères of Montreal and Lamson and Hubbard, as well as certain missions. These middle agencies provided a means for the state to strengthen its influence over the terms and conditions of relief. By 1918 the department had introduced the beginnings of a benefit system. In submitting accounts for reimbursement, the company and others could not exceed a standard family issue. At Fort Chimo, for example, the standard issue was $40.85 and included 3 bags of flour at $7, 20 pounds of tea at 50¢, 26 pounds of pork at 35¢, and 3 pounds of baking powder at 25¢. Agencies had to provide itemized lists that included the name of each recipient and the reason why relief was being provided. Middle agencies would be utilized to provide relief in remote areas for most of the first half of the twentieth century. As I discuss in the next chapter, this practice eventually came under scrutiny that led to complete government control.[136]

The Reed–Chipman correspondence was highly significant to the development of Indian relief administration, for several reasons. First, it provided the basis for a general relief system, despite the government's insistence that it neither wanted nor needed one. Once the company convinced the government of the need for a system of advance authorization, the government had no choice but to develop a coherent method of approving expenditures. It was relatively simple to adopt for the non-treated First Nations the policy already in place for the treatied. Over time, it would become evident that direct government administration throughout the system would be more efficient as well as more congruent with state objectives.

Second, the connection between the department and the company was an excellent example of the general relationship at the time between the political and economic levels of society. It was not unusual, for example, that men like Sir Donald Smith were both MPs and captains of industry. Like many of his confrères, Smith was a man of substance who saw government primarily as a supplier of goods supportive of the purposes of market capitalism.[137] Thus, at the top of post-Confederation society was a constellation of elites and their most trustworthy supporters, who consistently agreed on the overall objectives of the state though they sometimes disagreed about the means to achieve them.

As a good example, Reed and Chipman agreed that Indians had to be socially assimilated and that they had to adapt to the market economy (e.g., to wage labour). This twin objective was important for nation building. Their differences were about means. Chipman thought that Indian self-reliance could best be achieved by having the government subsidize the Indians' relationship with the company. Reed thought that this arrangement would undermine self-reliance and that the government should provide relief only in extreme cases. So a compromise was reached that offered advantages to both the government and the company; the company would be authorized in advance to provide relief for Indians, but only under conditions established by the government, and furthermore, the First Nations were not to be informed that the relief was government funded.

Third, the Reed–Chipman correspondence provides a good, early example of First Nations being perceived as objects of power and administration. Indeed, although Indians were the raison d'être of the correspondence, they were largely incidental to the correspondents' institutional objectives. This objectification of First Nations allowed Reed and Chipman to depict Indians in passing and in broad images. The issues were real, the victims less so. This approach was evident in the agreement that the Indians should not generally know about the provision of relief; the correspondents were presuming that they would take advantage of it and merely want more.

This pejorative view of the Indian 'other,' which was the operative truth for elite insiders, contrasted with representations given to outsiders such as Rousseau – for example, that Indians had never been more content and prosperous. Of course, no matter how First Nations were actually depicted, they were always thought of as a homogenous people who could be treated accordingly. Assimilation policy espoused liberal principles of individualism, yet its success depended on a reductionist view of First Nations – a view predicated largely on a notion of the state as a private club to which only 'the right people' could belong. This point of view made it possible to create subcategories of human beings and also to devise legal and bureaucratic means of judging them as worthy or unworthy.[138] The liberal revolutions of the eighteenth and nineteenth centuries had forced even the Tories to adapt to a new sociopolitical order that celebrated the equal rights of individuals, individual creativeness, and freedom from tyranny. Yet the government's conduct toward First Nations flew in the face of all this. The apparent inconsistency with liberal values can be explained partly by Eurocentric, imperialist views of 'other.'

A final point: The government's decision to give continuous advance authorization for relief helped the Hudson's Bay Company to develop its retailing empire. As settlement increased, the company's trading posts quickly evolved into principal sources of goods and supplies for settlers and Indians alike. Treaty annuities and general relief became critical and reliable sources of Indian purchasing power.[139] Much of the company's modern success, then, can be attributed to Indian subjugation and destitution, which was relieved by public funds.

Origins of Relief

In this chapter I have used case studies to analyse the beginnings of government relief policy for Canada's First Nations. I have concentrated on Quebec, Ontario, and the Northwest Territories because these three regions were most present in government archival materials for this early period. Nevertheless, in the documents examined there was nothing to suggest that policy was any different in either the Maritimes or British Columbia. For example, in 1880, in response to an inquiry from the undersecretary of state concerning relief to Nova Scotia Indians, Vankoughnet replied: 'Relief money is expended by the Agents in the purchase of necessaries for ... such of the Indians as are sick, infirm or aged and unable to attain their own living.'[140] Similarly, a 1910 directive to all new Indian agents in British Columbia stated in part:

> Nothing should be given to any able bodied Indians unless an equivalent in the shape of work or some other value is received from him or her for the article given ... In the case of very poor, aged or sick Indians, the Department will ... give such relief as necessary for the alleviation of their wants ...
>
> I have to impress upon you the necessity of ... exercising the strictest economy in ... granting of relief supplies ... Food should be given in extreme cases of destitution only and ... sugar, soap, tea, etc., should not be supplied except in case of sickness, which must be fully stated in body of voucher.[141]

Over the entire period 1873–1912, there were few general statements of relief policy. However, one circular issued in 1903 was consistent with the department's directives to individual agents:

> The Department desires that economy shall be exercised in supplying relief (as well as grain) to Indians of your Agency ... [Indians] should be given to understand that they must rely [on their] own exertions for their support, and when possible [provide for] their own poor.

> [Relief] should not be given except in cases of illness [or when] the applicant is, on account of other infirmity [unable to provide] the necessities of life; or in cases where the [provision of relief will] prevent actual suffering. Pork and [ ] to be ... allowed. No tea, tobacco [are to be] issued.[142]

Exceptions were made to the general policy when circumstances affected not just Indians but the population as a whole. In 1905, for example, an unusually severe winter in Nova Scotia prompted a directive from the secretary, J.D. McLean. In it he noted that 'the poorer class of people, not only Indians but whites,' had been unable to work as usual and thus found themselves so poor that they could not purchase seed grain. Consequently

> the Department has decided to come to the aid of the Indians ... The Department disapproves in a general way of assistance ... being furnished, but the circumstances this year are ... exceptional, which is the reason that the rule ... in the matter is being temporarily departed from ...
>
> You should ... give them [the Indians] to understand that need is only furnished this year because of the exceptional circumstances ... and ... in future they will be expected to rely solely upon their own exertions.[143]

In both 1906 and 1908, the department found it necessary to remind its agents of the conditions under which it was permissible to grant relief. Persons suffering from an affliction who could not support themselves

> should on no account be allowed to suffer for want of the necessaries of ... life, in the way of plain food and clothing ... If their relatives are able to keep them they should do so; but where this cannot be done or [they] will not do so, the Department expects its Agents to provide at all times for all aged, sick and infirm Indians, bearing in mind ... that the strictest economy must be exercised and care taken that the aid so given is not appropriated by those not in need or deserving of it.[144]

These statements, taken together, represent the department's essential Indian relief policy by 1913. In this chapter I have examined the policy's evolution through case examples. It is important to note that the treatment of Indian poverty during this period was in many ways no different from the handling of white destitution. It was thought that assimilation could only be accomplished if the expectations placed on destitute Indians were the same as those placed on destitute whites. At the same time, the fact that Indians were historically the 'other' constantly placed relief administration in the wider context of the white man's duty to elevate the Indian to modern society.

The state's assumptions about Indian poverty set the department on an irreversible course of welfare administration. These assumptions, made without regard for Indian perceptions, were based on a distinctly Puritan view of poverty as an individual, moral shortcoming. Few if any attempts were made to understand Indian poverty in historical and collective terms, nor was there any appreciation that Indian people perhaps did not perceive themselves as poor. In a market society where the ability to labour was essential and the production of wealth was dependent on the obedience of the working classes, the essential task was to instil in Indians ideas about the moral virtues of work, self-sufficiency,[145] and, presumably, the promise of eternal reward or punishment. Macpherson's description of the increasingly dominant, Puritan view of the poor in seventeenth- and eighteenth-century England has similarities to the operative principles of assimilation policy:

> The Puritan doctrine of the poor, treating poverty as a moral shortcoming, added moral obloquy to the political disregard in which the poor had always been held. The poor might deserve to be helped, but it must be done from a superior moral footing. Objects of solicitude or pity or scorn, and sometimes of fear, the poor were not full members of a moral community. Here was a further reason ... for continuing to think of them as less than full members of the political community. But while the poor were ... less than full members, they were certainly subject to the jurisdiction of the political community. They were in but not of civil society.[146]

Thus, Indian relief policy was merely one aspect of the department's self-ordained task, which was to raise Indians to the status of moral, honest workers; and it must be seen in the context of parallel initiatives in education (chiefly through Christian churches), in agricultural and industrial training, in the banning of alcohol on reserves, and in the eradication of 'heathen' cultural practices.

The fear of Indian dependence on the state was deeply rooted in the perceived consequences of dependence. In the opinion of Hayter Reed and many others, these consequences were already visible in Indian traits such as laziness, idleness, and indulgence in alcohol. Yet the custodial relationship imposed by the state on First Nations could not help but create a dependent condition, which was exacerbated by policies that directly or indirectly brought about their economic marginalization. The National Policy, the building of the CPR and CNR, the destructive impact of state-supported settlement on North America's ecology, the catastrophe of the Indian farm policy, and prohibitions on hunting and fishing – all of these created forces that were contradictory to the stated aims of the government's Indian policy. Yet when Indian policies repeatedly failed, Indians were implicitly or explicitly blamed as individuals.

Ironically, the Hudson's Bay Company saw an advantage in 'socializing' the costs of labour and challenged the entrenched fear of Indian dependence on the state – specifically, the fear of the cost of providing relief for unemployed fur harvesters. The government resisted establishing a 'general system of relief,' yet soon began to realize that firm, central control of relief policy could be an excellent lever in acculturating Indians to individual self-sufficiency. As a result of the agreement with the company, relief policy became more structured and explicit, especially during and after the administration of superintendent general Clifford Sifton.

Sifton concentrated on developing a strong, central organization headed by men who cared little about Indians but a lot about economics and departmental objectives. Typical of these men were James McKenna, Sifton's private secretary; Frank Pedley, deputy superintendent general from 1902 to 1913; and Duncan Campbell Scott, chief clerk and accountant, who would succeed Pedley in 1913.[147] These men represented an emerging class of elite public servants more modern in their approach to bureaucracy and organization but still driven by Victorian ideas and values about country and duty. Their impersonal conduct embodied the notion of rational authority and the belief in 'the legality of enacted rules and the right of those in authority to issue commands that have their basis in law.'[148] When Scott took over from Pedley in 1913, the stage was set for the consolidation of Indian subjugation and the transition to a new phase of Indian policy.

4

Relief Policy and the Consolidation of Subjugation, 1913–1944

Since the introduction of what is termed 'Responsible Government,' the authorities considered it advisable to appoint men to supervise the people, far removed from the larger centres of civilization, for the protection not only of the immigrant, but also to educate, christianize and protect the tens of thousands of people emerging from the darkness of superstition, idolatry and self-constituted authority, through which all nations passed, in earlier stages of history.

Excerpt from a proposed pamphlet by Thomas Deasy, Indian agent, 25 October 1920

Duncan Campbell Scott and the New Bureaucracy

Duncan Campbell Scott became deputy superintendent general of Indian Affairs in October 1913. On his appointment, he assumed control of a department that, like the rest of the nation, was wrestling with a fundamental transition from a world view rooted in religious values to one based on secularity and the promises of science.[1] Some writers, notably Titley,[2] attribute to Scott much of the department's overall direction between 1913 and his retirement in 1932. Yet he was mainly a representative of his times, and as such he reflected much of the era's confusion about the nature of the secular and the sacred.

By early-twentieth-century standards, Scott was a well-educated man. However, for financial reasons he had been unable to attend university. Nevertheless, as an accomplished poet and amateur musician he maintained an interest in the arts, and he was influential in the country's intellectual life. He was from a family of devout Methodists, but his own learning and interests had led him away from formalized religion. Even so, he retained a personal faith and adhered to many Methodist values.[3]

In many respects Scott was the paradigm of Weber's ideas about rational bureaucracy and the secularization of those moral imperatives – especially work values – which formed the basis for the modern capitalist state.[4] Because he believed implicitly in the value system, and thus the culture, that provided the context for the bureaucracy's operations, Scott was able to pursue unswervingly the goal of assimilating Indians into Canadian society – a society that he accepted on faith as superior. Indeed, Scott personified in frightening, ironic ways Weber's ultimate condemnation of the bureaucratic expert:

> No one knows who will live in this cage in the future, or whether at the end of this tremendous development entirely new prophets will arise, or there will be a great rebirth of old ideas and ideals, or, if neither, mechanized petrification embellished with a sort of convulsive self-importance. For of the last stage of this cultural development, it might well be truly said: 'Specialists without spirit, sensualists without heart; this nullity imagines that it has attained a level of civilization never before achieved.'[5]

Scott represented what was becoming *au courant* in the bureaucrat and the bureaucracy: impersonal obedience and action based on an *a priori* consent to the social order's foundation and goals. Thus, what mattered was not Scott the individual, but the *type* of person he and his employees embodied.

Scott emerged as an early prototype of Ottawa's later mandarin period.[6] Unlike most public servants of his time, he was appointed on merit, not through political patronage.[7] Scott's extensive career in the inside service and his superior writing, accounting, and clerical skills, which he combined with a cool, imperious nature, admirably suited him to the rational management of a large organization administering a difficult state objective. (The Indian Affairs bureaucracy, like the rest of the federal civil service, had grown significantly in size and complexity since the 1880s. By 1913, Indian Affairs in Ottawa was divided into six branches and employed 76 people; the outside field service had 651 employees. In comparison, during the 1880s and 1890s the department's inside service in Ottawa employed about 40 people and the outside service about 460.)[8] Scott was not so much an architect of Indian Affairs policy as he was an organization man determined to consolidate the administration of Indian policy in as efficient a manner as possible. Scott's determination to engineer Indian consent to civil society ultimately created the most odious and lasting characteristic of the Indian

Affairs bureaucracy: the denial of Indians as subjects and their transformation into faceless, amorphous objects of policy.

In this chapter and the following one, I review some dominant themes and events in relief and general administration from 1913 to 1944. These themes and events, notwithstanding my previous comments about the period, ultimately redirected Indian Affairs policy toward ideas about integrative citizenship and the assumption that Indians desired to be fully part of civil society. In addition, the First and Second World Wars, the Bolshevik Revolution, and the Depression of the 1930s overshadowed the Indian administration; in themselves, these were dramatic expressions of the capitalist state in crisis. This crisis affected state responses both to the First Nations and to Canadian society as a whole. The state feared that the working class would reject the dominant class, and it struggled to find peaceful or other ways to engender workers' consent[9]; in the same general way, it continued to perceive Indians as a potentially hostile force that required constant supervision and 'training' in the ways of white civilization.

Thus, as in the broad society the state attempted to quell or manage social discontent, so too any hints of Indian resistance were not tolerated. Outside influences on the state administration, including those emanating from both Indian and non-Indian interest organizations, though endured as inevitable, were at the same time resented and strategically ignored or torpedoed.[10] The fact that these influences emerged and became a factor in the department's conduct reflected a general change in all Canadians' expectations regarding citizenship and the state, a change spurred by popular disillusionment with the state after the First World War and promoted by new intellectual currents and activism.[11]

General Statements of Relief Policy and Administration, 1913–1944

Scott wasted no time in making his authority felt in his new job. On 25 October 1913, two weeks after his appointment, he issued a policy pamphlet with seventy points of instruction to all Indian agents. Following four general introductory items, he wrote for the fifth: 'It may be stated as a first principle, that it is the policy of the Department to promote self-support among the Indians and not to provide gratuitous assistance to those Indians who can provide for themselves.'[12] Very importantly, his next point attempted to clarify the state's legal authority over First Nations: 'The Indians of Canada are subject to the ordinary law, both civil and criminal, except in so far as the Indian Act makes special provision for their exemption.'[13] Although this item seemed to be stating the obvious (from the state's point of view), it was an essential principle of assimilation strategy, and in 1951 it was paraphrased in section 87 of the new Indian Act. Ever since, it has been a source of constitutional debate as well as resentment among First Nations peoples. In the context of this book, it is important because it later became part of federal efforts to convince the provinces to extend their welfare services onto the reserves.[14]

The remainder of the pamphlet provided specific instructions on nearly every imaginable area of Indian life. A constant theme was the agent's paternal role and his duties as the state's representative. From these instructions we can glean not only the department's specific objectives, but also the general flavour of the state's accepted role with respect to the individual and to social security. Items 25 and 26 addressed the issue of 'Occupations of Indians,' specifying that 'the Indians should be encouraged to settle on their reserves, and where feasible, to engage in farming, stock-raising, etc ... Those who cultivate the soil should be impressed with the advisability of saving enough seed to plant their land the next spring. In whatever occupations the Indians are engaged they should be encouraged in habits of industry and thrift.'[15] Item 45 provided instruction with respect to destitution:

> The Department will be willing to provide the actual necessaries of life to sick and aged Indians, or orphans and widows who are unable to work and have no means or no friends able to support them upon the facts being fully represented by the Indian Agent. In order to prevent suffering it may be necessary for an Agent to furnish a small amount of provisions without reporting, but in any such case the Agent should lose no time in laying all the facts before the Department.[16]

There was nothing new in this statement; policy had changed little since Vankoughnet's post-Confederation pronouncements. Still, this was as clear and concise a statement of relief policy as any before it. It consolidated policy in terms that applied universally across the country, and it signalled a resolve to pursue the policy within the context of the entire set of instructions, which themselves reflected the broad objective of assimilation. For example, item 27, on education, stated that 'earnest attention should be given by Agents to the administration of the schools, and efforts should be made to increase their efficiency. A lively interest on the part of the Agent in all the operations of the various classes of schools will do much to advance the standard of the work and its results.' An intended result of education was specified in item 69, which stated that 'agents in the West should in every way possible discourage gatherings which tend to destroy the civilizing influences of the education imparted to Indian children at the schools.'[17] Between 1913 and 1944, Scott and McGill would waver little from this policy statement. In their work, they focused on developing complex mechanisms to bring about the rational and cost-efficient implementation of relief goals.

The Beginning of Administrative Consolidation in the North

The organization of relief administration had changed little since the turn of the century. In the more settled south, where reserves were less isolated, the Indian agent was the primary administrator. In the north, where the fur trade was still a factor in First Nations' economies and where transportation was still difficult, relief administration was shared among the trading companies (predominantly the Hudson's Bay Company), the Indian agent and, at times, detachments of the Royal North West Mounted Police.[18] From the department's point of view, the northern administration was becoming increasingly cumbersome. When it relied on the company to administer relief, its sense of control was diminished. It could not be sure that its policies were being strictly followed (i.e., that Indians were not receiving benefits in addition to relief from the company and other traders). The department's ambivalence became increasingly apparent during the First World War. Ironically, a split within the company emerged over the same issue at the same time, and for similar reasons.

The First World War broke out in August 1914. In autumn of that year, directly because of the war; the British Board of Trade suspended fur auctions. As a result, the fur trade collapsed. The Hudson's Bay Company instructed its traders not to buy furs through the 1914–15 season, nor to extend credit to its Indian suppliers.[19] Ray states that the company's suspension of credit during this crisis was deeply resented by the Indians, who felt betrayed and deserted by a time-honoured partner. Since the Reed–Chipman agreement in 1897, the company had fostered Indian loyalty through the extension of credit, through relief paid from its own accounts, and through the distribution of government relief.[20] This instruction from London effectively eliminated any form of direct company assistance and left the department as the sole source of assistance.

Thus the department found itself facing a crisis in relief provision. Scott was quick to acknowledge the problem, but like most intermediaries of state benevolence, he sought to enforce firm controls. On 21 September 1914 he wrote to all Indian agents in those districts where sub-Arctic trade was still a factor that

> it is quite likely that a greater amount of destitution will be in evidence during the forth-coming winter, than was experienced in past years.
>
> It is therefore advisable that you should use your endeavours to convince the Indians of the necessity of bending their energies to the securing of *food* rather than fur ...
>
> Arrangements have been made by which, orders for relief for the sick and destitute, signed by authorized officers i.e. Indian Agents, Officers commanding Royal North West Mounted Police detachments, or other specially deputed persons, will be accepted by the Department as heretofore ...
>
> It is important to bear in mind that the Department does not propose to assist those Indians who are able to earn their own living, and this policy should be clearly understood by all the Indians, so that they will receive no encouragement to spend their time at the post in an idle and unprofitable manner.[21]

This circular provides several insights into the development of relief administration in relation to the fur trade. First, eligibility for relief remained the same despite the unusual circumstances. Destitution was a factor, but eligibility continued to depend on what category of person was destitute. The able bodied were expected to provide for themselves and their families, but the issue of where able-bodied Indians in remote areas were to 'earn their own living' was never addressed. In Canada and elsewhere, this expectation has always been a theme in the provision of assistance at times of economic crisis and employment. Those whom the crisis most severely affects are those deemed least eligible and most suspect when it comes to assistance.[22]

Second, the department was taking steps to limit Indian reliance on company supplies and had adopted a proactive and presumably less costly role in relief administration. In some northern agencies, relief was now distributed from the department's own supplies, which were sent ahead regularly in anticipation of seasonal need. Only after agency supplies had been exhausted were agents to authorize relief from the company. This approach to providing relief would later be proposed for every agency in the country. C.N.C. Roberts, a retired senior clerk, described the system in place when he first joined the department at Sioux Lookout, Ontario, in 1939. Merchant suppliers were chosen through a system of political patronage. He recalled that a clerk in one northern Ontario agency kept a thick register of merchants to be 'tapped' for building and relief supplies, hardware, funeral services and so on. After one federal election the clerk was told to expunge all the names on the register and gradually replace them with another approved list.[23]

Finally, Scott advised his agents in a later circular that their intelligent cooperation in the administration of government supplies should be sufficient to ensure the relief of destitution.[24] It is clear that he intended to avoid relying on the company if at all possible, mainly to save money and exert more control over relief provision. The company was well aware of the department's increased activity in providing relief and reacted to it with some uncertainty in subsequent years.

After the war, the fur trade entered a highly competitive phase that required the company to operate with far greater efficiency. Company people were divided over the issue of how to achieve this efficiency. Most traders advocated continued provision for Indians' economic well-being, the point being to retain their loyalty. London usually supported this position if, in its view, it suited the company's long-term interests. Commissioners in Winnipeg urged financial constraint to minimize debt and favoured shifting most of the financial burden of Indian welfare to the federal government. The traders' views prevailed until the early 1930s, when London relinquished control to Winnipeg. This set the stage for the government to assume the social costs of the fur trade and become the sole agent of relief in the north.[25]

The Consolidation and Rationalization of Policy and Procedures

Besides seeking to consolidate policy and to control the administration of relief in the sub-Arctic, the department began issuing circulars to all its agencies outlining in greater detail than ever before the procedures to be followed in assessing need and granting assistance. A circular issued in 1915 contains the makings of step-by-step procedures and a decision-making structure that would ultimately lead to set benefit scales and payments according to both family size and recipient category. The influence of Scott and his secretary, J.D. McLean, in moulding an ordered and accountable bureaucracy was nowhere more evident.

The circular's preamble stated three basic controls on relief. The first required agents to adhere to departmental procedures for relief expenditure; the second established procedures for presenting of relief accounts. The third forbade relief expenditure, except under unusual circumstances, without prior departmental approval.[26] The circular continued:

> When you are applied to by Indians for relief you should, make investigation ... into the circumstances of the applicant, before recommending the Department to grant assistance. If a case of destitution comes to your notice, where actual suffering would result were assistance not immediately afforded, you may give a small amount of aid, but in every case you should at once write the Department, stating all the facts of the case and the action taken. You should ... make a definite recommendation as to the further course which ... should be pursued and intimate the amount of relief which will be required.[27]

This wording began to formalize a process: Indians were to *apply for assistance* and their *circumstances* were to be *investigated* by the agent. In other words, the onus was on the Indian applicant to *prove* the existence of *need*. The agent was then to make a recommendation to grant assistance. There was an important distinction being made here – one that remains common to most bureaucracies – between the *spending* functionary (the agent), who assessed eligibility for an expenditure, and the *payment* functionary (Ottawa), who authorized the expenditure. It was recognized that in exceptional circumstances this distinction would have to be temporarily circumvented (but not avoided) and assistance immediately granted. This was an early instance of what most contemporary welfare systems refer to as emergency hardship.

Once payment was recommended – and again, this was payment in kind through a supplier – the agent was to recommend the *future disposition* of the *case*. This requirement implied a plan based on each case's individual merits. In this practice there is a hint of the future 'professional' social casework approach, one in which each applicant is treated methodically as a unique individual who, with correct intervention, will be able to rise above her or his circumstances.[28] This approach obscured the structural and collective oppression of First Nations; it also lent support to assimilation policy by applying a technical methodology. In this communication, which was sent out fully two years before Mary Richmond's early classic book on casework, *Social Diagnosis*,[29] it is possible to discern how simple it can be to link bureaucratic accountability with social casework principles.

The circular outlined in detail the accounting procedures to be followed in submitting properly authorized vouchers for payment, and it noted that failure to follow the procedures would result in the return of the voucher unpaid. After giving these instructions, McLean returned to the case problem approach:

> In cases where you recommend that relief be allowed you should inform the Department of the number of persons in the family, and state why they are in need of relief, and also state the amount required weekly or monthly, as the case may be, and also how long you think it is likely that relief will be needed.
>
> In all ordinary cases of relief only actual necessaries are to be supplied, and you will be held responsible for seeing that the merchants ... give only actual necessaries ...
>
> When Indians are tubercular, extremely old, or very ill, supplies of a more nourishing character may be allowed ...
>
> In every case where expenditure is authorized, the amount allowed must not be exceeded. You will be expected to comply strictly with this rule as well as to abide by all the foregoing regulations.[30]

This part of the circular was an elucidation of the earlier statement. And it was not wholly new – it was somewhat similar to Vankoughnet's 1893 circular.[31] The real difference was in the context in which the instructions were being presented. For the first time, relief policy was being stated as a complete process involving application, investigation, approval, exceptions, method of issue, reconciliation of accounts, and payment of suppliers. There was also an intimation that in the past, both agents and merchants had either exceeded approved amounts or issued items considered luxurious. The new regime placed the agent in a position where he was vulnerable both to his superiors and to wrathful merchants should payments be refused. Failure to abide by the policy could result in dismissal, and sometimes did.[32]

Directives like this increased the distance between the state and the First Nations. The administration's structure and organization became the primary concern; Indians were now simply hostages to 'the problem,' for which the organization had to find a 'solution.'[33] Dyck aptly describes the Indian agent's dilemma, although sad to say, for far too many there was no dilemma at all:

> The new employee of ... the Department of Indian Affairs encountered a set of existing bureaucratic roles, formally stated moral purposes and underlying institutional beliefs concerning the nature of aboriginal peoples and the ... appropriate ways of managing their lives. Whatever an individual employee's ... inclinations, the personal costs involved in ignoring or contradicting the formal rules and informal assumptions ... were usually sufficient to encourage conformity. Non-conforming employees were usually dealt with swiftly. For example, a newly appointed Indian agent who wrote to his superiors requesting that they inform the Indians ... that the repressive measures taken by him with respect to Indian dances did not originate with him, but were ... in accordance with policies established in Ottawa, was fired by Order in Council the following month.[34]

The dismissal of the Indian agent who questioned his role contrasts sharply with the sycophantic musings of Indian agent Thomas Deasy from whose proposed 1920 pamphlet the opening quotation in this chapter was taken. I quote from him again at length to show how deeply many agents internalized the liberal, imperialist assumptions underlying the department's work:

> Confederation, inaugurated in 1871, brought about the first endeavor to bring together, under proper management, the Indians of this country. Superintendents, and ... Indian Agents, were appointed, to supervise and care for the Indians, under Dominion Government control. The natives were placed in the position of 'Wards of Government,' while laws were promulgated for their government. Although Reserves were apportioned, to particular Bands of Indians, no restrictions were placed on the natives, so far as their field of labor, or of their usefulness, to themselves and to others, was concerned ...
>
> Their wars ended. Churches and schools ... appeared on the various reserves; while the laws of the realm applied to communities and individuals. It is strange, that the fifty years of preaching and teaching brought forth few able to take their places in the mission field, or in the schoolhouse, from amongst the natives. It is probable that a nomadic life interferes with the education of the young; but the Boarding and Industrial

Schools aid in the work, which has been interfered with in a measure, through the pupils returning to the environment of the Indian home ...

The Indian Agent is much misunderstood, by both Whites and Indians. His duties call for more than those of any other class of officials ... The Indians, as 'Wards,' should look upon their Agent ... in the light of a 'Father.' It is true that the Indian Agent is clothed with the powers of a Magistrate ... and requires compliance with the rules of law and order. He is governed in his public acts, by the 'Indian Act,' which is carried out for the betterment of all concerned ...

It is a mistaken idea, of many of the Indians, that an Indian Agent represents only the powers that control him. IIis duty should be to forward the work of civilization, in a straightforward, honest, manner. The 'Wards of Government' are approaching the day when they will be thrown on their own resources ... Over fifty years of education, and the aid of self-sacrificing missionaries, should be sufficient, to lead a people from 'wardship,' to an understanding of what is required of them, not only for the good of themselves, but also for the public good ...

The 'ballot' is only given to those who understand the exercise of its use. Education is the first requisite, and the government of a country endeavors to educate the masses to an understanding of the responsibilities imposed on them. A government is 'of the people, for the people.' On the Indian reserves ... schools have been opened, by the government, for the enlightenment of the people. Christian missionaries have sacrificed self, in an endeavour to bring about moral laws, to replace tribal customs and habits, which were detrimental to the well-being of communities and individuals. Men and women now understand that the laws of God, and man, are for their benefit, both here and hereafter.

Our Indians must understand that individuals make up communities. As the individual acts, in such manner will communities exist. The Indian has passed the days of tribal customs and habits. The footsteps of civilization are effacing the winding trail. The 'iron horse,' and 'fleeting vessels,' are crossing the praries [sic] and the trackless ocean. The day of emancipation, even from 'wardship,' is approaching rapidly.[35]

Deasy's platitudes seem today almost absurd, yet it was precisely this kind of unabashedly optimistic belief in the superiority of 'our' world compared to 'theirs' that was essential to the operations of the Indian Affairs bureaucracy. It is what gave Deasy and other agents a sense of authority over and above what was actually invested in them. All policies, from education to relief, were administered in the utter conviction that the agents were morally correct, that they were uplifting the backward races and contributing to the progress of humankind. Finally, Deasy's comments suggest that blind belief in the morality of the mission – based as it was on the self-evident truths of Western progress – carried with it an irritation, a hint that punishment would be forthcoming if those blessed with the opportunity to 'advance' should resist the department or fail to fall into step with the forward march of democracy.

From 1915 – the date of the circular – through the Second World War, relief policy remained largely unchanged, although it continued to evolve in structural complexity. For example, a May 1917 circular sent to the Indian office in Winnipeg for distribution to trading post managers in Treaty Nine provided important clarification regarding what constituted actual necessities according to the recipient's category of assistance. In the circular, McLean defined those eligible for relief as persons who were incapacitated because of 'illness, physical deformity,' or who were 'temporarily destitute through unavoidable misfortune.' He specified that 'no relief should be given to Indians who have able-bodied, unmarried sons, capable of supporting them.'[36] The bare necessities to be issued to eligible cases included 'flour, pork, or lard, tea in limited quantities and ammunition when the recipient is able to make proper use of it.' If ammunition was given, provisions issued had to be appropriately reduced. Clothing 'of the plainest and most serviceable nature' could be issued twice a year (summer and winter), but only in those cases where destitution was permanent. For seriously ill people, milk and sugar 'and such necessities' could also be given, but again, in 'limited quantities.'[37] McLean ended by cautioning that the department was considering sending inspectors to review relief issues and to disqualify undeserving persons. This threat reflected a general departmental concern – in part because of the war effort, but also because there nearly always was a concern – that relief expenditure was becoming excessive. To this issue we now turn.

Concerns about Dependency in the Maritimes and Overexpenditure in British Columbia

Over the fifteen years from late November 1915 to the early part of the Depression, the Scott administration hardened its resolve to curtail relief expenditures.[38] The inside themes of departmental frugality in matters of relief and the consistent blaming of Indians as idle beggars who needed constant exhortation to be self-supporting – themes that had been well established since Confederation – were now played on with even greater vigour.

As discussed at the end of the previous chapter, the reasons why Indians needed relief were never explored beyond those related to qualifications such as illness or age. Instead, the need for relief was understood in Euro-Canadian terms, as a function of wanton idleness; for this the best cure was either to deny benefits completely or to make them so paltry as to be undesirable. Departmental relief policy was informed by prevailing ideas about the proper relationship between the individual and the state – in particular ideas held by the dominant elites. That being said, assimilation policy was necessarily informed by conceptions of progress, industry, and the state; inevitably, then, principles of relief had to be integrated with instruction in the ways of liberal capitalism.

For the department to look good in Ottawa, it had to reduce and contain the costs of relief. By denying or reducing relief, it could demonstrate that Indians had already learned – or certainly were learning – the evident advantages and rewards of individual independence. Thus the department developed a deliberately contrived pattern of restrained expenditure, which it accompanied with proclamations of success. Unfortunately for both destitute Indians and the department, this made it much more difficult to convince anyone, including the federal treasury, that increased expenditures might be necessary. Titley writes that 'Scott's annual reports invariably sounded a note of optimism. Glowing accounts of progress in agriculture, education, and the adoption of "civilized manners" appeared with predictable regularity.'[39] Beginning in 1915, the Maritimes and British Columbia became the department's particular though not exclusive concern in its drive to reduce relief expenditures. Following instructions from Scott, McLean wrote to Indian agents in British Columbia on 23 November that

> expenditure in connection with relief of Indians in British Columbia has ...
> exceeded what was anticipated ... and as it is not the intention to ask Parliament to vote further funds for this purpose, it will become necessary for you to curtail the expenditure in this direction by giving relief to only the most deserving cases ... in the past ... there has been too lavish an issue of supplies to Indians and not only the really destitute have been furnished with supplies, but those who are able-bodied and capable of sustaining themselves have been assisted. If this continues the Department will have to refuse paying the accounts as there will not be funds for the purpose ...
> It will be necessary ... for you to exercise the strictest economy in the issue

of orders for relief and confine them to those Indians who through sickness, old age and infirmity and without relatives and friends to depend on, are unable to sustain themselves.[40]

This circular, which is so similar to many already cited, reflects some important themes. First, the department was concerned (as always) that relief be given only to the most deserving, *and furthermore*, that even this small amount might be too generous. Second, although the department used the term 'destitute' for operational purposes, it was never precisely defined. Presumably the common, dictionary understanding of the word applied – that is, 'without resources, in want of necessaries.'[41] That this was the case is clear from McLean's 1917 circular. This statement, which was analyzed in the previous section, included a definition of 'necessaries.' Still, this lack of a clear definition almost certainly contributed to sharp discrepancies of interpretation and expenditure among the agencies, missionaries, and trading posts. Because of these discrepancies the department tried even harder to micromanage first the level of benefits and later on the criteria for receiving them.

Third, the circular alluded to the concepts of the capacity and ability to labour. Both are critical to an appreciation of the reasons for destitution. In accordance with Euro-Canadian thought of the time, McLean believed that a person who had the capacity to labour – that is, who had the strength and skills to work[42] – should not be eligible for relief. But this view did not take into account a person's access to the means to put that strength and those skills to use.[43] In capitalist societies it is not enough to be able bodied and 'capable' of labour; if there are no jobs requiring a person's specific capacities, then strength and skills are moot. In British Columbia, for example, Indians' access to work fluctuated; it was highest in the early part of the twentieth century, but even then the work was mainly seasonal and increasingly vulnerable to 'the concentration of development in a few large centres and the concentration on "productive efficiency."'[44] McLean's admonitions, then, reflected Ottawa's increasing isolation from the field as well as the general tendency to view unemployment as an individual failure. Those admonitions were organizationally necessary, however, if economizing measures were to be consistently applied.

Fourth and finally, McLean harped on a theme common to residual models of relief – that is, that even those who might be eligible should first rely on the resources of family or friends. This theme, which persists today, even in the state systems of social assistance,[45] has its basis in the liberal understanding of community. There is no collective responsibility for the well-being of individuals; rather, needy individuals should seek their welfare mainly among those within their private constellation of intimate associates.[46]

The principal message in McLean's circular was that Indian agents in British Columbia needed to curtail relief expenditures, because at the pace they were being spent, the funds would be exhausted well before the end of the fiscal year. Few bands in British Columbia were receiving annuity payments. The funds voted by Parliament for British Columbia, which included relief funds, were allocated by departmental responsibility. Agents were asked to submit annual estimates; these were reviewed by the department before submission to Parliament.

Admittedly, the war was having some impact on the government's civil expenditures; even so, the Scott administration was being meanspirited. It is difficult to know what to surmise from McLean's comments. Were the agents profligate spenders? Had they underestimated their requirements? Had the economic situation in British Columbia worsened dramatically since their original estimates? The collapse of the fur trade in 1914–15 would have seriously affected bands in British Columbia's northern interior; and according to Carstens, economic conditions for the Okanagan nation had worsened because Indian farmers could not compete on an equal foooting with white settlers.[47] Most probably, given the authoritarian culture and methods of the central administration, the agents had been told to be economical in their estimates, and upon their receipt in Ottawa those estimates had been further revised before being submitted to Parliament.[48]

Whatever the specific events, calls for economy in the interests of the war effort strengthened Scott's resolve to control relief costs. By 1918, parliamentary appropriations for Indian relief in the Maritimes were the same as before the war, even though requests for relief were rising. Alarmed by this pattern, McLean wrote to the Indian agents in New Brunswick and Nova Scotia in April 1918 advising them that because spring was arriving, he expected to see a decrease in relief expenditures; they should 'keep the expenditure down to the lowest possible amount without inflicting suffering.'[49]

Apparently the agents did not try hard enough; two months later they were told that all relief had been cancelled for July, August, and September. The only exceptions were to be 'Indians disabled by illness or old age, who may be living alone, without any relative upon whom to rely for support, and except also in the case of orphan children.'[50] He gave as the reason that the department had decided that Indians in the Maritimes had come to rely too much on the department and that most of them should be able to support themselves through the summer months.

Why would Indians be seen as overly reliant on relief? McNaught observes that despite a robust wartime economy, by war's end all levels of government were operating under heavy debt loads. Most of the wealth produced during the war had accrued to business; meanwhile, farmers and workers suffered under rampant inflation and a decline in real wages. In the Maritimes, Indians were few; furthermore, they were marginal to the labour force and to agriculture. So it is not surprising that they had to rely on government support.[51] The same cancellation was reissued in 1919, together with a demand for an immediate reduction in relief and for the names and projected costs for those remaining on relief during the three-month period.[52]

Once Ottawa saw that it could cancel relief without any evident complaint from either the Indians or their agents,[53] it did so every year until 1931. This, despite healthier government revenues and the relative prosperity of the mid-1920s – a prosperity not shared by the Maritime provinces.[54] Indians in the Maritimes became hostage to other government spending priorities, including war debt charges, public works, and subsidies to the provinces.[55] Scott's own determination to do with less compounded the problem and led to a downward spiral in Indian welfare and neglect. By 1924, McLean had extended the cancellation of relief to all Indians in the Maritimes thought capable of work; he had also lengthened the relief 'holiday' to four months, from July to October.[56]

Scott's drive for economy and efficiency had especially targeted the Maritimes. In 1918 he instituted a review of the reserve system there. In Nova Scotia, a plan was developed to amalgamate bands in more central areas of the province. By 1925 the 'scattered Indians of Halifax County' had been concentrated on one reserve near Truro, with 'encouraging results.' The main obstacle to amalgamation, Scott stated in a letter to Dr Trefry, was the Indians' reluctance to give up their nomadic ways.[57]

In the mid-1920s, Dr Trefry was one of a few citizens who cared enough about Indians to make his views of their condition known to the department. He criticized the reserves near his home, alleging that they perpetuated the Indians' half-civilized state. His recommendation:

Do away with all the small reserves ... throughout the Province, choose a good situation of fertile Crown land, and collect all the Indians to it. Make every Indian family build a small home on that reserve, with house, well, outbuildings, garden, etc.; built to specification, under Government supervision. Build there a Community Hall, a small Catholic church, a school house and etc. as is found in Western Canadian mining towns. Insist on him producing so much garden produce as to comfortably supply his family; pork, etc. ... Have a Government farm there, as at the Poor Farms, with a large dairy and orchard, help for which is to be hired solely from among the Indians. Have an agency with the priest or school teacher, to supply American Tourists and sportsmen with guides. Have another agency to buy all canoes, baskets, axe handles and etc. as, as made by the Indians and such agency to obtain the highest possible market price for same.

This, although it may read a fantasy, is the only solution, whereby the health and moral of some hundreds of real fine potential subjects, can be made self supporting and at the same time improve conditions which are not only deplorable but a considerable expense to the Government without results.

Scott's reply to Dr Trefry noted that the department had been working on the issue of centralized reserves in Nova Scotia for some years.[58]

The drive for economy after the war also affected Indian health care. This, even though during Scott's administration the Indian population declined from nearly 128,000 in 1901 to fewer than 104,000 in 1915. After that it rose slightly, to 108,000 in 1929. This amounted to a net increase of only 5.9 per cent since Confederation.[59] In October 1919 – less than a year after four thousand Indians died in the Spanish influenza epidemic of 1918–19[60] – McLean advised all the Indian agents for Manitoba, and Kenora and Fort Frances, Ontario:

With reference to ... medical attendance on Indians, I beg to draw your attention to ... the policy of the Department to promote self-support among the Indians and not to provide gratuitous assistance to those who can provide for themselves, and this policy is extended to include medical attendance and medicines ... I beg to refer ... to Indians who visit Winnipeg and call upon Dr O.I. Grain for medical attendance ... In order to guard against abuses on the part of Indians it has been decided that Dr Grain should insist on all Indians calling at his office for treatment at the expense of the Department producing an order form from either their Inspector, Agent, or Medical Dispenser, on the Reserve. Orders should only be given to indigent Indians.[61]

A similar circular was sent to Indian agents in British Columbia in February 1920.[62] This followed a circular earlier the same month that had again exhorted the agents to exercise proper control in the expenditure of relief 'which action is most necessary in the interests of economy.'[63] McLean noted that some agents had curtailed their expenditures, and he expected all to do so. He followed this statement with a list of six requirements in relief administration. Items 4 to 6 outlined three new procedures: the agency relief list was to be reported semiannually; variances to the list were to be reported each month, along with the month's actual expenditures; and special reports were to be submitted if unanticipated causes, such as the failure of the fishing industry, created additional need.[64]

With Scott's general direction and approval, McLean continued his offensive on British Columbia. Early in 1922, with the 1921–2 relief allocation and potential overexpenditure in mind,[65] he wrote to the agents, directing them that Indians in 'fair circumstances' requiring hospitalization should pay for their own care and maintenance.[66] Then, in an unusual move, he wrote a letter clarifying the department's position with respect to the province's chiefs. All well-to-do Indians were expected to pay, he wrote, but this would result in greater benefits for those most in need, and this should be pointed out to band members: 'It is in the best interests of an Indian, as well as a White, community that the leading men belonging thereto shall be self-reliant and self-respecting, and the fact that they make payment of expenses which they incur will tend to that end.'[67]

In letters to agents, McLean expressed his satisfaction with the reductions in relief expenditures in British Columbia in 1922 and 1923, noting that those truly in need would now be benefiting the most.[68] His satisfaction must have been short-lived, because in September 1926 the department brought to the attention of all British Columbia agents what it considered excessive expenditure on relief. Seven months remained in the fiscal year, yet the parliamentary appropriation was running out. Without asking why,[69] McLean simply directed that the 'strictest economy' be employed: 'Only in most deserving cases should assistance be afforded ... be particular to see that all Indians who have earning powers provide for themselves and their families.'[70] This directive merely reinforced the Scott administration's philosophy. Over the years, the department had moved beyond the basic work test principle of less eligibility to no eligibility at all if there was a capacity to work. Consequently, need was deemed not to exist if the applicant worked – regardless of the wage earned – or if the applicant *could* work. Of course, the application of this policy was highly subjective. Although the basic intent was abundantly clear, it is difficult to assess from the archival materials available just how closely the agents adhered to it. Ottawa's relentless concern certainly reflected a belief that Indians and agents alike bore constant monitoring. To warn the agents in British Columbia yet again about expenditures, McLean wrote: 'Each Indian Agent should make a point of seeing how low he can keep expenses of this nature without inflicting suffering upon Indians deserving of assistance.'[71]

This theme was pursued again scarcely three months later by A.F. MacKenzie, who was acting for McLean. In a statement to all Indian agents in British Columbia, Ontario, Quebec, and the Maritimes, he wrote: 'It is noted in many instances that the policy of the Department ... is being disregarded ... Relief issues must be confined to necessities such as flour, beef, bacon, rice, oatmeal and lard. Sugar and tea should only be issued for special reasons.'[72] Still, the department required something more than regular warnings. The relief system was in fact fairly open-ended; there were no benefit scales to guide the agents in the amounts they should distribute.

About a month after Mackenzie's letter, the department clarified its position by providing a scale of relief benefits. The scale issued by MacKenzie on 22 February 1928 was the first broad attempt to define and rationalize relief costs by relating the type, quantity, and value of relief to the category of the recipient (see Document 4.1).

Elements of the scale were unclear – some differences between the Class 1 and Class 2 ration were not well defined – yet certainly the essential elements of a benefit structure were present, including a method for determining a family's ration based on the age of the dependants. From the department's previous directives, we can surmise that Class 1, the 'Adult Destitute Ration' included only those considered deserving – that is, unable to work. Thus, basic policy was translated into clearer terms.

It must be admitted that there was now a better recognition of health problems among First Nations and of the need to deal with them more adequately than in the past.

Scott was well aware of Indian health problems on the reserves and of those created by poor conditions in the residential schools.[73] Still, his own economizing, coupled with the budgetary restraint of the Borden and Meighen administrations, had only aggravated the situation. Furthermore, Scott had been embarrassed by various reports, including an especially damning tract, *The Story of a National Crime* by Dr P.H. Bryce, who as the department's medical inspector had in 1911 proposed certain preventive measures – measures that had been largely ignored.[74]

Document 4.1 Scale of food relief rations, February 1928

Class 1. Adult Destitute Ration (Monthly Allowance)

Flour	24 lbs.	Baking Powder	1 lb.
Sugar	2 lbs.	Salt	1 lb.
Tea	1 lb.		

Bacon, Pork, Fresh Beef, Fish, Beans, to the total value of $2.00. Maximum issue of Beef, – 15 lbs.; of Pork or Bacon, – 8 lbs. monthly.
Lard, Rice, Oatmeal, Molasses, Macaroni, to the total value of $1.20.

Class 2. Sick Ration

In addition to all or part of the Class 1 Ration, milk, eggs, rice, oatmeal and fresh meat may be issued to sick Indians. This issue is intended to provide the means for making soups and puddings, and should be supplied for the use of the sick person alone ...
Milk and eggs are allowed for tubercular Indians only. One quart of fresh milk daily and one dozen of eggs weekly is the maximum allowance. Where fresh milk is not available, one 12 oz. tin of condensed sweetened milk may be supplied in place of each quart of fresh milk.
Children under ten years are allowed half the adult ration; over that age full ration.

Class 3. Babies artificially fed or undernourished

Fresh milk, evaporated unsweetened milk, condensed or powdered milk ... may be issued in suitable quantities for the feeding of babies whose mothers are unable to nurse them or to supplement breast feeding. One 16 oz. tin of evaporated milk is equivalent to one quart of fresh milk. Tinned tomatoes may be issued for the use of babies where there is no available supply of fresh fruit ...

As in the past, it will be necessary for an Indian Agent to obtain authority from the Department before making relief issues extending over a protracted period. The Agent will have, as at present, authority to incur emergency relief when necessary up to approximately $5.00.

Source: NAC, RG-10, Red Series, vol. 3087, File 279,222-1B, Letter to all Indian Agents from A.F. MacKenzie, acting assistant deputy and secretary, Ottawa, 22 February 1928.

When the Liberal governments of Mackenzie King were more generous in their allocations, Scott took advantage and in 1927 created a medical services branch within the department. From this we can surmise that the influence and resources of this new branch were reflected in Classes 2 and 3 of the benefit structure. The new scale reflected the department's continued determination to contain and control costs. For the first time, however, special recognition was made of tubercular Indians and of babies who today would be termed 'at risk.' It was this scale that carried departmental relief policy into the Depression years and that became the point of departure for a fully developed welfare program.

Relief during the Depression: Self-Support in the Face of Adversity, 1929–1934

In the fiscal year 1929–30, total relief expenditure was $569,218. The following year, 1930–1, this amount rose sharply to $658,674 – an increase of about 16 per cent (Table 4.1). Still, on 23 April 1931 Scott sent out a circular to all the Indian agents in Ontario, Quebec, and the Maritimes stating that because of the dramatic increase in the numbers on relief, agents were immediately to reduce expenditures by removing names from the relief lists. They were to continue to do so as the season progressed. Indians who were able to work, he wrote, should be advised immediately so that they 'may at once obtain employment so that they may earn sufficient money to defray their living expenses.'[75] Then, about a week later, he issued a further directive to all Indian agents in the country which noted that because of reduced parliamentary appropriations, 'it will be necessary to avoid admission of Indian patients to hospital or sanitorium for treatment of Tuberculosis or Trachoma.'[76] To drive home his point, he reissued the 1928 scale of benefits.[77] The Depression had taken a firm grip.

It is useful, here, to review the general treatment of the unemployed in Canadian society during the Depression. According to Guest, the administration of relief during the early 1930s 'reflected the deep distrust of dependent people which ... pervaded both public and private charity.'[78] Morton's description forcefully highlights the havoc wreaked by perceptions driven by ideological excess:

> Relief procedures, designed to force the idle to work, crushed self-respect. Relief officials insisted that cars, telephones, pets, ornaments, comfortable furniture, and all but a single bare light fixture be sacrificed. Recipients

Table 4.1
Relief expenditures, Canada and Indian Affairs, 1929–1936

	Year	Relief exp.	% ± based on preceding year
	1929		
Canada		n/a	n/a
DIA		$569,218	n/a
	1930		
Canada		n/a	n/a
DIA		$658,674	+ 15.7%
	1931		
Canada		$21,000,000	n/a
DIA		$790,672	+ 20.0%
	1932		
Canada		$93,000,000	+342.9%
DIA		$748,587	− 5.3%
	1933		
Canada		$94,000,000	+ 1.1%
DIA		$682,690	− 8.8%
	1934		
Canada		$101,000,000	+ 7.5%
DIA		$676,342	− 0.9%
	1935		
Canada		$142,000,000	+ 40.6%
DIA		$716,130	+ 5.9%
	1936		
Canada		$135,000,000	− 4.9%
DIA		$786,830	+ 9.9%

Sources: Canada, Department of Mines and Resources, Indian Affairs Branch, *Annual Report, 1936–1937*, 194. Canada, Parliament, Special Joint Committee of the Senate and the House of Commons Appointed to Examine and Consider the Indian Act, *Minutes of Proceedings and Evidence* (Ottawa: Edmond Cloutier, Printer to the King's Most Excellent Majesty, 1946), No. 1, 16. A.E. Grauer, *Public Assistance and Social Insurance*, Study Prepared for the Royal Commission on Dominion-Provincial Relations, Table 3, p. 14, Reproduced in Dennis Guest, *The Emergence of Social Security*, 86. *Notes*: The federal fiscal year then, as now, began April 1 and ended March 31. Indian relief amounts are based on 80 per cent of the total welfare expenditure as reported by R.A. Hoey, director of Indian Affairs, to the Special Joint Parliamentary Committee on the Indian Act in 1946. Canadian figures for relief represent the combined contributions of federal, provincial, and municipal governments.

collected food vouchers, sought medical care from an over-worked contract doctor, and visited a municipal depot for issues of used clothing. Men shovelled snow, chopped wood, or pulled weeds for their relief benefits. Since women did not work, often no provision was made for their clothing or personal needs.

Table 4.2
Per capita relief expenditures, Canada and Indian Affairs, 1929–1936

	Year	Population	Per capita expenditure	% ± based on preceding year
	1929			
Canada		10,059,300	n/a	
DIA		*108,012*	$ 5.27	n/a
	1930			
Canada		10,217,100	n/a	
DIA		108,912	$ 6.05	+14.8%
	1931			
Canada		*10,376,786*	$ 2.02	
DIA		109,812	$ 7.20	+19.0%
	1932			
Canada		10,489,773	$ 8.87	+39.1%
DIA		110,712	$ 6.76	− 6.1%
	1933			
Canada		10,602,760	$ 8.87	same
DIA		111,612	$ 6.12	− 9.5%
	1934			
Canada		10,715,747	$ 9.43	+ 6.3%
DIA		*112,510*	$ 6.01	− 1.8%
	1935			
Canada		10,828,734	$13.11	+39.0%
DIA		113,684	$ 6.30	+ 4.8%
	1936			
Canada		10.941,721	$12.34	− 5.9%
DIA		114,858	$ 6.85	+ 8.7%

Sources: Canada, Department of Mines and Resources, Indian Affairs Branch, *Annual Report, 1936–1937*, 194. *The Canadian Encyclopedia*, s.v. 'Population,' by Warren E. Kalbach. James S. Frideres, *Native Peoples in Canada*, 140. A.E. Grauer, *Public Assistance and Social Insurance*, Study Prepared for the Royal Commission on Dominion-Provincial Relations, Table 3, p. 14, Reproduced in Dennis Guest, *The Emergence of Social Security*, 86.
Notes: Population figures in italics are Canadian or Indian Affairs census numbers. The other figures are crude estimates based on the absolute growth between the census years. For example, Indian Affairs counted Indian population every five years. Between 1929 and 1934 an increase of about 900 per year was assumed. The Canadian census was conducted every ten years. Indian per capita amounts are further approximated because relief amounts are not exact.

Misery on relief was deliberate public policy. Even at the depths of the Depression, editors and business leaders insisted that jobs were available if men would only hunt for them.[79]

For the first half of the decade, relief was administered in kind (i.e., food, clothing, fuel) or through the use of purchase vouchers. Only in the late 1930s did some direct cash relief come into use. Despite an estimated unemployment rate of 23 per cent by 1933,[80] the unemployed were seen as largely to blame for their own misfortune and likely to lose all incentive to be self-supporting if they became dependent on relief.[81] The effects of these attitudes were powerful, so much so that Morton derisively writes: 'Bred in the doctrine of self-help, individual Canadians seemed almost pathetically willing to accept responsibility for their plight. Some literally died rather than accept relief.'[82]

The federal government annually transferred to the provinces increasing amounts of grants and loans for relief, but it did so with the publicly stated assurance that each grant represented a temporary measure and would be the last.[83] Grauer's figures show that only in one year, 1934, did federal relief transfers decline from the previous year. In 1931 the net federal transfer for relief (loans and grants) to the provinces was $3 million. By 1937 it was $52 million – 17.3 times more than in 1931.

Federal and provincial government ineptitude and continued ideological rigidity favouring capitalist elites eventually led to widespread social discontent and political unrest.[84] For example, 1933 saw the rise of the democratic socialist movement in Canada with the formation of the Co-operative Commonwealth Federation (CCF) and the publication of the Regina Manifesto. Only when confronted with this ferment, combined as it was with the emergence of a new intellectual elite and the exigencies of the Second World War, did Ottawa begin to move slowly toward broader, more meaningful social reform.[85]

Indian Relief Policy, 1929–1934

The attitude toward unemployed Indians on relief differed little from that toward Canadians in similar circumstances. The Depression generated little sympathy for the First Nations; in fact, it contributed to their even greater neglect. On 1 August 1931, when it was thoroughly apparent to Ottawa that relief costs were again significantly higher than the previous year (Tables 4.1 and 4.2), Scott wrote to all Indian agents throughout the country instructing them that their primary duty was to promote self-support among the Indians. With the difficult economic circumstances in mind, he observed: 'At the present juncture it is necessary to direct attention to these instructions with increased emphasis. So important is adherence to this principle in carrying out your duties that the Superintendent General has directed me to state that its successful application is the standard whereby your services will be judged.'[86] There is no evidence of any such directive from the superintendent general, Thomas Murphy, to Scott. In fact, Scott's tenure in comparison to those before him was remarkable for the lack of written communication between the superintendent and his deputy. Such an extraordinary expectation would seem to have made the agents responsible for ending the Depression; and had the department strictly adhered to this benchmark, it is unlikely any would have been left in its employ!

One agent at Resolution in the Northwest Territories replied in writing, with pride and scarcely veiled criticism that 'our Indians ... are really trying, and succeeding in earning their living, in spite of hardships not met in the prairies, winter travels, long distances, scarcity of fur and food often, poor health, low prices for fur, and excessive prices for everything that they have to purchase.'[87] But he also conceded, probably to Scott's liking, that 'there are cases of clear mendacity, inherent in the race, which we cannot eradicate, a certain number of subjects who will never be any good; and these we try to push and see that they do work.'[88]

This letter notwithstanding, the desperate economic circumstances caused the department to relent in its unreasonable expectations. A.F. MacKenzie, who had replaced the retired McLean, soon wrote to all Indian agents in effect countermanding Scott's earlier instructions: 'in view of the Department's attitude in this matter, it is taken for granted that each Indian Agent is endeavouring to instil and further a spirit of independence among the Indians under his care, but in doing so he should not overlook the fact that at the present time many Indians as well as Whites are unable to find remunerative work. Cases of acute distress arising from unemployment should not be allowed to go unrelieved.'[89] MacKenzie's circular introduced a major though ultimately temporary change in policy: the able-bodied unemployed were to be given relief. It is worth noting that the department had relented on this matter once comparable treatment of unemployed Euro-Canadians made it defensible to do so.

The relaxation of policy did not last long. Scott retired 31 March 1932, and his successor, Dr Harold McGill, was not confirmed until the following October.[90] However, Scott's methods outlasted his tenure, and so did the departmental culture he had done so much to create.[91] Determined to prevent any further rise in relief expenditure, the department embarked on a new program of restraint.[92] In April 1932, MacKenzie issued a now familiar circular to all agents in Ontario and

Quebec instructing them to remove names from their relief lists.[93] The suspicion of widespread fraud in the north then kindled a new initiative on Ottawa's part to develop other methods for controlling local administration.[94] One possible method was to administer relief rations directly through a system of agency storehouses. Early in 1932, MacKenzie advised all Indian agents in the country: 'The Department has under consideration a change in the method of purchasing relief supplies for the Indians throughout Canada. The present system of local purchase is a costly method and it is thought arrangements might be made for the purchase in bulk of food supplies and clothing for the sick and destitute and which would be distributed as needed.'[95] At the time of this proposal there were two principal methods of administering relief: through purchase vouchers issued to local merchants, and through the direct issue of rations from either an agency storehouse or trading company stores. Although there were storehouses in many northern agencies,[96] the proposal to extend the system was not immediately acted upon, and possibly it never was. The building of storehouses at every agency would have been a costly endeavour for a government whose revenues were strained and whose political priorities lay in satisfying the provinces' and municipalities' demands for financial aid.

Under McGill's new leadership, the department began seeking still more ways to control relief costs. In June 1933, on the heels of the now annual request that agents remove names from their relief lists,[97] MacKenzie wrote a severe directive concerning economies in relief administration. This directive, though it acknowledged serious economic problems, was remarkable for its reversion to standard images of Indian idleness and aversion to self-support:

> I have to advise you that that in view of recent regulations concerning public economy, it is necessary that relief issued to Indians should not be in excess of minimum needs. The Department appreciates the difficulties with which our Indian Agents are confronted in dealing with this problem owing to continued lack of opportunities for employment, and also in part to the natural tendency to idleness on the part of a certain type of Indian. While it may not be possible for the Indian to earn sufficient money for their livelihood at the present time ... they could help themselves much more ... by the cultivation of gardens or by fishing where such is available.
>
> It is absolutely necessary that the amount of relief issued to able-bodied Indians should be drastically curtailed in an effort to stimulate them to partial self-support at least.[98]

This directive, it would seem, reduced the Depression to yet another call to duty. It reflected the perception that unemployment was not so much a problem for Indians as it was an irritating obstacle to the Indian agent's project, which was to make the Indians self-reliant. According to this directive, Indians were not people but rather objects of 'public economy.' This directive was the product of an utter bleakness of vision, of the simplistic ideologies that by this time had permeated the department. The Department of Indian Affairs was rapidly driving itself into a dead end, with the First Nations as its captive passengers. Jenness writes acerbically of the period that 'the Indian administration did not ask: its job was simply to administer, and, like many a custodian, it was so involved in the routine of its administration that it forgot the purpose of its custodianship.'[99]

The next targets for restraint were the destitute sick. In a September 1933 memorandum, MacKenzie advised all agents that relief for the sick was to be confined to three categories of persons: tubercular patients at home, undernourished nursing mothers and children 'less than about five years,' and exceptional, doctor-certified cases requiring a special diet.[100] Two further items provided clues about the department's motivation here. First, MacKenzie stated that the communication was not meant as a prescription of any definite ration for the sick: 'The object of this instruction is to reduce rather than increase ... expenditure on sick relief'; agents were not to assume it was an invitation 'for extending the supply.'[101] Second, and most telling, MacKenzie in his conclusion warned agents to ensure that sick relief provisions were not 'used as additions to the family food supply.'[102]

This memorandum strongly suggests that at some point between May 1931 and September 1933, the department had revised the Class 2 and 3 rations introduced in 1928. Admittedly, in the files researched, no correspondence was encountered that would indicate this. Whatever the case, the department had apparently decided that special rations for the sick were too expensive. What it either chose to ignore or refused to understand was that as basic relief expenditures decreased (Tables 4.1 and 4.2) because of deliberate miserliness, recipients and their families were more likely either to become ill because of deprivation, or to resort to extraordinary action to secure necessities.[103] So it is not surprising that as the 1930s drew to a close, Indians' poverty, hunger, and health became a concern among outside observers.[104]

The department's next cost control tactic was introduced in February 1934, near the end of the fiscal year. MacKenzie sent a circular to all

Document 4.2 Scale of relief entitlement for Indian agencies in Ontario an British Columbia, February 1934

Number in Same Family	Amount of Entitlement
Minimum of Allowance	$ 4.00 per month
2 or 3 persons	$ 6.00 per month
4, 5 or 6 persons	$ 7.00 per month
7 and 8 persons	$ 9.00 per month
9 and 10 persons	$10.00 per month

Add $1.00 supplementary for each person in a family above ten persons.

Allowable Foods For Purchase.

The commodities supplied should be restricted to the following items:

Tea, sugar, salt pork, rice, beans, molasses, macaroni, rolled oats, barley, lard, baking powder, flour, canned tomatoes, salt, yeast, dried peas, the cheapest cuts of fresh meat or the cheapest kind of fish.
Root vegetables or apples, of the cheapest variety, may be supplied only in cases where the Indians have had no opportunity of raising these products on their own lands.

Suppliers should be advised that MINIMUM LOCAL PRICES should be charged and Indian Agents should not certify vouchers unless this requirement is complied with.

Source: Adapted from NAC, RG-10, Red Series, Vol. 3087, File 279,222-1C, Circular to all Indian Agents in Ontario and British Columbia and accompanying letter from A.F. MacKenzie, secretary, 10 February 1934.

Indian agents in Ontario and British Columbia – the two provinces with the biggest First Nations populations – introducing a progressive rate structure that tied the maximum value of food relief rations to family size.[105] In developing this new scale (Document 4.2), the department was trying to establish a set of universal rates that could aid in the projection of estimates. The previous scale, issued in 1928, had only placed ceilings on the quantity of rations and on the value of certain items. The actual value of relief, therefore, varied from agency to agency. The variation was sufficiently embarrassing to the department that in 1932 it had issued a directive to agents in Ontario and Quebec, instructing them not to mention the value of relief issued and to ensure that only the approved rates of the issuing agency were used.[106]

The introduction of a ceiling entitlement was accompanied by two other changes. First, although the department continued to specify the allowable foods for purchase, it no longer specified the quantity. Thus the recipients could apparently choose to purchase any of the allowable foods in amounts suitable to their own needs up to the ceiling entitlement. Second, the department for the first time significantly decentralized its work by giving the authority to grant relief to the Indian agents themselves. Only when the agent wished to grant in excess of entitlement – perhaps in cases of illness – was he to request approval from Ottawa.[107] This change probably resulted from a deluge of field correspondence in Ottawa as the Depression deepened.

These changes allowed greater flexibility, yet they should not be construed as generosity toward or moderation of expectations about Indians. Primarily, they were experiments in the interests of organizational efficiency and fiscal control. They established a new level of rationalized relief administration that would eventually apply throughout the country and that would make First Nations even more concentrated 'objects' of bureaucratic oppression.

The Impact of the Depression and the Continuation of Relief Policies during the Second World War

After February 1934 there is a six-year gap in the central archives. The file series I have been reviewing end abruptly at that time, and no further material is available until 1940. However, analysis of other data and literature have made it possible for me to acquire some insights into the continued impact of the Depression on First Nations and on the development of relief administration during this period.

The Great Depression

In June 1936 the new Liberal government of Mackenzie King made the Department of Indian Affairs a branch of the Department of Mines and Resources.[108] This action was part of the federal government's continuing efforts to control its expenditures.[109] It also reflected the low importance now attached to Indian matters, and marked the nadir of First Nations' status in Canada. The creation of the branch brought some important organizational changes to the Ottawa office. The branch was still headed by McGill, whose title, however, was changed to director. Immediately below him was the departmental secretary. Below the secretary but directly accountable to the director were five services: Field Administration, Medical Service, Reserves and Trusts Service, Welfare and Training Service and Records Service.

The new Welfare and Training Service, in enunciating its philosophy and objectives, remarked

> that a worth-while welfare program must be ... educational in character ... The activities of the Division, therefore, are ... complementary, directed toward clearly defined objectives. These objectives, for a generation or two at least, will be the training of pupils to make the most of their available resources, with talents consecrated to the service of the bands to which they belong, and an adult Indian population proud of their racial origin and cultural heritage, adjusted to modern life, progressive, resourceful, and self-supporting.[110]

These glowing words obscured the real situation, which was characterized by Indians' continued resistance to assimilation and by the state's determination to press its objectives with greater resolve.[111] Of course, the government could hardly be expected to admit that its policies were abject failures. Even so, the language in this extract is disturbing in its misrepresentation. Could this have come from the same office that had been issuing endless memoranda reducing Indians to objects of fiscal management? This memorandum did not simply deny problems; it evoked the sense of a parade under one banner.

The new service had two divisions: welfare and training. The training division was responsible for administering Indian education. The welfare division, organized toward the end of the 1936–7 fiscal year, was responsible for

> the creation and cultivation of subsistence gardens and the extension of agricultural operations; the purchase of live stock and equipment; encouragement of arts and crafts and sale of handicraft products; the survey and development of territory suitable for the propagation of muskrats and other fur-bearing animals; purchase of trap-lines and leasing of timber limits, housing construction, administration of relief, and the care of the aged and physically incapacitated.[112]

Table 4.3
Approximate per capita relief expenditures adjusted to estimated numbers on relief

	Year	Canada	First Nations
Percentage of population on relief		20%	33.3%
Per capita relief expenditures	1932	$44.33	$20.30
	1934	$47.13	$18.05
	1936	$61.69	$20.57

Sources: James Struthers, 'Great Depression,' The Canadian Encyclopedia; Department of Mines and Resources, Indian Affairs Branch, Annual Report, 1936–1937, 194.
Notes: The Indian percentage is based on the estimated proportion of the population on relief in 1936/37. The Indian per capita figures include DIA cost sharing with Ontario for the Mothers' Allowance and reimbursements to the fur trade companies for relief as well as all other welfare activity expenditure.

This description of welfare activity provides additional insight into the departmental data in Tables 4.1 and 4.2. First, the departmental figures in Table 4.1 represent 80 per cent of the total welfare expenditure and are for relief only. The amounts available for other activities would have been completely minimal. Thus in 1936, for example, the amount spent on activities other than relief was about $197,000, or $1.71 per capita.[113] Second, the figures in Table 4.2 can be adjusted to reflect the per capita expenditure on the estimated portion of the population dependent on relief. Table 4.3 depicts this adjustment for the selected years 1932, 1934, and 1936. Although the figures are approximate, they accurately portray the wide gulf that was developing between Indian and non-Indian relief. Indian and non-Indian relief measures were similar in some ways. For example, many-able bodied First Nations people in need were being denied relief outright. Also, bands in Ontario and Quebec had been made responsible for relief payments from their own accounts[114] – a requirement that further impoverished them. In this way, they were being handed the same responsibilities as white municipalities. While historians rightly deplore the treatment of unemployed Canadians during the Depression, and the meagre amounts given them for relief, the brief analysis in Table 4.3 suggests that the treatment extended to First Nations was considerably meaner.

Northern Indian Income, Relief Expenditures, and the Changing Role of the Hudson's Bay Company

Another perspective on Indian relief expenditure is provided by Ray's examination of Indian income between 1922 and 1935. Ray analysed income from all sources (including relief) for three selected Indian groupings involved in the fur trade. The first group, the Woodland Indians – Indians in the southern belt of the trade southeast and southwest of Hudson Bay – had an income peak in 1926 of just over $2 million, which then steadily dropped to $800,000 in 1935 – a decline of 60 per cent. In the second group, Indians of northern Alberta, Saskatchewan, and Manitoba, income fell 66 per cent, from a high in 1924 of $880,000 to $300,000 in 1935. Finally, in northern Ontario, Indian income from all sources in 1935 was $500,000, a drop of 38 per cent from the peak in 1925 of $810,000.[115] During roughly the same period, 1922–34, government relief payments to all northern Indians declined 32 per cent, from some $242,000 in 1922 to about $164,000 in 1934.[116] Not only did relief payments not rise or remain constant in response to lower income, they actually fell.

The drop in northern Indian income was precipitated by several related factors in the inter-war years: increased competition among the fur companies, the rapid incursion of white trappers, and the depletion of fur-bearing animals and resulting conservation measures. In addition, the fur trade was – like the rest of the economy during this period – subject to many regional, national, and international fluctuations in production, price, and volume of sales.[117] As Indians became lesser players in the fur trade – a setback from which they would never recover – and more vulnerable to the trade's volatility, the Hudson's Bay Company, under considerable media pressure, proposed various solutions to the problem of their prolonged destitution.[118]

One of these solutions – the impetus for which emanated principally from London and the district trading posts – was the creation in 1925 of a development department to explore the company's future operations in Canada. Part of the new department's mandate was to review and make recommendations for the health and welfare of the company's First Nations and Inuit trading partners.[119] From Ray's brief account of the department's work, it is evident that two critical problems facing natives were identified: nutrition, and alternative sources of income. In the wake of this, the new department, under the direction of Charles Townsend, initiated two important projects. One was a Home Industry program; the other was a nutritional supplement program, meant only for their own Indian and Inuit customers.

The Home Industry program, begun in 1926, was intended to discourage idleness and maintain morale. It promoted the manufacture and sale of native handicrafts for tourists, especially during the slow summer months.[120] The nutritional supplement program was based on the company's own studies, which strongly linked Indians' malnutrition to their susceptibility to tuberculosis, influenza, and other infectious diseases. Company post managers distributed vitamin supplements, iodine tablets, cod liver oil, and 'a meal made from cod livers to those Indians who were regular customers.'[121] In late November 1927, Townsend met with Indian Affairs officials in Ottawa to discuss the company's initiatives and their impact on native welfare. Dr E.L. Stone, the Indian Affairs medical superintendent, entirely endorsed the company's new programs. Perhaps he was a man in despair of the rigid economies exercised by Scott and McLean, for he reportedly said that his 'Department was really in need of the Company's help' and 'had only the Company to turn to.'[122]

There followed then, a brief period of joint departmental and company initiatives to promote Indian health and cottage industries. The company attended to the needs of its Indian customers, and the department to those who were not part of the trading system. The health initiatives were reflected, for example, in the department's relief rate structure issued in 1928; the promotion and sale of handicraft products became part of departmental welfare expenditure as early as 1929.[123] These well-intentioned initiatives by Stone and Townsend were irritants both to the department and to the company's commissioners in Winnipeg.

The company had still not resolved the conflict between its London managing directors and its Winnipeg administrative committee over responsibility for Indian welfare. The Winnipeg committee took a hard business approach to the company's operations and thought that London was naive in regard to the conditions necessary to make the company an efficient enterprise in Canada. Its members opined that the complexity of competition and the uncertainty of Indian loyalty meant that the fur trade's social costs (i.e., Indian welfare) should lie with the state. In 1931 the London board bowed to these arguments and transferred the company's operational control to Winnipeg. That same year the development department was eliminated and the last source of the company's paternal humanism and mercantile reciprocity was gone.[124]

Indian Affairs, of course, was still convinced that almost any form of relief detracted from Indian self-reliance. After 1931, freed of the company's example, the department dropped the Class 2 and 3 rations from the relief scale and placed even stricter controls on sick relief. Thus, during the Depression years there was a disastrous convergence of the company's gradual withdrawal from Indian welfare with the department's harsh approach to relief. The effects of this convergence left the First Nations so economically and politically impoverished that by the end of the Second World War, they were the subjects of much national embarrassment and international concern. *The Economist,* for instance, wrote that 'the handling of native peoples throughout the world will be one of the foremost problems of the post-war settlement and it is a matter of surprise to Canadians to find that their policies with respect to the aboriginal native peoples of Canada ... scarcely bear comparison with progressive policies developed in other countries in recent years.'[125] The ensuing solutions to their plight would only further draw First Nations into a complex nexus of burgeoning government administration, academic study, and public interest.

Relief during the Second World War

There is little policy correspondence available on Indian relief during the Second World War; what material does exist suggests that practices were harsher even than those of the interwar years. A circular to all Indian agents – likely jointly authored by McGill and R.A. Hoey, superintendent of the Welfare and Training Service – introduced what had proven to be an utter failure in Canada during the Depression: the principle of work for welfare:[126]

> Relief allowances in the case of physically fit, able-bodied Indians should be cancelled not later than July 1. It is not the policy of the Department to provide able-bodied Indians with relief. All such Indians must undertake certain tasks either on the reserves or off the reserves. The cultivation of gardens, farm work, clearing land, road construction, drainage projects, wood-cutting, repair of buildings, caretaking, and fishing and trapping in certain districts are all tasks that might be undertaken.
>
> Rations may be supplied to Indians engaged in such work. In no case, however, will it be permissible to supply relief to an Indian who refuses to undertake the task assigned him by the agent.[127]

A new monthly ration scale, intended to bring complete uniformity to relief administration 'throughout the Dominion,' was issued simultaneously (Document 4.3). Agents were also warned that no payments would be made for rations issued that were not on the scale unless recommended by the medical officer and directly authorized by Ottawa.[128]

The circular, the accompanying scale, and a further letter of explanation in June 1940 provided the basic gist and tenor of Indian relief until the beginnings of reform in the 1950s. Of course, the war provided the department with yet another platform to call agents to their patriotic duty and to urge cooperation from them and Indians alike. Agents were instructed to cut down wherever possible on the issue of imported foods, to 'keep down relief costs and thus conserve public funds,'[129] and to beware of providing relief to those Indian families whose men had enlisted in the Canadian Active Service Force.

The relief scale and the issue of work for welfare are of particular importance. McGill, in explaining the new scale to the agents, observed that the ration lists had not been revised for some time, with the result that 'a number of agents are ... supplying rations to Indians on instructions received ... 9 years ago.'[130] This was hardly surprising, since there were at least two scales in existence: the 1928 scale (reissued in 1931 and revised between then and 1933), and the 1934 scale issued for Ontario and British Columbia.

The branch claimed that the revised rations were 'sufficiently nutritious to provide sustenance and maintain health.' In fact, those rations did not compare favourably with either of the other two scales. Despite a rising awareness of the importance of nutrition, no attempt was made to reintroduce the Class 2 and 3 rations; indeed, items like milk in any form, eggs, tinned tomatoes, root vegetables, and apples could not be distributed without Ottawa's authority. Ottawa continued to insist, as it had since 1873, that Indians cultivate their own gardens for fruit and vegetables. Some First Nation bands did succeed in raising sufficient quantities of garden foods to support themselves. Recalling his childhood in central Ontario during the Depression, an Ojibwa Nation elder, Ernie DeBassige stated that 'my Dad had a store, and at that time people had a four dollar per month ration and there were only certain things in the store they could have for that amount ... All people would buy would be ... things they couldn't grow ... Everybody had a garden and people had root houses, where they kept things under the ground; potatoes, turnips, and everybody cut wood, people salted barrels of fish ... and usually raised a

Document 4.3 Scale of monthly rations for Indians on relief, May 1940

No. of Adults	1	2	3	4	5	6
	Lbs.	Lbs	Lbs.	Lbs.	Lbs.	Lbs.
Ration						
Flour (2nd grade)	24	36	49	61	80	98
Rolled Oats	6	9	12	15	18	18
Baking Powder	1	1¾	1¾	2	2	2
Tea	1	1½	2	2	2	3
Sugar	2	4	5	7	8	10
Lard	3	5	8	10	10	13
Beans	5	5	7	7	8	8
Rice	2	3	5	5	7	7
Cheese	1	1½	1½	2	2	3
	$	$	$	$	$	$
Meat or Fish	1.00	1.50	1.75	2.00	2.00	2.25
Salt	10¢ or 15¢ per month per family					
Matches	10¢ to 20¢ per month per family					

Note: Indians under the age of 12 years shall be considered children, and over that age as adults. Issues of rations for each child, of flour, rolled oats, sugar, lard, beans, rice, cheese and meat or fish, shall be one half the quantities specified for one adult.

Departmental approval must be secured for special rations recommended by the Medical Health Officer in cases of sickness, and milk that may be necessary in the case of infants.

Storekeepers should be warned that if they vary without authority the items contained in this list they are subject to immediate removal from the list of firms authorized to do government business.

Source: NAC, RG-10, Central Registry, Vol. 7094, File 1/10-3-0, Memorandum from R.A. Hoey, Superintendent of Welfare and Training to accompany Circular C-118-1 to Inspectors and all Indian Agents from H.W. McGill, Director, Indian Affairs Branch, Department of Mines and Resources, Ottawa, 22 May 1940.

pig or two.'[131] Similarly, a band councillor from the Osoyoos Band of the Okanagan Nation recalled a period of relative self-sufficiency until the 1950s: 'The band had community gardens, cows, horses, chickens, ducks, and turkeys. There was still extensive hunting and trapping. The band traded with the white community for what it needed, or it sold furs.'[132] Yet it is hard to imagine how many bands could have produced sufficient quantities of vegetables and fruit to support themselves, especially in the sub-Arctic and wherever the Canadian shield extended. Even today, many bureaucrats living and tending a home garden in Ottawa are well aware of the obstacles imposed by bedrock.

While some items were added – notably, matches and cheese – other standard issues were deleted: yeast, macaroni, and molasses. Most critical, however, was that the quantity of rations was reduced in two ways. Half-rations were effectively issued for a longer period by raising the age of a child to twelve years from ten; and instead of the 1928 scale, which gave each adult a standard ration, adults' rations were graduated according to their number in the household. For example, the 1928 scale had allowed six pounds of baking powder in a household of six adults, whereas the 1940 scale allowed only two pounds. The dollar value of meat and fish rations had also been significantly reduced.

Finally, the purchase flexibility evident in the 1934 scale had been completely removed; not only that, but the ration quantities were now described as upper ceilings. In other words, recipients were to be issued rations *up to* the specified amounts. Whenever the issuing authority felt that the recipient had other resources, each rationed item was to be appropriately reduced.[133] Overall, the 1940 scale of rations was a further initiative by Ottawa – with ringing calls of service to the Dominion – to rationalize and control food relief in the interests of economy and in the endless pursuit of Indian individual self-reliance.

How did this actually translate in the field? The following description of relief day by Charles Roberts, the acting Indian agent at Norway House in 1941, provides a useful anecdotal picture of the combined method of providing relief (i.e., through the agency warehouse and local store), the assessment of eligibility, and problems of diet:

The shipments came in of salt pork and all this type of thing, and on relief day I had an Indian that worked on the staff. I think he was called an interpreter. He used to issue this stuff. People would come in with their little sugar bag or whatever and got their flour, bacon, and so on. It was based on quantitative value, a basic ration was so many pounds of this and so many pounds of that. And this salt pork – sow belly as we used to call it – the big thing about that was it was so important to the Indians because the deer meat and the fish that they were using mostly was so dry; they needed the fat and that's what made it so important.

Roberts explained how need was determined:

> You just sorta – well, you knew if they were employed or unemployed, and you knew if it was a widow or a young healthy man. You normally didn't give it to him. But it was a very hit and miss sort of thing. I suppose welfare is today to some extent. But you just did it. There was some of them would try to cow you into giving it them; some would sort of plead with you. You had to try to just bear your common sense to that.[134]

This description offers excellent insights into the nature of relief then and now. Today, public systems of social assistance are cloaked in apparently objective criteria for determining need; however, these criteria are premised on as subjective and ideological a conception of deservedness as the 1941 standard revealed by Roberts. More importantly, Roberts's depiction of his role demonstrates how relief systems established on the premise of individual culpability tend to place administrators in the position of powerful gatekeepers who are there to defend not only the rules of relief per se but also the system and ideology they represent.

Indeed, the anecdote is a good example of Foucault's thesis that power and resistance are best understood at the point of administration. An Indian who tried to cow or plead with an agent to give him relief was in effect resisting and/or challenging that agent's power over him. The agent in turn was subject to discipline – even the loss of his job – if he chose not to apply the rules. The system depended on the agent's loyalty as a willing participant in exercising power over the Indian, who after all symbolically represented a counterforce. An agent who 'resisted' the power of his superiors – who in effect disobeyed them – thus empowered the Indian he was dealing with not only individually but collectively as a representative of First Nations. The function of an Indian agent and the representation of that function were, therefore, critical to the summoning of an entire system of state power capable of enforcing, as necessary, the relationship of domination and repression.

The Second World War brought a return of prosperity to most of Canada, but for the Department of Indian Affairs, under the inflexible direction of McGill, it provided a further rationale for exercising public restraint. Between the fiscal years 1936–7 and 1943–4, welfare expenditure dropped almost 34 per cent to $652,090, or $5.19 per capita.[135] (The reported Indian population in 1944 was 125,686.) These figures could perhaps have been defended had there been substantial evidence of a general improvement in First Nations' social and economic status. There was, however, little evidence of this. In 1945, Indian Affairs reported that the 'income of the Indian has been steadily increasing in recent years' to about $16 million in 1944, an amount that constituted a per capita annual income of about $127.00.[136] In comparison, the average weekly wage for non-native Canadians in 1942 was $29.49. The unemployment rate was just 3 per cent. Thus, even a family of six would have had a per capita income about twice that on reserves.[137]

One other important change was mentioned in the 1940 circular: the work-for-welfare provision. Ironically, this change could be seen as a relaxation of past regulations that had denied relief completely to able-bodied Indians except for a brief period during the Depression. Relief would now be available to able-bodied Indians if they were willing to undertake specific types of physical labour in the community. More importantly, the work for welfare requirement marked the beginning of change in departmental thinking about on-reserve welfare and job creation.

The department's reason for implementing work for welfare was rooted in traditional prejudices of liberal and classical economics toward public welfare and its potential, unless vigilantly supervized, to undermine the individual's incentive to seek her or his welfare in the marketplace. In other words, Indians as individuals repeatedly had to learn that there was no such thing as a free lunch. Thus, Indian Affairs policy and the agents of its administration imported into First Nations cultures the stigma associated with economic dependence in Western society and then linked it to Indian inferiority and the burden of tutelage.

By the 1940s, however, the department had conceded that employment on and near most reserves was almost non-existent. The only way to 'teach the lesson' was to create situations of artificial employment external to the mainstream labour market and economy. An ideal method of doing this was through a program of public works that focused on the communities themselves. This would instill and maintain a sense of individual initiative and self-reliance; it would also, at a relatively cheap cost, develop and improve those communities. Work for welfare lasted throughout the Second World War but apparently did not survive as official policy much beyond 1950.[138]

There were probably two reasons for this. First, the program had done nothing to reduce dependence on relief, since Indian relief costs continued to rise steadily after the war.[139] Second, there was a more generous public attitude toward the right of individuals to state benefits, an attitude that stemmed from the more general concern, so prevalent after the war, for rights of democratic citizenship. Thus, there was less call for harsh measures to be applied to recipients of assistance; indeed, by 1956 the federal government had entered into cost sharing with the provinces for assistance to the 'employable' unemployed.[140] Despite the end of work for welfare, the idea of harnessing welfare to public works on reserves percolated in Indian Affairs for some time. This idea surfaced again in 1971 when the department instituted a new community works program that allowed – though it did not require – social assistance recipients to create a monthly wage for themselves by combining their monthly entitlement with other funding sources.[141] Called the 'Work Opportunity Program,' this was the first of a continuing series of attempts by the department to create employment opportunities on reserves and to develop marketable skills off reserves.

In the long term, two interrelated issues are relevant to the question of the First Nations' reactions to work for welfare: the cultural compatibility of Euro-Canadian forms of social assistance with First Nations cultures and social organization; and control over social policy, services, and administration. Since the late 1970s, studies of provincial and Indian Affairs social assistance programs delivered on reserve have pointed out the basic cultural dissonance between the programs and their recipient communities. The provincial programs and their Indian Affairs clones emphasize principles of individual rights and responsibilities, such as the right of the individual to a benefit based on proven need, balanced by the responsibility of the individual to become independent and self-supporting. First Nations state that social assistance programs have undermined their communities' interdependent and communal structures, and they complain that the 'social' in social assistance is meaningless. They reject the assimilatory bent of Euro-Canadian social assistance programs, and they correctly link their continuation to fundamental issues of control of culture and self-government. This stance is not a novelty; Quebec took an analogous position during the 1971 constitutional discussions and the 1986 Meech Lake Accord. What does all this imply about the meaning of work for welfare in many First Nations communities? In their view, work for welfare ought really to be a mechanism to return the interdependent notion of 'social' to social assistance. Indeed, ideally under terms of self-government, social assistance would be equivalent to a transfer grant to the community, to be utilized as a common resource for the mutual benefit of all members.[142]

5

Other Influences: The Transition to the Period of Citizenship, 1918–1944

To modernize Canada's Indian policy, a thorough transformation of public attitude will be required. The argument that the Indian should be treated as a free and equal citizen immediately arouses antipathy and scorn, so long has the public neglected the Indian, and so fixed has become the idea that he is an inferior person. But up to now Canadian Indian policy has done little beyond save the Indian from extinction. It has done little to open the way for his assimilation into Canadian society.

'The Canadian Indian,' reprinted from *The Economist*, 1944

A criticism of the Indian Affairs bureaucracy made by the Hawthorn report of 1966 – one which, I believe, was quite common – was that it was historically isolated from the wider organizational culture of the federal government and Canadian society as a whole. It operated as a realm unto itself, free of any meaningful criticism and oblivious to a changing Canada.[1] I think that this criticism, however, failed to account for the influence of outside organizations – including Indian organizations – politicians, and interested individuals. In particular, it failed to account for public collusion with the department's fundamental objectives.[2] More often than not, Canadians who criticized the department objected to its inefficiency in accomplishing the job, not to the job itself.

Like most bureaucracies, the department resisted outside interference, and it did not like being told what to do. It did not appreciate criticism, especially from its subject clients. Yet as long as it remained firmly in control of the administration and its propaganda, the department enjoyed sharing the burden of its unenviable task with citizens who were on its side. It even flattered those who appeared sympathetic to it. In the inter-war years there was considerable Indian political activity and resistance to Indian policy, which irked the essentially authoritarian department.[3] As well, 'concerned' Canadians were showing some incipient awareness about the situation of Canada's First Nations and about the administration's difficulties in accomplishing the tasks of assimilation. The changing level of concern for Indians and their movement toward full citizenship ultimately led to a barrage of interest and assistance from academics, professionals, and private organizations after the Second World War. I turn now to four episodes that I believe contributed to the department's evolution in the broader Canadian context and consequently to changes in its approach to social policy.

Indian Citizenship and the Social Service Council of Canada, 1918–1923

At the beginning of the previous chapter, I discussed the changing nature of Canadian society and its movement from a culture based in sacred values to one concerned with modernism, science, and the secular. Perhaps no other social phenomenon better exemplified this movement than the treatment of First Nations, which was rooted in Christian missionary imperatives but was increasingly confronted by the failure of Christian theology to convert Indians to the ideals of Western progress.

The struggle for social reform in late-nineteenth-century Canada, Cook contends, was largely a struggle over the relevance of Christian theology to modern, capitalist society. Many leading Christian thinkers argued that a new, practical application of theology, a new means of introducing Christ's teachings on earth, was required. This requirement gave rise to the rediscovery of Christ, the social reformer.[4] James L. Hughes, the progressive nineteenth-century Methodist educator from Ontario, wrote that 'men are beginning to understand the revelations of Christ in regard to the greatest ideal – community – and to believe that Christian principles are for everyday use; they are in fact the fundamental principles of all social evolution ... This ideal is making Christianity a vital force in the social and industrial organization of humanity and an essential element of a progressive civilization.'[5] The implication of this statement was a shift from predestination in Christian thought to an evangelical determinism; Christ was seen as an active rather than a passive saviour. Christianity was to be transformed into a code of ethical conduct for living in a profane world. Cook writes that 'this union of the sacred and the secular,' of Christianity and "progressive civilization," was destined eventually to give birth to the secular social science of sociology. ... If Christ was ... a social reformer, then the "perfect sociology" was obviously the central concern of Christian thought.'[6]

The task emanating from this point of view was to build a practical sociology of reform based on Christian thought. A Christianity that not only tolerated but seemed to provide the moral *raisons d'être* of capitalism, of exploitation, poverty, human waste, and suffering, was unacceptable to Canada's Christian reformers, and had to be replaced by one that, in practical terms provided the inspiration, organization, planning, and tools of social reform.[7] One such organization was the Moral and Social Reform Council of Canada, a broad-based coalition of Protestant churches and Christian organizations founded in 1907 to pursue the social reconstruction of Canada.[8] In 1913 it changed its name to the Social Service Council of Canada. The following year it sponsored the Social Service Congress in Ottawa, one of the largest, most stirring meetings ever held in Canada on issues of social reform.[9] The outbreak of the First World War deflated much of the congress's radical zeal; even so, the Social Service Council gradually evolved into a respectable social research body and a moderate advocate for social reform.[10]

One of the council's primary interests was the status of Canada's Indian peoples. Before the end of the war in 1918, the council's Indian Affairs Committee[11] adopted a resolution that, reflecting Indian enfranchisement through army service and the demands by some tribal councils for equivalent status, called for a survey into the 'whole problem of [Indian] citizenship.'[12] It was resolved that the survey should cover a range of issues affecting Indian citizenship, including 'existing treaty conditions for Treaty Indians to be recast; Problems of non-Treaty Indians; ... Indian lands, privileges, and rights in every province of the Dominion; Family life and the moral, social, and economic welfare of the native Indians; The relation of Federal and Provincial Governments to Indians.'[13] The council further resolved that a non-partisan, sympathetic commission on Indian affairs, comprised of members of the religious bodies engaged in Indian missionary work, would be set up to do the survey.

The council referred to its executive committee another resolution to dissociate the council from the Friends of the Indians, a voluntary association of white Canadians who supported the Nisga'a land claims in British Columbia. This was done in the interests of present and future working relationships with governments, since the Friends were perceived by the state as a somewhat subversive organization.[14] This was a curious position. The council obviously knew that the Friends were out of favour with Scott and the department. The resolution was clearly meant to appease Scott; yet earlier in the same meeting, the council had approved a motion of its Indian Affairs Committee confirming the Reverend A.E. O'Meara as a corresponding committee member. O'Meara – a lawyer and Anglican priest – was a well-known leader of the Friends of the Indians and believed by Scott to be the ringleader of Nisga'a discontent.

Early in May 1918, the council's general secretary, Dr T. Albert Moore, wrote to Scott, enclosing the minutes of the council's annual meeting and drawing to his attention the resolutions of the Indian Affairs Committee and the call for a commission. He continued: 'I write to say that we believe that this Commission would be of great value to the Government in helping to secure the proper advancement of the Indians to enable them to become intelligent citizens, capably and wisely using their franchise.'[15] In his reply, Scott requested clarification of the proposed commission's exact nature so that he might discuss it more fully with the minister, Arthur Meighen. The proposed one-year time frame was, he thought, unrealistic, given the survey's ambitious scope. In closing, he referred to an Indian Act amendment to facilitate voluntary Indian enfranchisement for those who no longer followed 'the Indian mode of life.'[16]

Moore was apparently buoyed by a later conversation with Scott, who offered him timely 'advice,' and wrote to him on 14 June: 'I understand that it is the hope of the Indian Affairs Committee ... that the Government of Canada will appoint and finance the proposed Commission ... and that the Council, or its Committee on Indian Affairs may have the privilege of consultation, or even nomination, as to its members. We ... recognize the necessity of this Commission carrying on in the utmost good-will with the Government, and have no thought of any other relationship.'[17] Moore continued by restating what the council had envisaged as the commission's scope, and concluded: 'The resolution ... was intended to open ... for consideration ... everything affecting the Indians. The specific ground to be covered by the ... Commission, however, would be a subject for decision on the part of the Government, after conference with the Council.'[18] So much for the revolutionary days of the Ottawa congress! The council's proposal had been carefully manipulated and co-opted by Scott, and Moore had acquiesced. Scott's real interest was to hasten the process of enfranchisement and assimilation.

Not satisfied with the 1918 amendment to the Indian Act, he and Meighen were planning a new amendment to enable compulsory enfranchisement.[19] A commission to air the overall condition of Indians in Canada, one that might point to a host of problems to be resolved – especially land claims and treaty rights – before full citizenship could proceed was not in the government's perceived interests.

The commission was going to rely on the government for funding, and Scott knew it. He replied to Moore on 17 June: 'I shall be pleased to bring your correspondence to the attention of the Hon. the Superintendent General as soon after his return as may be found convenient.'[20] It was a polite brush-off; it was never found convenient.

Nearly two years later, the Conservative government introduced Bill 14, which allowed for 'the enfranchisement of an Indian against his will following a report by a person appointed by the superintendent general on his suitability.'[21] The bill encountered immediate opposition from Indians and mixed response in the press. Because it created controversy, the bill was sent to committee. To Scott's horror, that committee invited submissions from interested Indians. First Nation communities argued, quite logically, that if they were intelligent enough as individuals to be considered suitable for enfranchisement, they were intelligent enough to decide whether they wanted it. The bill, they said, was a deliberate attempt to destroy them and their communities.[22] Scott bluntly agreed. 'Our objective,' he testified, 'is to continue until there is not a single Indian in Canada that has not been absorbed into the body politic, and there is no Indian question.'[23]

Amidst the furore created by the bill, Jack Forster, chairman of the Indian Affairs Committee for the Social Service Council, wrote to Meighen in an attempt to resurrect the commission, believing that such an initiative might rescue the government from an embarrassing situation. Forster wrote: 'We believe that if the Commission ... had been appointed the Bill now before you might have made some different and fuller provisions ... If the ... Bill be not immediately urgent, might it not be held in abeyance, that the Commission be appointed and the Bill revised after ... the results of the survey?'[24] Meighen's private secretary informed Forster that his letter and the 1918 proposal for the commission had been forwarded to the House committee for consideration. By separate letter, without Forster's knowledge, the secretary brought the revived proposal to Scott's attention.[25] Scott wrote to Meighen within the week: 'I would call your attention especially to my letter of the 25th of May, 1918, to Rev. Dr. Moore, and subsequent correspondence. I discussed this matter with you for a few minutes and we decided to take no action. To my mind the suggestion made in Mr. Forster's letter is not reasonable.'[26] No further correspondence ensued on the matter. The bill eventually passed Parliament in June 1920, but Indian hostility to it remained so great and the Conservative government so politically fragile that its provisions were never pursued with any vigour. After the Meighen government collapsed in 1921, the new Liberal government of Mackenzie King made the provision voluntary.[27]

Could the bill have been successfully amended under commission aegis? Probably not. A commission, even with government-controlled appointment of its members, would have stirred a great deal of antidepartment feeling as well as Indian objections to the entire custodial relationship between Canada and the First Nations. Such a response would not have satisfied the council, for it was firmly assimilatory and believed that social justice for Indians could be achieved only through their Christianization, 'advancement,' and citizenship. Scott and Meighen saw the council as a meddlesome ally who could make a troublesome situation worse. The council, of course, did not help its cause by its bumbling, naive approach to politics and power. It had severely weakened its position by rebuking Meighen for not having appointed the commission in the first place. Thus it was left with no role at all.

All of this was a hard lesson for the council, which had wanted to be a friendly advocate for Indian progress. After this failure, Dr John G. Shearer, the general secretary since 1918,[28] adopted new tactics for dealing with the department. First, instead of direct criticism or sweeping reform proposals, the council devised an issue-oriented approach and began conveying annual recommendations to the department for its interest and consideration. Second, the council presented a new image to the department, one that implicitly acknowledged the complexity of the department's tasks. This shift was evident in the council's careful scrutiny of the Indian Affairs Committee's recommendations prior to their approval. For example, Shearer in February 1922 sent Scott several recommendations approved by the council, with this covering letter:

My dear Dr. Scott:

I have pleasure in enclosing herewith a copy of the Report of the Indian Affairs Committee of the Social Service Council of Canada as amended and adopted by the Council itself.

You will note the various recommendations and I am sure they will receive your open-minded consideration. I hope also your approval.[29]

Two of the recommendations concerned standards of Indian education and legal procedures surrounding land claims in British Columbia – a dominant issue during Scott's administration. A third called for occasional articles on Indian matters 'to promote enlightenment of public opinion' in the council's journal, *Social Welfare.*

Scott replied with equal politeness and collegiality: 'I have to acknowledge the receipt of your letter ... inclosing the recommendations of the Social Service Council with reference to Indian matters. I have read them with pleasure and the Department will be mindful of them when considering policies and ways and means.'[30] He then commented on each of the recommendations; however, he was obscure in his reference to B.C. land claims.

The following year, 1923, Shearer again forwarded several recommendations; he also brought to Scott's attention that recommendations concerning land claims had been deleted because of the need for further study. The remaining recommendations were of the sort that Scott could easily accept. They included suggestions for the moral improvement and Christian citizenship of Indians, as well as for a system of direct deposit of treaty annuities in individual accounts, to encourage thrift and to prevent work interruptions due to the annual treaty payment gatherings![31] There was no reply from Scott, and Shearer's letter was the last important correspondence between the council and the department.

The relationship that had developed between the Social Service Council of Canada and the department was significant for several reasons. At some level the state, through the department, knew there was value in cultivating a relationship with an outside organization such as the council. By 1922 the council's membership had broadened considerably to include the Canadian Conference on Public Welfare and the Canadian National Association of Trained Nurses. Many members of its executive were lawyers and professors. In a Gramscian sense, it was important to have an organization nurtured by the civil level of society and of some intellectual stature, 'on side' and in fundamental support of state objectives. In other words, to ensure the dominant culture's hegemony, it was necessary to have a prominent, independent, national body that, by offering considered input into the department's work, actually helped legitimize the state's relationship with the First Nations. Miliband writes that 'it needs to be stressed that "hegemony" is not simply something which happens, as a mere superstructural derivative of economic and social predominance. It is, in very large part, the result of a permanent and pervasive effort, conducted through a multitude of agencies, and deliberately intended to create what Talcott Parsons calls a "national supra party consensus" based on "higher order solidarity."[32]

The department could accept council recommendations on relatively non-controversial issues pertaining to self-reliance, education, and so on, since these in effect reinforced the state's own objectives. It must also be remembered that the leading member churches of the council were intimately involved in the provision of Indian education. More importantly, it was better to encourage the council to relate with the department than with First Nations, since such a relationship – as amply demonstrated by the reviled 'Friends of the Indians' – could only result in agitation, challenges to state dominance, and (eventually) public doubt about the state's legitimacy. The state's 'invitation' to the council, then, provided the latter with a sense of importance and justification, while committing the department to nothing.[33] The department could accept recommendations 'with interest' or 'put them under advisement' and thus appear to be encouraging the council's work; the council could feel that it was both a friend to the Indians and a trusted department advisor.

Shearer, who had helped found the council and was one of its strongest proponents, died in early 1925. The council disbanded that year, and other, parallel interest organizations subsequently became strong national bodies.[34] The legacy of the council's relationship with the department is very important. It dispels the common perception of an entire public unaware of Indian matters and of a department hermetically sealed into its own world. Also, that relationship laid an important foundation for future ones between organizations not unlike the council – or what the council had become – and the department. In the high period of citizenship after the Second World War, the department would turn to academics and influential voluntary organizations as allies for support and consultation. Chief among the latter would be the Canadian Welfare Council and the National Commission on the Indian Canadian, later to become the Indian-Eskimo Association of Canada. The role of the Canadian Welfare Council is more fully examined in chapter 8.

The Extension of the Mothers' Allowances to Reserves in Ontario, 1921–1940

This part of the chapter briefly reviews the history and significance of the extension of the provincial Mother's Allowance to Ontario Indian reserves. The Ontario Mothers' Allowance was the result of a widespread campaign by women's organizations in the post–First World War period for the provision of state benefits to destitute, principally fatherless, families. Although initially resistant to the idea, Ontario and many other provinces could not defend the inequity 'caused by war pensions being available for families made dependent by the war, but not others similarly poor.'[35] Also, the province was anxious to encourage women to leave their wartime workplaces and go home to replace the diminished 'stock of healthy males.'[36] The Ontario Needy Mothers' Allowances Act was passed in 1920 and instituted in October of that year.[37]

Shortly after Ontario began administering Mothers' Allowances, W.G. Frisby, the executive secretary of the Mothers' Allowances Commission, wrote to Duncan Campbell Scott enclosing a copy of the legislation and asking him to determine whether any widowed Indian women were eligible for the allowance.[38] Scott then sent a general letter of inquiry to all Indian agents in Ontario, detailing the basic conditions of eligibility for the allowance and asking them to advise him whether there were any women on their reserves who might qualify.[39] At the same time, he wrote to A.S. Williams, the department's legal clerk, asking his opinion about the legislation and the eligibility of Indian women for the allowance.[40]

Williams took over a month to reply. His letter was a seminal, early statement of some of the issues concerning federal and provincial responsibility for Indian persons and the applicability of provincial laws on reserves. He wrote, in part:

> Indians residing outside of a reserve would, I feel sure, come within its provisions because they are then in the same position as any other resident of the province, but it is very doubtful if Indians residing on a reserve would come within it and I am inclined to think that they would not.
>
> There is nothing in the said Act specifically debarring the Indians from its benefit, but I do not think that this Act was intended to apply or would apply to those living in any territory situate within the province over which the laws of the province generally do not apply. Under this Act one half of the allowance paid by the Province is charged against the Municipality in which the person who receives such allowance resides, and as the Indian reserves and the Indians residing thereon are not subject to municipal taxation ... I do not think that such Indians would be considered as residing within the municipality within the meaning of this Act.
>
> The Commission ... may take a different view of the matter and be dis-

posed to treat the Indians as all other residents of the province. If the Commission were disposed to grant an allowance to some Indian women ... it would bring the matter to an issue for determination.[41]

Williams's letter identified three key issues in arguments that would emerge between the federal and provincial governments concerning constitutional responsibility for and jurisdiction over Indians.[42] First, he stated that an Indian living off reserve was, in effect, a citizen of the province and entitled to the same benefits as any other resident of that province. An Indian living on reserve, however, immediately raised the question of whether provincial laws applied to lands and people often considered outside provincial jurisdiction. Second, he raised the problem of defining laws of general applicability. Was a law generally applicable to Indians if the province said so and if certain conditions were met – in this case, the test of municipal status? Third, by stating that the province could decide to make Indians eligible to apply, he was implying that social welfare was a matter of provincial jurisdiction and that only the province could decide on eligibility. In making this statement – however obvious it might have sounded – Williams was raising the possibility that the provinces might be responsible for Indian social services.

Scott wrote to Frisby in late March 1921, stating that he understood, through his own representatives, that the province was prepared to extend Mothers' Allowances to reserves. He asked Frisby to confirm this, and inquired whether local governments would be responsible for half the cost of the Indian allowances as specified under the act.[43] Frisby replied in great detail, outlining the critical provisions of the act and the municipal and county jurisdictions responsible for payment. Indian reserves, he noted, did not generally fall within these recognized jurisdictions: 'Moreover, it does not seem fair that municipalities which receive little revenue from a Reserve should be taxed for the allowances of beneficiaries within the Reserve.'

Like many others, Frisby seemed to be ignoring that residents of reserves close to cities and towns contributed much to the local economy and indirectly to the tax base as customers of the local merchants. In fact, much Indian relief was probably a direct boon to many municipalities. Nevertheless, how could the letter of the law find Indian women eligible for Mothers' Allowances if Indian reserves could not be considered eligible for cost sharing? Frisby's letter made a bold proposal: 'May I ask you therefore ... so that the matter may be placed before the Commission if the Dominion Government would, through your Department, consider assisting the Province in this matter and relieving the municipalities or the Province from the payment of an amount which represents half the amount of allowances granted to beneficiaries resident on Reserves within the several Counties.'[44] Scott did not challenge Frisby's assertion that reserves did not generate revenues for local municipalities. Instead, he simply replied positively on 25 April 1921: 'I think that if any allowances are given to Indian mothers under your Act that the Department should become responsible for the payment of the moiety which is provided to be paid by the municipality. Where Indian bands have trust funds which are sufficient to bear the contribution it will be charged to such funds, but in other cases the Department will supply the amount from Parliamentary appropriation.'[45] This correspondence set in motion what was to become a unique relationship between the federal and Ontario governments with respect to Indian social services, and one that Ottawa subsequently hoped would become the basis for Indian welfare policy in other provinces.

Why was this agreement important to Indian social welfare and to federal Indian policy? Visible in Frisby's letter are the roots of Ontario's position concerning the applicability of provincial welfare law on Indian reserves. As long as reserve communities or the federal government could fulfil municipalities' financial responsibilities, provincial services could be extended. Apparently, Ontario was less concerned about the constitutional implications of its position on Indian social services than it was about the ability of reserves to pay their way.

From Ottawa's perspective, the extension of provincial services offered two possibilities: the reduction of direct relief costs through cost sharing, and the furtherance of Indian assimilation through absorption into Ontario social policy. Since 1884 the federal government, through the Indian Advancement Act, had been trying to turn Indian band councils into quasi-municipal governments by granting 'advanced' bands powers beyond those accorded under the Indian Act. These efforts had met with stiff resistance from bands in Ontario and elsewhere, since they were seen as a further intrusion into traditional forms of government and as another attempt at assimilation.[46] It is reasonable to speculate that the powers of the superintendent general to access Indian trust funds for provision of relief,[47] together with Ontario's proposal to treat individual band members as if they were residents of a municipality, simply offered Ottawa an 'end around' method of pursuing the Indian Advancement Act's frustrated objectives.

Frisby quickly confirmed Scott's correspondence, stating that the commission had agreed to the proposed arrangement.[48] In October 1921 the first allowance was paid to a mother on the Cape Croker Indian Reserve. She received $10 per month, with half that sum remitted by the department to the province. By June 1922, seven mothers on reserves in Ontario were receiving the allowances. The number peaked in 1935 at seventy-one, but dropped to twenty-one the following year.[49] In 1937 – probably because of the strain on municipal finances during the Depression – the provincial act was amended so that the province paid 100 per cent of the costs. As a consequence, Ottawa made no contributions between 1 April 1937 and 31 March 1939. This manoeuvre affected the two governments' relationship, and after a complaint from the Ontario minister responsible for the commission, Ottawa made a retroactive payment of 50 per cent of the allowances during the two-year period.[50]

A new agreement was then reached: Indian Affairs would reimburse the province 100 per cent of the costs of the allowances paid to mothers on reserve, and Ontario would pay 100 per cent of the costs for those off reserve. By then, the monthly allowance paid to mothers in cities was $40, in towns $35, and in rural areas $30.[51] Under McGill's direction, Indian Affairs requested cancellation of the allowances in 1940 – presumably without consulting either the affected bands or the recipients. After that, Ottawa provided direct relief to families living on reserve, and Ontario ceased to pay the allowance to Indian mothers living off reserve.[52] McGill's extremely mean attitudes toward relief probably contributed to Indian Affairs' eventual withdrawal from the program. That being said, the program's initial success in extending provincial welfare services to reserves made it a model for the era of postwar citizenship. The program also worked well as a tool for integrating Indians into Euro-Canadian society.

The Special Parliamentary Committee on Postwar Reconstruction and Re-Establishment: The Indian Population, 1944

Mackenzie King's Liberal government was concerned about the social and economic security of postwar Canada. A country that had barely stirred from the Depression had been thrust into the Second World War without having reformed in any meaningful way either the relationship between capital and labour or the state's role in that relationship. The government's pressing fear was that after the economic boom generated by the war effort, the country would slip into another depression and that thousands of demobilized troops, on returning home to unemployment and poverty, would form the core of a social revolution. At home, these fears were exacerbated by rising public support for both the CCF and the Communist Party and by a powerful and socially conscious female labour force. Overseas, Canadian troops had learned quickly through contact with other allied soldiers that reforms in Britain and the United States had left Canada a backwater of social and economic injustice.[53]

Mindful of these pressures for reform, King pursued an artful course of appeasement that enabled him to appeal to both capital and labour without entirely satisfying either. During the war years, his government established a large number of research and advisory bodies and parliamentary committees, whose purpose was to make recommendations for Canada's postwar reconstruction.[54] Prominent among these was the special House of Commons Committee on Postwar Reconstruction and Re-establishment, formed in 1944 to hear testimony and receive briefs from government officials and interested organizations and individuals regarding issues affecting returning veterans. A special interest of this committee was the future of Canada's Indians.

In the literature on Canada–First Nations relations little mention is made of this committee's attention to Indian matters. Many writers have argued that it was the Joint Parliamentary Committee on Indian Affairs, appointed in 1946, that brought the 'forgotten Canadians' to prominent public awareness, but this was simply not the case.[55] By this time, many Canadians from all walks had some awareness of Indian issues, albeit within a narrow context. That being said, nothing compelled them to pressure for social justice. Aware they may have been, but most were either indifferent or too preoccupied with their own social security to be concerned about Indians. It was Indians' disproportionate numbers in the armed forces that changed public attitudes toward egalitarianism. By war's end, the principles of collective citizenship had awakened a more profound discomfort about Canada's public policies toward its First Nations.

Indian matters came to the committee's attention because of its responsibility to inquire into the needs of Canada's returning veterans. By early 1944, 2,383 Indian adults had enlisted in the armed forces – about 2 per cent of the total registered population.[56] Available evidence indicates that the committee conducted hearings on Indian Affairs over two days, on 18 and 24 May 1944. The 18 May hearings focused mainly on Indian Affairs' initiatives in assisting the fur trade, on fur conservation, and on how to protect Indian lands and trap lines[57] from white competition. There was also some discussion of general employment opportunities for Indians off reserve, including an unchallenged claim by one senior Indian Affairs official that there were almost no unemployed Indians in Canada.[58] By day's end, having recognized that the fur trade would not ensure First Nations' economic salvation, the committee had begun discussing Indian home industry – in particular the economic viability of handicrafts.

The Indian Affairs Branch under Public Scrutiny

The hearings of the following week resulted in heated controversy and a swarm of press comment and public correspondence concerning the status of Canada's Indian peoples. The committee, it seemed, was not so accepting of the previous week's testimony, during which the department had tried to paint a somewhat optimistic picture of its policies and of the benefits that Indians were daily deriving from them. On the second day, 24 May, the primary witnesses before the committee were T.R.L. MacInnes, the secretary for the Indian Affairs Branch and McGill's immediate junior, and R.A. Hoey, the superintendent of Training and Welfare Services. MacInnes, according to his own testimony, had been with Indian Affairs for thirty-two years; Hoey was a former education minister in Manitoba. The chief questioners were George H. Ross, MP for Calgary East, and Dorise Nielsen, a CCF MP from Saskatchewan.[59]

Early questioning, which set the tone for the day, placed Indian Affairs on the defensive – a role to which it was obviously not accustomed. Ross began by asking MacInnes about the actual relationship between the government of Canada and the First Nations, the level of autonomy – especially judicial – granted to Indian bands, and how it compared with that in the United States. Ross was clearly impressed by the American policy, which permitted a limited exercise of tribal justice. MacInnes replied in vague terms that Indians exercised a level of autonomy under the general supervision of the Indian Act and a somewhat higher level under the Indian Advancement Act.

With respect to justice, MacInnes said that he understood from his own conversations with the Indian commissioner in the United States that the system there did not work well. The Indians reportedly played one system off against the other, using whichever one best suited their purposes at the time. Visibly irritated with this answer, Ross shot back:

In 1934, President Roosevelt, speaking about Indian Affairs, used these words: 'Certainly the continuance of autocratic rule by a federal department over the lives of more than 200,000 citizens of this nation is incompatible with American ideals of liberty. It is also destructive of the character and self-respect of a great race.'

Then ... in 1940 the Commissioner of Indian Affairs in making his report speaks of the Indian way of disciplining their own members, he speaks of working out satisfactorily.[60]

This statement seems to have rattled MacInnes, who danced around it. Moments before, he had derided the American system; now he stated that he was not really at liberty or qualified to speak about it. He then claimed that Canada's Indian population was too small and scattered for such a system, and that in any case, Indians in Brantford, Ontario, for example, would nearly always choose Canadian justice over their own.[61] Some unpleasant cracks were beginning to appear in the department's testimony, and the committee knew it.

The focus of the questions moved to Indian education. Nielsen took a powerful, uncompromisingly critical position. Considerable discussion followed regarding the appropriate setting for Indian education (residential versus day), its compulsory nature under the Indian Act, and its funding, including per capita amounts for children. On this last point, Nielsen raised a sore issue when she quoted a brief submitted by a church committee on Indian education:

In the days of the depression, cuts were made in the per capita and were progressively restored ... This restoration did not last very long, and by unilateral action an arbitrary cut in the authorized pupilage was made ... retroactive from January 1, 1940, so that no school can be paid 100% of its attendance ... Without discussing the need of economy, the churches would point out that the sufferers are either the Indian children, who must be denied an education, – or the churches who ... must devote some of their resources to seeing to it that the Indian children have an opportunity for an education ... the government should remember that this is ... elementary education, and that the very thing for which the United Nations are fighting is being denied to Indian children.[62]

Hoey tried to blame the Depression era cuts on the federal finance minister and the general climate of austerity. However, he could offer no explanation for the reintroduction of cuts in 1940. Nielsen had made an important point. She then moved on to the objectives of Indian education generally, and for girls in particular:

> I ... remember talking last summer ... to an archdeacon of the English church who was looking after Indian ... schools and I was ... appalled at his attitude ... He complained of the numbers of girls whom they educate in their schools ... He said, 'Of course, we train them and ... they are best fitted for domestic service.' He said, 'We send these girls into good homes ... eventually they marry and go back into the reserve, and you should just see their homes after a little while.' It seems to me that there is something wrong with our whole attitude towards these young girls. Why should Indian girls be more fitted for domestic service than any other type of girl? Why should we not endeavour to fit these young girls ... in the usual life of the country and to go into various forms of service?[63]

This statement drew no response from either MacInnes or Hoey. However, it generated sympathetic comments among the other committee members. Nielsen continued:

> I am ... opposed to the idea of just educating the Indian people to take on the rough kind of work. Why not give them every opportunity and facility, if they are capable of absorbing it? I do not like the attitude ... so many people seem to have towards the Indian people, that they will educate them to a certain limit, and then if they go back to the reserve ... it is through some fault of the Indians themselves. I do not believe that it is. The reason ... many of these girls ... revert ... to ... slatternly sort of women when they go back to the reservations is that they have not the economic means of keeping a home. It is not any fault of the Indians themselves.[64]

A committee member asked her what could be done about it. Nielsen's reply and subsequent comments, soon to be echoed by many, touched on the core objective of Indian policy in the postwar period: equal opportunity in education and employment to enable social integration:

> Break down a lot of the prejudice, and see that Indian people have the same right of employment as anybody else; see that the girls do not have to go back to the reserves but that gradually the younger generation of the Indian people are absorbed into the life of Canada, that they live in cities like the rest of us. I think that speaking of that younger generation of

Indian people, we should bring them up to take their part in the general life of this country and forget about the reserves. You [Mr Hoey] spoke about the Indians having freedom and not being wards of the government. In my opinion they have the same kind of freedom that there is when men are free to sleep under bridges ... or on park benches ... In this church brief ... they have ... the kernel of the whole problem. They say among Indian people, 'There is no pressure of public opinion which looks on illiteracy as a disgrace nor can either the Indian parent or the Indian child be as sure as the white that education is likely to be of any economic advantage.' They do not care about education. Many of them feel why should they care, and go back to the reservation. I think that is our fault because we have not made it as easy for them as it is for our own people to get out into ordinary civilized life.[65]

Nielsen recommended a complete change in Indian policy, which she described at that time as 'still in the horse and buggy stage [while] the rest of the world has gone by.' Then she addressed Hoey directly, drawing him to her side with a sympathetic olive branch: 'I have no quarrel with the officials of the department. I think they are doing the best they can under the circumstances ... You cannot do many things you think should be done.' Hoey was moved. 'It is the toughest task I have ever undertaken,' he said, 'the most discouraging. There is no sense of appreciation, no sense of recognition.' A committee member interjected: 'You mean by the white people?' 'By anybody,' Hoey replied. 'I got a letter from an Indian woman ... Her boy was killed overseas and I enlarged a photo snap and sent it ... to her ... I got a letter of appreciation from that woman, and that is the first letter of appreciation I got from any source in the department in eight years.'[66]

Hoey's comments were remarkable because they laid bare the relentlessly authoritarian structure that permeated the Indian Affairs Branch and its treatment of Indians and staff alike. A field agent stood to lose his job at the least sign of disagreement or disobedience; the junior layers of the headquarters staff had to be just as wary. The department was so infused with this culture of unswerving loyalty that no one dared voice a new point of view; indeed, no one at any level of its structure thought it possible. What was required was precisely a vehicle like the committee – that is, a sanctioned group that was free to ask questions, to level criticisms, and to probe for dissent and the possibility of change.

Any idea that Hoey had been shedding crocodile tears was dispelled by MacInnes's testimony. MacInnes was of the old guard, a man who required complete control of every situation, and a man with more opinions about Indians and what was best for them than was probably advisable for a government official in a public inquiry. It was Nielsen's comments about what had to be done that eventually captured the imagination of the media and the public, but it was MacInnes's that inspired a furore as well as a debate on the future of First Nations in Canada.

MacInnes opened the second part of his testimony with a lengthy statement about what a fine race he thought the Indian people were. He declared that in his long association with Indians, he had found that the Indian 'as an individual is equal to the individual of any other race in the world in his potentialities and possibilities, his mental, spiritual and cultural equipment.'[67] He went on to describe what he thought were good examples of successful Indians: the high steelworkers of Caughnawaga (Kahnawake) and the fishermen of the West Coast. 'There is fair proof,' he said, 'that the Indian can get along pretty well if he is out on his own and uses his own self-reliance and initiative: but it is very true that there is a depressing and retarding reserve psychology, a substandard economy.'[68] Mr McDonald, MP for Pontiac, asked him if he thought this was due to an inferiority complex. 'It is a dependency complex,' MacInnes replied. Some discussion followed around the problem of dependency. To help the committee understand the problem, MacInnes, adopting the role of mentor, depicted a relationship between dependency, the existence of reserves, and the future of Indian policy. It would be a depiction he would not forget. The reserve, he said,

was established to provide for [the Indian] a place where he could be protected against despoliation and exploitation. It was a sincere ... move, and it was for a good reason that it was done. But while it may be still necessary as a protective measure in western Canada where the Indians have only been 75 years or less in contact with whites to any extent, where they have not really overcome the first shock of their contact with civilization, on the other hand, in eastern Canada, where the Indians have been in organized districts and familiar with the white man and white man's ways and general life of the community for 200 or 300 years, there does not seem to be any justification for our staying in the Indian reserve business. It is retarding them. Its value is weakening. It is like the child who has passed the weaning stage. If you try to keep him pap fed from then on, he will sicken and deteriorate. Those Indians in eastern Canada ... should be divorced from the reserve system entirely and put on their own. It is their only salvation ... It would be good if we had a little push from the legislative body to do something ... to speed up ... the process of making the Indians a regular part of the Canadian community, without any separate ... substandard special status.[69]

MacInnes's remarks instantly provoked press comment and a flurry of public debate. Editorials and radio newscasts took him to task; letters to the editor in the country's major papers expressed varying points of view about reserves and Indian policy. Charles Camsell, Deputy Minister of Mines and Resources, wrote to McGill, demanding that he caution MacInnes concerning his remarks.[70] McGill defended MacInnes, saying that the press had 'stretched' his testimony and that he had nowhere suggested a change in policy. At any rate, McGill concluded, was MacInnes to be instructed what to say or not to say to a parliamentary committee?[71] Camsell was furious. He firmly rebuked McGill and said that as a public servant, MacInnes ought to have known what opinions he could or could not express in public. There was no justification for MacInnes to have offered an opinion on the subject of reserves, Camsell wrote.[72]

But the damage had been done. The department's problems, the failure of its policies, its inertia, and its inability to modernize the relationship between Canada and the First Nations were in full public view. The committee subsequently received many letters from the public expressing views on the situation of 'Canada's Indians.' Whether they thought that the government had 'kept the Indian down' or that the Indian had to 'bring himself' into the twentieth century, they were unanimous in one view: the solution for Canada's Indians lay in their full integration into Canadian life.[73]

The committee, for its part, found no fault with the Indian Affairs Branch, which, it thought, performed its job tirelessly, with inadequate funding and with little interest or knowledge shown by the government or the House of Commons. At one point, a committee member had said to Hoey: 'I think the committee wants to help you. We have never had an opportunity like this before to get the background of what you are up against. Every year the Departmental estimates come in and they are very meagre. Very likely you do not ask enough. Perhaps you have not been asking the government to do what you would envision should be done yourself.'[74] As was described throughout the previous chapter, the fault of funding lay precisely with the department's legacy of meanness and unwillingness to present its case – and thus the plight of Indian peoples – strongly to Treasury Board. Every Indian Affairs official had been carefully schooled in economy and thrift. Still, the uniqueness of its work allowed the branch to turn criticism into sympathy and provided its public critics with a way to avoid acknowledging their own implicit collusion.

The New Voice of Canada

On balance, the committee was a positive force. At the conclusion of its hearings it called for a complete parliamentary inquiry into the subject of Indian administration in Canada.[75] There can be no doubt that this call and the publicity generated by the hearings in part prompted King to create the 1946 Special Joint Parliamentary Committee on the Indian Act. What appeared in the work of the committee on reconstruction – and especially in Nielsen's comments – was a reflection of the changing Euro-Canadian society of the mid-1940s. Nielsen embodied the new voice of Canada and the evolution of the liberal state from its protective to its developmental function. Hers was the voice of secularism, of social science and human development. She spoke directly to those principles espoused by Mill and Dewey – individual equality of citizenship and opportunity, and the power of education to liberate, self-actualize, and empower. Her opinions, though generous and humanistic, were derived from the liberal vision of individual freedom, and they were intended to inspire Indians to obtain their social and economic welfare as free and equal individuals in the democratic state.

At a different level, and with the benefit of knowing recent history,[76] it is possible to understand that Nielsen was not speaking to Indian hopes at all, but rather to the hopes of Euro-Canadians in the postwar period. Moreover, her aspirations for Indians were another product of Euro-Canadians talking to other Euro-Canadians about what was best for Indians. Indians were talked about, but none was heard from. It is curious that the committee members could not perceive this contradiction, even at the time. Even as they decided that Indians needed equality of citizenship, the implication was that Indians were inferior. This thinking simply reformulated postwar paternalism at a more acceptable level and set Indian Affairs on a new, but paradoxically familiar, course of custodial intervention.

The Appalling State of Indian Health

Dr Percy Moore's testimony before the committee, and his recommendations, would, in tandem with Nielsen's articulation of basic developmental principles, become central to postwar policy objectives for Indians. Dr Moore was the superintendent of medical services for Indian Affairs; his extensive research into Indian health and nutrition would soon become critical to the 'health and welfare' ethos that was beginning to guide the department's thinking. Dr Moore appeared on 24 May in the afternoon and presented the committee with an overview of the medical services administration and the general status of Indian health. His testimony did much to expose how the profound neglect and parsimony of the Indian Affairs administration was exacerbating Indians' poverty, despair, and sense of denigration, especially in British Columbia and in the country's remote northern areas.

Moore began by stating that on the whole, the medical services available to Indians in the south were quite adequate. The problems arose farther north, where hospitals were fewer (there were fifteen hospitals throughout the entire administration) and doctors and nurses were scarcely available.[77] Moore described a desperate situation; as many as thirty Indian bands, accounting for as many as 1,200 people, received a visit from a doctor for half a day once a year if they were lucky. Many of the bands received a doctor's visit of the same duration once every two or three years.[78] Dr Moore stated that although the problem of adequate medical care was critical, the real issue was one of public health and health education, since the diseases his administration spent most of its time treating – tuberculosis, trachoma, and venereal and nutritional deficiency diseases – were preventable. At one point in his testimony, Dr Moore provided statistics from British Columbia showing an Indian tuberculosis mortality rate ten to seventeen times the provincial average. He also provided data, pulled from recent studies and case reports across the Canadian north, that indicated the presence of almost every known disease related to nutrition deficiency.[79] The only exceptions were scurvy, pellagra and beriberi.

Dr Moore's testimony, unlike any before it, gave the committee members an absolutely frank and straightforward account of living conditions and health standards among First Nations. What were becoming internationally famous studies on nutrition provided indisputable evidence to back his argument that the Indian Affairs Branch must be modernized and properly funded. Dr Moore testified: 'In 1942 a study was made ... of the food habits and state of nutrition of some 400 Indians at Norway House. The foods eaten consisted largely of white flour, lard, sugar, tea, fish and game, the fish and game usually not being plentiful. The diet was markedly deficient in most of the vitamins and some of the minerals.'[80] What the committee did not know, and what the doctor refrained from saying, was that this diet was standard relief issue.

Dr Moore proposed four structural solutions to Indian health problems. First, a properly funded Indian health service should remain under the Indian Affairs Branch, where it would be integral to overall Indian Affairs administration and to the intersecting problems of Indian policy. He opposed the idea of including Indian health services under the Department of Pensions and National Health, although he firmly believed that Indian health and medical services should be equal to those provided to every other Canadian.[81] Second, the availability of Indian medical services should be expanded by adapting the Australian 'flying doctor' model to Canada's north. Third, a nursing service should be created for the reserves that, besides providing a basic level of health care, could accomplish the more important tasks of health education and promotion. It could also develop needed programs such as nutritious school lunches. Besides this, either the Indian Affairs Branch or the provinces should hire welfare officers, who could be given special training to work with Indian peoples and thus assist the nurses in their work.[82] Fourth, his team of medical experts should keep conducting nutritional studies. This was important, Dr Moore believed, because the studies of Indian nutrition in the James Bay region of Ontario and Manitoba were beginning to form the basis of a comprehensive plan for improving the overall health and living standards of First Nations throughout Canada.

In Moore's testimony can be detected the methodology needed to actualize Nielsen's vision of Indians as full citizens of Canada – that is, the methods of medical and social science. Indeed, he had identified the need for trained welfare workers and public health nurses as critical to Indians' future. But his nutrition studies did more than that; they inspired an awakening of academic interest in Indian psychology, sociology, and anthropology such that by the end of the 1940s, the country's universities were entertaining Indian research proposals and clamouring for grants in unprecedented numbers.[83] Dr Moore represented the new, professional voice of the bureaucracy. Indian Affairs administrators had failed so far, but not because their objectives had been the wrong ones. Rather, they had failed because they had been insufficiently guided and informed, and as a result they did not fully understand the difficulties facing Indians in their adjustment to civilization. Like any modern institution, the Indian Affairs Branch needed a base of scientific knowledge on which to build successful programs for Indian integration. This base could be developed by hiring more professionals and by securing the consultation and independent research of leading academics. Postwar Canada was poised to provide it with both kinds of people.

Active Resistance: The Jules Sioui Affair, 1943–1944[84]

The challenges the department most resented, and that it tried to deal with most firmly, were those initiated by the First Nations. This is not surprising. After all, Indians were not a typical client group; in the recesses of historical consciousness, they were a group that had to be tamed and managed lest they begin entertaining thoughts of asserting old ways and reclaiming old lands. The state's anxiety over armed or political Indian uprisings had never gone away, and it continued to drive in irrational ways the government's responses to perfectly rational objections to wardship, tutelage, and the denial of historical rights.

The interwar regimes of Scott and McGill set an especially harsh tone when it came to dealing with Indian political protest. Of course, from the state's perspective there was good reason for harshness. In the minds of men like Scott and McGill – and of their overseeing superintendents – it was not logical to permit dissent if the state's ultimate objective was, in effect, the annihilation of the First Nations. Acknowledgment of the aims of Indian political organizations would have amounted to a contradiction to that objective as well as a tacit admission that Canada's Indian policy had failed. Force was no longer the immediate method of quelling Indian protest, nor was it necessary; administrative and legal coercion served the same purpose. Thus, whenever Indians organized politically or mobilized legal resources to press land claims and fishing and hunting rights, the senior bureaucracy usually tried to frustrate or discredit their leadership and their causes.[85]

Various strategies were employed by headquarters to minimize protest and any disruption of the 'efficiency' of the Ottawa administration. Indian delegations were actively discouraged from visiting Ottawa. This was accomplished through Ottawa's insistence that the Indian agents deal with complaints and dissent locally and, if this proved impossible, by subverting the dissent itself. The method of subversion was nearly always the same. Regarding the public, Ottawa would seek to divide the Indian community into 'good' and 'bad' Indians. The 'good' Indians were in the majority; they were loyal and trying hard to advance themselves and be like their white brothers. The 'bad' Indians were prey to outside agitators who either were not Indians or were influential Indians who had lost their 'Indianness' and might be considered white.[86] These strategies had limited success during the 1920s; however, they gained effectiveness after a 1927 amendment to the Indian Act forbade bands to pay lawyers or organizers to make claims against the government.[87] The amendment effectively restricted Indian political organization beyond the band level.

McGill's deputy superintendency reinforced the authoritarian and imperious approach of his predecessor, Scott. Scott had issued a circular early in his administration that set the course for his nineteen-year tenure; in the same way, McGill on assuming office issued a statement after he had assumed office that clearly specified his direction:

> For some time there has been a progressive increase in the number of letters received direct from Indians on reserves, both by the Honourable the Superintendent General and at this office, concerning matters which should come before the Indian Agent in the first instance. This practice of Indians attempting to deal directly with the Department is undesirable as it involves unnecessary waste of time and interferes with despatch and order in the [conduct] of official business ... The Indians should be instructed to bring matters that concern them to the attention of the Agents.[88]

Major Harold Wigmore McGill, MD, was a politician and surgeon from Calgary, Prime Minister Bennett's hometown. Just before his appointment he had been a sitting Conservative MLA in the Alberta legislature.[89] The archival documents suggest a bigoted, authoritarian man. In this sense he was like Scott, albeit without Scott's depth or cunning. He seemed incapable of introspection or discourse, and he hid behind the trappings of his office to keep Indians at bay. At worst, he seemed not in the least interested in First Nations and thought their existence a complete nuisance, an aggravation that interfered with his administration. At best, he thought that Indians, who were at the bottom of the Indian Affairs hierarchy, should accept with simple gratitude the state largesse extended to them. The above directive, then, was entirely consistent with the barriers McGill would erect to keep Indians in abject subjugation and away from the locus of power. Not surprisingly, First Nations' testimony during the 1946 Special Joint Parliamentary Committee identified this directive, more than any other, as representing the extent to which they had been politically repressed and left without rights or recourse beyond their Indian agents.[90]

McGill and his senior colleagues thought that Indians would behave in an insatiable manner if their complaints were heard or satisfied. Furthermore, they believed that their complaints were either ill founded or the result of their own intrigues. The following excerpt, from an early 1941 memorandum to his deputy minister concerning an investigation of complaints at the St-Regis (Akwesasne) reserve near Montreal, captures the essence of McGill's attitude:

> The chief contributing factor to the difficulty of administering this agency is the ... intrigue that goes on among the members of the band. It is probable also that the Indian Affairs Branch has been over considerate in receiving delegations and listening to complaints ... Delegations of Indians should be received only by pre-arrangement with the Indian Agent, and as a rule the agent should accompany any ... Indians desiring audience. The holding of investigations and the patient reception given delegations of Indians only tends to bring forth more complaints and dissatisfaction with existing conditions.[91]

His letter did not deal with merits of the complaints, only with the nature of the complainants. By the end of the year, McGill had issued a general notice to Indian agents – especially to those responsible for Mohawk agencies in eastern Canada – which, he instructed, 'you should display in a conspicuous place in your Indian office':

– NOTICE –

INDIANS VISITING OTTAWA WILL NOT BE GRANTED INTERVIEWS WITH DEPARTMENTAL OFFICIALS UNLESS SUCH INTERVIEWS HAVE BEEN ARRANGED BY THE INDIAN AGENT, OR UNLESS INDIANS SEEKING SUCH INTERVIEWS ARE ACCOMPANIED BY THE AGENT HIMSELF. OBSERVANCE OF THIS REGULATION, BY INDIANS, WILL AVOID UNNECESSARY EXPENSE AND INCONVENIENCE.

DIRECTOR.[92]

The letter was a form letter adapted to each agency's particular circumstances. Indian Agent A.D. Moore was told that while there had been no problem with the Tyendinaga (Mohawks of the Bay of Quinte) he should nevertheless impress upon them the meaning of the notice. The agents for Caughnawaga, Oka, and St-Regis were told unequivocally that Indians were to be discouraged from visiting Ottawa 'to discuss matters of a trivial character and matters that should be discussed by them with the agent.'

The Conventions

In 1943, in this context of political repression and the general neglect of First Nations, Indian resistance began to mount to its greatest intensity since the mid-1920s. The catalyst was concern about their rights with respect to compulsory military service and exemption from income taxation. Sometime in August or September 1943, Jules Sioui, a member of the Huron Nation and chief executive of the Comité de Protection des Droits Indiens, issued a general, bilingual notice of invitation to the chiefs of all First Nations in Canada (see Document 5.1). The notice was quickly brought to McGill's attention by one of the agents.

Even though this committee – in light of the restrictions imposed by the Indian Act – had carefully proposed an independent meeting to be funded entirely through the delegates' donations, McGill issued a stern warning to all Indian agents across the country:

> The person who signed the circular is not a chief of the Jeune Lorette Band. He is an agitator and trouble-maker with whom the department has had a great deal of difficulty over a considerable period. Although he is a member of the band and an Indian under the law, he is physiologically a white man with no perceptible Indian characteristic ... There are many of these legal Indians who retain their status because of paternal descent, but who actually have lost all trace of Indian blood. They are often the most prominent among the leaders of movements in support of alleged ancient Indian rights and other claims ... I sincerely hope that none of the Indians of your agency will waste their time and money by travelling to this meeting or becoming involved in ... Mr. Sioui's organization.[93]

Sioui had not claimed to be chief of the Jeune Lorette band, but McGill, in his fervour to discredit him, had misread the notice. In McGill's letter can be seen wonderful evidence of the state being hoist on its own petard. It was surely not Sioui's fault that the Indian Act defined him as an Indian. McGill had operated on Euro-Canadian assumptions and popular images about what Indians ought to look like rather than on who Indians actually were.

Sioui, then, was a 'bad' Indian out to dupe the 'good' Indians who were not yet sufficiently advanced to recognize a crook in their midst.

Document 5.1 Notice to all chiefs issued by Jules Sioui, English portion

---

PROVINCE DE QUÉBEC

CANADA

COMITÉ DE PROTECTION DES DROITS INDIENS

Quartiers généraux au Village Huron de Lorette

Head chief:–

This letter advises you that a general meeting of the chiefs of our Nation will take place in Ottawa, on the 19th day of October next. I do claim the presence, at Windsor Hotel, of two or three delegates from each one of our reserves.

The impact of these perilous moments compels us to draw-up serious reforms. We have to establish such reforms in order to put a betterment in the Indian situation, and this, without delay, if we want the maintenance of our rights in our proper country.[a]

A urgent affirmative answer is requested. A financial help will be welcome as this rally and the works to be performed are very expensive and their cost rests rather heavily on our shoulders.

Sincerely,

JULES SIOUI,
chef exécutif du – C.P. – chief executive,
Case postale Loretteville P.O.B.,
Comté de Québec County.

Source: Adapted from NAC, RG-10, Red Series, Vol. 3212, File 527,787-4, Indian Conventions Held in Ottawa 19–21 October 1943 and 5–7 June 1944.
[a]The phrase 'our proper country' was apparently a literal translation from the French. The closest meaning in English – significantly – is 'our *own country*.'

This was clearly a time for Indian agents to exercise their custodial duties. But there was far more at stake here than 'good' and 'bad' Indians. These were merely images based on ideology. The real problem, which was understood but not well articulated, was the falsification of history. Every time the possibility of sustained Indian protest arose, there was the real threat that history would be reconciled with the truth and that Indian policy would be exposed for its complicity in Indian dispossession.

The Indian agents complied faithfully with McGill's directive, agreeing with his assessment of Sioui and assuring him that they were discouraging their Indians from attending. These attempts to undermine the October conference succeeded only in part. Attendance was low but not insubstantial. The conference also attracted a great deal of favourable press. The Ottawa *Evening Citizen* reported that several of the delegates met briefly with J.W. Pickersgill, Prime Minister King's private secretary, with whom they left a petition demanding that their rights relating to military service and income tax be observed. Other papers reported that some delegates met with J.A. MacKinnon acting for the absent Thomas Crerar, the Minister of Mines and Resources, who was responsible for Indian Affairs. MacKinnon made no concessions, however; he simply reiterated the government's position that Indians were British subjects and liable to military service.[94] Nevertheless, Sioui had achieved a modicum of success. He and the delegates felt optimistic, and they announced that a follow-up conference would be held in June 1944.

The battle lines were drawn. The McGill administration was determined to undermine Sioui and the chiefs and to prevent the June conference from being held. At the very least it wanted to stop the delegates from seeing any government officials. McGill apparently thought his future depended on his ability to protect his minister from embarrassment. On 24 May, using the opportunity presented by the Special Committee on Postwar Reconstruction, T.R.L. MacInnes introduced Sioui into his testimony on dependency and Indian reserves. 'Do you know that in Quebec,' MacInnes asked rhetorically, 'there are reserves where there is hardly a person with a dark complexion, where many of the people have red hair, blue eyes, freckled faces and speak French?'[95] Referring specifically to Ancienne-Lorette, Sioui's home, he continued:

That reserve is made up of Hurons who were survivors of the mission of Lalemant and Bréboeuf[*sic*] ... They have been bred absolutely white. They are completely miscegenated. There is no trace of Indian about them. Yet they talk about their Indian rights and their ancient Indian history. One of their number who styles himself as a leader of all the Indians of Canada, who is going to bring a big convention of Indians here, Jules Sioui, is no more of an Indian than I am; not nearly so much so, to my mind. I am sure I have a lot more Indian about me than he has.[96]

With the Sioui conference less than two weeks away, it was no wonder that Deputy Minister Camsell was furious about MacInnes's remarks; he had given Sioui more ammunition for Indian rights than probably Sioui could have thought possible, and in doing so he had publicly embarrassed the government.

The next day, the department issued a new circular to the field drawing its agents' attention to the September 1943 letter and again cautioning them about the dangers of Sioui and 'his so-called Indian Protection Committee.'[97] Indians of their agencies were again to be advised not to attend the meeting, because it would be a waste of their time and money. The circular then attempted to invoke loyalty to higher authority:

> In the name of the Minister of Mines and Resources ... it is their patriotic duty ... to remain at home and do their utmost to assist in the war effort, and to refrain from travelling across the country at the beck and call of any agitator ...
>
> It is felt that the better and more representative Indians who are loyal and respectable members of the community would not wish to cause unnecessary annoyance to the government at a time when all attention ... should be directed towards the great drive for victory.[98]

These invocations obviously fell on deaf ears. On 5 June 1944 the convention began with two hundred delegates in attendance, including Sioui, Andrew Paull, a powerful Indian organizer from the Squamish band in British Columbia, and Chief John Tootoosis, a highly influential Cree from the Poundmaker reserve in Saskatchewan.[99] From the reports and correspondence on file, they were more than a match for the government. Despite flurries of memoranda from the branch warning various levels of authority not to receive them, the delegates managed to get the attention of the governor general's office. Unnerved by this audacity, the branch called in the Royal Canadian Mounted Police; but according to documents on file, the Mounties thought Sioui and his followers were well within their civil rights and did nothing to intervene.[100]

The convention took place around the time of the D-Day landings, and, of course, the media and the country as a whole were absorbed with the invasion and Canada's role in it. This made the public's interest in the convention all the more remarkable. As a vehicle for publicizing aboriginal rights, for establishing a new, First Nations national political organization, and for gaining the attention of the minister, Thomas Crerar, it was a ringing success. The *Journal* in Ottawa reported on 8 June:

A resolution asking that Dr Harold W. McGill director of the Indian Affairs Branch, Mines and Resources Department, be placed in some government department other than Indian Affairs was passed Wednesday afternoon by the convention of nearly 200 Canadian Indians at the Y.M.C.A. The move was requested on the grounds that 'our progress is hindered by his kind of administration.' The resolution will be presented to Prime Minister King, to Resources Minister Crerar and the Civil Service Commission.

During the afternoon session the Indians organized the North American Indian Brotherhood, an organization that will embrace all Canadian tribes and many United States and will keep Indian problems before the government ...

During the day the delegation met Resources Minister Crerar and presented protests against military call-up and income tax.[101]

Thomas Crerar was sixty-eight years old and soon to be appointed to the Senate. According to Rea, his views of First Nations peoples and of the Indian 'problem' were fairly conventional. Rea states that although Crerar had some understanding that Indian policy had failed, he had no idea what new direction Indian policy should take.[102] His speech to the delegates at the convention however, would seem somewhat to contradict Rea's assertion.

Crerar spoke to the delegation at some length. After seventy-seven years of Canadian Indian administration, the mere fact that he was present and that he delivered a prepared address was a significant concession. The First Nations had finally re-established what they considered a fundamental and historical right since the Royal Proclamation of 1763 – a direct link with the Crown.

Crerar's Speech: New Directions for Old Policy

Crerar's speech represented a major concession to the Indian leadership; it was also a clear indication of the King government's future direction in Indian Affairs. The text reveals that he had been thoroughly briefed about the recently concluded Committee on Reconstruction hearings. To emphasize Indians' dependence on the state and to set the context for the statement of intent to follow, he began with a review of Indian Affairs expenditures:

The Government today appropriates for Indian Administration over 5½ million dollars a year ... What struck me is this: as our Indian population increases and it is increasing, this burden will grow unless some satisfactory means can be found of making the Indians of Canada self-supporting or self-supporting in as large a degree as possible ... Now I am sure that the Indians are just as anxious as anyone else is to make their own livelihood, to become useful citizens in a country which, after all, is our common country. It may be, and doubtless is, true that your ancestors centuries ago roamed over this country and owned it, but in the process of time that changed and I think there is an obligation resting upon the people of Canada to see that the Indians are fairly treated and do everything possible to assist them to become useful citizens in the community ...

You may not agree with me, but I look forward to the time when the Indians of this country will become full citizens of Canada. I know that many of you do not wish to do that.[103]

There are several points worth gleaning from this wonderfully political text. Throughout the speech, Crerar referred to the Indian delegates in the third person. The thrust, conscious or not, was clear: Indians would remain objects of policy. His critical message – which he delivered obliquely – related to Indian sovereignty. First, he mythologized that sovereignty as something that had perhaps existed 'centuries ago.' This immediately asserted Euro-Canadian dominance; it took what had been real until very recent times and transformed it into a phenomenon submerged in time far beyond memory. He then observed that 'in the process of time that [ownership] changed' as though, like evolution itself, the shift had been the inevitable result of civilization and progress. He then stated his New Deal. Because Euro-Canadians owned the land, they now had a moral obligation to treat Indians fairly and to help them become, in the liberal, utilitarian sense, self-supporting citizens of the community – that is, of broad Canadian society. He further suggested that citizenship in the liberal sense was a contractual obligation: Indians had to reciprocate fair treatment with an honest effort to become 'useful' citizens.

Underlying the politeness of Crerar's speech was an unmistakeable message – that the issue of Indian sovereignty was dead. Indians, he implied, had a choice: they could become useful, self-reliant citizens of Canada, or they could languish in collective obscurity. Crerar was saying that whether Indians agreed or not, the objective of Indian policy would continue to be assimilation. The state would find more positive ways to achieve goals such as equality of opportunity and citizenship for Indians, but its basic policy would not change.

The Importance of the Sioui Convention

The great significance of the Sioui convention was that it happened at all. Not since the mid-1920s, when F.O. Loft led the League of Indians of Canada,[104] had the First Nations enjoyed a prominent national presence. However, the state's resolve to contain Indian political activity through the 1927 amendment to the Indian Act, coupled with its increasingly mean neglect of Indians, had created 'forgotten Canadians' who could overcome their condition of absolute oppression only through surrender to assimilation or through resistance and organized opposition.[105] Sioui was no fool; he understood Canada's changing mood. Quebec had bitterly resisted conscription in 1942, and in that previous battle for its rights, Sioui saw an analogy for Canada's First Nations. He correctly assumed that Canada's chiefs would respond positively to an appeal against the injustices suffered by their people. Thus, despite Ottawa's efforts to discredit the committee, the issues prevailed, as did the resolve of the First Nations to confront the state on them. Between 5 and 7 June 1944, the First Nations had presented their perspective on their problems in a full public forum, and the people of Canada had heard.

A second important outcome of the convention was the creation of the North American Indian Brotherhood (NAIB) which aimed to represent the broad interests of all Indian peoples in Canada and the United States. The formation of the NAIB amounted to a defiance of state restrictions on Indian political activity. Since the formation of the brotherhood in 1944, there has never *not* been a national First Nations organization for any significant period. As a national organization, the brotherhood lasted only six years, but the idea of such an organization stayed alive, and eventually resulted in the founding, in 1982, of the Assembly of First Nations.[106]

It can be argued that the three events – the committee hearings, the Sioui convention, and the founding of the NAIB – helped spark the federal government's reconsideration of its generally coercive strategies for bringing about assimilation. The government's awareness that a new relationship with First Nations was needed is evident in D.J. Allan's short note to a branch official who was visiting the Christian Island agency: 'The whole Jules Sioui affair requires to be handled with gloves, my own view being that to treat Indians harshly here would most certainly force them into an organization which is not particularly in favour at the moment.'[107] For one thing, if assimilation strategies obviously had been successful, there would not have been an Indian convention in Ottawa. For another, it was now abundantly clear that health and welfare problems on the reserves were the result of state neglect and underfunding. These problems could not be permitted to continue in such an obvious way.

The reserves, initially created to protect and educate Indians, were now part of the problem. The solution, from the state's perspective, was to develop programs that would enable Indians to leave the reserves and take their places in Canadian communities as equal, useful citizens. If such programs could be made to work, and if Indians could be made to feel an attachment to Canada, their spontaneous consent to civil society would follow. To achieve any of this, their confidence would have to be gained. This could be done, first, by instituting a full parliamentary inquiry into Indian Affairs, and second, by making an immediate gesture to show that a new era was at hand. Within the year, Dr Harold W. McGill had retired as director of Indian Affairs.

Conclusion

The previous chapter cited cases to illustrate how the Canadian state consolidated its control over Canada's First Nations. This chapter reviewed four episodes that contributed after the Second World War to a new direction in Indian policy (i.e., the extension of citizenship rights). Read together, these two chapters juxtapose the unalterable, inflexible administration of the earlier period against the rising tensions generated by new, external influences.

Relief expenditure between 1913 and 1944 can best be understood in terms of the state functions of control and coercion. The provision (or non-provision) of Indian relief was not a positive function of state legitimation; rather, it was meant to control Indian behaviour and coerce the able bodied into the marketplace. Indian relief was primarily a social expense, the purpose of which was to maintain the pacification achieved during the post-Confederation period and to teach Indians the principles of individual self-reliance, often through harsh measures. Relief was limited to minimal, monthly food rations and occasional plain, essential clothing. According to C.N.C. Roberts, shelter needs were considered only on an *ad hoc* basis, and even then were limited to a roll of tar paper or a window pane.[108]

The stringent market philosophy in administering relief policy brought little success; what success there was, was confined mainly to southeastern Canada – specifically, southern Ontario – where there was some access to employment, including jobs in the United States.[109] In the rest of the country, Euro-Canadian prejudices and the isolation of First Nations – especially farther north – resulted in the virtual confinement of Indians to their reserves.[110] The reserves took on the atmosphere of workhouses defined by geography rather than by walls. Just before and after the Second World War, thinking outside Indian Affairs came to see the reserves as part of the problem, although not in the same way that they had been in the post-Confederation era. Then, the reserves were to have formed part of the assimilating transition; indeed, they were to have disappeared as enfranchised Indians acquired individual portions of them or sold their portions to other buyers.[111] By the late 1930s, new observers began to see the reserves and the reserve policies of the Canadian government as the reasons that Indians were being held back. The reserves had bred slumlike conditions, ill health, despair, and suspicion. There were no employment opportunities on them, nor did they offer any access to technical training. Canada had created its own system of crushing apartheid.[112]

To a large degree, relief policies had masked the continuing lease or sale of Indian lands to settlers and capitalist interests,[113] and provided poor compensation for that and for the relentless incursion of whites into traditional Indian economies.[114] Indians were left with less and less viable land and with fewer economic tools for their collective welfare, and while this was playing out, relief policies turned their attention away from dispossession toward survival in the twentieth century. The government and the Indian affairs bureaucracy had knowingly orchestrated both these processes, not in a purely conspiratorial sense, but in response to the demands of an expanding capitalist state with both political and bureaucratic arms. Hawthorn alluded to this when he observed that the people who worked in Indian Affairs were white Canadians who, when they were not sitting at their desks as agents of the state, were citizens with allegiance to that state.[115] They thought in Euro-Canadian terms, and they consented to the state's fundamental social and economic objectives. Thus, the functions of the state bureaucracy and its bureaucrats were far from neutral; they sprang from the state's ideological hegemony.

In the first half of the twentieth century, many Canadians outside the Indian Affairs bureaucracy grew concerned about the extent of Indians' exclusion from Canadian society. As the notion of Canadian citizenship began to take hold in the interwar years, attention to the situation of

Indians increased, mainly among a somewhat disaffected element of the university-educated bourgeois.

In the early 1950s the English sociologist, T.H. Marshall, having reflected on the emerging welfare states, proposed a theory of social citizenship as the mediator between the equalizing tendencies of political democracy and the inequalities produced by capitalism. By the height of the postwar period, his argument had become the central ethos guiding liberal democratic thought. Marshall theorized, *ex post facto*, that the 'answer to the problem of capitalism versus democracy was the welfare state.'[116] He also posited that the welfare state was largely an invention of the twentieth century and was the final stage in the evolution of rights and responsibilities in liberal states. Political and civil rights had been well established by the late nineteenth century, he argued. In the twentieth, what was required was a concept of social rights, an institutionalized set of entitlements derived from belonging to the state and from exercising responsibilities associated with the state.[117]

Marshall remains a key point of departure in terms of understanding conceptions of citizenship. Turner observes, however, that in the context of the development of nation-states – not all of which are liberal – citizenship has become more difficult to typify, especially in light of the changes that global capitalism is bringing to how citizenship is constructed.[118] His discussion of problems associated with modern state citizenship is helpful in setting the context for Canada's Indian policy after the Second World War. Turner defines citizenship as 'that set of practices (juridical, political, economic and cultural) which define a person as a competent member of society, and which as a consequence shape the flow of resources to persons and social groups.'[119]

Turner carefully highlights the importance of 'practices.' Citizenship is as much a social construction, an active notion, as it is something bestowed or conferred. He also emphasizes citizenship as central to the question of equality and the distribution of wealth. He concludes that 'In general ... citizenship is ... about the nature of social membership within modern political collectivities.'[120] These statements immediately pose important questions with respect to First Nations as captive minorities within a white settler society. First, what is the measure of active membership? Second, how is attachment or belonging assessed? It follows from Turner's ideas about the practice of citizenship that the answers to these questions determine to some extent how resources are distributed to First Nations.

Turner is not unaware of this dilemma. He is careful to point out that the idea of modern citizenship is primarily a part of the history of the Western democracies. As such, it represents an aspect of classical thought in sociology – furthered by modern theorists like Parsons – as it struggled with the problems of alienation and urban industrialization: 'If the historical evolution of European societies had been from community to association, then we can see citizenship as a secularized version of the more primordial bonds of tradition, religion and locality. The emergence of citizenship is the emergence of those forms of social participation which are appropriate for a society ... no longer grounded in *Gemeinschaft* relations.'[121] The secularization of 'belonging' clearly went hand in hand with the evolution of the liberal state, and of the notions of contract, individual status, utility, participation, and choice. To the extent that citizenship was the result of the secular development of the modern nation-states, then it necessarily excluded those who fell outside that framework – that is, aboriginal groups within white settler societies. In this sense, Turner continues: 'Aboriginal groups are faced with the choice of either separate development within their own "state" or some form of assimilation into existing patterns of citizenship. While the first alternative looks like a version of apartheid, the second ... involves the inevitable destruction of aboriginal cultures. In these circumstances, citizenship begins to look like a repressive rather than progressive social factor.'[122] The notion of citizenship as a subjugating force is, I think, a valid one – especially so in the case of Canadian assimilation policy after the Second World War.

For aboriginal societies, the problem of citizenship is not simply one of individual versus collective rights or even of sovereignty. The longer indigenous societies remain subject to, are continuously influenced by, or begin to absorb the cultural imperatives of the dominant society, the more complicated becomes the dilemma of inclusion versus exclusion. Crerar's speech was tactically brilliant in this regard. When he appealed to Indians to be 'useful citizens' in 'our common country,' he was making a new statement about inclusion and social harmony. He was appealing to a sense of social membership and of active belonging based on the liberal assumption that this was Indians' need and Indians' desire, just as it was for all other individuals.

Because the state redefined the Indian 'problem' as one of citizenship and inclusion, it inevitably invited the interest and response of fellow citizens. This was especially so among the more bourgeois and privileged, who could help marshal the necessary resources and assist the government in constructive ways to promote Indian citizenship.

Thus, respectable groups like the Canadian Welfare Council and the Indian-Eskimo Association of Canada, together with knowledgeable individuals from social science centres, rushed in earnest to the task of Indian integration.

For the First Nations, the postwar era introduced a new, intensified form of state subjugation. The church, long influential in Indian education, began to decline in importance. In the vacuum thereby created, the secular, civil level of the state allied with the political level. Instead of salvation and moral improvement, Indians now required social adjustment, modern education, and opportunity. To those ends, Indian social welfare policy also planned for the full integration of Indians into 'our common country.'

6

Citizenship: The General Context of Postwar Indian Welfare Policy

The Indian affairs branch used to use the word assimilation, but recently we have been using the word integration. It seems to fit more in with the feeling that the future of the Indians is to become ordinary citizens of the country but still retain their culture and background and those parts of their history and environment which they wish to retain.

Testimony of Indian Affairs Branch Director H.M. Jones,
Committee of the Senate and House of Commons on Indian Affairs, 2 May 1961

During and after the Second World War, the federal civil service bureaucracy began to change rapidly in size, functions, and complexity. These changes were a consequence of the needs identified – principally by the 1937–40 Royal Commission on Dominion-Provincial Relations – in order to revitalize and redefine Ottawa's role in the country's social and fiscal affairs. The changes were also propelled by Ottawa's greater role in economic planning and enterprise during the war. It can be argued that no other period in Canadian history altered Canadian federalism so profoundly. Simeon and Robinson describe how Canada evolved from a classical federal state, decentralized and laissez-faire at all levels, to become a modern federal state, centralized and broadly interventionist.[1]

During the first eighty years of Confederation, much of the federal government's behaviour toward Indian peoples could be understood in the context of classical federalism and attitudes about the state's role in individual lives. These attitudes changed abruptly after the war. Baffled by the failure of its assimilation policies, the state set a course of benevolent intervention with the goal of extending citizenship to Indian peoples and bringing about their dispersal and integration into Canadian society. Enriched funding, the search for new solutions, and systematized approaches to the problem of assimilation gradually altered the Indian Affairs bureaucracy. In the process, a state presence different from the one between the wars, but just as pervasive, was slowly unleashed on First Nations communities.

The different kind of state paternalism that emerged was less dominated by particular personalities and more associated with planned programs, positivism, the promise of professionalism, and applied social science. The state determined to become a friend of the Indian but an enemy of the 'Indian problem.' The Indians were not to be blamed for their failure to assimilate; it was their living conditions and the effects of those conditions that generated the problems and that were to be the objects of state intervention.

The First Nations had a mixed reaction to the postwar era. On the one hand, they welcomed the new spirit of optimism, and they recognized an opportunity to address historical grievances and to take advantage of new state benefits and programs. After years of subjugation under narrow-minded and mean-spirited administrations, the promise of a 'square deal' and of increased citizenship rights had a certain allure. This was the tone of many of the Indian briefs and much of the testimony at the Special Joint Parliamentary Committee hearings on Indian Affairs, held first in 1946–8 and then in 1959–61. On the other hand, First Nations did not unconditionally accept the new benefits and increased rights; they continued to resist federal attempts to integrate them into the mainstream. Dyck writes that 'reserve leaders in some parts of the country (notably in Saskatchewan) warned their people that this might be the first step in a plot to do away with the special status and rights of Indians and to turn reserves into municipalities that would soon be taken over by non-Indians.'[2] First Nations understood that in the final analysis, the war against the Indian problem was really a war against them. For the next quarter-century, until the publication of the *White Paper* in 1969, First Nations quietly but resolutely resisted concerted federal efforts to include them as simply one part of the emerging Canadian mosaic. C.N.C. Roberts, a former Indian Affairs functionary, remembered that he and many of his colleagues were well aware of Indian resistance to government policies: 'Assimilation was the word and the people in Indian Affairs thought that this would be the ideal wonderful thing. But Indians had other thoughts on that. They wanted to stay under the federal government [as opposed to dealing with the provinces].'[3]

Beginning in the 1950s, Indian social policy and social assistance programs, increasingly reflected the broad objectives of citizenship and integration. For some time, the Welfare Division was central to these objectives and was the dominant division within the Indian Affairs Branch. Self-reliance and individual independence were still the underlying goals of Indian social assistance, but the emphasis shifted away from harsh admonishments to be self-supporting toward a search for ways to make these goals achievable in physical, social, and economic terms. To this end, the branch began broadening its operational environment to harness the expertise of outside organizations and of sympathetic academics. The rest of this chapter places post-war Indian welfare policy in the context of prevailing Euro-Canadian thought by reviewing some important threads of the 1946 Special Joint Parliamentary Committee on the Indian Act and the resulting addition of Section 87 to the revised act. The three chapters that follow this one explore key developments in social assistance policy is the context of these new but carefully controlled influences.

The Special Joint Committee of the Senate and the House of Commons Appointed to Consider and Examine the Indian Act, 1946–1948

The previous chapter argued that the Parliamentary Committee on Postwar Reconstruction together with the Sioui affair essentially set the course of postwar Indian policy. This being so, the 1946–8 special joint committee provided the government with a forum where that policy could be aired for public endorsement. The joint committee was established in May 1946 following the recommendations of the reconstruction committee, but only after considerable public and Indian agitation for a Royal Commission into Indian matters. Chief Andrew Paull, President of the North American Indian Brotherhood, testified on 27 June 1946: 'But this is not the kind of committee we asked for. Now while we are prepared to speak to you and present our grievances to you I want this to go on the record; we asked for a Royal Commission to investigate "you" and "me."'[4] The committee was set up primarily to make recommendations for revising the Indian Act. It was authorized to examine eight matters covering a broad scope of Indian issues, from 'treaty rights and obligations' to 'any other matter or things pertaining to the social and economic status of Indians and their advancement, which ... should be incorporated in the revised Act.'[5] The committee was chaired by D.F. Brown and had twenty-six members – seven senators and nineteen MPs.

It divided its hearings into three phases: Indian Affairs Branch, 1946; Indian, church, and other organizations, 1947; and revision of the Indian Act, 1948.

The committee's conduct augured the behaviour of the Indian Affairs Branch for the next twenty-five years. It remained firmly in control. Indians and other organizations were invited to air their opinions or submit proposals; from these, the committee could pick those which most closely fitted its own agenda. The evidence given by the Indian Affairs Branch was primary and represented a statement of the government's position and policy directions. The Indian submissions – especially those concerned with historical grievances – were considered least relevant or not relevant at all; those from established Euro-Canadian organizations were given greater weight and were incorporated into the committee's four reports.[6]

One of the first issues to confront the committee – and whose resolution was an indicator of how Indians would fare from the proceedings and recommendations – was whether there ought to be continuous Indian representation at the hearings in the form of a watching brief. On the first day the committee met, Mr Castleden, the CCF member for Yorkton, Saskatchewan, moved:

> Whereas the amendment of the Indian Act will establish, for years to come, the type of control which will determine the standards of life, training and, perhaps, the very existence, of these subordinated human beings to whom democracy is denied in Canada ... Therefore be it moved that this Committee immediately invite the Canadian Indians to send at least five Indians to represent the following five parts of Canada: (1) British Columbia and Alberta; (2) Saskatchewan and Manitoba; (3) Ontario; (4) Quebec; and (5) the Maritime Provinces; to sit in on all the deliberations of this Committee with watching briefs and to be available to be examined as witnesses under oath.[7]

This motion next came up on 4 June 1946. Castleden was told it could not be resolved until the committee had settled the question of a liaison officer for all Indian persons and organizations wishing to appear before it. Castleden thought the chair was stonewalling him. He persisted: 'When will the matter be decided whether or not we should ask Indians to come and sit in with a watching brief?' Brown retorted: 'Once we have obtained authority to engage a liaison officer or counsel.' A testy exchange ensued. Then another member, Mr Blackmore, opined that a liaison officer would be helpful in advising them on the merits of Castleden's motion. He went on: 'I think anyone who has sat with a group of Indians all through a long day and endeavoured to get them to come to a unanimity of view on one thing must realize the possible dangers with which Mr Castleden's resolution might be involved. I am not for or against it, but I would like to have an entirely open mind on the matter.'[8] Castleden replied: 'I am not asking that these Indians who may come in with watching briefs do anything themselves other than to come here, sit here and watch the deliberations of this committee ... It will not be a matter of deliberation for them, but merely to watch the interests of Indians, as this committee proceeds.'[9] The government members seemed determined to stop Castleden's motion, fearing, it might be surmised, that if they allowed Indians in with a watching brief, it might derail the government's carefully prescribed agenda.

When the motion was considered again, on 21 June 1946, Castleden stated in the minutes that the committee had 'gone forward and discussed treaties, health, welfare, education, training, field supervision and other things of deep concern to the Indians,'[10] yet there still was no Indian representation. Clearly annoyed by the committee's failure to take action, Castleden made a strong statement for his motion:

> These people have been suppressed and have been under pretty rigid dictatorial control. They have never had any avenue of official appeal against any action against them. They have never had a voice ... It seems to me that any committee of this nature, which is going to affect the lives of these people for so long, would be well advised to invite the Indians of Canada to send ... five representatives here.[11]

Castleden sensed that the motion was being thrown into limbo and said he would not allow it to be tabled without a vote: 'If the committee turns it down, I will put up a fight. Democracy must rule. If the committee decides they will not have Indian representatives sit in, then that is that.'[12]

At this point, the exasperated Brown let down his political guard and revealed his own and the majority's bias against the motion: 'We must be practical. There is no use in our adopting a theoretical and impractical viewpoint. What we must do is get representations made to this committee in an orderly and systematic way ... We have considered that matter [of five Indian representatives] in committee and we have not reached a decision as yet; we see the impractical nature of the suggestion.'[13]

Brown knew he had blundered and began to back-pedal, reassuring Castleden that the motion would be considered at a later date. Because the motion was at subcommittee, Castleden was finally forced to agree to wait. Still, he commented acerbically that the 'trouble with the later date is that we are already going ahead with reports, receiving recommendations and discussing matters of importance; and they [Indians] are not now here.'[14]

Six days later, the motion was brought before the committee, together with a recommendation from the subcommittee. The subcommittee shrewdly stated that the committee should be prepared to invite five Indian representatives to the committee provided that 'some practical way could be found to select such delegates.'[15] Castleden suggested that the NAIB and other Indian organizations be asked to name delegates. The committee could then select delegates from the names submitted. Castleden agreed to put this suggestion in writing to the subcommittee; it would then come to the committee for final approval.[16]

Castleden wrote his letter to the committee clerk on 3 July 1946 but became suspicious when it was not placed on the subcommittee record. When the full committee met on 9 July, he requested that his letter be put on record. This request triggered resentment among other committee members, who felt they were being upstaged by Castleden's crusade. His behaviour was seen as impugning their sincerity as committee members. One member said: 'I fear that the impression is going out all over the country that Mr Castleden alone is fighting the battle of the Indians.'[17] The reality was that most committee members did not want – as they put it – 'immediate' Indian representation, even though they could proudly state for the public record that in principle they were for it. They accused Castleden of holding a gun to their heads.[18]

The subcommittee's fifth report, including Castleden's letter, was then adopted, at which point the committee considered his original motion. In the discussion, the chair cited the words of an Indian who had appeared before the committee as evidence for his own perspective:

THE CHAIRMAN: I think it is safe to say that every member of the committee is in favour of the principle of having Indian representation here, but there has been no feasible manner presented to this committee either by the members of the committee or by others. We had the Rev. Mr Kelly who spoke to us as a representative of the Native Brotherhood of British Columbia ... and he was opposed to having Indian representatives here at this time.

MR. GIBSON: He displayed a lot of common sense.

THE CHAIRMAN: I think that every member of the committee ... is absolutely in favour of having representation of the Indians, but there is no feasible manner which has been shown to this committee.[19]

A careful analysis of Kelly's 27 June remarks, however, shows him to have been in favour of Castleden's motion. Kelly, a member of the Haida Nation, had appeared through a special arrangement, and many members had listened to his testimony somewhat selectively. The Native Indian Brotherhood Kelly mentioned was largely composed of north coast fishermen. Kelly had stated that because of the start of fishing season, the appearance of the brotherhood to present its brief and testimony would be most suitable after 1 October.[20] His position on an Indian presence for a watching brief was entirely different. On that matter he stated:

> The last thing I want to mention is this. A member very generously offered a motion I think ... to say that Indians be represented in this committee ... If that were acted upon ... once again I should like to submit that instead of one member representing British Columbia and Alberta, it would be a natural division ... for one member to represent British Columbia and one member to represent the three prairie provinces ... That is the point I want to make.[21]

Clearly, Kelly favoured the motion. Castleden unaccountably did not contradict Brown's misrepresentation of Kelly's testimony. This failure cemented the defeat of his motion.[22] When Castleden's motion was defeated, Brown introduced a new one, which easily carried: 'That whilst this committee is happy to welcome to any open meeting any person interested in the proceedings of the committee, it is not of the opinion that at the present time the work of the committee would be facilitated, or expedited, by authorizing the constant attendance before it, with watching briefs, of any number of Indians or other representatives.'[23] Therein lay the committee's objectives. The government agenda would prevail and the Indians would neither dictate nor influence it.

Unfortunately for the government members, the Canadian Press ran an unfavourable story about the committee's decision. Brown was miffed, and he wanted the committee to contain the damage. On 11 July he brought two particular clippings to the committee's attention, one from the *Toronto Star* and the other from the Owen Sound *Daily Sun-Times*. The 9 July *Star* article stated:

A resolution by G.H. Castleden (C.C.F. Yorkton) that five Indians be appointed immediately to serve on the committee with watching briefs was defeated today after a stormy discussion at the parliamentary committee on Indian affairs.

In presenting the resolution Mr Castleden said: 'We don't get a proper picture of the Indian problem unless we have Indians here to listen to the departmental evidence and then give us their opinion of it. The Indian hasn't been given a square deal. Here is an opportunity to give him British justice.'

William Bryce (C.C.F., Selkirk) said that, since the Indian Act was going to be amended to improve the conditions of the Indian, 'surely he has a right to sit in on this committee.'[24]

Brown, who was now clearly agitated, stated that when he assumed the committee chair, he had asked all members to set aside their political differences in the interests of the Indians. Then, with reference to the news reports, he implied that some committee members were trying to pit one class of Canadians against another, were trying to create unrest among Canadians, and were acting as traitors to the country.[25]

Castleden was not present to hear this bombast. Bryce did not respond immediately, but when he finally did, he took Brown hard to task. He rebuked Brown for making his statements without Castleden being present:

I had never thought that I would live long enough in Canada to have somebody tell me that I had been treacherous to Canada ... I could never wear that cap. As long as I am on this committee I will never let anyone deprive me of my right of saying what I think is right ... May I say that when we were in the subcommittee we took a vote and everyone voted for throwing the motion out but me. You [Brown] appealed to me to make it unanimous ... I said ... I would be agreeable ... if we would let the main committee decide the matter, and the matter was brought back to the main committee.[26]

Brown tried to defend himself, but the damage he sought to control was worsening. The committee had to find a way to soften its rebuke of Indians and to regain the semblance of a functioning body. The government could not afford this embarrassment. A cabinet member on the committee, the Honourable Mr Stirling, brought the discussion back to the press reports: 'It seems to me that it is ... our duty to point out that the report which appeared in two newspapers ... is wrong, and we want to put the matter right.'[27] Douglas Harkness, the Progressive Conservative critic of Northern Affairs and Natural Resources, and a committee member, concurred: 'I feel that such a report will undoubtedly do a considerable amount of damage and will shake the faith of the Indians and the people across Canada ... The sooner we deny what appeared in those articles the better it will be for Canada and the Indians at large. I favour Mr Stirling's suggestion that the matter be taken up in the House.'[28]

This episode has been emphasized here because it tells us much about how the government intended to treat First Nations for the foreseeable future. The government intended to promote citizenship, and this necessarily involved promoting among the public the idea that although First Nations were a shamefully deprived minority, they were still backward peoples whose steps forward into modern society required careful guidance and management. The joint committee was an all-party committee; that being said, the government controlled its agenda and had no intention of allowing it to render recommendations except those which would further that policy and that image of Indians. This, I think, was the reason why the committee rejected a particular phrase in Castleden's motion, the one that went 'immediately invite the Canadian Indians to send.' The Indian Affairs Branch was to be the primary witness for the rest of 1946, and the government feared that a watching brief on its policy would become destructive. This was precisely the spectre raised when Castleden stated: 'We don't get a proper picture of the Indian problem unless we have Indians here to listen to the departmental evidence and then give us their opinion of it.' Most committee members thought that Indians should have opinions about their treatment but that they should be invited only to make circumscribed submissions about it. They were not sanctioned to challenge their political and social position, which had already been determined. Thus, the defeat of Castleden's motion effectively disempowered the collective voice of First Nations.

Finally, Brown's call for committee members to set aside their political differences was important because it amounted to a plea for the committee to adopt a neutral position. In actuality, there was nothing neutral about the position he wanted the committee to take; it was meant to be an exercise in state legitimation. By 'setting aside political differences,' the committee further narrowed the scope of possibilities for First Nations: Indians could accept what was on offer in the form of civil, economic and social rights from the state, but they could make no substantial political claims on it as a people.[29]

The Testimony of the Director of the Indian Affairs Branch, Robert A. Hoey

Hoey succeeded McGill as director of the Indian Affairs Branch in 1944, which meant that in 1946 he was the branch's principal witness before the joint committee. The structure of the branch had not changed significantly since its earlier reorganization under the Department of Mines and Resources. However, the number of its employees had decreased from 1,189 in 1936 (65 in headquarters, 1,124 in the field) to 810 in 1946 (71 in headquarters, 739 in the field). It was a sign of Indian neglect that during the war years Indian Affairs had substantially shrunk while the Ottawa civil service as a whole grew significantly.[30]

In his extensive brief to the committee, Hoey's main objective was to present an overview of the situation of Indian peoples and of the branch. Having done so, he enhanced this overview with a fifteen-year plan for bringing about Indian integration. For this discussion, the most important aspects of Hoey's testimony are those relating to the welfare program – especially relief – and to the branch's fifteen-year plan.

Hoey began by stating that until the Second World War, relief administration had consumed most of the time and money of the annual parliamentary appropriation for Indian welfare. Indian relief expenditure would also have included Allowances for Aged Indians. Indians were not covered by existing (1927) federal legislation for old age pensions. They would later be covered by it under both the Old Age Security Act and the Old Age Assistance Act of 1951. During and since the war, he went on, relief expenditure had dropped by about 11 per cent as a proportion of the total appropriation. Hoey attributed this drop to increased employment for the able bodied.[31] Two problems in particular concerned the branch, he said. The first was the definition of 'Indian' under the Indian Act, and the second was the responsibility for relief of Indians living off reserve. In the case of the first issue, Hoey referred to Indian women who had lost their status through marriage. If they were widowed or deserted, these women often returned destitute to their reserves. There they found that they were ineligible for relief because they were not legally 'Indian.'

With respect to unemployed Indians living off reserve, Hoey pointed out that most municipalities did not accept responsibility for Indian welfare and that the Indian Affairs Branch did not have the administrative capacity to provide it. In some instances, municipalities provided assistance on the understanding they would be reimbursed. Such arrangements seemed only 'to encourage other Indians to take advantage of this service.'[32] Branch officials, Hoey continued, thought that once an Indian had resided off reserve for eighteen months, he or she should become the responsibility of the municipality. 'It is unnecessary to add,' he testified, 'that the provinces, with one or two exceptions, and the municipalities do not take kindly to this suggestion.'[33]

These two problems, both of which focused on the issue of citizenship, would be critical to the development of the branch's relief policy over the next twenty years. For example, the problem of relief for 'non-Indian' Indian women raised the question of provincial jurisdiction and laws of general application on reserve. The issue of Indians living off reserve raised basic questions about citizenship and civil rights. Ultimately, both problems raised an even more basic question: If Indians were to be considered citizens of the country and of the provinces in which they lived, should not the provinces be responsible for their welfare? The issue of provincial responsibility had been publicly addressed as early as 1943, when Major D.M. MacKay, commissioner of Indian Affairs for British Columbia, in a speech to the Vancouver Institute, called for the extension of provincial services to Indians. Mackay later became branch director. By the mid-1950s, the issue of provincial responsibility had become a dominant theme whenever Indians' issues were discussed.

Hoey turned next to a general discussion of ways to secure Indian welfare and advancement. First, he reminded the committee that Indians were not at all homogeneous in economic and cultural achievements; here, he drew stark comparisons between those in 'certain sections of Ontario ... and in British Columbia' and those 'nomadic bands in the north who still live in tents, dilapidated shacks or tepees.'[34] These latter Indians, he testified, had a special claim on the resources of Canada for their 'gradual advancement.' Hoey then raised the general problem of Indian advancement and its relationship to the branch's work. He left no doubt about his admiration for American Indian policy, and he quoted Commissioner Burke of the U.S. Bureau of Indian Affairs in his forward to the book *The Red Man in the United States*. Burke, it seems, caught for Hoey the essence of what Indian Affairs ought to be doing in Canada:

Practically all our work for the civilization of the Indian has become educational: Teaching the language he must of necessity adopt, the academic knowledge essential to ordinary business transactions, the common arts and crafts of the home and the field, how to provide a settled dwelling and elevate its domestic quality, how to get well when he is sick and how to stay well, how to make the best use of his land and the water ... how to work for a living, save money and start a bank account, how to want something he can call his own, a material possession with the happiness and comfort of family life.[35]

Here can be seen the degree to which liberal ideology had become reified not simply in the minds of the bureaucrats – for whom, in Weber's sense of social action, it brought meaning to their work – but in the general public consciousness. This was the commonsense understanding of the world, and most nearly approaches, I think, what Marx meant by phenomenal form, the appearance of reality and the source of false consciousness. Subsequent remarks show that no one on the committee questioned these basic assumptions; it did not occur to anyone to do so.

Hoey then focused on the centrepiece of his brief, a 1928 report titled *The Problem of Indian Administration* that had been prepared for the U.S. Department of the Interior and was commonly known as the Meriam Report. The report had been the basis for the reform of Indian policy in the United States, and it had been largely incorporated into the Indian Reorganization Act of 1934.[36] Hoey's testimony indicates that he considered the situation of the First Nations in the United States and Canada as analogous, but American Indian policy as superior to Canadian. He immediately turned to the recommendations of the Meriam Report in order to impress the committee with their importance. His deliberate reading of them undoubtedly was meant to represent the new direction of the Indian Affairs Branch and the essence of postwar Indian policy. The Meriam recommendations were like a guide to socialization into industrial, liberal society:

The fundamental requirement is that the task of the Indian Service be recognized as primarily educational, in the broadest sense ... and that it be made an efficient educational agency, devoting its main energies to the social and economic advancement of the Indians, so that they may be absorbed into the prevailing civilization.

The Service must have a comprehensive, well-rounded educational program, adequately supported ... This program must provide for the promotion of health, the advancement of productive efficiency, the acquisition of ... ability in the utilization of income and property ... and the maintenance of reasonably high standards of family and community life ... Since the great majority of the Indians are ... to merge into the general population, it should cover the transitional period and ... endeavor to instruct Indians in the utilization of the services provided by public and quasi public agencies for the people at large in exercising the privileges of citizenship and in making their contribution in service and in taxes for the maintenance of the government ... By actively seeking co-operation with state and local governments and by making a fair contribution in payment for services rendered by them to untaxed Indians, the national government can expedite the transition and hasten the day when there will no longer be a distinctive Indian problem and when the necessary governmental services are rendered alike to whites and Indians by the same organization without discrimination.

In the execution of this program ... care must be exercised to respect the rights of the Indian. This phrase 'rights of the Indian' is often used solely to apply to his property rights. Here it is used in a much broader sense to cover his rights as a human being living in a free country.[37]

In many ways, Chamberlin correctly observes, the Meriam Report simply revisited old themes, such as self-reliance and thrift, using a different lexicon. But two ideas were different. First was the idea that being Indian and being American were not necessarily mutually exclusive. Indians could retain certain of their collective rights – here referred to as their property rights – but they were to see those rights as a point from which to embark on a course of individual citizenship. Ultimately, their individual or 'human' rights were paramount and infinitely preferable. Still, as with Euro-Americans, these rights were best achieved from within the security of strong, stable communities.[38] Second, citizenship as an idea had to be made into something tangible, accessible, and visible. This was not possible as long as Indians remained the isolated endeavour of the Indian Service. It could be achieved through a comprehensive program of education in citizenship led by the national government and supported by the active cooperation of all other levels of government. These two ideas had captured the thinking of the Canadian government and were now being happily articulated by Hoey.

Hoey next presented the committee with a master plan for implementing these ideas. He saw the plan as requiring budget increases for the next fifteen years, to a maximum of $25 million per year, after which point the amount would gradually decline. Hoey and the branch envisaged an aggressive intervention in Indian communities during these fifteen years, highlighted by the repair and revitalization of Indian schools and education, new health programs to combat tuberculosis and other communicable diseases, the construction of new housing, the building of access roads, the development of community infrastructure, and the erection of community halls for recreation and adult learning. Indian economies were to be assisted through the employment of better qualified farming instructors and the broadening of the fur conservation program. Indian lands anticipated to be under further pressure in the postwar era were to be protected from alienation as far as practicable. Finally, Indians were to be encouraged to take more responsibility for administering their own affairs. This might be accomplished, Hoey remarked, by allowing them to administer their own Family Allowances and by helping them beautify their own communities. 'It is difficult to understand,' he mused, 'how the Indian can develop as a citizen physically or mentally, in the absence of these and other related responsibilities.'[39] The theme of community beautification has persisted in Indian Affairs' policy. It recalls attempts to have Indians build beautiful gardens, the hallmarks of civilization. In the postwar era the garden became the suburb.

Hoey's summarizing statement made the following observations. Like the statements of his many predecessors, these reminded the committee of the white man's burden:

> Finally, let me state that when we turn to the Indian population and to the consideration of ways and means whereby conditions on Indian reserves might be improved, the problems confronting us appear to lend themselves in the main to a well thought out, long-range program. The education and ultimate assimilation of the Indian population will be, in my judgment, a slow and painful process and one that will likely demand the exercise of devotion, self-sacrifice and patience ...
>
> Fortunately for us, we live in an age when scientific research, or to speak more accurately, the results of this research, is enabling us to rapidly overcome the obstacles once created by time and space.[40]

There were many connections between the Meriam Report and Hoey's statement of the branch's policy. The emphasis on education beyond its traditional sense, the branch's role in Indians' economic and social advancement, the idea of citizenship as a transitional process, the protection of Indian lands for utilitarian purposes, self-administration as an exercise in responsible citizenship, and the emphasis on Indian community and family life – all of these themes were obviously adapted from Meriam.

Since the Indian Reorganization Act of 1934, however, American Indian policy had had mixed success. According to Chamberlin, there were inherent problems in attempting to strengthen First Nation internal governance mechanisms and economic self-sufficiency on the one hand, and expecting assimilation to occur as a consequence on the other. Indeed, stabilizing the group as a way to promote assimilation ultimately ran contrary to the American ideals of rugged individualism and personal liberty:

> The difficulty was that tribal self-governance and economic self-sufficiency were ... so dependent upon non-native standards and decisions that they quickly became little more than a disarming daydream which created a dangerous illusion of stability among some native groups. And it was dangerous quite simply because it was an illusion and eventually resulted in a repetition of ... defeated expectations and feelings of bad faith ... It was ... true that the new Indian social and economic structures were extremely vulnerable. They were established ... to effect the assimilation of the native people 'into modern life.' Yet they were in many ways in direct theoretical opposition to the immensely powerful ideological forces in American society which defined modern life and the liberties it allows, as well as the kind of happiness it envisages.[41]

In other words, this American approach to achieving assimilation resulted in a reinforced and much resented group dependence on government regulation and largesse. This problem was not evident to Hoey or the branch; that, or it was evident and they chose to ignore it. Canada, then, was set to establish yet another paradox in its own Indian administration. The first paradox, described in chapter 2, involved the creation of 'Indian' as a separate legal status for the purposes of assimilation. The second paradox would fuel the government's eternal fear of Indian dependence; it would also require more programs to combat the very dependence it had created.

Hoey and the branch were not alone in their thinking. Brooke Claxton, the Health and Welfare minister under Mackenzie King, appeared before the committee on 6 June 1946 and spoke to his department's extensive brief on Indian Affairs. Claxton's comments were important. Since 1945, his department had been responsible for Indian health services; it had also been instrumental in including Indians in the Family Allowance program.[42] As one of the principal architects of Canada's welfare state, he had an enormous influence in shaping the overall environment of Canadian citizenship and hence the place of Indians within the state. Of particular significance was Part VII of his department's brief. Item 54, General Observations, specified the department's solution to the Indian problem:

> It is evident that the health of the Indians and Eskimos of Canada is insepa-
> rable from their general welfare and economic standing. These matters do
> not come within the jurisdiction of this department, but we have seen
> enough of the problem to recognize its ... complexity. It is important to
> remember that one of the greatest factors in self-reliance is provision of
> adequate food and shelter for one's dependents. Such surveys as have been
> made indicate consistent nutritional deficiencies in Indians as contributing
> to their inferior health and economic status. Improved nutrition can be
> brought about by education and by improvement in economic standing
> itself. Government assistance should ... aim at putting the Indians and Eski-
> mos in a condition in which they can themselves gain a better living as the
> basis for good health, greater welfare and a better life. Indians living in
> organized communities should have advantages similar to those of the
> white people living in those communities.[43]

Claxton's message reiterated the assumptions underlying the Meriam Report, which Hoey and the branch had already adopted. The primary one was that Indian health and economic and social standing could be substantially advanced if their communities were stabilized and if economic opportunities were made available to them as individual wage earners. Claxton also identified two principles of Indian welfare – principles that would become essential to the federal government's integration strategy. First, Indian dependence should be understood as a result of lack of economic opportunity in the same way as dependence would be understood in the case of Euro-Canadians. 'Their duty ... was to become self-sufficient,' Chamberlin wrote in his analysis of the Meriam Report, 'or else to become dependent *in the same way* as others were becoming dependent, with the spread of social security and welfare schemes.'[44] The second principle was comparability. Claxton spoke to the issue of Indians living in off-reserve communities and of the need to ensure that they were treated like other Canadians in similar circumstances. This was a critical statement. First, it addressed an issue that concerned the branch and gave it the added clout of a new and powerful federal department that had extensive dealings with the provinces. Second, although the principle pertained to the situation of Indians off reserve, it established the basis for the development of Indian welfare policy on reserve. This was that all social services available to Canadians in their respective provinces should be available to Indians in their own communities, either through the extension of those services onto the reserves or through their provision in a comparable manner.

The real implication of this position was that in most respects, again, Indians were to be treated no differently from their Euro-Canadian counterparts. Like Euro-Canadians, they had since Confederation been held individually accountable for their own misfortunes. Now, in the postwar period, they were to be regarded as legitimately dependent citizens if employment was not available. The crux of the matter was, however, that Indian dependency was different from dependency in the Euro-Canadian mainstream. In the rush to social justice, postwar Indian policy was about to negate that difference and effectively obfuscate the historical status of First Nations.

First Nations' and Other Organizations' Submissions and Testimony

During the committee's two years of sitting, it received briefs and heard testimony from hundreds of individuals and organizations representing First Nations and Euro-Canadian points of view. This section provides a very small sample of these presentations. The First Nation selections have been chosen quite randomly except for the testimony of Chiefs Andrew Paull and Tom Jones, representing the NAIB. Euro-Canadian submissions were picked deliberately. Of special interest was the joint submission of the Canadian Welfare Council and the Canadian Association of Social Workers, because their submission strongly influenced the committee and its recommendations.

Euro-Canadian submissions included brief letters of approval of the committee's task and complaints that Indian Affairs policies left mainstream services no alternative except to refuse to deal with Indians. For example, a letter from Toronto's Danforth Avenue United Church Women's Association simply endorsed the 'work' of the committee, and a letter from the Creston Valley Hospital Association blamed the Indian Affairs Branch for the hospital's having to refuse admission to sick Indians. It claimed that it was $64.50 out of pocket for emergency treatments![45] Another brief, from Vancouver's University Branch of the Canadian Legion of the British Empire Service League, called for Indian representation in the Dominion Parliament and the provincial legislatures and for policies to promote Indian's 'economic freedom.'[46] Finally, a submission from the Society for the Furtherance of B.C. Indian Arts and Crafts linked the welfare of Indians to a revival of their traditional handicrafts ('highest of the known primitive art of the world'), to the education of their children in a culturally sensitive manner, and to a 'modern program [of planned] social services' that would 'requir[e] a scientific approach ... and trained personnel' and that would be available to Indians just as they were to other Canadians.[47]

As might be expected, the great majority of the Euro-Canadian submissions dealt with Indians' citizenship and with their status vis-à-vis non-Indian Canadians. Typical of these was the brief of the Vancouver branch of the Canadian Civil Liberties Union, which spoke from a well-informed perspective and grappled with the history and unique status of Indians in Canada. Ultimately, however, it could not propose a solution radically different from that of the nineteenth-century humanists and protectionists. In particular, the CCLU struggled with the meaning of the term 'assimilation.' Thus, the union recommended in its submission the following long-term objectives for Indian policy:

To educate, train and condition all Indians in such a manner –

(5) a. (1) That they shall be equipped adequately to maintain themselves in their own traditional economic activities or in new and modern ones, under the conditions of white competition.

(6) a. (2) That they shall both welcome and be equipped adequately to accept the rights, conditions and responsibilities of citizenship.

(7) b. (1) To liquidate the reserve system gradually and according to a plan, or plans approved by the Indians ...

b. (2) And in, and as an automatic part of this process to transfer the Indians or bands from their state of wardship to a state of full citizenship with all its rights and privileges.

(8) c. To work out ... a mutually acceptable and just plan to extinguish ... all obligations (financial, social, economic and educational) which the government is under exclusively to the Indians.

(9) d. To establish a state of affairs in which the Indians will stand in the same relationship to the government as do Canadian citizens in general.

...

(11) f. To effect the assimilation of the Indians, or, in other words, their transition from the present state of wardship to that of citizenship, in such a way as to encourage such Indians as wish to do so, to retain such identity of blood, culture, skills and organization as they are capable of maintaining.[48]

The union felt compelled then to elaborate on its definition of assimilation:

> There is no reason why those Indians who wish to do so, should not retain whatever elements of their Indian heritage they wish ...
>
> In becoming assimilated, the Indians need only to add to the background they already possess, the abilities, outlook and knowledge that are necessary if they are to participate independently and responsibly in Canadian life.
>
> But we are convinced that ... the Indians really have no choice. They must become assimilated (in the sense in which we use the word) if they are to survive ... Unless, individually, they are able to adapt themselves to the society in which they exist, they are doomed to eventual racial submergence.[49]

The union's position was, I think, one that most Canadians at the time found eminently sensible and just. Its acutely liberal position advocated the retention of cultural heritage as a matter of individual choice and recognized as inevitable the slow relinquishment of collective rights in favour of individual, free, and independent status within the modern nation-state. This position held out liberalism as the humane saviour of peoples, yet it never fully explained how people as individuals could retain pride in their cultural heritage when all vestiges of their collective existence were dismantled. Still, it was an element of the received wisdom of the day, and it represented, in part, the meaning the federal government eventually ascribed to the term 'integration.'

The union's position included an aversion to the reserves, which it referred to as depressed 'plague spots' giving rise to slumlike conditions, poor health, and low morale. Reserve conditions should be 'remedied for the sake of the country' as well as for the Indians, the union's brief stated. It was axiomatic that the source of Indian welfare had to come from the outside, like a cure for a disease. The Indian Affairs Branch ought to develop 'superior conditions' on the reserves 'which will allow the Indians to advance to ... superior levels.' The problem, according to the union, was that Indians didn't have a visible and measurable material standard that they could use to assess their progress: 'Until the Indians have developed superior leadership and the ability to view their own situation with foresight, detachment and intelligence, it is unlikely that they will be able to see the advantages of many changes that are necessary before full assimilation can be accomplished.'[50]

These sorts of statements fed directly into government thinking and provided support for its position. Like the Meriam Report, the union's brief directly connected Indian material progress with Indian advancement and happiness. Within the liberal, utilitarian world view, it was obvious that raising the standard of living on the reserves would provide the necessary security for Indians to leave their old ways behind.

More troubling was the patronizing nature of the union's position, notwithstanding its underlying liberal philosophy of self-actualization and choice. The proposals the union was making would have had the effect of perpetuating the very dependency whose eradication was being sought. As long as there remained in the Euro-Canadian mind the image of Indians as childlike and backward, Indians would remain eternal wards of the state. This view of the 'other,' rooted in Western imperialism, was constantly being promoted as the chief obstacle to Indian progress. The same view was useful for state legitimation, because it diverted attention from issues of sovereignty and from the history of dispossession. At the same time, the acceptance and promulgation of this view by the state's civil level – reflected also in briefs from other citizens', church, and professional groups – revealed both the strength of spontaneous consent and the power of the dominant classes in postwar Canada.

Perhaps no other brief from a professional organization carried as much weight as the joint submission of the Canadian Welfare Council and the Canadian Association of Social Workers. In hindsight, it could well be that in the long term no other brief presented to the committee offered a more damaging perspective. The weight accorded to the council's brief can be attributed to the new importance of state social welfare and to the emergence of social work as one of the first professions in 'applied' social science.[51] The Canadian Welfare Council and the Canadian Association of Social Workers were seen as advocates of the Marsh Report, of universal welfare programs, and of the programs' harmonizing and equalizing influences.[52] In their view, the First Nations' plight was the result of the absence of universality; it also exemplified the ills suffered by any disadvantaged group within Canadian society.

The brief began with an overview of the many problems affecting Indian communities. It cited poor living conditions reflected in inadequate housing, high mortality rates, severe malnutrition, primitive home life, low standards of education, substandard foster care provided through the residential schools, and inadequate assistance for funds such as old age pensions and direct relief.[53] The submission also identified five problems related to child welfare. Of particular importance was the fifth of these:

> Owing to the fact that wards of the Dominion Government are not eligible for benefits under provincial legislation, Indian children who are neglected lack the protection afforded under social legislation available to white children in the community.
>
> Instances could be multiplied. No matter what phase of individual opportunity or family situation is considered, the Indians are at a disadvantage by comparison with other groups in the Canadian community.[54]

Here, then, was the crux of the problem: If provincial welfare law was not applicable on the reserves, how could Indian peoples receive the level of services enjoyed by non-Indians and thereby rise to desirable standards of individual and family life? The expectation that Indians would adopt Western standards of individual and family life was to be balanced with equal access to the social services and tools of acculturation that would make the change possible. The expectation also implied that there had to be a point at which the state could say: 'Passed: assimilation complete.' All of this was as senseless as the legislation to encourage the gradual civilization of the Indians that had been passed by the United Canadas in 1857. Standards might be set, but could anybody meet them, including those who set them?[55]

The council proposed five 'necessary changes' in First Nation communities to prepare Indians for assimilation. The first of these, under the rubric *Improvement in Living Conditions*, borrowed from Hoey's earlier testimony and evoked (though it never referred to) the Meriam Report:

> Within the framework of a long-range plan we consider it necessary that the Canadian Government should undertake an imaginative and aggressive program to improve the conditions of life among the Indian population. This may best be achieved through co-ordinated efforts in the ... fields of education, nutrition and economics, the whole program being planned as a unit. Health and welfare services should be developed in relation to the fundamental needs mentioned above.[56]

The brief, whose author was clearly cognizant of federal testimony, rubber-stamped an extension of the fur conservation projects. It also endorsed a well-funded agricultural training program. Furthermore,

Indians should be guaranteed the full opportunity to participate in the 'economic activity of the general Canadian community' through an end to discrimination and 'the widest possible educational and cultural opportunities.'[57]

The brief also turned its attention to federal–provincial relations and to the need for social services to be developed on the reserves. The council challenged the provinces to become involved in Indian issues for their own best interests. Social conditions on the reserves 'may infect surrounding communities over a wide area' the brief warned, while the 'setting aside of large tracts of land as Indian reserves is ... often a problem to the development of the province and its resources.'[58] The council then urged greater cooperation between the provincial and federal governments. It noted that the provinces were in the best position to provide effective services to reserves, and it appealed to governments' sense of economy by identifying the savings that could be achieved by avoiding a duplication of services.

Finally, with clear reference to Dr Moore's suggestions to the postwar reconstruction committee, the joint brief recommended a simple, three-point plan for developing professional social services on the reserves. First, Indian Affairs should hire 'thoroughly qualified' welfare specialists in headquarters to work with other specialists in health, education, agriculture, and so on. Second, the welfare specialists should be complemented in the Indian agencies with at least one trained social worker, who would work with the professionals representing the other fields. Third, the social workers in the agencies would provide general welfare services, including child and family welfare, recreation, and adult education.[59]

The council and the association concluded with nine recommendations, all of which had been implicit throughout the document. Still, I will highlight four because they found their way directly into federal policy and thus reflected the developing relationship between the branch and national organizations of stature. One recommendation was for 'the full assimilation of Indians into Canadian life as the goal of the Government's Indian program.'[60] To reach this goal, it was further recommended that the federal government negotiate with the provinces to secure the extension of their health, welfare, and education services to the reserves. Two separate recommendations called for the branch to hire welfare specialists for headquarters and trained social workers for the field. The importance of these recommendations – indeed of the entire brief – was not that they were original but rather that they agreed with what was already becoming evident in federal Indian policy. The Canadian Welfare Council and the Canadian Association of Social Workers had provided the state with legitimation of its political intent; it had also mapped out a way for the state to achieve its goals.

Briefs and submissions from the First Nations were from individual bands or tribal groups or from national or provincial organizations. Nearly all the band submissions followed the same format, addressing each of the committee's eight themes of inquiry in order and often using identical or similar phrases. For example, to the theme 'treaty rights and obligations' a frequent response was, 'It is our desire that these rights and obligations of the Federal Government towards the Indians, be at all times respected and fulfilled.'[61] Briefs from the Indian Association of Alberta, the Union of Saskatchewan Indians, and some other organizations were considerably more expansive and detailed.[62]

Some briefs rejected outright the authority of the committee and the government of Canada over their lands and governments. For example, the written brief of the Mohawk Nation of the St-Regis Reserve (Akwesasne) began: 'We, the Chiefs of the Mohawk Nation who swear allegiance to the Six Nations Confederacy, as the only true government of our people, having assembled in council, have decided to call the attention of the Joint Committee ... to the following facts.'[63] The statement continued:

(1) We occupy our territory, not by your grace, but by a right beyond your control.

(2) We hold original title.

(3) We have never voluntarily submitted to the domination of the Canadian government, and have never been conquered by it in a just war.

(4) According to International Law, no nation can legislate over another without first acquiring title to the land.

(5) Canada considers itself a democratic country. The basis of democracy is the rule of the people governed by the law. We submit that we, the people of the Mohawk Nation can find no bona-fide evidence that we had a voice in preparing the original Indian Act or in its revision. Since we reject the premise that the Canadian Parliament can make laws over us, it is only justice that said Parliament should denote the legal basis for enforcing its laws on the reserves.

(6) The burden of proof must be borne by you, for we wish to hold to the status quo which was established in the first encounter of red man with white.[64]

This kind of position, of course, found little favour with the committee, which was interested only in those First Nation submissions which conformed to its citizenship agenda. The committee was prepared to listen to grievances, but it heeded only those which acknowledged the full authority of the Canadian state and which the government could be seen to respond to positively or with reservations, as it chose.

Challenges to Canadian sovereignty were not always as direct as the one just noted. That being said, most of the First Nation submissions reflected a certain wariness of and ambivalence toward citizenship if it was going to be based largely on the existing conditions of enfranchisement. Indians desired to free themselves of wardship status, but they rejected citizenship to the extent that it would cost them their status, rights, and heritage. This was seen by them as too great a price. They felt no rush to be Canadian, no immediate urge to identify themselves as Canadian first and foremost. Even so First Nations did not wish to be treated as second-class human beings. The briefs often emphasized this point by asserting Indian equality with whites while simultaneously emphasizing their separateness. The Fort Chipewayan Cree, the Dog Ribs of Fort Rae, the Ohamil Band in Laidlaw, British Columbia, the Fort Alexander Reserve in Pine Falls, Manitoba, and the thirty-two Ojibwa bands covered by the Robinson-Huron Treaty in Ontario, all rejected compulsory enfranchisement, although some, including the Fort Chipewayan Cree and the Ojibwa, thought citizenship should remain a matter of personal choice.[65]

The right to vote met with the same mixed response; some thought that alternative methods ought to be developed for Indian representation in Ottawa. The Ohamil Band expressed a desire for the right to vote so long as their privileges were retained.[66] Most of the Robinson-Huron bands favoured the right to vote with the same proviso; however, the Sucker Creek Band and bands from the north shore of Lake Huron thought that special seats should be allocated in Parliament to protect their interests. The Whitefish River and Mississauga bands rejected the vote entirely.[67] The Fort Chipewayan Cree and the Fort Alexander Reserve rejected the right to vote but asked for paid representatives in Ottawa to speak to their interests.[68]

The issue of poverty on the reserves inspired a nearly unanimous response in favour of the provision of adequate social security. In particular, all the bands agreed that there was an urgent need to extend the federal old age pension to Indians, since the elderly were at the time receiving only relief rations. For example, the Fort Chipewayan Cree stated in their brief:

We would like to have old age pension, like white people ...

For our old aged relatives, we would ask the old age pension from the age of sixty ... besides necessary clothing, housing and wood fuel.

And if the old age pension is not to be given to us, we ask for every old people of sixty, a greater amount of rations, and some extra food supply for a decent living. We have all our life a very hard life, and we would like to enjoy like the white people, the privileges granted to them in their old age.[69]

Their brief also called for a broader range of adequate benefits for all band members in need:

We appreciate generally what was done for our sick people, we desire to have it continued, by the decent help in rations and clothing, housing and fuel wood. When the man is sick and has a big family, the help should be proportionate.

For the blind people, besides the double rations supply, nothing was done so far. It is really too bad, because they are the most destitute in this country.

So we ask the Government to give them either a far greater help for the rations, which are insufficient to them, or the old age pension ...

For the destitute people, we want you to keep helping them decently adding in the amount of rations.[70]

The Ohamil Band stated: 'We think the Department should grant the old age pension to our Indian people. We also think there should be a pension for widows, because many of them have large families to keep.'[71] The Robinson-Huron Ojibwa expressed a desire for benefits comparable to those provided to whites, and implied that relief being provided to their members amounted to a form of discrimination. Chief Meawasige testified that the delegates at the tribal forum held to develop a position for their brief had agreed that their 'old people were not being sufficiently well taken care of.'[72] He continued:

The Indian is often destitute in old age. While he might have cheaper housing than the whites, that was balanced by the fact that he had often to pay much more for his food, since he lived in remoter areas and transportation increased the cost. All agreed we should have old age pensions, mothers' allowances, relief, on an exact par with the whites and not be discriminated against.[73]

But it was the Fort Alexander Band that perhaps made the most eloquent request for the old age pension: 'The Indians, living side by side with the Whites, should not be in an inferior and dejected state when they reach their last winters on earth, but they should be treated as well as their brethren of poor means.'[74]

The presentations of the provincial and national Indian organizations were fundamentally consistent with the positions of the bands and tribal councils. The ambivalence about 'being Canadian' was a constant thread. The NAIB, in addition to its oral presentation, submitted a number of written recommendations, including one that would abolish the policy of terminating treaty rights upon enfranchisement. It also noted that Indians were not prepared to discuss the right to vote; instead it recommended a study of how Indians might have their own representation in Parliament.[75]

Chief Andrew Paull's testimony – and in particular his choice of language – helped enlighten this latter recommendation. He never referred to First Nations as Canadian; rather, he spoke of their being British subjects and – because of formal and informal treaties – of their being equal in status to Euro-Canadians.[76] When he referred to committee members, to the Canadian government, or to Canadians generally, he used 'you,' and he consistently referred to First Nations as 'we.' In this way his testimony imparted a sense of parallelism, of 'you' and 'us' together on this continent called North America. With respect to equal status, Paull remarked: 'Why does someone make a treaty with somebody? You have to be equal to somebody before you can make a treaty with somebody. We say to you now that those Indians at that time were your equal when they made the treaty. Now maybe that is something you hate to swallow.'[77]

This theme was especially striking when he compared Indians' loyalty to the treaties with what the brotherhood considered white treachery:

We charge the government of Canada with having abrogated these treaties without telling us they were going to abrogate them. Please tell your Prime Minister that he has committed a crime in doing that. Treaties are abrogated when those who sign them go to war against each other. We did not go to war against you ...

This government ... exceeded ... their authority when they transferred the natural resources of the province of Ontario to the government of Ontario, because in that conveyance they violated and they abrogated the terms and conditions of the treaties that were made with the Indians in the province of Ontario.[78]

Paull pursued the 'we–you' theme in his discussion of Indian agents – a discussion that was really an entree to the demand for self-government under the aegis of the Canadian state. 'In Canada today,' he testified, 'there is no Indian who can become an agent or anything like that ... We have Indians ... who have a greater degree of learning than the illiterate Indian agent who supervises and administers your laws over those Indians. That ... must be stopped.'[79] How was it to be stopped? Paull continued:

> We are of the opinion that the Indians should be given self-government ... We mean that there should be an Indian council which would meet, and there would be no Indian agent there when the Indian council meets, and we believe there should be a provincial council, and that provincial council should be responsible to a central board of governors in Ottawa who are not responsible to the government in power, but who are responsible to the parliament of Canada.[80]

Implicit in this statement was not just the ambivalence that First Nations felt about their Canadian identity; the suggestion was that the only just solution to the predicament of Indian dependency was a political one – specifically, the restoration of Indians' traditional capacity to control their own affairs and destinies.

In a seemingly contradictory stance, many of the First Nation organizations requested a social security program comparable to that of their 'white neighbours.' They needed this because of their desperate impoverishment in the market economy and the discrimination they experienced in it. Chief Paull, for example, recommended to the committee that 'you ... extend in all mercy the hand of kindness and include Indians in all old age pension laws that the government of Canada will enact.'[81] The Indian Association of Alberta observed in its brief that Indians were treated discriminatorily by the federal government. When it was expedient, Ottawa considered Indians full subjects of the Crown, responsible to serve in the military. Yet in other situations, Indians were considered wards of the Crown and thus ineligible for the social benefits accorded to all others.[82] Furthermore, the Alberta association saw discrimination in the provinces' failure to provide them with services and strongly implied that Indians should be eligible for provincial social benefits.[83] This, however, was not a position generally shared by other First Nations organizations or bands, who saw the federal government as solely responsible for their welfare.[84]

In the social welfare section in its brief, the Union of Saskatchewan Indians was especially critical of the ration system of relief, calling it inadequate and a factor in Indian inequality with other Canadians. The brief described in detail the current scale of rations and stated: 'This schedule of supplies indicates that entirely inadequate provision is being made at present to meet the needs of Indians who, being human beings, have the same hungers, and suffer the same pains from the elements, from illness and old age, as others.'[85] The Saskatchewan Indians recommended that the ration scale be changed to provide a fully adequate, nutritious diet that included essential vitamin content. The union identified the federal government as responsible for Indian welfare and recommended that it 'finance and extend to them the benefits of Old Age Pensions, aid to the blind, mothers' allowances and all other social benefits that may be provided, from time to time, by legislation, for Canadian citizens.'[86]

The Catholic Indian Institute of British Columbia took a position in its brief similar to that of the union: 'We are far behind other Canadian people in the matter of health and social welfare, We ask that funds be provided by Parliament to set up a good system of medical care. We want our Indian reserves visited regularly by medical doctors and nurses.'[87] The institute called for the federal government to build new hospitals and housing; it also developed a short critique of Indian Affairs' relief policy and its effects on the Indians of British Columbia:

> Relief and pensions have been denied to the Indians on the pretext that the small amounts granted to the Indians could be supplemented by their privileges of hunting, fishing and trapping. This plan failed to take into consideration that most applicants are ... incapable of enjoying those privileges; also that these privileges are seasonal and do not provide a subsistence standard of living at all.
>
> Much hardship has been endured by us in recent years ... If the B.C. Provincial government can give its people generous pensions, there is no good reason why the Canadian Parliament can not do so for the B.C. Indians. Subsistence relief provided by the Indian Department has been cut very low, and in many cases denied altogether ... The low incomes of most Indian families have prevented these families from supporting their aged or sick relatives.
>
> Much suffering and misery has been caused among the Indian and much bitter criticism of those responsible for the care of us – even much of the sympathy aroused among white people who knew of our condition,

and their insistent demand that these things be set right, which has brought about this Joint Committee, was caused by callous administration and the denial of social benefits to Indians in recent years.[88]

The institute asked for Indian pensions comparable to those for Euro-Canadians, with amounts set in the Indian Act, free from the arbitrary administration of Indian Affairs. Like the Family Allowance, all forms of social security – including Old Age Pensions, Widows' Allowances, and disability and relief benefits – should be payable in money and should not be charged against the reserves themselves.[89]

This latter point, regarding the branch's practice of charging relief against bands' trust accounts, was an especially sensitive one, and had also been addressed in the brief of the Indian Association of Alberta and in the NAIB's testimony. It involved two issues. First, Indians resented the government's control over band membership and the expenditure of band trust funds through the Indian Act. This government control of both membership and expenditures effectively deprived bands of the right to govern their own members. Chief Tom Jones, the NAIB treasurer, testified:

Those trust funds were created because we ceded certain types of lands and as a consequence a certain capital amount was set up in trust ... from which we get interest money ... The position we take ... is that the Department of Indian Affairs has no right to admit anyone to membership in our band and in that way make them eligible to participate in the distribution of the interest money ... There is too much high-handed dictatorial action taken with respect to saying who shall benefit from those funds. We are the ones who are appointed to look after the welfare of our people, but that is one instance in which our rights have been invaded.[90]

The second point was noted by the Indian Association of Alberta. Eligibility for the Old Age Pension in Euro-Canadian society was individually means tested,[91] and the costs of the pension were in effect 'charged against the individual property of the recipient.'[92] Yet for elderly Indians, for whom the only social assistance available was relief, the costs of benefits were charged against community property, the trust funds. In contrast, Indians in the United States were, according to the association, eligible for all social benefits provided by the government from the public treasury. This discrepancy, the Association stated, arose because Canada's federal government had decided it would be too difficult to administer pensions on the reserves. 'Is Canada unable to discover how these benefits are administered in the United States?' the Alberta brief pointedly asked.[93] Still, the basic problem alluded to in the Alberta position was that the Canadian government had found it cheap and expedient to maintain Indians in abject poverty by providing menial relief to *all* Indians regardless of age. In addition, it charged them collectively for the costs of their poverty, for which, according to policy, they were individually responsible.

In the position of the Indian bands and organizations, there was an apparent contradiction between their ambivalence toward being Canadian and their desire for the same or comparable social welfare benefits as Euro-Canadians. Was the contradiction real? The First Nations' position was consistent with the historical relationship they understood to exist between themselves and the federal government: that it was the only government responsible for their welfare and for protecting their status and rights as the country's original peoples. Even the Indian Association of Alberta had not explicitly asked for an extension of provincial services, despite its allusions to them.

If there was a naiveté in the First Nations' position, it was that they failed to appreciate fully the means to the end in the federal position. In other words, by accepting social security measures, they would be collaborating in policies aimed at integrating them into Canadian society. On balance, First Nations were captive not only to their poverty but also, like everyone else, to the period and to the promise of a better and more secure future. They did not foresee the intrusive effects of social welfare measures on their cultures; instead, they saw their provision as an acknowledgment of their status and as a means of promoting their self-determination. For its part, the joint committee, like most of Euro-Canada, interpreted Indian ambivalence about citizenship as Canada's failure to make Indians feel a part of the country. Its final recommendations concerning Indian welfare and other aspects of its mandate would directly reflect that interpretation.

Report of the Commission on Indian Affairs, 1946–1947

In 1946, a submission by Berry Richards, the MLA for The Pas, Manitoba, in consultation with the chief and council of The Pas Indian Band, recommended that the committee visit as many of the reserves as possible to understand first-hand the conditions of First Nations communities. 'Unless this is done,' he wrote, 'your committee will not properly appreciate the size and complexity of the problem it is called upon to solve.'[94] Whether his recommendation spurred the government to action is moot. What is certain is that on 11 October 1946, the King government appointed a ten-person Commission on Indian Affairs under the Inquiries Act. The commission, whose members were all from the existing joint committee, was given a mandate to conduct committee business by visiting selected reserve communities in Quebec and the Maritime provinces. Within ten days of its appointment, the commission began its work, and on 8 July 1947 it submitted its final report to the government. The report was prepared as a submission to the joint committee.[95]

Over the course of eighteen days, from 20 October to 6 November 1946, the commission conducted hearings at nineteen reserve communities: ten in New Brunswick, six in Nova Scotia, one in Prince Edward Island, and two in Quebec. The commission's findings and recommendations were reported according to the eight categories of inquiry followed by the joint committee. The commission reported a general aversion to the idea of enfranchisement among older Indians, who feared the loss of rights and privileges 'to which they have become accustomed.'[96] The younger Indians, and especially ex-servicemen, understood the advantages of enfranchisement, 'but, unfortunately, in their formative years ... were not shown ways ... of helping themselves to become other than "wards of the Crown."'[97] This latter statement was pivotal to the commission's recommendations, nearly all of which revolved around this dilemma and how it could be resolved through Indian advancement. What social and economic advancement meant however, was dispersion. In the Euro-Canadian view, so long as Indians remained as collective entities outside Canadian society, they would remain implicitly primitive. The whole question of protecting their rights had become hopelessly confused with the idea of their wardship.

Citing its visits to several Micmac and Malecite reserves, the commission referred to the Indians' loss of their ancestral fibre, energy, and initiative as if somewhere in their distant past they had possessed all the attributes of enterprising, self-made men. The solution, the commissioners decided, was already contained in R.A. Hoey's testimony to the joint committee on 30 May 1946:

We agree with the view expressed by Mr R.A. Hoey to the 1946 Joint Committee (Minutes of Proceedings and Evidence, pp.27, 28): that 'consideration of ways and means whereby conditions on Indian reserves might be improved, and the problems [which confronted] us, appear to lend themselves in the main to a well thought out, long-range programme.' if [*sic*] the Indians of the present and future generations are to be so advanced educationally and economically that they will be able to enjoy the rights and privileges of, and assume all the obligations of, Canadian citizenship.[98]

The final objective, the commission's report continued, was Indian assimilation and a reduced need for special services to Indian peoples. Finally, the report stated that during this assimilation, 'much as it will cost, Canada has a moral responsibility and a legal obligation to meet with regard to the provision of our Indians with all necessary social services.'[99]

During their reserve visits, the commissioners reported, Indians often told them that they received neither old age nor blind people's pensions and that they had asked for these to be provided. But the most common complaint on every reserve concerned the distribution of welfare and relief: 'Your Commisioners do feel that many improvements can be made in this regard and are confident that the Indian Affairs Branch is endeavouring to make it as easy as possible for deserving Indians to be given every needed assistance to receive that amount and kind of direct relief as will make the recipient healthy and comfortable.'[100] The commission recommended that the old age pension be provided to Indians and that the amount and variety of relief rations be increased so that 'the Indian diet may meet the standards of competent nutritionists.' No recommendation was made for a blind person's pension, despite the provision for one under an amendment to the Old Age Pensions Act in 1937.[101]

The commission also called for the implementation of a housing program – a need that Hoey had identified in his testimony to the joint committee.[102] Furthermore, it recommended higher qualifications for Indian agents who must possess – besides an uncommon dedication to duty, the right skills, and aptitude – 'a good working knowledge of social welfare.'[103] It appealed to the government to assist the Indian Affairs Branch in every way to employ qualified professionals, including social service workers. This was important, the report concluded, because the 'Indians of Canada must be permitted, and helped, to maintain themselves and their dependants with at least the same minimum standard of good health and living conditions as are considered necessary for their Canadian neighbours.'[104]

The commission's report was remarkable for its parroting of Hoey and Indian Affairs' 'new' policy. As a self-proclaimed fact-finding mission of the joint committee, the commission did little to modify the latter's work. It did, however, establish a presence in First Nations communities and thereby lent credence to the committee. A further point of great significance: the commission's conclusions revealed that the joint committee, barely one year into its mandate and still having to hear from a host of Indian and Euro-Canadian organizations, had already made up its mind. Despite the commission's own recommendation that the Indian Act not be revised until the committee had heard from all other interested Indians and Canadians, the balance of the hearings and submissions would all be window-dressing. By including the commission's report, the committee had already thrown its full support behind government policy and the Indian Affairs Branch.

The Special Joint Committee on the Indian Act presented its fourth and final report to Parliament on 22 June 1948. The report was divided into two parts; the first contained eight specific recommendations concerning revisions to the Indian Act; the second made various recommendations covering twelve areas relating to Indian concerns and administration. With reference to the Indian Act, the committee's recommendations began with this statement: 'All proposed revisions are designed to make possible the gradual transition of Indians from wardship to citizenship and to help them to advance themselves.'[105] Among its proposed revisions to the act, the committee recommended that Indian band councils be given greater responsibility for self-government and that this should lead toward the goal of municipal status within their respective provincial jurisdictions.[106] The committee also recommended that the revised act make it 'the duty and responsibility of all officials dealing with Indians to assist them to attain the full rights and to assume the responsibilities of Canadian citizenship.'[107]

Through the committee, the state was saying that the implementation of full citizenship should not only be a part of Indian policy, but that it should be the statutory duty of those charged with its administration. The mere fact that this statement was made confirmed the state's implacable position on citizenship – and *ergo*, assimilation. The committee did make limited concessions to Indians' wariness – ascribed mainly to older Indians – but the idea that Indian citizenship was a mandatory objective remained paramount. It had simply been reduced to another phase in the continued domination and subjugation of Indians.

The committee also recommended that the government consider the granting of a pension to aged, blind, or infirm Indians.[108] Then, in its final recommendation, it made what likely was its most influential statement about the direction of postwar Indian policy:

Your Committee ... recommends that the Government consider the desirability of placing on the agenda of the next Dominion–Provincial Conference, for consideration by the Provinces, the following matters:–

...

(b) Health and Social Services;

...

Your Committee realizes that ... the above ... are matters which, normally, are dealt with under provincial legislative powers. However, it should be possible to arrive at such financial arrangements between the Dominion and Provincial governments as might bring Indians within the scope of such provincial legislation, in order that there be mutual and co-ordinated assistance to facilitate the Indians to become, in every respect, citizens proud of Canada and of the provinces in which they reside.[109]

No other recommendation reflected as clearly as this one the state's determination to resolve the Indian 'problem.'[110] It represented a significant departure from what many Canadians – and certainly most Indians – understood to be an exclusive federal responsibility. Certainly, it was not a recommendation that represented the majority view of the First Nations as it was expressed in their oral testimony and their written submissions. Rather, this was the view that had been articulated principally by both the federal government and by Euro-Canadian organizations such as the Canadian Welfare Council. The central state was now poised to envelop the First Nations in a final process of absolute hegemony.

The clearest signal of the government's approval of this joint committee recommendation was the introduction of Section 87 into the new Indian Act of 1951. Section 87 was not especially new; rather, it expanded on and cast in legal terms what Scott had stated in his policy pamphlet, which he had issued thirty-eight years earlier:

Subject to the terms of any treaty and any other Act of the Parliament of Canada, all laws of general application from time to time in force in any province are applicable to and in respect of Indians in the province, except to the extent that such laws are inconsistent with this Act or any order, rule, regulation or by-law made thereunder, and except to the extent that such laws make provision for any matter for which provision is made by or under this Act.[111]

The introduction of Section 87 brought no real change to how the government understood Indian subjection to ordinary law. It did, however, clearly manifest an awakening to the importance of the principles that Scott's pamphlet had enunciated and their relevance to Indian assimilation. It had become vital to reinforce policy with the law.

Arguably, the idea of including Section 87 had been inspired by the American experience under the Social Security Act of 1936. That act 'had universal application and involved Indians with the States, [and] had reduced certain areas of special federal relationship.'[112] The Social Security Act followed hard on the heels of the Indian Reorganization Act of 1934. The Indian Affairs Branch in Canada was well aware of the new directions in American Indian policy, so there can be little doubt that both the government and the branch were similarly aware of the inclusiveness of the new American initiatives in social welfare. Besides its obvious jurisdictional implications, the Social Security Act had produced another important result for the United States government: it had reduced the costs of Indian administration by involving the states in Indian welfare.[113] The chance to reduce costs would look tempting to any government.

Section 87 must therefore be seen in three lights. First, it was a tool of assimilation policy, a means for the federal government to limit its constitutional responsibilities toward First Nations and force the provinces to accept responsibility for resident Indian citizens. One of the most important of these responsibilities would be social services. Second, it was a statement in law that either implicitly denied federal responsibility for Indian affairs, or served notice that certain as yet to be determined matters would be transferred to the provinces. Of course, Section 87 (now Section 88) did not immediately oblige the provinces to become involved. Nevertheless, it forced the issue into the open and allowed both levels of government and the courts to develop a complex set of arguments concerning laws of general application and where federal constitutional responsibility for Indians began and ended. Third and last, it was a way for the federal government to reduce the direct costs of Indian administration by transferring them to or sharing them with the provinces. In short, Section 87 was to be an instrument of transition from wardship to citizenship that might allow the federal government to divest itself eventually of responsibility for Indians, except in regard to the protection of rights assured by the Royal Proclamation of 1763. Even then, it was hoped that such protection would only be for as long as the Indians felt it was necessary.

Conclusion

This chapter has argued that the basic course of government policy was clearly established sometime late in the war years. Consequently, the Special Joint Committee on the Indian Act was not so much a forum to create a new direction in policy, as it was an opportunity for the state to articulate what had already been set in motion. It provided a public arena for the government to share with the Canadian people its individualistic vision of the place of Indians within Canadian society, and it minimized Indians' attempts to speak against it. Indian positions, in fact, were only minimally incorporated into this vision, and only – as in the case of old age pensions – when they accorded with the government's intentions.

The committee was itself a tool of state propaganda; it was meant to enlist public consent to the state's agenda. Throughout the hearings there was an underlying patronizing tone toward Indians, a sense that they were being humoured in the manner that adults adopt with precocious children. This was especially evident in cases such as the committee members' discussion of the Castleden motion and their treatment of the St-Regis (Akwesasne) Mohawk submission. This treatment left Indians at best as supplicants to the proceedings, at worst as bystanders hoping for something better than the preceding years of relentless repression. It was precisely in this relationship between hope and the benevolence of the state that First Nations' political and psychological disempowerment lay; nowhere did this become more apparent than in the advent of the Indian welfare state.

7

The Influence of the Social Sciences: The Secular Understanding of the 'Other'

What is this so-called 'Indian problem?' In essence it is this: the Indian is too often considered an outsider in our society. His reserve is palisaded with psychological barriers which have prevented close social and economic contact between Indian and non-Indian.

It is the policy of the government to help the Indian, caught in an age of transition, to adapt himself to a larger and more complex society, to be able to earn a living within that society if he wishes to do so.

But there are many factors which inhibit the Indian in his adaptation to a mid-twentieth century technological world. Most are but dimly understood.

Indian Affairs Branch, Department of Citizenship and Immigration,
The Indian in Transition: The Indian Today, 1962

One of the chief research difficulties encountered in a study of post–Second World War Indian administration arises from the growth and complexity of the Indian Affairs Branch. At headquarters, enriched funding and the development of new and existing programs resulted in a dramatic increase in correspondence with educational institutions, international bodies, the media, other public and private organizations, and the Canadian public, not to mention assorted federal and provincial government sectors. Much of the earlier, apparent simplicity of branch policy was lost as officials grappled with a variety of influences and as branch programs began to develop their own unique requirements. As professional expertise within the branch grew, holistic approaches to the Indian 'problem' became less and less possible as each area claimed its own special knowledge. Assimilation remained the objective, but what exactly that meant and how best to accomplish it became matters of considerable discussion.

These many influences pose a dilemma: How can the development of Indian social welfare policy be presented in the context of their competition within the minds of senior administrators? Because it is impossible for me to account for all influences, I will focus in the final section of this book on those which were most germane to the outcome of welfare policy by the mid-1960s. These will include the roles played by the social sciences, the Canadian Welfare Council, and, to a lesser extent, the Indian-Eskimo Association of Canada. The role of the social sciences is presented separately because they set the overall tone and context for the department's new-found energy and policymaking, especially in the twenty years that followed the Second World War. The role of the Canadian Welfare Council – whose membership and staff included practising social scientists and elite social administrators – is explored separately in chapter 8 as part of the development of modern welfare policy in the 1950s and early 1960s. Finally, the role of the Indian-Eskimo Association, an outgrowth of the Canadian Association for Adult Education, is discussed in chapter 9. The association's work seems especially pertinent to the development of welfare policy – in particular, to ideas about community development, welfare, and integration that emerged during the 1960s. The role of the Indian-Eskimo Association was complex and problematic. As a predominantly Euro-Canadian advocacy organization purporting to speak to the interests of Indians, it behaved at times almost as a partner of the government.

Acculturation and the Influence of the Social Sciences[1]

In the immediate postwar period, the overriding external influences on the work of the Indian Affairs Branch were the social sciences. These influences would persist as many practitioners were absorbed into the bureaucratic structure.[2] The influence of the social sciences in the public service reached its zenith during the 1960s and early 1970s. In many respects the social scientists were the explorers and missionaries of the mid-twentieth century, the new interpreters of the 'other' to the European mind. The potential of applying various social science disciplines to the problems of Indian administration became apparent in a 1942 study of Indian nutrition conducted by Dr Frederick Tisdall at Norway House, Manitoba, and reported by Dr Percy Moore to the Parliamentary Committee on Postwar Reconstruction. In his report, Dr Tisdall 'envisioned a battery of specialists tackling the Indian problem in one or two specific groups.'[3] As a consequence of that study, the Canadian government mounted a comprehensive survey of Indian bands living around James Bay in northern Ontario and Quebec. The James Bay Survey was conducted by a research team of doctors, dentists, and two social anthropologists, all under the general direction of Professor G. Gordon Brown, an anthropologist at the University of Toronto.[4]

This survey was initiated in 1947 with the full blessing of the joint parliamentary committee. According to one of the researchers, John J. Honigmann, it was 'a major attempt to integrate the points of view of diverse sciences and to apply those disciplines to administrative problems.'[5] Also according to Honigmann, the idea of applying a social science, anthropology, to the administration of cross-cultural situations had first been applied 'fruitfully' by the British – though he did not specify where – and later by the Americans in their Indian administration.[6] Of course, anthropologists had long been studying First Nations and Inuit in Canada. Among the most prominent of these were Franz Boas, Diamond Jenness, and T.F. McIlwraith. Jenness, for example, thought his work useful in assisting government policy – indeed, his assessment that Indians generally were headed for extinction helped legitimate the state's position on assimilation.[7] In the postwar era, however, Indian Affairs became more active in soliciting and/or funding studies and utilizing social scientific knowledge of First Nations cultures to assist those nations in adapting to Euro-Canadian society. The James Bay Survey awakened a flurry of interest in academic Canada and alerted the government to the necessity of funding only those studies that would advance or legitimate the state's aims regarding Indian integration. To paraphrase Peter Kulchyski, this was social science in the service of the state.[8]

A letter from Forrest E. LaViolette, a sociologist at McGill University, to Herbert Marshall, the Dominion statistician, reflected this new interest. LaViolette told Marshall about a current series of studies, sponsored by the Canadian Social Science Research Council, 'dealing with the Canadian Indian and his position in contemporary Canadian life.' LaViolette continued that 'this initiative on the part of the Council came about as a result of the war experience of the Department of National Defence, of the new responsibilities of the Department of National Health and Welfare, of the new concern on the part of the Department of Indian Affairs, and of the increased interest on the part of the general public.'[9] The possibility that the many studies underway might be lost to the overall goals of the government prompted R.A. Hoey to write to Dr Hugh Keenleyside, the Deputy Minister of Mines and Resources. In his correspondence, Hoey supported a suggestion from Dr Morton of the National Defence Research Board that closer links be developed between the board's research and the activities of the branch:

> There are a number of projects that naturally come to one's mind when ... research comes up for discussion. The scientists I have interviewed appear to be ... interested in psychological and sociological studies with the object of securing information relating to the temperament of the Indian, his innate inertia, his nomadic instincts, lack of frugality, etc. It is perhaps well that we should have thorough understanding of these before we undertake a program aimed at the legitimate exploitation of the resources to which the Indian claims ownership. But even at this stage, research work in forestry, fish culture, educational effort and the dietary habits of the Indian, and his available food supply, might very profitably be undertaken.[10]

Hoey's memorandum, besides showing an enthusiastic response to the National Defence proposal, brings to light in an innocent way the state's underlying objective and the potential usefulness of the social sciences in its achievement.

Why was it now so important to integrate Indians into the Euro-Canadian mainstream? Was it simply the moral imperative of citizenship? Clearly, capital and the state worked together on economic development[11] and, so that dominant class interests could pursue that objective, it was constantly necessary for the state to expedite economic penetration into native territories with the least resistance possible. This could be done, it was surmised, by gaining the confidence of the general public in the promise of Indian citizenship and betterment,[12] and by inducing First Nations' consent through their inclusion into civic society. In effect, the goal of postwar Indian policy was to transform First Nations into a new level of civil society, one from which they would see that participation in the exploitation of their lands was in their own interests. One role of social science, then, was to help lay the foundations for a civil level of native society. This required, first, a scientific 'understanding' of the Indians, and second, the application of that understanding to the development of programs necessary for their adaptation to the dominant Euro-Canadian society. There were several ways this might occur. For Indians in the south, the principal goal of assimilation policy was to connect them as individuals to the labour market. Regarding the north, it was thought that Indians would either leave the reserves for the cities or that, by establishing a more sedentary lifestyle, they would form the basis for a new labour force as the resource economy expanded.

Also implicit in Hoey's memorandum was the modern, Euro-Canadian perception of what the non-European 'other' lacked and what the Euro-Canadian believed was authentic human nature – that is, those characteristics of possessive individualism which formed the core of the modern, liberal state. Hoey was stating plainly what was believed by the administration: that there was an innate Indian nature or psychology that prevented successful assimilation. Innate characteristics were separated from those which might be considered purely cultural, although innate characteristics presumably did something to shape Indian cultural expression. Thus, the other role of social science – derived from the first – was to sort out these qualities in order to determine what was preventing Indians from advancing. That is, was it their culture or their innate character? Which counted more? And could any of their 'innate characteristics' be modified, minimized, or eliminated to prepare them for assimilation?

Dr Keenleyside agreed with Hoey that Indian psychology should be included in the research; such research would surely interest the branch. In January 1948 he wrote to C.J. Mackenzie, president of the Canadian Social Science Research Council, asking him whether the council might be interested in expanding its focus of Indian research beyond sociological and anthropological studies to include psychological ones as well. Mackenzie replied that it would, noting that although the council had not up till then considered psychology a part of its interest, its experience with psychologists during the war had been so positive that their inclusion in Indian research might well be worth supporting.[13]

During the Second World War, much of the research on Indian behaviour began to centre on the effects of malnutrition. Dr Moore and others had published some early findings in the *Canadian Medical Association Journal*; in 1948, preliminary results of a new study, the James Bay Survey, were published in the same journal.[14] In September 1948, Giff Swartman, superintendent of the Sioux Lookout agency, wrote to headquarters, enclosing correspondence he had received from one of the local physicians, Dr L.C. Bartlett of Favorable Lake, Ontario. Dr Bartlett wanted to caution the branch against relying too heavily on Dr Moore's thinking about malnutrition and to bring to its attention psychiatric theory that he thought relevant to the advancement of Indians: 'You will recall that several years ago, in an article in the Canadian Medical Journal, Dr. Moore concluded that some of the traits attributed to the Indian as a racial characteristic, such as shiftlessness, indolence, etc., might actually be the result of chronic fatigue from malnutrition. I have another thought on the subject.'[15] Drs Moore and Bartlett did not disagree about the symptoms, but their diagnoses and prescriptions were clearly different. Dr Bartlett continued, freely blending a rather amateur understanding of Freud with allusions to Watsonian childrearing:

> It occurred to me that I have never yet seen an Indian parent punishing his child in any way. On looking into it, I find that they actually very rarely enforce any sort of discipline at all; the child merely obeys all his whims, and the parents cater to them at will. It is the path of least immediate resistance to let the child have his own way. ... Contrast this with a white child's upbringing.
>
> Is it unusual, then, that the child should grow up with no sense of responsibility to anyone but himself? In adulthood, he merely continues to do as he pleases, usually the path of least resistance. He works when he feels like it, eats when he is hungry, but makes no store for tomorrow, etc. These are still childhood patterns, and I suggest that they have persisted into adulthood because at no period of his life was he taught to discard them and aim at adult thinking and discipline.
>
> In support of this we have the observation that Indians who have been brought up in a better environment, eg. a good school under a good teacher, who tried to do more than teach reading and writing, usually show more initiative, and usually have more sense of responsibility towards other people than do Indians raised entirely in native ways.[16]

There is no evidence that Dr Bartlett's musings were ever translated directly into policy. That being said, the idea that Indian children could benefit from European childrearing principles certainly was well entrenched in the residential schools. Later, in the 1960s, the idea would be given still more weight when disproportionate numbers of Indian children were placed for fostering and adoption in white homes.[17] If Dr Bartlett's views represented a rather simplistic application of child development theory, those of Marcel Rioux did not.

In November 1949 – the year the Indian Affairs Branch was transferred to the Department of Citizenship and Immigration – Rioux, a cultural anthropologist at the National Museum in Ottawa, conducted a study of the social customs of the Iroquois at the Six Nations Reserve near Brantford, Ontario. In the course of his study, Rioux developed an extensive questionnaire on childrearing practices and family reactions to newborns. F.J. Alcock, the museum's chief curator, submitted the questionnaire to branch officials, informing them that it would be administered by the schoolteachers on the reserve, who would 'fill in the questionnaire, after having observed the behaviour of a certain number of families.'[18] This was a necessary protocol, because the teachers were employees of Indian Affairs. In addition, all studies of Indians on the reserves had to be approved by the branch. The questionnaire contained ninety-four questions, many of them highly sensitive and intrusive in nature (see sample in Document 7.1).

So sensitive was the questionnaire that Mrs R.A. Farmer, representing the Local Council of Women in Brantford, wrote a letter of protest to Ross Macdonald, the Speaker of the House of Commons. In it she stated the council's strong disapproval of many of the questions and opined that they infringed on the respondents' private lives.[19] But standards of respect that applied to the dominant culture were dismissed in the interests of science and progress when applied to the 'other.' Alcock replied to Farmer:

> It is thought that there is a close relation between the way children are brought up and the way they will later behave as members of a group; the aim of these studies on child social adaptation is to find the roots of actual adult behaviour with a view of eradicating the sources of maladjustments. ... The behaviour, which we justly consider as intimate, has a wide influence on other aspects of human behaviour and should be investigated if a full understanding of a given society is to be arrived at. The best example ... of the good effects of this type of enquiry is that of the Navaho Indians who have been studied in this manner by members of the Peabody Museum of Harvard. These Indians are now dealt with by administrators with a full comprehension of their point of view and will in the near future be completely integrated into the active life of the country with their complete consent and satisfaction.
>
> The Iroquois of Brantford have been chosen ... because of their great culture achievements and because it is thought that in understanding the way they have accomplished their cultural transition this knowledge could be used and applied to some other groups who have not achieved so much.[20]

Indians had been reduced by the state to objects of paternalistic

Document 7.1 Questionnaire on childhood among the Iroquois, excerpts

---

B. *Prenatal Period*

11. How is the announcement that a woman is pregnant received by members of the family?
12. Is the behaviour of these people towards the expectant mother changed? ...
14. Does the couple continue to have intercourse?
15. Is there any belief associated with pregnancy? Dreams, forerunners, belief that the coming baby represents the soul of an ancestor.
16. What measure does the mother take to have a good-looking and healthy baby? ...
18. Is there any means known to foresee the child's sex? ...

C. *Birth*

20. Opinion of older people towards hospitals ...
25. If delivery takes place at the Hospital, describe what happens before, during and after the entry in the hospital ...
27. When the delivery takes place at home, what happens? (Full description of the event).
28. How is the cord cut, and with what instrument? ...
31. Does any member of the family leave the house during the delivery? ...
35. Are there any special practices in the family in connection with the childbirth? ...
47. Is there much attention shown to the baby?
48. How is he nursed. Breast or bottle-fed? ...

D. *Month 2 and 3*

71. At what time does the exposure of sex cease?
72. Is there any curb to self-manipulation? ...
79. Is the temper of the child controlled, encouraged or ignored?

Source: NAC, RG-10, CR Series, Vol. 8616, File 1/1-15, Part 1, Anthropological Research, 'Questionnaire on Childhood among the Iroquois,' prepared by Marcel Rioux, included in correspondence to D.M. McKay, Director, Indian Affairs Branch, Department of Citizenship and Immigration, from F.J. Alcock, Chief Curator, National Museum of Canada, 21 November 1949.

administration, and now social science was reducing them to objects of study – specifically, to subjects participating in the development of knowledge for their own good. There was no question here of what the final outcome ought to be. At issue was whether the methods to achieve it could simply be better developed and refined and the Indians made more willing partners in their own demise.

The 'demotion' of Indians to scientific objects made it possible to justify denying their claims to cultural and social integrity. Almost any study could now be justified, as long as it promised to shed light on Indians' dependence and their perceived aversion to acculturation to liberal society and the work ethic. In the context at hand, it was thought that by studying Indian childrearing patterns, some insight might be gained into their future predisposition to self-discipline and self-reliance and, consequently, into the likelihood that they would require social assistance as adults. In the specific case of the Iroquois – a supposedly advanced people – lessons could be learned that might be transferable to those Indian nations considered less advanced. This was a curious logic on Alcock's part, for if, as he claimed, the Iroquois had already made a successful transition, how would understanding their childrearing practices be any more helpful to policymakers than simply teaching those used in Euro-Canadian culture? It seems that Alcock was being less than forthright with Mrs Farmer, and that Rioux's real interest was, indeed, the stubborn reluctance of the Iroquois to embrace the Canadian nation.

Rioux's was typical of the interest of many sociologists, anthropologists, and psychologists who were making proposals to the government to study First Nations communities and cultures. Throughout the 1950s, many graduate students approached the branch about conducting summer research; this, of course, was the fieldwork part of their studies. Nearly all these requests focused either on native languages or on acculturation and barriers to it.[21] By 1951, the many government departments and agencies involved in Indian matters had agreed that a representative panel was needed in order to assess the merits of the study proposals and judge their fit with the overall aims of Indian policy. To this purpose, the Advisory Panel on Indian Research was established in January 1951, chaired by T.F. McIlwraith from the University of Toronto's Department of Anthropology.[22] The member groups on the panel were the National Research Council, the Dominion Bureau of Statistics, the Canadian Social Science Research Council, the Department of National Health and Welfare, the Civil Service Commission, and the

Indian Affairs Branch. Shortly after its first meeting on 27 January 1951, McIlwraith wrote a memorandum to all the panel members to set in writing the agreed upon terms of reference: 'The primary function of the Panel is ... a clearing house for information on research, especially in the field of the adjustment of the Indians to changing conditions.'[23]

The panel's tasks were to consult with potential researchers and with the government agencies it represented, to advise on the suitability of research proposals, and to distribute the findings of those it had approved. Many panel members worked in government agencies whose policies directly affected Indians, and were to bring policy changes to the panel for discussion. The panel could then adjust its criteria for assessing research proposals in order to accommodate these changes.[24] Discussion about a method of adjusting research criteria continued during later panel meetings; these culminated in the fall of 1951, when Colonel H.M. Jones, the Superintendent of Welfare Services for the Indian Affairs Branch, raised the issue of new policies resulting from the revised Indian Act.

The activities of the Indian Welfare Service had been considerably expanded, he said, and social workers had been appointed in all the country's administrative regions. In addition, the effects of the new act's significant changes would require study.[25] Dr Morton picked up on Jones's concerns and suggested that the panel develop a comprehensive list of problems to guide it in selecting research projects. The discussion, led by Jones and Dr Morton, then focused on the need for a 'master plan' that could be followed to match proposals with identified Indian problems. Such a plan could also help interpret scientists' findings in ways that would be of assistance to administrators.[26]

One of the first studies to gain the panel's approval was a testing of Indian intelligence by D.J. Penfold of the University of Western Ontario. Penfold was interested in the educability of Indian children. Dr Morton reported the results of Penfold's research to the panel in October 1951.[27] Morton abstracted from those results, and concluded:

It could be inferred that in so far as immediate ability to meet white educational standards is concerned the Indian child is retarded, and this is true to some extent even when age is neglected in grade-for-grade comparisons. On the other hand abilities of the Indian child expressed in a form less directly dependent on verbal tools or on the use of symbols more familiar to the white appear to be as high as for white children. Thus it could be judged that, given equal stimulation and comparable environment, the

Indian child might be expected to be as educable as the white. This condition is not granted at present, but could be in the future; it would probably require, however, much more than the provision of better facilities for academic education alone.[28]

Here then, was a perfect example of how the panel proposed to work. The identified problem in this case was Indian education and educability. The study suggested to administrators a twofold approach: one, develop programs to counteract the cultural disadvantages experienced by Indian children when they encountered white education, and two, develop broader measures to promote general Indian acculturation and integration. Science would thus help the Indian.

Another research project typical of those which interested the government came from Dorothy Woodward, an anthropology student at the University of Toronto. She proposed an ambitious three-month study of the Chippewa at Sarnia, Ontario, which would focus on their adaptation to urban life. She hypothesized that Indians' claims that there was racial discrimination in hiring practices was probably a misinterpretation. Instead, poor results occurred because of '[the Indian's] failure to incorporate the work ethic and his lack of industrial training.'[29] Furthermore:

> The charge of descrimination [*sic*] against the Indian may be confused in the mind of the Indian as racial descrimination [*sic*] *per se*. The real factor probably lies in the lack of the work ethic stemming from the survival of cultural factors handed down as the remnants of another way of life. This phenomenon is not different ... from that which is taking place in ... formerly rural Quebec. The world view of the Indian ... is out of kilter with the psychological demands of industrial society.[30]

There was no evidence that Woodward's study was approved or conducted, but her thinking on the topic of the Indian and the work ethic was quite representative of the branch's. In addition, her double-standard for Indian culture – 'sensitive' to its uniqueness on the one hand, and dismissing it as an out-of-kilter remnant on the other – was in line with the branch's own way of thinking.

An acerbic response by the branch to a project proposed by its new companion, the citizenship department, demonstrated this double-standard. In 1954, A.E. Thompson, a regional liaison officer with the Citizenship Branch of the Department of Citizenship and Immigration, sought approval to develop a project on Indian citizenship. His proposal could not be found in the Indian Affairs file; however, its content can be ascertained from the correspondence that he wished to attend courses at universities in Washington and Chicago that would provide specialized knowledge in Indian integration. He would then adapt this knowledge to develop a pilot project in Canada. The Citizenship Branch asked Indian Affairs for its opinion of Thompson's proposal. Indian Affairs dismissed the proposal entirely, and one senior bureaucrat implicitly accused the Citizenship Branch of entering its exclusive jurisdiction.[31] An especially contemptuous judgment of the proposal by J.P.B. Ostrander, superintendent of the Welfare Service, was more than just hostile:

> The whole submission implies that the long succession of capable and conscientious officials who have worked with and studied the Indians for the past hundred years ... have learned almost nothing and it remains for a rather mediocre official of another Branch to provide the answers to most of the questions which have long puzzled us.
>
> Mr Thompson ... demonstrates ignorance of the real needs of the Indians, for example, encouragement to develop the Potlatch, tribal dances and other aboriginal customs would be a retrogressive step amongst the people who have for one or two generations accepted Christianity.[32]

Ostrander's indignation exposed the branch's own ineptitude and mediocrity! His statement also represented the opinion of senior administration about Indian cultural practices, notwithstanding that Parliament had removed any legal proscription of them. The tone of Ostrander's reply permeated Jones's response to Citizenship.

> The statement [by Thompson] that the Indian is a member of a 'demoralized group' without pride in their own institutions, culture, heritage, etc. is an opinion not shared by this Administration. By and large Indians are a proud people very much conscious of their racial heritage and privileges, real and imaginary, in Canadian society ...
>
> We do not discourage participation in any truly cultural native ceremony, although you will recall that certain ... ceremonies ... were unlawful under the former Indian Act ... However, special 'Indian days' and exhibitions ... have had a detrimental effect and interfere with work and study. Fortunately, our younger Indians who have had the benefit of education are less attracted to such events than were their fathers ...

> Mr. Thompson's proposals are, in actual fact, a resumé of the ... policies of the Branch.[33]

In the responses of Jones and Ostrander can be detected the administrative equivalent of Woodward's academic hypothesis about the Sarnia Chippewa: that their culture was a 'remnant from another way of life.' The branch disdained Thompson's proposal; not only that, but it continued to be highly suspicious of Parliament's decision to allow the practice of cultural rites, a decision that in their view could only result in the regression of the Indian and be counterproductive to the goal of integration.

Throughout the 1950s, then, studies conducted for Indian Affairs centred on problems of Indian adaptation and transition to Euro-Canadian society. They were tailored to the state's needs rather than to a sympathetic appreciation of the situation facing First Nations. Most professed to be objective studies, but nearly all were implicitly biased toward ideas of liberal progress, modern society, and what Indians lacked – either in their social environment or in their nature – that would enable them to become successful citizens. One study, by the Reverend William Baldwin, applied a structural-functional analysis to the social problems of an Ojibwa band in Ontario. Using Durkheim's concept of anomie and Parsons's systems theory, Baldwin contended that in their former way of life, the Ojibwa had developed institutionalized responses that enabled them to adapt to changes. The source of their contemporary social problems, he had found, resided in their failure to develop new institutional (i.e., normative) behaviours consistent with their new socioeconomic environment. Thus, they had been unable to achieve a new equilibrium and were now in a state of 'anomie.'[34] Another study, typical of this bias and proposed by Dr Frank Vallee, Director of Research for the Citizenship branch, intended to examine the 'social and economic situation of Indians living in a place like Edmonton,' with a special emphasis on Indian employment and the effectiveness of rehabilitation programs. The study, Dr Vallee thought, could give 'a general picture of Indians in the city – their living conditions, leisure habits, examples of successful and unsuccessful adjustment.' H.M. Jones, the officious director of Indian Affairs, thought this study most worthwhile, although file evidence does not reveal whether the study proceeded.[35] Not until the early 1960s, in an effort to preserve what was rapidly becoming lost, was there any significant movement toward an appreciation of native cultures. According to the Indian Affairs files at

least, it was European rather than North American scholars who spearheaded this change.[36]

The best summary of the intent of the postwar studies can be gleaned
from Professor Harry B. Hawthorn's 1954 proposal for a special study of
the Indians of British Columbia – a study that later gained much favour
with Indian Affairs.[37] Indeed, its general methodology was later incorporated into a general survey of the situation of all First Nations in Canada. Hawthorn wrote that 'long-range planning in the field of Indian
administration calls more urgently than ever for a non-partisan, systematic, comprehensive and reliable investigation of the present economy
of Indian groups, of their progress towards self-responsibility and self-
reliability, of their attitudes towards the general Canadian way of life, as
well as of the attitudes of other Canadian groups and individuals
towards them.'[38] Treasury Board approved Hawthorn's proposal in mid-
March of 1954. The proposal arose from the creation of a special fund
by the Department of Citizenship and Immigration in the fiscal year
1953–4, whose purpose was to assist studies of Indians from a 'citizenship standpoint to form the basis on which to judge advancement to the
point of readiness for enfranchisement.'[39]

Another research direction was proposed in 1959. Professor W.J. Morris at the Department of Anthropology of the University of Toronto proposed a comprehensive survey to the Indian Affairs Branch. His survey
of Canada's Indians would be broader in scope than Hawthorn's British
Columbia study, not only in its sample population but also in the number of factors to be considered as affecting the adaptive capacity of First
Nations. The Hawthorn study had confined itself to the effects of federal legislation; in contrast, Morris hypothesized that all 'formal legislative requirements determine the nature of adjustment possible for an
enculturating indigenous population.'[40] By this he meant the impact of
provincial as well as federal legislation, and the total environment
spawned by legislation in the different jurisdictions, including the emergence of provincial and voluntary welfare agencies. Morris was especially critical of Hawthorn for failing to take into account this total
environment, and he believed that many of his recommendations were
irrelevant as a consequence. Morris's proposal was apparently not
approved; yet it was he, more than any other researcher – including
Hawthorn – who squarely identified the constitutional division of powers as an important issue in Indian integration. In 1964, at the request
of the Indian Affairs Branch, Hawthorn began a comprehensive survey
of Canada's Indians for the federal government, one that included

many of the factors identified in Professor Morris's earlier proposal. It is not known whether Hawthorn was aware of that proposal. What is certain is that the federal government now wanted a full picture of the political, legal, social, and economic environment of Indians in Canada.

The James Bay Survey

The James Bay Survey, conducted between 1947 and 1949, was until the 1954 Hawthorn study of Indians in British Columbia the most comprehensive and influential of all studies affecting Indian Affairs policy, especially Indian social welfare. In this discussion, reference is made to John J. Honigmann's 1951 account of the James Bay Survey published in the *Dalhousie Review*. Honigmann was a student anthropologist at the University of Toronto during the course of the survey and was one of the researchers assigned to the Attawapiskat Band of Cree at Attawapiskat, Ontario. His paper is especially interesting because of its extensive discourse on what he perceived to be the revolutionary nature of the study in comparison to traditional approaches to anthropology established in the nineteenth century. 'In this paper,' he wrote, 'we will be concerned with how contemporary patterns of thinking about man are related to problems of human administration. Particularly how they are related to the government of people who follow a way of life different from that of the administrators.'[41]

Honigmann began by outlining the premises of nineteenth-century anthropology and their effects on colonial administrations. Essentially, he maintained, early anthropology was based on the 'quasi-scientific' belief in sociocultural evolution and in the inevitable progress of all cultures toward the ultimate state of Western Civilization. Teaching backward peoples the ways of the West could hasten this evolution. This, according to Honigmann, was what Indian Affairs administrators were trying to do when they introduced husbandry as a replacement for hunting and gathering, a mode of existence considered to be at the lowest rung of human organization. In contrast, modern social anthropology has 'come to replace the belief in cultural evolution with empirical laws concerning the processes through which social life maintains itself and changes.'[42] Equipped with knowledge gained from other kinds of studies about human behaviour, the anthropologist now viewed man's place not as the 'lord of the universe but rather as a single variable in a most complicated field of forces.'[43] Thus, the James Bay Survey was an attempt to understand the total field of forces affecting Indian cultures and to set in motion the processes by which, according to the newly identified empirical laws, social change might occur.

Utilizing Dr Tisdall's earlier findings on Indian malnutrition as the focal point for intervention, the James Bay Survey team postulated two possible solutions: one, continue food relief policies that would alleviate the problem but not solve it; or two, improve people's capabilities to become self-supporting.[44] This latter, preferred approach required knowledge about 'what makes the Indian tick, what motivates him.'[45] To acquire this knowledge and to gain insight into changes in food production and consumption, G. Gordon Brown, the survey leader, proposed 'to put two communities under observation for a calendar year and watch what happens not only at any part of the year, but through the whole annual cycle. In other words, the first task was to obtain the facts of the way of life.'[46] Two anthropologists, Honigmann and Kerr, would spend one year in the communities. The second task, not mentioned by Honigmann, was to conduct a medical survey of the same communities.[47] The two James Bay communities – Attawapiskat, Ontario (Honigmann), on the western shore, and Rupert House, Quebec (Kerr), on the southeastern shore – were selected based on their 'pronounced dependence on relief [and] adjacency to Toronto.'[48]

The organization of the study was guided by three principles that incorporated 'contemporary patterns of thinking shaping the methods of the sciences and promising to influence the arts of human administration.'[49] The first principle was the fundamental unity of human life. Man was to be conceived no longer in particularizing terms such as economic, rational, or biological man, but rather in terms such as organismic or holistic, which reflected the 'simultaneous interplay of biological, nutritional, emotional, social, and cultural forces.'[50] In this sense, health was defined as a function of geography, human constitution, traditional habits of subsistence, and the size of the group. The latter factor affected the potential for economic cooperation.

To illustrate the study of health according to the first principle, Honigmann described the role of the biologist in specifying the symptoms of malnutrition and of the anthropologist in identifying how learned behaviour patterns had led to the neglect of once useful food resources. The problem, Honigmann asserted, was that the Indians had learned to depend on European foods when fur-bearing animals and game were depleted; now, when traditional foods had been replenished, they remained dependent on European foods.[51] Indians were unwilling to return to traditional subsistence patterns; the social scientists interpreted this as a failure on their own part to understand how to alter desire, how to motivate a change in behaviour.[52] Part of the solution, Honigmann wrote, was to show the government administrators how to induce changes in Indian behaviour in such a way that they could remain true to their own democratic values (i.e., refrain from direct manipulation of people). Honigmann seems to have equated democracy with the politics of choice; Indian behaviour would change based on alternatives, among which some would be self-evidently more desirable than others. But if the administrators were to motivate changes in behaviour – changes that would lead to assimilation – was this not simply a form of manipulation? Here was another example of the object/subject syndrome whereby the state, through social scientific means, engaged the object of study as an active participant in the real objective: the domination of the object.

The second principle was to understand the 'total situation' of human behaviour in its external and subjective reality. To illustrate this, Honigmann noted that the Attawapiskat were not starving in 1947 or 1948, yet 'they believed themselves both on the brink of starvation and neglected by the Federal government. Psychologically they were ... troubled, anxious, and insecure, conditions no doubt related to the fact ... they had seen their ... resources dwindle in a period of over-trapping as well as to the fact ... the government was ... sharing their anxiety by pursuing a generous relief policy.'[53] It was not clear from this assertion what solution the researchers had proposed, nor what value there had been in treating fear of starvation as a subjective experience. Implicit in Honigmann's language was the suggestion that Indians needed to be weaned from relief with the assurance that life really was not as bad as they perceived it to be. The lesson for government administrators was not to respond in the manner of compliant parents acceding to the fears of the child, but rather to foster and encourage healthy responses to uncertainty.

Honigmann then made an extraordinary leap from the 'totality' of the immediate situation of the Attawapiskat to their position in the entire postwar world. The researchers had decided to consider all the influences in the lives of the James Bay Cree, including the remote ones. Honigmann observed that 'Canada's bush Indians are far less "bushed" or isolated than is commonly supposed. Together with the rest of the population of our shrunken globe they are intensely bound up with their contemporaries. Realization of this complex "social field" is of paramount importance for planned change.'[54] This statement seemed to indicate that the researchers' earlier concern for a return to traditional patterns of subsistence had been obviated by the greater need for 'planned change' – a euphemistic allusion to the Cree's necessary adaptation to modern society. Honigmann and the other researchers were apparently ignorant of the fact that the Cree had been adapting to influences far beyond their own lands since the time of first contact. Blinded by the project of science, the researchers were oblivious to their own biases and assumptions.

The study's third principle was the recognition of the part played by culture in resisting or facilitating change.[55] Why, Honigmann posed, do cultures resist change? First, he noted, there is a reluctance to expend energy on learning something new. Second, proposed changes are usually 'incongruent with the ideas, values, skills, or patterns of organization familiar to the group.'[56] Here, Honigmann gave an especially undiscerning example:

> It is ... likely that a fundamental mistake occurred when gardening was introduced with the expectation that men would undertake planting ... Traditionally in Attawapiskat culture men engage in the more spectacular and least humdrum occupations – hunting, trapping, travel, large scale marketing. Women do the routine work, including net fishing and cooking ... Probably plant husbandry would be more successful than it has been in Attawapiskat if the women were placed in charge of the gardens.[57]

This depiction of the Attawapiskat demonstrates the problem of objectifying the 'other.'

Clearly, Honigmann reduced the failure of gardening to gendered role division. Indian Affairs officials obviously had made a fundamental error in assigning gardening tasks to men. Although Honigmann attributed this error to a failure to understand traditional Cree culture, arguably he was drawing on his own assumptions about gender and the division of labour in any culture, including modern, Western culture. According to Honigmann, men were used to 'spectacular' occupations (real or productive work), whereas women were best suited to those which were 'humdrum' (routine or domestic work). It didn't occur to him that sustenance gardening was probably not a viable proposition for any culture on the shores of James Bay.

Honigmann remained unaware of his assumptions. The issue for him and the James Bay team was to find ways to help the Attawapiskat learn skills in innovation. Thus, the task of the James Bay team was to educate government administrators to help the Attawapiskat change in a manner that would be self-determined and democratic. This change would occur once the Cree recognized that it would be to their material advantage.[58] This dilemma about change and innovation became the genesis of a new approach to government administration. Honigmann said, with reference to the American experience under the Indian Reorganization Act, that 'assimilation is a policy both difficult to realize as well as basically undemocratic. Yet nobody desires to withhold from native societies techniques that would enhance their control over the environment or traits that members of those groups are anxious to adopt. The policy of internal development ... has come to replace assimilation as a doctrine of cross cultural administration.'[59] Successful change would occur, the James Bay study concluded, if it was congruent with the Cree way of life and reflected goals the Cree thought were desirable. On the basis of this conclusion, the research team recommended that material development occur from within the culture rather than from without.[60]

On the surface, this conclusion seems reasonable and forward-looking. Actually, community development as an administrative strategy is clearly situated within its rationale. Yet the underlying objective of such a strategy – Indian adaptation to and integration with Euro-Canadian society – must not be ignored, any more than the fundamental fact that a strategy of intervention was required in the first place. It is ironic that community development ideally is a method of self-determination and actualization yet is often used as a form of indoctrination to preferred paths.

Thinking like Honigmann's was delusory. The survey had set out deliberately to find out 'what made the Indian tick' because government and academia alike were concerned about Indians' dependency and their apparent lack of desire to change. Researchers embraced a notion of 'holistic' or 'universal' man – a liberal idea from the Enlightenment which, when boiled down to its Euro-Canadian essence, still seemed more related to utilitarian or economic man than to any other. They shuddered at using manipulation – a method 'not acceptable in Canadian administration' – and then recommended a strategy to do precisely that. If, as the state and academia paternalistically averred, Indian survival lay in change and in the unfolding fabric of Canada, and if Indians and Indian culture by nature resisted change, then a method of inducing change had to be found. In an insidious fashion, then, Indians were to be manipulated by principles of self-determination to an accommodation of Euro-Canadian society so that they appeared satisfied and, principally, so that state objectives were satisfied.

This, Honigmann proclaimed, was the great contribution of science and scientific method:

> We maintain that scientific methods can develop and thereby change the Indian's traditional culture to the point where it is not a slavish imitation of the white man's but where it represents a unique and satisfying instrument, both adjusted to its milieu and at the same time not radically divorced from tradition. The success of such a program rests ... with imaginative and sympathetic administrators who may themselves be trained. It demands continuous application of social scientific and other knowledge. Above all it calls for men who believe that social science can be successfully applie [*sic*] to human administration.[61]

The training of government administrators in these ideas began in the two communities during the course of the survey. The training, however, was not necessarily openly welcomed, and at first the branch was more concerned about changing the thinking of their own personnel than that of the Cree. According to Major C.A.F. Clark, an educational survey officer with Indian Affairs in Ottawa, Euro-Canadian culture could be equally resistant to change. In a report on a 1948 field trip to the James Bay agency, he discussed a meeting he had had with Brown and his two field researchers.

> Their findings and recommendations would not irritate a person accustomed to objective scientific discussion, but I left them advice that they should take into account the reactions of two types of minds often found in personnel employed in Indian education and welfare activities:
> (1) those with a positive philosophy which tends to make them heedless of or even hostile to scientific opinion which has not received ecclesiastical sanction;
> (2) those with a mass of experience which they have not been able to organize ... so as to be able to do a progressively better job and who will resent what might appear to be a criticism of their achievements.
> The organized opposition of such people might deter the authorization of further surveys ...
> Professor Brown and his associates will likely urge [that] workers in the Indian field ... receive at least sufficient instruction in sociological anthropology and allied subjects to give them 'sophistication' in those subjects and in their dealings with the aborigines.[62]

Conclusion

The role of the social sciences in shaping welfare policy after the Second World War was most pronounced in two parallel directions. First, the social sciences underpinned the continued development of a rationalized relief system that was aimed both at satisfying requirements for adequate nutrition and at furthering Western notions of family and male responsibility for employment and support. They also set the course for Indian citizenship by providing new ideas about community development – ideas that would lead directly to strategies involving the provinces and the extension of their services to the reserves. Most important, however, was that the social sciences introduced a new culture into Indian Affairs that allowed the government to reinvent paternalism based on the 'benevolence' of secular understanding, knowledge, and the tools of social engineering. The social sciences simply furthered the state's aims and provided the knowledge and rationalization to legitimate state activities in First Nations communities.

8

The Emergence of Indian Welfare Bureaucracy, 1945–1960

Well, we didn't choose Canada and we didn't choose to be Canadian ... We are governed by the Indian Act: our independence has been taken from us ... You see we are up against so much ... there was a time up until the fifties that we survived ... But then the big machinery came and it displaced us. The logging trucks destroyed our traplines. After machinery came welfare.

Mary John, Elder of the Stoney Creek Indian Band, British Columbia, 1990

Healthy and Wise: Indian Welfare Policy and Administration, 1945–1958

In his testimony to the 1946 joint parliamentary committee, R.A. Hoey, the director of the Indian Affairs Branch, stated that throughout the Second World War expenditure on Indian relief had steadily declined. In the fiscal year 1945–6, he noted, just 68.6 per cent of the total welfare appropriation in Indian Affairs had been spent on direct relief. Hoey offered no data on how many Indians received this assistance. Instead, he merely asserted that the decline in expenditure was the result of increased employment for able-bodied Indians.[1] Without these numbers, and considering the branch's historical meanness, it is impossible to determine the extent to which need had really declined and thus to assess the accuracy of Hoey's testimony. It *is* possible, however, to develop a framework of analysis around it.

The per capita welfare expenditure in 1945–6 was about $7.15, or 16.5 per cent less than it had been in 1935–6 (Table 8.1). When the actual amount spent on relief in 1945–6 is compared with that in 1935–6 the results are more dramatic. For example, if no more than 33 per

Table 8.1

Comparison of approximate per capita relief expenditures, Indian Affairs, 1935–6 and 1945–6

| Year | Per capita expenditure according to % population[a] on relief[b] | | |
	Expenditure	100%	33.3%
Total expenditure[c]			
1935–6	$983,537	$8.56	$25.71
1945–6	$913,651	$7.15	$21.46
Actual expenditure[d]			
1935–6	$786,830	$6.85	$20.57
1945–6	$626,765	$4.90	$14.72

Sources: Canada, Department of Citizenship and Immigration, Indian Affairs Branch, A Review of Activities, 1948–1958 (Ottawa: Queen's Printer, 1959), 2; Canada, Department of Mines and Resources, Indian Affairs Branch, Annual Report, 1936–1937, 194; Canada, Parliament, Special Joint Committee of the Senate and the House of Commons Appointed to Examine and Consider the Indian Act, Minutes of Proceedings and Evidence (Ottawa: Edmond Cloutier, Printer to the King's Most Excellent Majesty, 1946), No. 1, pp. 8, 11, 16.
[a]The Indian population in 1936 was about 114,858. In 1945–6 it was approximately 127,830 based on the 1944 Indian census and a growth rate of 1.7 per cent.
[b]It is not known what percentage of the Indian population actually required relief in 1946.
[c]Total expenditure represents all welfare expenditures including relief.
[d]Actual expenditure represents actual relief expenditure or 80 per cent and 68.6 per cent of the total welfare expenditure in 1936 and 1946 respectively as reported by Hoey to the 1946 special joint committee.

cent of the Indian population of 127,830 was on relief in 1945–6, the per capita expenditure was $14.72, or 28.4 per cent less than what it would have been for the same proportion of the population in 1935–6. In 1936 about one-third of the on-reserve Indian population was on relief. Data on actual relief expenditures as a proportion of the welfare appropriation were not provided in the annual reports for either 1936 or 1946.

Hoey's assertion that the reduced expenditure on relief was a result of increased employment among able-bodied Indians was probably true to some extent. The Canadian postwar unemployment rate remained below 3 per cent – and generally below 2 per cent – until 1954.[2] There are no unemployment rates for Indians during the same period, or any data concerning their labour force participation rate. More recent data indicate that historically, Indian unemployment rates have been higher – up to two-and-one-half times higher – than in the general population, and also that their labour force participation rate has been lower. In 1972–3, the earliest year for which it is possible to find data, the Indian social assistance dependency rate was estimated at 57 per cent, compared to a rate of about 6 or 7 per cent in the general population. In 1981 it was estimated that the rate had increased to 59 per cent.[3] Andrew Siggner assessed occupational data for Indians based on the 1981 census of Canada and found that the Indian unemployment rate was 17 per cent. This compared to the national average of 7 per cent; furthermore, the Indian participation rate in the labour force was about 46 per cent, compared to the general rate of 65 per cent. More recently, Frideres made similar comparisons using data from Statistics Canada prepared for the 1995 Royal Commission on Aboriginal Peoples. He noted that in 1991 the unemployment rate for aboriginal people was just below 25 per cent, compared to just over 10 per cent for all Canadians. Similarly, the labour force participation rate for aboriginal people was 57 per cent, compared to almost 68 per cent for all Canadians.[4] It is probable that in 1981, the high Indian unemployment rate combined with the low participation rate contributed to the high dependency rate and that this pattern has persisted. It seems, then, that the comparable rate of dependence in 1972 would have been a product of similar unemployment and participation rates.

Because of the lack of data, it is impossible to say that similar statistical rates existed in the immediate postwar period. Nevertheless, it seems reasonable to conjecture that some version of them existed and that they were tempered only by the generally low unemployment rate, by the continued prevalence of primary industry, and by benefits extended to returning veterans. Based on the later postwar data and on the consistently higher rates of dependence experienced by First Nations during the Depression, it is unlikely that Hoey could have substantiated his claim. Instead, it was policy and its administration that principally accounted for the low expenditure on social assistance.

That this was so is largely supported by the 1966 Hawthorn Report, which referred to the testimony of the head of the Welfare Division to the joint parliamentary committee in 1947. 'The low priority attached to welfare in the early post-war years,' the report stated, 'is apparent in Branch policies and public statements ... Welfare consisted mainly of relief of severe destitution ... relief policy has been characterized by concern for the taxpayer and a fear that liberal relief payments would harm Indian character and work incentives.'[5] The report then quoted the testimony of the head of the Welfare Division:

> The general policy of the division is to encourage and assist Indians to be self-supporting rather than to furnish them with direct relief ... Because of this, the scale of relief supplied to able-bodied Indians must err on the parsimonious rather than on the generous side. Our instructions to agents state that relief is not the right of any Indian but is given at the pleasure of the Branch to prevent suffering. We also state that in no instance are the quantities of relief allowed to be sufficient to remove the incentive to obtain employment where and when available.[6]

This position was not very different from how relief was generally viewed in Canada, and it was entirely consistent with Indian Affairs policy since Confederation. Indeed, the position of the branch simply conformed to Ottawa's rejection of social insurance as a method of welfare planning in postwar Canada.[7] Dennis Guest writes that after the Marsh Report of 1943 had been thoroughly laundered and its comprehensive qualities bleached beyond recognition, the federal and provincial governments moved to establish a social security system whose essential character was residual. Approaches to income support continued to emphasize needs, means testing, and targeting the 'deserving.' In his assessment of the above testimony, Hawthorn reported that relief during this period 'was granted by the Branch as a matter of grace as the Indian Act fixed no direct obligation on the government to provide social welfare benefits.'[8] This statement apparently implied that unlike other Canadians, the First Nations were captive to the voluntary benevolence of the state. Really, their status with respect to a 'right to welfare' was – and is – no different from that of the general population of Canada. It may well be that Canada's governments, both federal and provincial, have a constitutional obligation to provide welfare benefits to their citizens; in practice, however, they behave as though no such obligation exists.

Indian welfare was probably more harshly and tightly administered; that being said, the principles of deservedness underlying eligibility applied to First Nations and Euro-Canadians alike. This point is critical. Had Indian welfare policy been substantially different, the contrast would have been detrimental to assimilation strategies. Indians, therefore, were expected to conform like other Canadians to the government's full employment policies. Relief for the able-bodied would be minimal and temporary.

Hawthorn's analysis of Indian welfare policy in the mid-1940s also verified that work-for-welfare policies were still being followed. In all probability, this practice contributed to the low expenditure on relief. The report quoted a 1947 internal branch document dealing with its welfare practices: 'It is not the policy of the Indian Agent to provide able-bodied Indians with relief. If relief is necessary for such individuals they are required to undertake certain tasks either on or off the reserve, such as cultivation of gardens, farm work, clearing land, road construction, draining projects, wood-cutting, or other tasks at the discretion of the Indian Agent.'[9] Relief in the early postwar period, according to Hawthorn, was nearly always in kind and the value was 'deliberately kept low in order to ensure that a welfare payment would be of an amount below the earnings of the lowest paid wage-earner.'[10] The numbers of Indians considered able bodied generally represented over 50 per cent of the First Nations population. That fact, in combination with either the denial of benefits or the provision of absolutely minimal benefits, would clearly have resulted in a decline in absolute relief expenditure.

Two other factors bear mention in assessing Hoey's claim. The first relates to the source of relief expenditures. Hoey stated in his testimony to the joint committee that the amount spent on relief in 1945–6 was based on the welfare appropriation voted by Parliament.[11] However, the branch's annual reports from this period (on which the figures in Table 8.1 are based) did not differentiate between band fund and parliamentary expenditures, nor did they make any mention of band funds used for relief. Thus, the figures for 1946 in Table 8.1 *could* represent a combined amount, though this is probably not the case. The branch, like other federal departments and agencies, reported only on expenditures for which it was directly accountable to Parliament – that is, the parliamentary appropriations. Assuming that the 1946 expenditure shown was only the parliamentary appropriation, the need for relief was thus presumably greater than Hoey admitted.

Second, the Family Allowances Act, introduced in 1944 and implemented throughout 1945, may also have placed further restraints on relief expenditures. Among the general population, the opposition to the introduction of the allowances – led principally by Charlotte Whitton – had centred on whether or not a universal cash payment might simply encourage wasteful spending and untoward behaviour on the part of recipients.[12] This would not have been lost on officials in Indian

Affairs. The department did not trust Indians to manage their own funds, and it had always feared that any relief beyond the bare minimum would foster a pernicious dependence on the state. All of this prompted the branch to introduce controls over the administration of the allowances – controls not encountered by other Canadians.[13] Control over the allowances enabled the branch not only to regulate their distribution but also to contain its own relief expenditures. There is no direct evidence of this, but the corroborating evidence – in particular the significant reduction in relief per capita expenditure – suggests that this was the case. So, it might be concluded that immediately after the war, Family Allowances for registered Indians were used as a form of relief rather than for their intended purpose (i.e., to supplement wages to assist in providing minimum requirements to children).[14]

For all the rhetoric of a new deal for Indians during the war, there is little evidence that one was in place immediately after the war. Relief policy continued to be driven by the dogma of liberal political economy. In late 1947, however, a new Welfare Division was created from the Welfare and Training Service,[15] and by 1949, welfare expenditures had begun to rise sharply. In the fiscal year 1948–9, total welfare service expenditure was over $2,300,000, an increase of nearly 154 per cent in the three years after 1945–6.[16] Much of this increase can be attributed to a new housing program, which in 1948–9 accounted for 28 per cent of the total welfare expenditure. The remaining 72 per cent, or $1,665,600, was spent on various operational costs and on direct relief (see Table 8.2).

The branch did not report direct relief costs, but obviously these no longer accounted for 68.6 per cent of the total expenditure reported in 1945–6. How, then, can we estimate relief expenditure for 1948–9? From the branch's annual report for 1948–9, we know that salaries and miscellaneous items accounted for 2.4 per cent of total expenditure. Hoey's 1946 testimony to the joint committee revealed that operational costs such as freight, equipment, and maintenance accounted for 13.4 per cent of expenditure at the time. If those percentages remained constant and were applied to the total 1948–9 welfare expenditure, the balance remaining for relief would have been 56.1 per cent, or $1,300,282 (Table 8.2).

This assumption is supported in part by C.N.C. Roberts, a former Indian Affairs official, who spoke of the rapid change in welfare appropriation by the late 1940s:

Right after the war ... about forty-six, we got into these VLA houses. Veterans could get assistance of which about twenty-three hundred and some-

Table 8.2
Calculation of approximate Indian relief expenditures, 1945–6, 1948–9

Category	1945–6	1948–9[a]
Total welfare expenditures	$913,651	$2,317,415
Miscellaneous	$58,474 (6.4%)	$53,787 (2.4%)[b]
Freight, maintenance, equipment, etc.	$122,429 (13.4%)	$310,534 (13.4%)
Housing and repairs	$105,983 (11.6%)	$651,812 (28.1%)
Direct relief	$626,765 (68.6%)	$1,300,282 (56.1%)
Relief per capita	$4.90	$9.53

Sources: Canada, Department of Citizenship and Immigration, Indian Affairs Branch, *A Review of Activities, 1948–1958* (Ottawa: Queen's Printer, 1959), 2; Canada, Department of Mines and Resources, Indian Affairs Branch, *Annual Report, 1948–1949*, 200; Canada, Parliament, Special Joint Committee of the Senate and the House of Commons Appointed to Examine and Consider the Indian Act, *Minutes of Proceedings and Evidence* (Ottawa: Edmond Cloutier, Printer to the King's Most Excellent Majesty, 1946), No. 1, pp. 8, 11, 16.
[a]The reported Indian population in 1949 was 136,407.
[b]In 1948–9, this category covers salaries and miscellaneous.

thing was non-repayable if they proved up and did what they were supposed to do. So Indian Affairs gave that same amount of money to veterans and a house would be built with that as the nucleus and then some from appropriation.

Laval Fortier was deputy minister at about that time and he made an announcement at some meeting he attended where we were going to put much more money into the housing budget and those of us who were working had been niggardly apportioning out this *small* budget. You know, we said ... how was he going to get all that money! But the money came through and the appropriation just kept increasing year after year.

I think it was Laval Fortier who criticized what we had been doing. We were quite proud of our good record. He said, 'Yeah, you got a good record, but it's so small.'[17]

Roberts, then, confirms the branch's penny-pinching culture. He also directly identifies housing as the primary source of new monies and as the impetus for the gradual relaxation of hard-line attitudes toward welfare spending. New housing accounted for a substantial portion of the increased expenditure; however, the branch's 1948 annual report identified rises in commodity prices and costs of services as other contributing factors.[18]

Although relief decreased as a proportion of overall expenditure, it increased dramatically in actual and per capita dollars (Table 8.2). The 1948 report did not directly account for relief expenditure, so it is difficult to explain this sudden rise. However, D.M. McKay, the former Indian commissioner for British Columbia, who had replaced Hoey as branch director, provided some clues in his summation of Indian socioeconomic conditions during 1948:

> Good progress was made during the year towards the ultimate goal of affording the Canadian Indian opportunities equal to those of fellow Canadians of the white race ...
>
> Economically, the lot of the Indian followed the pattern of other Canadians ... the Indian shared fully in the national prosperity. Wages were high, crops abundant, and there was but little unemployment ...
>
> A small monetary monthly allowance to aged Indians was a new welfare project put in operation ... Three thousand eight hundred and fifty old people were in receipt of this allowance.[19]

These observations were typical of the branch's annual reports – indeed, of almost all public Indian Affairs materials – in their propensity to see the condition of First Nations through rose-coloured glasses.

McKay's introductory comments were followed by reports from each of the branch's eleven regions. These reports were more cautious about the circumstances of First Nations. Trapping revenue had been down everywhere because of depressed world prices, or smaller catches, or both. Across the country, revenue from agricultural production and income from employment had varied considerably. Flooding had severely affected the livelihood of Indians in British Columbia's Fraser Valley. Employment on the prairies was barely mentioned; only in Alberta had 'many' Indians worked – specifically, on a power project at Spray Lakes and on farming operations in the northern United States. Oil revenues had continued to 'contribute income to Band Funds,' although six new wells had yielded no commercial production. Indians in southern Ontario had reportedly prospered in both agricultural and industrial employment. With few exceptions, those in Quebec, the Maritimes, and the two territories had not experienced a good economic year.[20]

The new Allowances for Aged Indians (AAI), which were distributed monthly, were an especially important development. Indians were not eligible for the existing old age pension, which was funded largely by the federal government but administered by the provinces.[21] First Nation briefs and testimony, and the recommendations of the special commission to the joint committee concerning the destitution of elderly Indians, had evidently had some impact, for in 1948 the branch introduced its own version of a pension. The AAI remained in place until 1952, when Indians were brought under the provisions of the new federal Old Age Security Act. According to a later internal report of the Department of Indian Affairs, the AAI in 1951 – just before its replacement by Old Age Security – had been paying elderly Indians $25 per month.[22]

If, as McKay reported in 1948, 3,850 Indians were receiving the AAI, then a monthly allowance of $25 would have cost the branch $1,155,000, or almost 89 per cent of the relief expenditure depicted in Table 8.2! Since the AAI was being extended to elderly Indians as a supplement to their monthly relief rations, then conceivably the entire relief expenditure was being directed at elderly Indians! McKay stated in the annual report, however, that relief monies had also been expended to relieve general hardship in the north. Furthermore, despite the continued mean-minded attitude toward general relief, it must also be assumed that relief – especially for the sick – was being provided elsewhere. So it is difficult to arrive at a satisfactory accounting of the 1948 relief expenditure. It is possible that the AAI expenditure was not included in the annual report, but it is more likely that the allowance was less in 1948 than in 1951 and that bands with sufficient funds were being expected to meet the costs of both general relief and the AAI.

Two important points can be gleaned from this analysis. First, the sharp rise in relief expenditure, and especially in per capita expenditure, was probably due to the introduction of the AAI. Unchanged were liberal ideas about individual self-reliance as the means to achieve integration and independence. First Nations' socioeconomic conditions were still being described in predominantly individualistic rather than collective terms. Second, the government's requirement that Indian bands pay for all or some relief from their own trust accounts remained in place despite many complaints to the joint committee that this was an undue hardship. There was no internal correspondence concerning this question, but it can be inferred that there were two possible reasons why. One, it was feared that paying relief from parliamentary appropriation would simply foster the dependence the branch was seeking to discourage. Requiring bands to fund their own relief would encourage them to maintain a sense of independence by instilling an aversion to relief as a drain on their own resources. Two, there would be considerable savings to the federal treasury.

This second reason involved a constitutional issue: How might the provinces interpret a federal decision to provide Indian relief exclusively by parliamentary appropriation? The federal government had never assumed statutory responsibility for Indian welfare; rather, it had 'wandered' into the provision of relief from band funds, which it administered by default because none of the other jurisdictions, provincial or municipal, had been willing.[23] In the documentation reviewed, there was never any evidence in the post-Confederation period to suggest that the federal government thought to do otherwise. Not until 1920, when the Ontario government offered to include Indian women under the Mothers' Allowance, did Indian Affairs became aware of the possibility that other jurisdictions might assume responsibility for Indian welfare. Then, in 1946, presentations at the joint committee – especially the submission of the Canadian Welfare Council – generated new federal thinking about provincial responsibility for Indian welfare. Thus, by 1949 the federal government was less certain whether it should accept sole constitutional responsibility for Indian peoples. If Ottawa decided to pay all relief from parliamentary appropriation, the provinces might interpret this to mean that the federal government was accepting responsibility for Indian welfare and that the full integration of Indians was not possible. For the federal government, this conclusion would have been unacceptable.

Immediately after the war, welfare expenditure remained extremely frugal. Whatever Hoey claimed, relief was being denied to Indians thought capable of work, whether or not work was available. By 1949, expenditure had dramatically risen, but this rise was largely due to an infusion of new funds for housing and for elderly Indians, not to any changes in attitudes or policy. The federal government continued to be fearful of encouraging what it saw as innate Indian dependency and of hindering Indians' adaptation to market principles. By 1949, this position was in conflict with a general inclination to treat Indians with greater generosity and to extend to them the benefits already enjoyed by Canadian citizens.

We now proceed to 1952, the first year after 1940 for which archival material on Indian relief policy and administration is available. Significant changes had already occurred; two of these, the creation of an entirely separate Welfare Division and the branch's transfer to the Department of Citizenship and Immigration, I have already noted. The new Indian Act had been passed in 1951; the same year, Parliament also passed the Old Age Assistance Act and the Blind Persons Act, which, in direct response to joint parliamentary committee recommendations, included Indians in their provisions.[24] Both acts became effective 1 July 1952. Thus, by 1952 Indians were included in all four major federal social security initiatives: Unemployment Insurance, Family Allowances, Old Age Pensions, and Blind Persons Allowances. Finally, by 1950 the branch had six professionally trained social workers located in head-quarters and in the field.[25] As well, a new superintendent of the Welfare Division, Colonel H.M. Jones, had just been appointed. According to C.N.C. Roberts, Jones came into Indian Affairs from outside the federal service. Within three years he would be appointed branch director, a position he would hold until his 1963 retirement. Roberts gave a first-hand description of Jones:

> He had been working in a liquor store in around the Bay of Quinte some-where. I think there was a lot of political drag when he got in. He was all right. He was sort of cunning and didn't get himself into trouble. He got along all right. But he wasn't a hard man to work for, really.
>
> He wanted to be called Colonel Jones. I had a friend who was active in the military. One day I asked him something about this colonel business and he said, 'Well, he really has no right to use it.' He'd retired and what-ever kind of commission he was ... it retired with him. He wanted it [the title] to stay on. I used to do it, I'd call him [colonel] because I was working there, and my bread and butter was sort of depending on it.

In *Making Canadian Indian Policy*, Sally Weaver also provides some interesting insights into Jones's administration:

> After the war, the branch's military tradition was most conspicuous in the person of Colonel H.M. Jones ... The analogy of the branch as a 'command post' during Colonel Jones' years was apt; senior officials addressed him as 'Colonel' and stood up when he entered the room ... His style of leader-ship was foreign to civil servants outside Indian Affairs, and those who felt the branch was an anachronism sometimes referred to it as 'Colonel Jones' lost battalion.' Directives flowed from the top down to the superintendents on the reserves, line authority being highly respected.

Weaver is not entirely correct in suggesting that Jones's style of leader-ship was foreign to the rest of the civil service. Jones was, however, a car-icature of how the civil service operated.[26]

The New Ottawa: Relief Policy in 1952

One of Jones's first initiatives was to issue a new policy document, 'Welfare and Relief Assistance for Indians.'[27] Consisting of five legal-size pages, this document was the branch's first unified 'policy manual' on welfare and relief measures. It continued the rationalization of relief policy that had begun in 1915. The manual included a general statement of program intent and the standard procedures to be followed for regular recipients. In addition, it addressed the special treatment of tubercular Indians and provided regular and special scales of rations. Finally, it provided directions on the use of discretion for additional benefits in the case of illness and emergencies and for the provision of special items such as clothing, fuel, and the payment of transportation costs and indigent funerals. Of special importance was the addition of policy and procedures for the care of incapacitated adults, especially the elderly. Milk was added to children's rations, and the dollar values for meat and fish were increased; otherwise, there was no major change in rations from the 1940 scale (Table 8.3; also, Document 4.3).

The new manual pointed to several questions that both the branch and the Welfare Division would grapple with for the next twelve years. First, how much greater a provision of benefits and services could there be without discouraging individual self-reliance? Second – related to the first – should benefits be administered in kind or by cash, and how adequate should they be? Underlying both these questions of course, was the running issue of domination and the branch's need to exert control over the relationship between First Nations and mainstream society.

In the general policy statement, these concerns began to emerge within a distinctly different, less dogmatic approach to relief:

> Relief assistance in kind may be provided indigent Indians when necessary to alleviate distress and hardship. Direct relief is not payable in cash but through provision of food, fuel, clothing, household equipment, care of the helpless, or other assistance as necessary in individual cases. The type and amount of help depends upon the requirements of the Indian, his location, physical well-being, availability of country food, and ability to provide for himself. The basic principle is the welfare of the individual and every effort must be made to avoid discouraging initiative and self-reliance.[28]

The difference was evident in the facts that relief was generally *permissible* and that able-bodied Indians were not excepted. The *welfare of the*

Table 8.3
Scale of rations for Indians on relief, March 1952

Ration	1 Adult	2 Adults	3 Adults	4 Adults	5 Adults	6 Adults
	Lbs.	Lbs.	Lbs.	Lbs.	Lbs.	Lbs.
Flour (Vitamin B)	24	36	49	61	80	98
Rolled oats	6	9	12	15	18	18
Baking powder	1	1¾	1¾	2	2	2
Tea	1	1½	2	2	2	3
Sugar	2	4	5	7	8	10
Lard	3	5	8	10	10	13
Beans	5	5	7	7	8	8
Rice (or potatoes up to an equivalent value)	2	3	5	5	7	7
Cheese	1	1½	1½	2	2	3
Meat or fish	$2.50	$3.75	$4.50	$5.00	$5.50	$5.75
Salt	10¢ or 15¢ per month per family					
Matches	10¢ or 20¢ per month per family					
Milk	One pint of milk or equivalent in evaporated or powdered form per day for each child of an indigent family 12 years of age and under.					

It will be noted that the above scale indicates quantities for adults only which should be reduced proportionately for minor children.

Source: NAC, RG-10, Central Registry, Vol. 7094, File 1/10-3-0, 'Welfare and Relief Assistance for Indians,' Indian Affairs Branch, Department of Citizenship and Immigration, Ottawa, 4 March 1952, p. 1.

individual and the unique *circumstances of each case* were to guide the Indian superintendent – the new term for the agent – in assessing the need for relief. Furthermore, cash relief – never mentioned in any previous policy statement – had apparently become an issue for discussion. This was probably because the Family Allowance was already in many cases being paid by cheque, as was the AAI. Benefits under the Old Age Assistance Act, soon to supplant the AAI, would also be paid by cheque.

Another concern, nutrition, was evident in the description of procedures to be followed in determining need. With reference to the scale of rations described in Table 8.3, the manual stated: 'This list is not all inclusive and by its ... nature cannot be rigidly applied ... Reasonable substitutions ... which do not entail increased cost nor affect nutritional value are normally acceptable. In some areas, for example, local foods of high nutritional value are available ... and should be substituted for items on the authorized scale when such substitutions would be advantageous.'[29]

Concern with nutrition was also reflected in further directions given to the superintendents when it came to assessing health and medical circumstances. 'In the case of ill health, absence of country food, special illnesses such as diabetes and other conditions, additional foods over and above the authorized list may be required. In all such cases, reference should be made to the nearest medical authority for recommendations as to the exact foods and quantities ... In emergencies necessary additional foods may be provided without prior authority.'[30] Finally, special attention was paid to the nutritional requirements of tubercular Indians in their post-hospitalization period of convalescence. The special diet for these persons was to supplement regular relief and was to be provided on a weekly basis (Table 8.4). The concern with nutrition was tied to the results of many studies conducted by both public and private bodies that had overwhelmingly linked Indian ill health and high mortality rates to destitution. Moreover, nutrition was much in vogue in the postwar baby boom years. Ottawa was looking for ways to 'grow' the Canadian population in anticipation of a rising demand for labour.[31]

Despite the greater flexibility, many themes present in Indian relief policy since Confederation persisted. There was the continued admonition to the field to promote individual Indian self-reliance. There was a decentralization of decision making for general relief, but Ottawa maintained a high degree of control over exceptional cases involving illness or the non-availability of country foods. 'In all such cases,' the manual stated, 'reference should be made to the nearest medical authority for recommendations ... and a special authority number must be quoted on the voucher submitted in payment.'[32] In addition, headquarters maintained control over special benefits: 'Indian Superintendents are required, except in cases of grave emergency, to secure prior authority from Head Office before undertaking the supply of fuel, ... foods in addition to the authorized scale, clothing and blankets, household equipment of all kinds and care for indigent or helpless Indians.'[33]

The control of costs, however, remained the most persistent theme; in fact, it seems that the issues of self-reliance and of expenditure authority flowed naturally from this overriding concern. It stood to reason that in cases where Indian bands could be made responsible for providing for all or a portion of their own welfare, then costs could be contained and self-reliance encouraged. Similarly, if both Indians and the field saw benefit provision beyond basic relief as an extraordinary measure, then it followed that costs could be more effectively controlled. This was most evident in the treatment of country foods – that is, local fruits and vege-

Table 8.4
Scale of weekly rations for tubercular Indians, March 1952

Item	Amount
1. Milk	
fresh	7 quarts
evaporated	7 16 oz. tins
powdered	2 lbs.
(check possible duplication if other relief food supplied)	
2. Tomato Juice, Grapefruit Juice, or Vitamized Apple Juice	2 20 oz. tins
3. Potatoes (check for duplication if other relief food supplied)	5 lbs.
4. Carrots and/or Peas (mixed or separate) or Tomatoes	3 No. 2 tins
5. Meat or Fish (check for duplication if other relief food supplied) (Fresh or Canned)	3 lbs. Edible portion,
(This amount may be cut if game and fish are plentiful.)	boneless.

Source: NAC, RG-10, Central Registry, Vol. 7094, File 1/10-3-0, 'Welfare and Relief Assistance for Indians,' Indian Affairs Branch, Department of Citizenship and Immigration, Ottawa, 4 March 1952, p. 2.

tables, cultivated or wild, available to Indians as a natural part of their diets. The procedures further stated, 'If the Indian family or individual is in a position to provide any of the items shown on the ... scale through his own efforts, these items should not be supplied at the expense of the Indian Affairs Branch and the scale of foods should be revised accordingly. For example, Indians in areas where game and fish are plentiful should not be supplied with these commodities if they are physically capable of hunting or fishing.'[34] This requirement pertained not only to those eligible for general relief but also to tubercular Indians and their families. Thus, with respect to the special scale shown in Table 8.4, the manual noted:

In some parts of the country, the foods shown on this diet are readily available locally and can be procured by the Indian concerned through his own efforts. In the event that the medical authorities recommend provision of this special diet for an entire family, it is necessary that the quantities specified for the individual be reduced proportionately as the size of the family increases. Such a proportional reduction is not indicated in the scale as the ... reduction can be best left to the judgment of the individual Superintendent.[35]

There was little sense to be made of this direction. Presumably a tubercular individual required the amounts specified in the special scale, and it would seem only logical to *increase* them proportionately, not decrease them.

More problematic was the range of discretion given to the superintendent, not only in these but in all cases where he thought the availability of country foods or the likelihood of an Indian being able to hunt or fish were great. One significant problem recognized by the joint committee in the administration of Indian Affairs was the lack of control exercised by bands over local matters and the resultant maladministration by many Indian agents. Reforms within the new Indian Act – specifically, the expansion of the powers of band councils under Section 81 – were a weak attempt to redress this problem, and in any case they did not apply to welfare matters. Consequently, an area in which bands and their individual members were especially vulnerable – that is, their collective and individual destitution – remained firmly within the control of the Indian Affairs Branch and of the local superintendent.

That this had become highly problematic was evident in the Hawthorn Report, which observed that the field was now far more conservative in its views of relief than the Ottawa administration:

> The typical Branch relief philosophy in the field, as distinct from the opinions of Ottawa headquarters officials, appears to be that Indians should be granted minimum financial assistance under the tightest administration possible in order to discourage Indian dependency on government subsidies. Again and again we were told that most Indians were chronically dependent on relief for their livelihood and that higher rates and more lenient administration would only aggravate this dependency.[36]

Hawthorn did not ask why this was so, nor did he seem to notice that it was headquarters that propounded the principles which guided the field. It was all very well for Ottawa to hold more generous views concerning relief, but these would amount to nothing, even if they were articulated in policy, if they were not enforced. While Ottawa was articulating a humanistic view, its officials were imposing tight controls on field expenditure, promoting individual independence, and restricting the capacity of bands to respond to their economic marginalization.

Two other expense control points are worth mentioning. The branch consistently sought ways to reduce rations when country foods were available. But how were values to be assigned to these foods? It was more convenient to develop a ration scale based on the quantity of food rather than on its dollar value. Indian superintendents were instructed to authorize relief by the type and quantity of food, not by its actual dollar value.[37] Later, the branch moved toward a cash relief system, but even then it remained reluctant to abandon country foods. As a consequence, the method for attributing a market value to them became a matter of constant debate.

The second point is concerned with the government's mean-spirited and paternalistic control of band trust funds. The new Indian Act denied bands any decision-making authority over welfare matters;[38] not only that, but relief policy specifically warned superintendents not to provide rations unnecessarily 'at the expense of the Indian Affairs Branch.'[39] This was an extraordinary statement, since relief was often at the bands' expense, not the branch's. Yet one policy applied to both sources of funds. The statement reveals how much the branch dominated the lives of First Nations and how the organizational culture supported the belief that the government should control expenditures of their resources.[40] The management of Indian monies was – and still is – clearly defined under the Indian Act. Section 61(1) of the act states: 'Indian moneys shall be expended only for the benefit of the Indians or bands for whose use and benefit in common the moneys are received or held, and subject to this Act and to the terms of any treaty or surrender, the Governor in Council may determine whether any purpose for which Indian moneys are used or are to be used is for the use and benefit of the band.'

In concluding this section, it is important to note that the policy statement of 1952 was a more positive approach to Indian welfare, although the emphasis remained entirely on the individual Indian's ability to be self-reliant in the marketplace. Still, the services and benefits offered were more comprehensive. For the first time, various problems were being addressed in one document and services intended to mitigate their effects were being identified. Beneath this turn to benevolence was a troubling trend: the enrichment of services was the first indication of the branch's new direction, which was, to provide Indians with services comparable to those available to other Canadians. A minimal improvement in their material well-being might accrue from more generous benefits, but it would come at the price of a continued assault on their collective identities. There would no longer be any mistaking the federal objective, which was to treat Indians like other citizens of Canada and thus hasten their integration and eventual disappearance.

Nutrition, the Department of National Health and Welfare, and the Introduction of Cash Benefits

By late 1954, Jones had been appointed director of the Indian Affairs Branch and the position of Welfare Division superintendent had been filled by J.P.B. Ostrander. There were few changes in relief policy and administration between 1952 and 1954, but beginning in 1955 and through to late 1958, a flurry of activity ensued, centred on the scale of relief rations and their adequacy in relation to recipients' nutrition. There was a fear – especially within the Indian Health Service, which was lodged in the Department of National Health and Welfare – that Indian nutrition would be undermined by the substitution of cash benefits for rations. Continued concern over Indian nutrition and its relationship to disease and high mortality rates[41] coexisted with the pressure to make Indian welfare benefits and administration conform with those enjoyed by Euro-Canadians under the various provincial and municipal systems. These standards were constantly brought to the branch's attention through its association with the Canadian Welfare Council's Public Welfare Division, a body whose role is discussed in the next section of this chapter.

Late in 1954, Jones received a letter from Dr Percy Moore, director of Indian Health Services, who was acting on the advice of Dr L.B. Pett, chief of his department's nutrition division. In his letter, Dr Moore urged the branch to promote the use of bannock mix or improved flour.[42] Perhaps feeling the pinch of the minor recession of 1954,[43] Jones replied to Dr Moore in early 1955 stating that this would only be possible by including these items in the standard relief rations. This addition 'would be a substantial increase in relief costs which would be difficult to finance.'[44] He suggested instead a program to influence Indians 'to the extent of wishing for a flour which would produce bannock of increased nutritional value.'[45] Dr Moore might have been somewhat puzzled by this comment. Within two weeks he had written again to Jones, this time suggesting a third scale of rations for persons who 'require more than the ordinary scale of assistance but less than the T.B. rehabilitation ration.'[46] Jones replied that policy allowed Indian superintendents to be flexible in adding foods according to individual circumstances, so another scale of rations was not necessary.[47] It can only be surmised that Dr Moore was annoyed by this exchange. In 1956, an Interdepartmental Committee on Relief and Tuberculosis Rehabilitation Rations was established, comprised of representatives from Indian Affairs, Indian Health Services, and the Arctic Division of the Northern Administration and Lands Branch, Department of Northern Affairs and National Resources. The Arctic Division was responsible for providing relief to the Inuit (Eskimos). The Department of National Health and Welfare, Indian Health Service, was also responsible for the Inuit.[48]

The most influential member of the new committee was clearly Dr Pett from Health and Welfare's nutrition division. At a meeting on 13 July 1956, Dr Pett was there to engineer the approval of his own recommendations, which were the major items on the agenda. These were to include on the general scale a new ration for greater caloric content and the addition of tomatoes as a source of Vitamin C. The committee first adopted a statement of general principle:

> It was agreed that as a basic principle when a government agency accepts responsibility for relief rations, there must be a balanced diet to keep the recipient in reasonable health. The problem of what the recipient does with the ration cannot be legislated upon or directed, rather it is a matter of education.[49]

The committee then approved the addition of tomatoes – or, where this was not possible, the provision of a Vitamin C tablet – and a high calorie food (not identified in the minutes). At the same time, it rejected 'as excessive' a scale of rations proposed by the Citizens Committee of Aklavik and the Chief of Eskimos, although it approved an internal suggestion to enrich the diet of expectant and nursing mothers.[50] Jones acted promptly to authorize the inclusion of tomatoes, but no mention was made of Vitamin C tablets.[51] There is no evidence that he authorized either of the committee's other two recommendations, and it is likely that he did not, falling back instead on the discretion accorded to the field superintendents.

The branch's reluctance to alter its ration scale apparently forced the committee to recommend a controversial alternative that ran counter to other branch initiatives. In late 1956, after considerable discussion, the Department of National Health and Welfare concluded that in order to ensure good nutrition, it would be desirable to issue specified foods as a substitute for the Family Allowances. The scheme was to apply to Indians and Inuit where the Family Allowances were already administered in

kind.[52] Instead of being applied to children's clothing or other necessary supplies, it would be used on a discretionary basis to supply recommended foods. The scheme likely originated with Drs Pett and Moore,
who, in paternalistic fashion, remained highly dubious of the Indians'
ability to spend money wisely in the interests of their own health. On 3
December 1956, Jones advised the field that where the Family Allowances were administered in kind – and he probably also meant those
administered through the agency trust accounts – foods on a list prepared by Dr Pett might be issued as an alternative to regular Family
Allowance benefits.[53]

Using the tone of the wise and patient doctor, Pett reminded all those
in authority of the purpose of the Family Allowances and of their
responsibility for its administration. The Jones/Pett directive undermined the purpose of the allowances and reaffirmed Indian wardship; it
also 'formalized' the conversion of the allowances into what they had
long been *de facto* – an alternative form of relief and (from the Branch's
perspective) a means of restraining expenditure. If Indian integration
and citizenship were to be achieved, then both Indian Affairs and the
Indian Health Service had subverted one of their primary agents, the
universal demogrant. Still another problem smouldered beneath this
one: the obvious struggle between the two departments to control the
agenda for Indian welfare. To understand this struggle, we must look
for a moment at the branch's initiative to pay relief by cheque.

As stated earlier the Family Allowance issue seemed to run counter to
other branch initiatives. This was because in 1956 the branch had
decided on a limited experiment to issue relief by cheque to Indians in
need. To do so required the permission of the Treasury Board. This was
obtained on 30 November 1956.[54] The project was restricted to 'about'
10 per cent of the indigent population at the following monthly rates:
'$18.00 for one adult, $15.00 for each additional adult (including children over 12 years of age), $12.00 for each child 12 years of age or
under.'[55] Also, each agency superintendent was granted the discretionary authority to exceed the rates for special cases. Because of the experiment's limited nature, each interested agency had to apply through its
regional office for permission from Ottawa to issue cash relief.[56]

The project's initiation in April 1957 brought with it a further rationalization of procedures, the introduction of forms, and a method of
calculating entitlement and of deducting income and country foods.
The goal was 'to meet the circumstances and requirements of Indians
who can be relied upon to purchase essential items of food with a mini-

mum of supervision. It will also permit the capable Indian housekeeper to secure the best ... value for her relief dollar.' For the first time, Ottawa required the head of the household, identified as the man, to apply for assistance, but advised the agency 'when feasible' to issue the cheque to 'Indian mothers to assure that they are used to the best advantage.'[57]

Up until this time, scales of family rations had been presented as a matter of fact and without comment about family roles. The advent of cash relief suddenly introduced the 1950s Euro-Canadian, consumer family: father, the breadwinner and conduit for outside income; mother, the dependent homemaker, shopper, and efficient inside manager. Relief in kind had obviated choice; the introduction of cash made it necessary to delineate the individual, working family's relationship to the external capitalist economy.[58] Thus, even where employment was not available the paradigm was needed so that cash relief would be understood as a substitute for job income, and so that the proper household gender roles could be developed and maintained. Even the terminology was changing; relief was now sometimes called 'assistance,' as if to imply its more supportive yet temporary nature as a source of income in periods of unemployment. In these senses, the new cash relief policy was meant to promote assimilation into the liberal state.[59]

There was also a new requirement: regional supervisors were to ensure that all income or potential income in cash or in kind be considered in determining eligibility for relief assistance.[60] The assessment of income and country foods against entitlement effectively introduced a crude means test; it also amounted to an abandonment of the principle of less eligibility in favour of employment incentives. 'These people,' the policy stated, 'should not be discouraged from taking employment, nor should they be penalized to the extent of having their entire monthly earnings deducted from the monthly food entitlement.'[61] Then, with reference to the rates, the policy statement continued: 'The maximum amounts indicated ... shall be reduced by the value of available country food, farm produce and supplementary income from other sources, in excess of one-third of the maximum allowance permissible. Family Allowances shall not be taken into consideration when computing income.'[62] Once eligibility had been established, the supervisors were to monitor the adequacy of the scale of assistance 'to ensure ... the maintenance of a decent standard of living for the Indian and his family.'[63]

Shortly after the cash assistance program was introduced, the branch amended it to include an alternative provision: assistance through dollar value vouchers.[64] This amendment was piloted in the Maritimes[65] and was intended to be a step toward assistance by cheque. The voucher system had been used between the agencies and local merchants; in contrast, the dollar value vouchers were to be issued directly to the recipients, who would then redeem them at stores of their choosing for food and necessary household items. In addition, up to 1 per cent of the total value could be used for luxury items. Although luxury items did not include cigarettes, candy, and so on, the purchase of these items had to be specially authorized if they exceeded 1 per cent. Finally, the vouchers could be prorated for a partial month or even weekly entitlement. In every other respect, the policy governing the dollar value vouchers was the same as for cash assistance.

It was in the context of these new policy developments that a meeting was convened in the late summer of 1958 between the nutrition division and Indian and Northern Health Services, Department of National Health and Welfare, and the Welfare Division, Indian Affairs Branch. The purpose of the meeting, apparently called by Health and Welfare, was to clarify the relationship between relief administration and high nutritional standards. Health and Welfare believed that the standards were being eroded by the new method of assistance. The meeting, held in Dr Pett's office, was dominated by Health and Welfare officials: of the eight who attended, only two – J.H. Gordon, the new chief of Welfare Division, and C.N.C. Roberts, his senior clerk – were from Indian Affairs.[66] Gordon had been appointed sometime in 1956. According to Roberts, he was somewhat Jones's lackey: 'Gordon was rather despised by a lot of the staff. He catered to Jones. He used to rush into Jones's office in the morning and open his window and do all this kind of thing, and it paid off. He was recommended by Jones at the appropriate time to step up because he had done all this sort of batman [duty].'[67]

According to Gordon's report to Jones, the initial discussion was hostile as Health and Welfare objected to the branch's plans to do away with the ration scale.[68] Health and Welfare was concerned about Indian Affairs' plan to move completely to the cheque and dollar value voucher system as the method of administering assistance. Gordon, when asked to explain the branch's plan, offered a four-point rationale. First, the ration scale was cumbersome; it had become too difficult to keep adjusting with various foods. Second, a method that permitted the recipient to shop around for the best food value would 'bolster his dignity and self-respect.' Third, the current scale did not meet infants' nutritional needs – an acknowledged area of concern to Health and Welfare. Fourth and finally, the scale was also deemed inadequate for a single person.[69]

Gordon then described the new system of relief. It was to include a rate increase to $22 for the first adult living in the family, to bring the rates 'more into line with provincial practices.'[70] Furthermore, safeguards were to be introduced to ensure that a range of foods was purchased, and strict administration was to be imposed on any who abused the new system. In anticipation of the objections of Health and Welfare, Gordon then proposed that the health authorities in attendance develop a shopping guide using specimen budgets to show an 'appropriate distribution amongst the various types of foods.'[71]

A general discussion of the issues then ensued. Clearly, the Health and Welfare officials were acting on the instigation of Dr Moore. In his report to Jones, Gordon wrote: 'Dr. Willis gave great emphasis to Dr. Moore's opinion that ... payment in cash was both undesirable and premature. He wanted to know what safeguards we proposed ... as we moved away from relief rations, to ensure that every dollar was ... spent for foods which would benefit the family.'[72] In an attempt to appease Dr Moore, Gordon pointed out that the cash relief system had been underused in 1957–8. Only 4.5 per cent of total relief assistance had been through cheque issue – well under the maximum 10 per cent that had been permitted. Consequently, Gordon averred, the branch did not expect cash relief to exceed 12 per cent of relief expenditure in 1959–60, and 'it ... would be restricted only to those areas where Indian Affairs ... was ... confident that ... Indians would use the money to the best advantage.'[73] Gordon took pains to underscore this point to Jones: 'I made it a point ... to assure Dr. Moore that payment by cheque will ... be developed on a highly restricted basis. It is a special privilege accorded to Indians who give evidence of ability to manage their own affairs.'[74]

Those present agreed that there was no objection to the dollar value system as long as it included safeguards to ensure the purchase of the right foods and as long as it provided the means to place abusers 'on strict nutritional control.'[75] This 'agreement' could be interpreted in two ways: as a continuation of firm Indian management, and as a bureaucratic stalemate in which Health and Welfare opposed the new system but had to take a 'wait and see' approach. Although Gordon reported to Jones that everyone seemed to think that the new method of relief administration 'would be an improvement and an advance,'[76] no such opinion was alluded to in the minutes.

The remainder of the meeting focused on the rate of Indian infant mortality, which, Indian Affairs was told, was five times that of the non-Indian population.[77] Health and Welfare officials resorted to their nutritional expertise to fire heavy rounds at Gordon and Roberts. Dr R.A. Armstrong of the Indian and Northern Health Service emphasized the relationship between malnutrition and high rates of mortality and disease in childhood. He argued that health education and a better relief system could reduce the two to three million dollars spent annually on the care of sick Indian children. Apparently ignorant of actual practice, he opined that Indian parents ought to use the Family Allowance as a relief supplement.[78] The meeting concluded with a general agreement that Dr Jean Webb and Dr L.B. Pett would prepare a poster or booklet on the special requirements of infants under two years. The material was to explain 'in the simplest manner possible the categories of foodstuffs that the Indian should look for in using his relief credits ... It was emphasized that this health educational material [be] prepared so as to be extremely lucid and ... should be set out in semi-pictorial fashion with a minimum of written material requiring study.'[79]

Gordon's concluding comments about the meeting dwelt mainly on the differences of opinion he had detected among Health and Welfare officials and on the costs of implementing their proposals. The differences between the two departments were apparent. Indian Affairs was concerned about costs, about implementing a new system with minimal interference, and about maintaining the relationship between relief and liberal political economy. Health and Welfare was interested in nutrition, education, and the reach of its professional expertise – money was of little object. Relief was a means to a medical end, something that the doctor could prescribe and expect those less knowledgeable to administer by following the instructions. From the tone of the minutes, it is clear that Health and Welfare had little respect for Indian Affairs and felt that Indians would be far better off directly under the Health Service. Both departments had a common belief in the childlike ignorance of Indians and their need for firm and kindly guidance in reaching full and responsible citizenship in the liberal state.

The Relationship with the Canadian Welfare Council, 1955–1960

The 'progressive' changes in relief policy and the development of an articulated system of assistance can be linked to the branch's cooperative relationship with the Canadian Welfare Council – in particular, with its Public Welfare Division. On 9 February 1955, Dr E. Govan and C.A. Patrick, Secretary to the Public Welfare Division, met with Stan Bailey, a rehabilitation officer with Indian Affairs, and J.P.B. Ostrander at

Ostrander's office. Ostensibly, the meeting was convened to discuss two items: ways the organizations could work together to reach their shared objectives, and the state of rehabilitation services available to handicapped Indians.[80] Both organizations, however, had other agendas.

Ostrander wasted little time in advancing the branch's real agenda: 'to move steadily ahead in a positive welfare program aimed at assisting the Indian people to become integrated as fully as possible into Canadian life.'[81] The council could help the branch in achieving this goal. Considerable discussion ensued regarding the barriers to integration. Dr Govan put forward the idea of local interest groups in each community (meaning cities and towns) made up of 'welfare minded citizens including one or two Indians.' These groups could find ways to help Indians adjust to the community. The council agreed to consider studying 'the problem of public education concerning the integration of Indians' and establishing the proposed interest groups.[82] The council had not yet succeeded in advancing its underlying agenda at the meeting.

At the time, the council was spearheading a national campaign to have the federal government contribute to the funding of public assistance for the employable unemployed.[83] The recession of 1954 and an accompanying higher unemployment rate had contributed to the highest numbers of applicants for public assistance since the Depression. Once unemployment insurance benefits ran out, recipients had nowhere to turn except to their provincial or local municipal welfare departments. In a follow-up letter to Ostrander, Patrick decided to woo Indian Affairs with the suggestion that federal involvement in public assistance would be an incentive to municipal and provincial administrations to assist Indians: 'One of the problems faced by Indians is that applications for financial help when they are unemployed are practically always refused by the municipal government on the grounds that they feel the care of Indians to be a federal responsibility.'[84] He continued:

> Our policy statement on the subject issued in 1953 indicates the need for the Federal Government to participate in a public assistance program. Only when the Federal Government makes a contribution to public assistance will it be able to set certain minimum requirements for the granting of assistance. If, and when, the Federal Government discusses this problem, one of the conditions it seems to me should be that public assistance will be available to Indians wherever they apply for such help.[85]

Ostrander seemed irked by Patrick telling him how Indians were treated off reserve. He replied that in his view, Indians who had residency in municipalities away from reserves were already entitled to the services of ordinary taxpayers. Furthermore, Section 87 of the new Indian Act made provincial law applicable on the reserves. Despite his officious petulance, Ostrander conceded what was *de facto* the case:

> It is understood that some municipalities do not wish to recognize the principle I have outlined ... and rather than provide assistance ... on the same basis as other residents ... advise needy Indians that return to their reserves is in their best interests because help will then be ... available. This is a negative and a damaging method of solving the social problems of individual Indian families. I feel your Council could be most helpful in the development of better public understanding leading towards general acceptance of the Indians as an ordinary citizen subject to the same taxes and therefore eligible for the same services.[86]

Ostrander did not mention the added costs faced by the branch when Indians returned to reserves for relief. He also ignored Patrick's request for support and managed to twist Patrick's concerns so that they suited the branch's agenda.

The importance the branch accorded this potential ally was evidenced by the attendance of the director, Colonel Jones, at the next meeting. Jones seized the opportunity to put forward the Indian Affairs agenda. His vision was of all Canadians assisting Indians to 'become integrated into the Canadian way of life.' This job, he stressed, 'should not be the responsibility of simply a few Federal Civil Servants.'[87] As the branch strove to improve Indians' standard of living every effort must be made, Jones continued, to help the Canadian public accept the Indians as equals. Phyllis Burns, the council's director of welfare services, interjected that she thought the council had a special role to play in that regard since it could interpret Indian Affairs programs to the general public – something the branch could not freely do.[88]

At this point, Jones provided more insight into the branch's thinking about Indian integration when he acknowledged the truth of Patrick's assertion that more often than not, Indians were denied assistance by municipal authorities. Bailey reported Jones's comments: 'he [Jones] is ... anxious that if an Indian requires help of a welfare nature, this help should be given, irrespective of who finally pays. He went on to say that the idea of the Indian being a "ward of the Government" is gradually breaking down. The Branch is making every effort to destroy this concept ... The Provinces are gradually coming to the point where they are recognizing the Indian as an ordinary citizen of the Province.'[89] Jones's statement had a certain internal logic: if Indians were merely wards of the federal government then they were a federal responsibility, but if they were full citizens then they were a shared responsibility. Welfare services would be the litmus test. Still, the issues of responsibility, wardship and the scope of the Indian Act were – and remain today – not nearly so clear-cut! Whatever their assertions of liberal freedoms, Jones and the branch remained protective of their turf, and Indians were only as free as the branch thought they ought to be.

The final issue discussed was the question of the branch's membership and participation in the council, in particular, the council's Public Welfare Division.[90] At this time in Ottawa, it was not considered unusual for public servants to belong to outside organizations for work-related purposes. In fact, it was sometimes deemed essential. Jones was anxious that the branch be involved in any council work to examine Indians' social problems. Patrick explained the council's committee structure to Jones and indicated that the branch would first want to become involved in local committees working on specific problems. Burns said that it was likely that an Indian committee would be formed, and Jones said he would be glad if a branch representative could be on it. Burns then returned to her original suggestion, that is, that the public be educated about Indian Affairs through its publication, *Welfare.* Jones assured her that he would guarantee the preparation of any article she wished.[91]

Although both groups continued to meet regularly, no Indian committee was ever formed, and there is no evidence that any publicity submitted by the branch was ever used by the council.[92] It is possible that the council was discouraged from writing any material after an imbroglio involving Ostrander and Burns. Burns, a trained social worker, had prepared a draft memorandum, 'Services for Indians Leaving Reserves,' based on the meetings about the problems faced by Indians settling in non-Indian communities. In the memorandum, Burns had referred to non-Indians as 'whites.' Ostrander assailed her for this and wrote her a lecture on politically correct terminology: 'You will note that in correspondence from this office the word "whites" is never used. The use of the word was made to sound ridiculous ... by the Joint Parliamentary Committee ... wherein it was shown that negroes, chinese and other races were classified with the "whites" and Indians were ... a separate group.' Burns contritely replied that she knew 'we no longer speak of "Indians" and "whites." I would not want the memorandum to have ...

circulated with this ... error.'[93] By 1956, the tenth anniversary of the formation of the Public Welfare Division, contact with the council had considerably waned. In his annual report, the chairman simply listed Indians among the problems reviewed in the division's work. 'The Board,' he wrote, 'presently has committees working on all but the problem of the Indians.'[94]

Jones was annoyed by this perceived snub; he was also concerned that the branch had paid the membership of eight social workers in the field and had reaped no dividends from the investment. Gordon, the new acting Superintendent of Welfare, explained to him why there was no committee. The absence of an Indian committee, he said in a report to Jones, was the result of a council decision in 1950 that had created the current committee structure. The board of governors at the time had decided to see what developed from the new Indian Act before addressing Indian issues formally. The matter had been reviewed once since then, but there was no interest among the members in altering the board's original decision.[95]

The council's reluctance to form an Indian committee can also be explained in the context of the years 1955–6. The council at that time was embroiled in a campaign to establish better social security measures for the unemployed, and its energies – especially those of the Public Welfare Division – were very much focused on this issue. It wanted federal civil service support for its position, but Indian Affairs, over the two years of contact, had simply not offered any. It is likely that the council had decided to limit its attentions to those government agencies which would support it. In 1956, the federal government passed the Unemployment Assistance Act and the council began to show a renewed interest in Indian Affairs.

Jones was miffed; even so, the branch needed to cultivate a relationship with the council. In its pursuit of citizenship and integration for Indians through social welfare measures, the branch could benefit from the council's expertise. Then there was the fact that the council would provide the branch with a cloak of prestige as well as access to its 'peers' in welfare administration. Because many senior welfare administrators from the provinces were involved in the council, there would be opportunities to promote the extension of provincial services to the reserves and to keep abreast of developments in social assistance administration.

In 1957, Gordon attended various council functions, including its annual meeting in Ottawa. One workshop he informed Jones he would attend was a discussion on new developments in public assistance.[96]

That the branch relied on the council for information about welfare matters was strongly implied by Jones in a letter to Eric Smit, the executive secretary of the council's Family and Child Welfare Division. Jones was replying to a council questionnaire seeking suggestions about topics for an upcoming conference, 'Certain Issues In Social Security.' Jones wrote that the branch was most interested in two subject areas: the effects of residence on social security and general issues affecting public assistance such as provincial–municipal responsibility, benefit levels, and categorical versus general approaches.[97] Jones continued: 'You will appreciate that these matters affect ... those Indians who ... enjoy benefits of ... public assistance programs on the same basis as other Canadians. The questions also have implications in meeting the needs of Indians for welfare services and assistance when they are living in non-Indian communities.'[98]

Activity between the two agencies continued through 1958, and in 1959 the council's advice was reflected in the branch's new relief policy. The council, impressed by the branch's introduction of the cash/voucher scale of benefits, asked the branch to submit an article to the Public Welfare Division's *Bulletin*. Jones agreed, and in his letter to R.E.G. Davis, the council's executive director, he thanked the council for its cooperation.

The article, 'Major Revision in Social Assistance for Indians,' demonstrated that the branch had been doing its homework and had entered the modern world of social assistance. In the article, the branch highlighted both the new method of administering benefits and the elevation of assistance standards so that they were in 'line with those applied in regard to non-Indians in similar circumstances.'[99] The article went on:

> The ration system in terms of stimulating and preserving individual initiative and independence has many undesirable features ...
>
> The scale established under the new system is based on a study of minimum nutritional requirements, relief scales in effect in non-Indian communities, and standards maintained by self-supporting Indians living on reserves ...
>
> In addition to making more adequate provision for Indians who because of circumstances beyond their control are unable to achieve income independence, Branch programs to help Indians become self-supporting and contributing members of society show marked expansion. Efforts are being directed towards rehabilitation of the physically and socially handi-

capped, academic and vocational training of young people, and toward better employment opportunities through the operation of a Placement Program.[100]

The article could as easily have been written as the guiding philosophy for *any* Canadian public welfare department. Its most basic and blind assumption was that Indians ought to be provided assistance in a manner comparable to non-Indians in similar circumstances. It is difficult to understand how in the late 1950s the circumstances of non-Indians could still be thought of as similar to those of Indians. But this is precisely the point, and simply underlines the pervasiveness of liberal culture in informing the thought of policy thinkers and policy makers.

The policy of citizenship and integration had caused the branch to turn, not to First Nations, but to Euro-Canadian social policy groups such as the council for direction and for models of public welfare. Beneath the 'new' approach was a continuation of the old approach, except that a more benevolent form of welfare would help Indians become happy, productive citizens. The exchange between Jones and Davis is extremely important because it points clearly to the Canadian Welfare Council as the branch's major source of information for its postwar welfare policy.

From 1959 to 1961, the branch and the council enjoyed a close, collaborative relationship. Indian welfare was elevated in status within the council, and branch officials were sometimes asked to address local committees of the Public Welfare Division to explain Indian policy. One such address captured the direction of welfare policy and its relationship to Indian communities.[101] The presenter, most probably A.G. Leslie, said that the branch had come to understand the importance of the Indian community, which for the time being was a source of security for the average Indian. Many Indians, the official noted, would 'continue to cling to their own society either because of personal preference or lack of opportunity.'[102] Echoing the U.S. government's Meriam Report, he stated that the key to successful integration policy was to support Indian communities so that their living standards would rise to those of non-Indian communities. In this way the barriers between the two would break down and enable 'full social and economic intercourse.'[103]

A four-part approach to Indian integration was necessary. One, develop Indian leadership. Two, provide economic opportunity and physical improvements (including housing and, where necessary, community relocation). Three, provide social assistance benefits 'patterned ... upon those available for non-Indians to facilitate eventual integration into the provincial welfare program.' Four, expand Indian education, integrating Indian with non-Indian children wherever possible.[104] The policy envisioned in this address would foster a strong relationship between community development and welfare services. But it would be a highly manipulative form of community development, one designed to *manage* First Nations according to the state's overall strategy for 'solving the Indian problem.' Indian leaders, in the manner of puppet politicians, were to be trained to show their people the path into the twentieth century. Welfare services based on non-Indian models would be a statement of citizenship and also would hasten Indian absorption into provincial systems and economies.

Similarly, the presenter continued, off-reserve jurisdictions must soon recognize their Indian residents as equal citizens and extend to them their full services. In this context, the successful integration of Indians into the Canadian mainstream was dependent on participation, 'not only by all three levels of government ... but also ... by industry, private citizens and voluntary organizations. It is the policy of the Indian Affairs Branch to avoid establishment of parallel services on behalf of the Indians, and to take advantage, wherever possible, of resources provided for adjacent non-Indian populations.'[105] No clearer statement of the purpose of Indian welfare policy could have been made. Welfare services would help Indians join the broader society by erasing any perceived advantage to remaining in their own communities. For this strategy to succeed, the provinces would have to participate by extending their services to Indians on and off reserves. By 1965, the federal government would be prepared to entice them monetarily to do just that.

In the meantime, the branch, through the Canadian Welfare Council, continued to develop its expertise in public welfare administration. In mid-April 1959, Norman Cragg, the new executive secretary to the Public Welfare Division, extended an invitation to the branch to make a presentation on its recent welfare initiatives to the council's annual meeting.[106] At that meeting, the council also undertook to develop a statement of standards in social assistance administration and to sponsor a project to develop methods of compiling public welfare statistics. Known as the Project On Public Welfare Statistics, it soon became a forum for public welfare administrators across the country to discuss mutual concerns in the administration of social assistance programs. Gordon, representing Indian Affairs, became involved in the project. In the fall of 1959, for example, he attended a meeting of the Public Welfare Division national committee specifically to comment on the work done thus far in developing statistical forms.[107] Samples of forms and data collecting devices were exchanged, many of which the Indian Affairs Branch began to adapt for its own use.

In this way, the branch, through the council, began sharing its problems with other public welfare bodies. One of the main problems was the difficulty it had in administering an assistance program to a small, scattered population. In Gordon's view, this difficulty was undermining Indian integration. In a lengthy letter to Cragg, Gordon explained the reasons behind a new Indian Affairs initiative. The branch, he wrote, was overly identified as the sole government agency responsible for Indian welfare. Because Indians already received various cost-shared allowances through the provinces, the federal government had decided to negotiate agreements with other jurisdictions and voluntary agencies to extend their welfare services where they were adjacent to Indian communities.[108] From the council's perspective, this was a welcome development. It confirmed the value of its collaborative relationship with Indian Affairs; not only that, but the government was now following its recommendations to the 1946 joint committee. The Indians – both the government and the council thought – were truly in transition.

9

The Indian in Transition: Social Welfare and Provincial Services, 1959–1965

The central problem is this: How can the oppressed, as divided, unauthentic beings, participate in developing the pedagogy of their liberation? Only as they discover themselves to be 'hosts' of the oppressor can they contribute to the midwifery of their liberating pedagogy. As long as they live in the duality in which *to be* is *to be like the oppressor,* this contribution is impossible.

Paulo Freire, *Pedagogy of the Oppressed*

The Indian Affairs Branch and Welfare Division: Policy and Organization, 1959

In the ten years since 1948–9 the Indian Affairs Branch had evolved into a much larger organization. The total staff complement had increased nearly 115 per cent, from 946 in 1948 to 2,031 in 1958–9. A good portion of this increase involved the addition of teachers in the field. Children's education was seen as the primary means of effecting integration. Within the general administration, however, staff had increased by about 44 per cent, from 563 to 810. Of these, 597 were in the field, where they were responsible for eighty-nine agencies in eight regions. This amounted to an increase in field staff of 34 per cent. The 213 people in Ottawa represented an 80 per cent increase over the ten years. Program specialists in many areas such as social welfare, education, and economic development were located not only in Ottawa but also at each of the eight regional offices.[1]

The First Nations comprised 571 bands, which occupied 2,226 reserves encompassing 5,897,177 acres of land. The Indian population had increased by about 3 per cent per year over nine-and-a-half years, from 136,407 in 1949 to 174,242 as of 31 December 1958. The increase in Indian population, combined with the expansion of Indian Affairs programming, resulted in a 168 per cent increase in branch expenditures, from $10,379,427 in 1948–9 to $27,851,230 in 1957–8. The per capita expenditure had similarly increased, from $76.09 for each Indian in 1948–9 to $159.84 in 1957–8.[2]

Furthermore, changes had been made in the Welfare Division, which had been created from the former Education and Welfare Division in late 1947. A new Economic Development Division then emerged in 1958 from programs within the Welfare Division. By then, Welfare Division had redefined its basic objectives. The new ones were as follows:

(1) to improve social and economic standards in Indian communities by providing encouragement, assistance and guidance to individual Indians and to band councils;
(2) to promote the extension and adaption [sic] of the normal range of economic and social resources of non-Indian communities to the reserve community, with the long range objective of full economic and social intercourse between Indian and non-Indian communities;
(3) to assist Indians who have the necessary training, ability and interest to find employment and acceptance in the non-Indian community;
(4) to ensure that Indians who have established themselves in non-Indian communities have full access to the normal economic and social resources available to non-Indian citizens in the communities.[3]

These four objectives indicate the thrust of Indian policy by the late 1950s and early 1960s. They contain the two basic federal government objectives that had been articulated all during the 1946–8 joint committee hearings, those being, to ameliorate conditions on the reserves and to facilitate Indians' transition to mainstream society. These objectives guided the development of relief policy and its eventual linkage in 1963 and 1964 to the planning and implementation of a comprehensive community development program for Indians.

As one result of all this, the number and complexity of the programs with which the Welfare Division was involved had considerably increased. Reflecting this, there were nine social workers in the regional offices to consult with staff on social welfare matters; these nine in turn had a trained supervisor in Ottawa. The division continued to supervise the administration of Family Allowances; it also monitored the receipt of other categorical allowances administered by the provinces.[4]

Table 9.1
Numbers of families and children in receipt of Family Allowances and their method of payment, 31 December 1957

		Method of payment			
Families	Children	Cheque direct	Cheque c/o agent	Agency trust acc't	In kind
19,855	57,526	17,819	1,319	383	334

Note: The total value of Allowances issued was $4,411,852 or $6.39 per child per month.
Source: Canada, Department of Citizenship and Immigration, Indian Affairs Branch, *Annual Report, 1957–1958*, 54.

The division also funded the care of aged Indians in private homes and institutions, and provided funding, training, and residential support to disabled Indians in urban settings. Through local Children's Aid Societies, Ontario in 1956 became the first province to extend child welfare programs to reserves. Welfare Division thus began funding and monitoring these services. On-reserve housing continued to grow. Although the number of units built had declined by 1957–8 to about the same number as in 1948–9, from 1,197 to 814, the actual annual welfare expenditure had increased 136 per cent. Finally, the division was becoming involved in safe and 'accepted' forms of community organization. The Indian Homemakers' Clubs, mentioned earlier, were one example. In addition, carefully selected Indians with 'demonstrated leadership qualities' were being funded to attend special seminars under the Leadership Training Program.[5] Relief assistance remained the division's central program in terms of both expenditure and policy direction. In its summation of activities over the previous decade, the branch noted that relief costs had increased substantially. This increase could be attributed mainly to 'the increased cost of commodities' and 'such other factors as improved standards of relief, wider coverage, major interruptions in traditional economic patterns, chronically depressed fur prices, and restricted access to country foods attendant upon the shift to employment for wages.'[6] The branch's annual report for 1957–8 also highlighted the dramatic rise in relief costs over the previous year: 'Public assistance was necessary for many Indians, normally able to provide for their subsistence because of unemployment, in rural and urban areas. This factor, in addition to such others as

Table 9.2
Number of recipients of allowances by categorical type,
31 December 1957

Type of allowance	Number of recipients
Mothers' Allowances	262*
Blind Persons Allowances	271
Disabled Persons' Allowances	212
Old Age Assistance	1,660
Old Age Security	4,517

*In Quebec (74) and Ontario (188) only.
Source: Canada, Department of Citizenship and
Immigration, Indian Affairs Branch, Annual Report,
1957–1958, 55.

higher food costs, population growth and the introduction of higher standards resulted in a 33% increase in direct relief expenditures.'[7] These quotations provide some insight into the relationship between Indian relief and the dominant capitalist economy. The 'interruptions in traditional economic patterns' had been going on since well before Confederation. After the Second World War, Indian Affairs responded to these 'interruptions' with programs agreeable to modern sensibilities, but it continued to play the same role as always: it was an army of occupation.

The purpose of Indian policy continued to be to facilitate economic dispossession and social displacement. Its intention was not to help First Nations develop solutions to these things. This was the darker meaning of Indian policy. The cultural banners of humanitarianism and the applied reason of social science were mere masks obscuring the real task, which was capitalist expansion. For inasmuch as Indian policy sought ways to teach Indians the ways of liberal society, to civilize them in the name of progress, to integrate them into Euro-Canadian society, to make them equal citizens of the state, it constantly supported their exploitation and marginalization. Thus, the nature of Indian dependency resides in the relationship between the hegemony of capitalist processes and the legitimizing policies of the state that these processes engender.[8]

The new policy of issuing relief by cheques and by purchase vouchers was emphasized both in the 1957–8 annual report and in the ten-year review of activities conducted in 1958. In describing the new policy, the

Document 9.1 Representation of Treasury Board Minute No. 539372,
26 November 1958

The board approves the following scale of welfare assistance to indigent
Indians to be provided (a) in cash or (b) in kind, by way of a dollar value
authorization or direct commodity orders, effective 1 April 1959:

	Per Month
One adult	$22
Each additional adult or child over 12 years of age	$15
Each child 12 years of age or under	$12

The board also approves that additional assistance be granted in isolated
and semi-isolated areas by Indian agency superintendents, with the
approval of the department, up to 75 per cent of the maximum allowable
in the above scale for approximately 3 per cent of the relief cases and up to
30 per cent for approximately 10 per cent of the relief cases.

Source: NAC, RG-10, CR Series, Vol. 7094, File 1/10-3-0, 1958.

annual report – in language suggestive of social work philosophy and
ethics – highlighted the importance of placing 'more responsibility on
the Indian family to manage its own affairs' and of 'maintaining the
morale and self-respect of persons who must accept help.'[9] The *Review of
Activities*, published about a year later, reported that the 1958–9 fiscal
year would be the last in which food rations were issued as a form of
relief. The fiscal year after that, about 12 per cent of all indigent cases
would receive cash benefits, while the remainder would receive relief in
the form of purchase order vouchers. In addition, recipients would
receive a guide to good nutrition 'based on Canada's Food Rules' and
developed with the cooperation of the Department of National Health
and Welfare![10]

The authority to abandon the old scales of ration relief in favour of a
dollar value voucher system based on a scale of rates came from Treasury Board in November 1958 (Document 9.1). Besides allowing the
branch to take this step, the board granted the rate increase that Gordon and Roberts had called for in their September meeting with Health
and Welfare officials (see chapter 8). In the branch's opinion, the
experiment begun in 1956 had been a success. The movement toward a

fully articulated, rationalized system of relief based on provincial models was nearly complete. So too was the objectification of First Nations. The ongoing application of liberal welfare procedures continued to erode First Nations' collective autonomy; it also made each individual Indian a dependent object of professional intervention.[11]

Driving Home the Point: Welfare and Liberal Capitalist Values

Following the implementation of the 1958 Treasury Board minute, social assistance policy became even more complex. This was clearly reflected in the 1959 revision and expansion of the social assistance chapter in the Indian agency field manual.[12] Most telling was the chapter's articulation of liberal values, which was occasionally infused with misgivings about Indians' capacity to adopt them. For example, in a general statement of principles, the administrator was advised to issue cheques and vouchers to those Indians 'who can be relied upon to purchase essential items of food with a minimum of supervision,' as well as to ensure that 'welfare aid given in this manner is not abused.'[13] The head of the household, defined as the man 'responsible for the support of his family,' was still required to apply for assistance, but in addition he was not to 'delegate this task to his wife or some other person'[14] and consequently shirk his role as breadwinner.

Of particular importance was the definition of 'household' in terms of composition and dwelling. The single residence and the private, nuclear family were central to determining eligibility. Deviants, such as unmarried mothers, were dealt with in Euro-Canadian ways acceptable at the time. As well, administrators were in effect instructed to treat extended kinship systems as separate households under one roof: 'A household shall be considered as comprising a family unit or a single person when that person lives alone and maintains a self-contained living establishment. An unmarried mother and her children living with her parents shall be considered as part of the household of her parents. When two families live under one roof but each continues to exist as a separate entity, they shall be considered as being separate households.'[15] For the first time policy defined dependants in terms of their relationship to other family members and employability. The spouse of the household head was considered a dependant, and so was a child sixteen years or younger who was still in school. Others over sixteen could be considered dependent only if they were too ill or disabled to accept employment. Other employable household members over sixteen were required to accept available employment, while single employables were required to accept employment regardless of its distance from home.[16] The use of the term 'employable' to replace 'able bodied' was notable. It reflected, first, the terminology of the new Unemployment Assistance Act and, second, the fact that the dynamics of employment were shifting away from primary industry toward the growing secondary and service industries located in the south. The growth of knowledge-based employment was expanding the definition of employability.

These revised definitions of household and employability created a logic for the relationship of social assistance to the Indian family and the wage economy. Expectations about employment could now be made clear; furthermore, income from various sources could be differentially assessed. For example, Indians who were receiving Old Age Assistance or Disabled and Blind Persons' Allowances were now expected to support themselves from that income; they were no longer eligible for additional relief. They were not considered members of the household when family eligibility was being determined, nor was their income considered available to the family. This resulted in an even more fractured view of the Indian family, since it required that the needs of the non-pensioned spouse and dependants be considered separately.[17]

The means test remained as it was in 1957. Eligibility was determined by measuring entitlement against employment income and other resources, using a formula that included expenses and incentives to remain employed (Document 9.2). When the means test was being applied, income from Family Allowances was exempt, but unemployment insurance and other forms of government transfer payments – including War Veteran's Allowances – were not. If a child was being supported by foster care payments, amounts over a certain limit were deducted from the family's entitlement. Limited overages were also introduced for recipients who under the old system had received rations with a value that exceeded the new rates, or whose communities were designated by reason of geography to have a higher cost of living.[18]

The overages were offset, however, by a new regulation that explicitly introduced the principle of treatment comparable to that of adjacent non-Indian communities: 'If the scale of assistance ... is higher than the municipal or provincial rate in any area, the amount of assistance given must be so calculated that Indians will not receive more than non-Indians similarly situated in near-by communities.'[19] There were two exceptions to this last regulation. First, if the non-Indian rate was inadequate, 'consideration' could be given to linking the Indian Affairs rate to

Document 9.2 Example of application of 1959 means test for social assistance

A family of two adults and five children twelve years of age or under, the family's cash income from Unemployment Insurance being $113 per month and legitimate monthly expenditures for fuel and rent being $28 and $35 respectively.

Maximum monthly food allowance –		
Head of household	$22.00	
Wife	15.00	
Five children at ($12 × 5)	60.00	$97.00
Gross monthly income –		
Unemployment Insurance		
4⅓ weeks at $26.00 per week	$113.00	
Less fuel wood	−$28.00	
Less rent	−$35.00	
Net Income	$50.00	
Subtract ⅓ of maximum monthly		
food allowance (⅓ of $97)	33.00	
Amount by which maximum monthly		
food allowance should be reduced	17.00	$17.00
Net monthly food allowance payable	$80.00	

Source: NAC, RG-10, CR Series, Vol. 7094, File 1/10-3-0, Relief Food Policy 1888-1963, Circular No. 97, Re: Relief Administration, Dollar Value Orders, and Agency Cheque, Chapter 13.01, Indian Affairs Branch Field Manual, p. 3, Ottawa, 27 February 1959.

another provincial benefit such as Mothers' Allowances. Second, where social assistance was paid entirely from a band's revenues, the band council was permitted to set its own rates. If these were less than the Indian Affairs rates, the band was to be encouraged to set rates sufficient for adequate nutrition.[20]

Assistance was administered through each of the eighty-nine agency offices. Despite the increased complexity, the agency superintendents and their assistants – usually clerks – continued to be the direct adminis-trators.[21] Myriad regulations and forms guided them in reporting and accounting procedures.[22] There were seven forms used for the adminis-tration of basic social assistance alone. A principle of the new voucher/cheque system had been to afford recipients greater consumer choice and independence, yet Ottawa continued to maintain a roster of approved merchants for each agency.

The roster – which continued to be a pork barrel – could be circum-vented only if no merchants had been named for an agency. If assistance was paid mainly from a band's revenues, 'the wishes of the band [could] be taken into consideration.'[23] This, then, was the Indian Affairs system of social assistance in place by 1959. It would be applied across the coun-try without any changes until 1964.

The Anomaly of Ontario

Ontario was an important exception to this general pattern of welfare delivery on Indian reserves. Following the recommendations of the 1954 special select committee of the Ontario legislature inquiring into Indian civil rights, the province began entering into agreements whereby Ottawa would reimburse the province for the costs of provincial and municipal social services extended to Indians on reserve. This process culminated in 1959 with an amendment to the Ontario General Welfare Assistance Act (GWA) that granted a quasi-municipal status to Indian bands to enable them to administer the act on reserves.[24] More importantly, the particular form this initiative took provided the branch with an opera-tional paradigm for developing social policy in keeping with Section 87 of the Indian Act and the overall objective of integration.

The branch very much hoped that under the terms of the Unemploy-ment Assistance Act, the provinces would be encouraged to provide social assistance to non-Indians living on reserves.[25] Of particular con-cern were Indian women who had lost their status under the Indian Act, children of Indian origin (whose mothers had lost their status) in the custody of either their mothers or their status relatives, and non-Indian children in the custody of Indian women. The branch, it should be noted, was not empowered by Treasury Board to provide assistance to people of non-Indian status. The provinces, in contrast, treated all resi-dents on Indian lands as a federal responsibility. Thus, non-Indian reserve residents were technically ineligible for assistance from either jurisdiction. Jones was anxious to resolve this issue and in February 1959 wrote to his deputy minister, Laval Fortier, that 'there is nothing in the Act which would prevent the province or municipality from qualifying for the 50% subsidy for any assistance provided on behalf of non-Indians resident on the reserve.'[26] However, because the Unemployment Assistance Act did not oblige the provinces to extend their services to non-Indians on reserve, Jones felt stymied. In his memorandum to Fortier he contemplated a confrontational course of action: 'Under the circumstances I could see no way in which the Unemployment Assistance Act could be of immediate help to us unless it was decided at a high level to approach the provinces directly with the request that they recognize responsibility for non-Indians on reserves.'[27]

Fortier apparently objected to this approach, and Jones conceded that it would not be wise to challenge the provinces. Instead he suggested that the Department of National Health and Welfare might use its leverage to influence them to extend their services. Fortier raised this possibility with Dr G.F. Davidson, then the Deputy Minister of Health and Welfare:

> I have in mind the possibility that our objectives might be kept in mind in general discussions with the provinces in day to day administration and that, should the Act be opened up on the basis of a larger Federal contribution, we would then be in a favourable bargaining position to secure concessions ... I am not optimistic that a program of aid for non-Indians on reserves can be developed if it is contingent upon municipal contribution. I do think ... we could make progress in establishing provincial responsibility. I would be grateful for any service you may ... render in this regard.[28]

A brief spate of activity followed during which a fundamental strategy was developed to involve the Cabinet – a necessary step if the provinces were to be brought to the negotiating table.[29] The real significance of Fortier's and Jones's correspondence is that it provides an inkling of the branch's next policy thrust. No sooner had it introduced its new social assistance policy in February than it began to formulate a strategy to divest itself of the responsibility. By April the branch had been advised of Ontario's proposal to extend the provisions of the General Welfare Assistance Act onto the reserves, with the costs of social assistance for Indians to be shared with the federal government. This news triggered negotiations with Ontario and raised the possibility that the other provinces might extend their social assistance services to all residents of Indian reserves.[30]

The August Memorandum to Cabinet and the Joint Parliamentary Committee, 1959–1961

Ontario's decision to extend its social assistance services prompted the Indian Affairs Branch to conduct a quick survey to determine the climate for similar initiatives by the other provinces. In a memorandum to Fortier, Jones commented on the survey results, noting that the western provinces were not likely to follow Ontario's lead. Their reluctance, he surmised, was linked to reports that they were moving away from municipal to provincial service delivery systems. This was because the municipalities could not afford the costs of 'qualified staff ... now recognized as a necessary part of any welfare program designed to meet the needs of persons dependent on public assistance.'[31] The Ontario model, based as it was on a municipal service system, was therefore not appropriate for them. Jones thought that in the short term, an agreement limited to Ontario might prove useful if the branch could learn some of the administrative complexities from this experiment. In the long term, he concluded, 'the inclusion of Indians in expanding provincial programs ... will prove to be a better solution to the whole problem of [the branch] ensuring treatment and assistance of standards comparable to that provided non-Indians.'[32]

At this juncture it should be noted that there were really two issues at hand. One was the issue of responsibility for social assistance for Indians living off reserve. The other was who was responsible for social assistance for on-reserve Indians – an issue further complicated by non-Indians living on reserves. Generally, the provinces took the position that constitutionally, Indians were a federal responsibility wherever they lived. Non-Indians living on reserve lands were also considered a federal responsibility by the provinces since lands reserved for Indians were constitutionally under federal jurisdiction. As we have seen, in the post-war era the federal government had begun to take the position that Indians should be treated like any other Canadian citizens with respect to welfare and like services. Consequently, Indians on and off reserve lands, as well as non-Indians on reserves, should be eligible for provincial welfare services. By the mid-1950s non-Indians living on reserves generally were not being extended services by either the federal or provincial governments, whereas Indians living off reserve were generally not eligible for provincial or municipal services.

There was a cautious tone in Jones's memorandum to Fortier. This caution was probably rooted in two branch concerns. First, any initiative that gave even minimal autonomy to the bands raised concerns about their readiness to assume such a mantle of responsibility. Their lack of readiness could lead to spendthrift behaviour and a failure to meet their peoples' needs. Second, it was possible that provincial rather than municipal service systems would be more cost effective – perhaps even of minimal cost to Indian Affairs. It might be more prudent to see how the welfare systems evolved in other provinces before rushing into agreements with them.

In the end, the hesitation at moving forward with the other provinces was outweighed by the need to develop policies to support integration, and by the need to forge an agreement with Ontario that would make funds flow to support the extension of services. Given that such an agreement had to be negotiated, it made sense to develop one that in the long run would have application to the other provinces.[33] Beginning in May 1959 and over the next three months, a series of draft proposals were written. In early August a final document was sent to Cabinet for approval.[34]

The memorandum to Cabinet provided the most unequivocal statement of Indian social welfare policy and its relationship to integration since the end of the war. It also implicitly proposed that First Nations become third-party objects of contractual arrangements between Ottawa and the provinces; in this sense, its aim was to destroy their autonomy while promoting Indians' individual rights. The memorandum began with some general statements about the objectives of the Department of Citizenship and Immigration with respect to Indian peoples:

1. It has been the objective of this Department over the years to secure, for Indians, eligibility for the same welfare benefits and treatment enjoyed by other Canadian citizens in the various provinces.

2. This objective is based upon the conviction that differentiation between the treatment and benefits provided for Indians and those available to other citizens is undesirable. It is considered that Indians cannot achieve full citizenship if, because of their status, they are denied access to services available to all other citizens. In addition, it would be costly to attempt to establish services for the widely scattered Indian population which would duplicate provincial welfare services for other Canadian citizens in adjacent areas.

3. Indians who have established residence in non-Indian communities are liable for the same taxes as non-Indians and, in the view of the Department, should have access to all community and provincial services on the same basis as non-Indians. There seems ... no case for financial participa-

tion by the Federal Government in regard to welfare services on behalf of Indians in such circumstances.

4. In regard, however, to Indians on reserves and in their own communities, the Department of Citizenship and Immigration has assumed responsibility for essential welfare services in the past. Extension of provincial services to these areas, therefore, entails financial agreements with the provinces in regard to the cost of benefits and the costs of administration.[35]

The branch could never resist wording that implied that it shouldered the burden of history. From the memo's opening remarks, readers could not but believe that the branch had ceaselessly been seeking the welfare of Indians in provincial jurisdictions.

The text provided a rationale for the new direction in social assistance and general Indian policy. In the memo's item 2, for example, the segregation of Indians was depicted as undesirable and their full citizenship as impossible if their status was used as a barrier to services enjoyed by other Canadians. The assertion in item 3 that Indians living in non-Indian communities were arguably not a federal responsibility simply heightened the possibility of offloading Indians as a cost borne entirely by the federal treasury. Item 4, however, recognized that there was a price for provincial involvement in Indian services on the reserves and that financial inducements would have to be extended in order to entice the provinces to play ball.

The memorandum stressed this point again in item 7, which noted that the Unemployment Assistance Act alone was not a sufficient incentive for the provinces. It made a completely unsubstantiated claim that there was 'substantial evidence of the willingness of most provinces to consider agreements with the Department of Citizenship and Immigration.'[36] A final item 8 pointed to the necessity that any agreement reflect both the varied conditions of Canada's Indians and the differences in provincial legislation.

What, then, did the branch advise the minister, Ellen Fairclough, to recommend to her colleagues? Of three recommended courses of action, the second was the most important. The first was that the federal government continue to insist that Indians resident in non-Indian communities be eligible for the same benefits and services as non-Indians. The third, which was not implemented but which was to resurface five years later, sought to have the Department of Citizenship and Immigration assume the appropriate share of costs of social assistance for bands with insufficient funds.

But it was the second recommendation that set the blueprint for the next phase of Indian social welfare and integration policy. It advocated

> that the Department of Citizenship and Immigration be authorized to negotiate with provinces for the extension and administration of provincial welfare programs and services to persons residing on Indian reserves and in Indian communities, rather than attempt to develop special welfare services, on the basis that:
> a. the Department ... will contribute toward the costs of provincial welfare benefits, over and above the Federal contribution payable under terms of the Unemployment Assistance Act or other Federal legislation, and
> b. the Department ... will assume all, or such proportion as may be necessary of the costs of administration for the extension of provincial welfare services to Indian reserves and Indian communities.[37]

Significantly, the recommendation referred in general to persons who were resident on reserves; in this way it hoped to account for non-Indians as well as Indians. Still, the importance of the memorandum and its second recommendation was that it was a piece of social engineering, a 'how to' for Indian integration.

Until this time there had been no concrete plans, except in education, to achieve assimilation or integration.[38] Indeed, until the memorandum, policy had never really risen above platitudes. The thinking was similar to that of the tourist who expects his or her host to understand English if it is spoken more loudly. The imparting of ever more liberal philosophy to Indians would somehow make them get the message and disappear into the mainstream. This clearly had not happened. The failure of assimilation policy by the late 1950s was most evident in the enfranchisement statistics since Confederation. From 1867 to July 1958, only 10,497 Indians had become enfranchised, with about half that number doing so since 1951. Only two bands had become completely enfranchised.[39] The development of a strategy linking the final objective to specific actions was the essential achievement of the August memorandum. Social policy directed at Indians would continue to individualize them, but for the broad purposes of integration, they would be reduced to one faceless entity dealt with in broad-brush strokes.

By January 1960, Cabinet approval of the memorandum had still not been obtained even though negotiations with Ontario were in progress. Gordon was concerned that the branch was out on a limb. The memorandum had been intended to deal with the immediate Ontario situation as well as with the rest of the provinces.[40] In the annual report for 1959–60, the branch claimed that negotiations were underway with the provinces to integrate reserves into their welfare programs. The amendment to the General Welfare Assistance Act was in effect, and some bands were already participating. This meant they were paying 100 per cent of the costs of social assistance in anticipation of an 80 per cent reimbursement from the province. The remaining 20 per cent was wholly a municipal responsibility – that is, a band responsibility. Yet the Indian Affairs branch had no real authority in place to advance operating funds to a band or to cover the 20 per cent share if a band was unable to do so. Under the Ontario General Welfare Assistance Act, the province shared basic social assistance costs with the municipalities. The provincial share was 80 per cent and the municipal share was 20 per cent. It was not evident from the file under study when provincial reimbursement of the bands occurred, but certainly it would have had to occur before the end of each fiscal year. Subject to a satisfactory submission of band expenditures, the province would reimburse 80 per cent of those expenditures which complied with provincial requirements. The band, like other Ontario municipalities, was then responsible for the remaining 20 per cent. Unlike the municipalities however, bands generally did not have the power of taxation on reserve.

Underlying this concern was Gordon's fear that without an agreement in place, the department would lose control over how Indians expended their funds:

Mr Band's [deputy minister, Ontario Department of Public Welfare] insistence upon dealing directly with the Band Council, as he would with municipalities, seems to bar us from exercising adequate supervision or control; ... we provide the money and the band spends it in accordance with Ontario regulations. The province really accepts no financial risk ... because if the actions of the Council do not meet their standards they can simply refuse to pay the 80% subsidy ... The objective is to place financial responsibility correctly to ensure that the provincial scheme ... goes hand in hand with financial commitments. Otherwise, we are placed in the position of assuming full financial responsibility for any errors in administration which might ... result from an unwise and too rapid extension of this program, while the province ... is only too likely to press for these extensions because of the favourable publicity which this attitude would bring to them.[41]

To solve the funding difficulty, it was decided, on Gordon's recommendation, that subject to Section 68(1) of the Indian Act, bands with sufficient and *responsibly* managed revenues would negotiate directly with the province. The department would only be involved with those bands whose revenues were not sufficient to cover the 20 per cent municipal share, or with those which did not satisfy Section 68(1) but for whom the province thought it appropriate that they participate in the new arrangement.[42]

Although the lack of funding authority was a problem, Gordon's remarks were curious in light of the memorandum to Cabinet, of which he was the principal author. Its third recommendation was that the department be authorized to cover some or all of bands' costs.[43] In his correspondence we can glimpse the underlying operational culture of Indian Affairs. Inasmuch as Welfare Division drafted the memorandum to Cabinet, there was a surface appearance of pursuing the directions recommended by the joint parliamentary committee of 1946–8. Because the stated intention was to get the provinces to extend their services, jurisdictional issues outwardly consumed the branch. Inwardly, however, these issues were tinged with a distrust of the actions of other departments and governments in their dealings with First Nations. Also, Gordon's remarks were another indication of lack of faith in the readiness and capacity of Indian bands to govern themselves. This distrust suggested a more basic issue – that the Indian Affairs Branch was reluctant to accept any suggestion that it relinquish its role of guardian and spokesperson for Indian people. Indeed, that continues to be the paradox and the plague of the Indian Affairs mandate.[44]

The Joint Parliamentary Committee, 1959–1961

Cabinet approved the memorandum in March 1960.[45] While the memorandum was being drafted, another joint parliamentary committee on the administration of Indian Affairs had opened hearings in Ottawa. This second committee had been convened in response to continuing problems over land claims and to embarrassing, international criticisms of Canada's treatment of its native peoples.[46] Since 1948, no government had acted on the joint committee's recommendation that a land claims commission be established. The second committee sat periodically for two-and-a-half years and produced a final report and recommendations in 1961. In 1960 and 1961 the branch prepared two background briefings for the new deputy minister, George F. Davidson, so that he would be fully cognizant of the branch's position before the committee. At the request of Ellen Fairclough, in May 1960 Davidson had been transferred over to Citizenship and Immigration from Health and Welfare. Davidson stated that Fairclough had been 'increasingly dissatisfied with Laval Fortier.' He described Fortier as

> a very intelligent person, very quick to the point of giving the impression that he was almost impulsive. He reacted quickly to everything you would put in front of him. Sometimes one was left with the impression that his decisions were reached without probing the full implications of what the reaction would be. My relations with him were always good. He was a personal friend of mine at the time. He had been a military officer and had certain of the military attributes as did Colonel Jones to the Nth degree!

Fairclough had asked Diefenbaker for Davidson to replace Fortier to help restore the department's image following the botched deportation of a Russian refugee. Davidson recounted:

> I was brought over there *not* for Citizenship, *not* for Indian Affairs, but for Immigration, and I was pitchforked immediately into the Chinese immigration scandal. That was my main concern during the period. I was only there from May 1960 to January 1963. The degree of my responsibility – not in theory, but in fact – for Indian Affairs was relatively slight. I neglected Indian Affairs, you might say, because Colonel Jones was there. He had more or less the confidence of Ellen Fairclough, to the extent she wasn't impressed by him, she was scared of him!

Davidson's recollection of Jones provides some insight into Fairclough's fear: 'He was a frozen-faced military type, bleak. His impersonal presence was what impressed you most. He was cut and dried. You felt there was very little warmth or humanity in him, although there was more than appeared at the surface. But he acted more as a stern father in his outlook on Indian Affairs than he did as a humanitarian. You wouldn't slap Hubert Jones on the back!'[47]

The first briefing prepared for Davidson outlined the impact of economic conditions on Indian communities in Canada: the second provided a summary of branch policy and strategy to extend provincial welfare services. In both briefs there was repeated reference to the government's policy on Indian integration.[48] The briefs to Davidson seem to have been *pro forma*, indicating to him what the branch intended to say to the committee. Davidson did not recall appearing before the committee, and a review of the committee's proceedings and evidence did not show that he had.

The first brief, dated 30 November 1960, was in memorandum form from Jones to Davidson. Appended to the text were two welfare expenditure tables. One compared Indian trust fund disbursements between 1950–7 and 1957–60; the other made comparisons over the same periods for expenditures from parliamentary appropriations. The latter table also included a two-year projection to 1962. Despite a substantial increase in welfare expenditures between 1950–7 and 1957–60, Jones was reluctant to attribute this to changing economic conditions. 'Although the years 1950 to 1957 are ... a period of economic expansion, with some ... recessive tendencies in ensuing years, it could not be said that these changes in economic conditions have had a major impact on the activities of the Branch. The statistics for these two periods do not, therefore necessarily illustrate the response of the Branch to changing economic conditions in the country, but rather reflect the change in emphasis in the programs of the Branch.'[49] Jones apparently meant that increased expenditures were mainly the result of more benevolent approaches to administering on-reserve assistance beginning in April 1957, rather than variable economic conditions. Following this assertion, however, he wrote,

> The changing conditions in the Canadian economy affect the Indian population perhaps more than any other ethnic group in the country. In times of full employment the Indian is absorbed in the labour force wherever he fits in ... When economic activity slows down and unemployment rises the Indian labourer will likely be among the first to be laid off.
>
> *No statistics are available* on the changes in employment of the Indian labour force as a result of the general economic conditions in the country. However, these changes are reflected, at least to some extent, in the welfare expenditures by this Branch.[50]

It is unclear what Jones was trying to convey. First he asserted that there was no relationship between economic conditions in Canada and Indian welfare expenditure. Then he stated that economic conditions indeed affected Indians more than other groups and that increased expenditures most certainly reflected changed conditions. Finally, he conceded that he had no real data on which to base either statement! Davidson, who had no real recollection of the brief,[51] would have been hard pressed to make sense of it.

The relationship between Indian welfare expenditure and general economic conditions, and the questions posed by any serious analysis of this relationship, completely escaped Jones. For Jones the issue was not that relationship; instead, it was the need to create Euro-Canadians from Indians. Thus, he was intent on explaining to Davidson the solution to the 'Indian problem.'[52] He continued:

> Another important item in this program [i.e. capital expenditure from the Indian Trust Fund] is the construction of roads, because they open the reserves for further development and make it easier for the Indians to visit neighbouring municipalities where they can do business and seek employment opportunities. The development of roads on reserves is also closely linked with the education program ... More ... school bus routes are needed each year to permit ... Indian pupils to attend schools, and ... to enable them to reach municipal schools.[53]

Jones was especially pleased that these capital expenditures created employment for Indian men and concurrently provided them with opportunities to learn 'useful trades, such as carpentry' and to 'become proficient in handling heavy road building equipment.'[54] The intent of increased capital expenditure became evident later in the correspondence: 'As part of the preparation of Indians for integration, increased attention has been given during the past few years to the reduction of Indian dependence on Government aid. In part this is ... fostered by giving bands greater control and responsibility for the conduct of their own affairs. During the years 1959 and 1960 control of expenditure of Revenue monies has been transferred in whole or in part to 22 bands in Canada.'[55] Jones's proud boast was that about 3.8 per cent of all bands in Canada had some control over the expenditure of their revenues. This 'control' would have been limited by definitions of allowable expenditure. At least seventeen of the twenty-two bands were in Ontario, where they were paying their 20 per cent share of provincial social assistance![56]

Jones went on to describe the recent creation of an Economic Development Division:

> A new Division devoted exclusively to economic development came into full operation ... in February 1960, and has assumed responsibility for co-ordinating and directing the various programs having to do with the economic well-being of the Indians ... In all programs of economic assistance

to Indians, as contrasted with welfare relief measures, increasing emphasis is being placed ... on the repayment ... of the assistance provided. This approach is intended to encourage a spirit of independence and self-reliance, and to make clear the basis on which government aid is extended.[57]

This was a mid-twentieth-century statement of Indian policy and the spirit of its implementation since Confederation. Like their predecessors, Jones and the head of the Welfare Division, J.H. Gordon, were convinced that Indian welfare dependency was intrinsic to the provision of relief assistance. The best way to prevent such dependency was to avoid giving assistance in the first place or to make it conditional on individual performance and repayment. It was not difficult to conclude from this that the solution to dependency was to integrate Indians into the Canadian social and economic mainstream. Integration could be achieved by opening Indian communities to development and by providing access to white settlements where the best education and employment opportunities were to be found.

Jones and Gordon were apprehensive that Indians were coming to rely on federal assistance, with no appreciation of its origins and limits. Besides providing economic and educational initiatives that would teach Indians the value of an earned dollar, the extension of provincial welfare services onto reserves would reduce isolation, create linkages to the local labour market, and serve as a force for promoting citizenship. On 20 June 1960, for example, Gordon, now considerably influenced by his activities at the Canadian Welfare Council, mailed to the regions a discussion pamphlet, *Social Security Leads to Dependency?*[58] The pamphlet focused on the issue of the modern welfare state, its European roots, and the problems of employment, social security, and individual dependency in a postindustrial economy. It made no reference to Indian welfare. In his covering correspondence, Gordon suggested that 'while the pamphlet does not attempt to provide answers to the various questions which may be asked or which trouble the minds of many persons regarding social security, it is certainly thought provoking and will, I believe, assist our welfare administrators to place in proper perspective the problems confronting Indians applying to them for assistance.'[59] The 'problems confronting Indians' that Gordon alluded to were those faced by all employable welfare recipients: job skills, motivation, work habits, access to labour, and so on. Gordon's message seems to indicate that he saw no real difference in welfare dependency between Indian and non-Indian recipients.

The second brief to the deputy minister, which outlined the branch's welfare policy, was also prepared by Jones in consultation with Gordon in January 1961. The brief must be interpreted in the context of his November memorandum on the impact of economic conditions on Indians and his recommended solution to 'the Indian problem.' Jones began by describing the August 1959 memorandum to Cabinet as the seminal document governing Indian welfare policy. He then presented an ambivalent and confused appraisal of the progress made with the provinces since the memorandum was approved as a basis for action:

In the provinces ... there is now general acceptance of the position taken by this department ... that welfare services and programs should be available to Indians on and off the reserves and that it would be both undesirable and uneconomical for the federal government to duplicate provincial welfare legislation or for this department to create a parallel organization ... to service the small, widely scattered ... Bands. There have been important advances in the acceptance of ... responsibility ... for Indian citizens in all the provinces since the last Joint Parliamentary Committee Hearings ... in 1948. The long-term prospect ... is for further gradual extension of services ... It seems obvious, however ... that full extension of services is some years distant in most provinces.[60]

The fact of the matter was that there was little evidence that the provinces were willing to accept the principle of extending services. Negotiations with Ontario had apparently stalled, and there was no evidence of communication with any other province. Jones did acknowledge the impasse and its consequences: 'There are at present broad areas of need on Indian reserves in many of the provinces not covered by services available in non-Indian communities ... This situation is likely to continue for a considerable period ... unless ... progress in extension of provincial services can be accelerated.'[61]

The solution, he thought, lay, not in expanding the branch welfare services, but in influencing the joint parliamentary committee to support the principle of extended provincial services. A committee statement to that effect would place public pressure on the provinces. 'I believe this matter to be a major issue in Indian Affairs administration,' he wrote, 'and vital to the advancement and progress of the Indians ... I consider the alternative of enacting special Federal legislation ... would be retrogressive. I feel, therefore, that this matter should be reviewed by the Joint Committee.'[62] To this end he proposed to Davidson that he

[Jones] appear before the committee and make the case for the branch. In an earlier committee appearance, Jones had already made a statement on this issue: 'What we have in mind as a policy – and the minister made an announcement about it in the house not too long ago – is to bring the full provincial welfare resources to the reserves rather than to set up parallel staffs and organizations. We prefer to make arrangements with the provinces and to have them give to Indians the same services on reserves that are available to non-Indians off reserves.'[63] He identified three strategic issues that required internal discussion and agreement before he made another appearance before the committee: the method of negotiation with the provinces; financial considerations; and residual branch responsibilities.[64]

Jones told Davidson that he favoured a federal–provincial conference. Piecemeal negotiations with the provinces would result in unwieldy and fragmentary resolutions to issues that he believed required one solution. To entice the provinces to the conference table, the federal government would have to enrich the financial incentives. In an oblique reference to planned talks on what would eventually be the Canada Assistance Plan, Jones wrote: 'I think it would be ... advantageous if the proposals offered to the provinces could coincide with any plans there may be for further extension of federal financial responsibility in regard to provincial programs comparable to the sharing of costs under the Unemployment Assistance Act Agreements.' It was then his hope, if this were done, 'to secure a financial agreement with the provinces which would retain a degree of provincial sharing in all costs both benefits and services, extended to Indians and to Indian reserves.'[65] The branch would then retain only residual responsibilities to cover any temporary gaps in provincial coverage.[66]

During the spring of 1961, shortly before the committee's final report, the Indian Affairs Branch made several substantial presentations to the committee. Jones appeared again on 2 May 1961. He emphasized branch policy on the desired relationship between Indians and the provinces, and he stressed the critical role that welfare services could play in that relationship: 'I think the extension of provincial services and jurisdiction must eventually come. I do not believe that Indians can be treated as people apart indefinitely. There must come a time when they are accepted fully into the larger community ... The process must be developed by stages and there is one field ... where I believe it might come first. I would suggest that this is in the field of welfare.'[67] Several days later, as part of an overall summary, Gordon delivered an important brief concerning welfare division functions. It was instructive for two reasons: first, he clearly articulated the branch's welfare policy, which the branch recommended that the committee accept; and second, he provided clear insights into the thinking that guided the policy.

Gordon began by citing Ellen Fairclough's April 1960 statement to the House of Commons, which announced the federal government's readiness to negotiate with the provinces to extend provincial welfare services to the reserves. Fairclough had said that the federal government would assist with the costs of extending services to ensure that those services were not duplicated. Duplication, she had said, would result in Indian people being set apart from other Canadians.[68] 'This statement,' Gordon continued, 'is of fundamental importance to the welfare division and I believe the principle enunciated is widely accepted. Indeed three provinces and a number of major organizations have endorsed this ... view and have urged [its] acceleration.'[69] Among the national organizations that endorsed this stance were the Canadian Welfare Council, the Anglican and United Churches of Canada, and the Indian-Eskimo Association of Canada. Among the provinces, Ontario had endorsed the principle and was also practising it. British Columbia had provided a weak, somewhat confused endorsement, and Saskatchewan had also endorsed the extension of services. This optimistic overview, however, was offset by the difficulties the division had encountered in negotiating with provincial welfare departments. Gordon testified:

> Most provincial departments face demands for existing services which limited staffs and budgets are barely able to meet. Important sectors of provincial welfare programs depend upon participation of municipal and private agencies ... it is often difficult for reserves to fit into this pattern ... The costs and other implications vary from province to province depending upon a ... variety of factors including general attitudes; the ratio of Indians to the general population; and the number of Indian communities ... in areas ... expensive to service because of remoteness, depressed economic conditions or where ... no provincial administrative machinery now exists. In addition, there has been ... apprehension amongst provincial welfare staffs at the prospect of an addition to present heavy case loads of persons in the unfamiliar settings of reserves.
>
> The consequence has been that ... a good deal of resistance has been encountered.[70]

Yet Gordon remained adamant that the goal of the Welfare Division was to transfer its services and become redundant. He described the federal responsibility for Indian welfare services as transitional and necessary only until Indians had full access to provincial services. He said that 'the department has endeavoured to avoid the build-up of a large specialized welfare staff and organization. Also there is no specific welfare legislation respecting Indians either in the Indian Act or by other federal statute.'[71]

Having distanced the branch from the future administration of social welfare, Gordon was quick to define the philosophy of its current program: 'The ... program places much more responsibility upon the individual Indian; changes the task of the Indian superintendent from administrator to educator (nutrition – proper use of the food dollar – wise purchasing, etc.) and brings the standards and procedures into line with practices in non-Indian communities.'[72] He described how related social services must encourage Indians to be self-reliant and to re-enter the work force:

> In the field of public assistance the maintenance of the self-respect of the individual ... [of] his initiative and will to help himself is the most difficult of all the tasks assigned the Indian Affairs ... field officer. This function is particularly difficult where Indians feel there is an inherent right to full support from the Canadian taxpayer under the treaties and where the standard of living which can be achieved through the best efforts of industrious Indians is only slightly above subsistence levels.
>
> There is no easy nor quick solution to this problem. The basic reasons for dependency must be identified and recognized by the individual and the community and joint efforts made to correct them. It is important to avoid lower standards of assistance by comparison with ... non-Indian communities but, at the same time, not to set standards higher than the levels employed Indians can achieve through their own efforts ... The program must meet the needs of the temporarily unemployed factory ... and white collar worker from ... urban reserves and those of the illiterate trapper who depends ... upon country food and the harvest of natural resources.[73]

Gordon's testimony raised the familiar fear that Indians would think of social assistance as a matter of historical right. Instead of acknowledging the unresolved historical issues, it was easier to deny or ignore them, to depict Indians as still engaged in learning the ways of modern society, and to equate their situation with questions of labour market opportunity. Social assistance served two apparently paradoxical purposes. It was an inexpensive, controllable method of compensation. Yet it was also a method of instruction in liberal political economy and hence integration. It could be both precisely because it obscured – in the public's mind, at least – the issue of collective rights and historical grievances.

The branch stated its desire to be free of a welfare program, yet it stated with equal force its objectives in providing one. Gordon's assumptions about the application of welfare programs in Indian communities were entirely ethnocentric. Indians were simply unemployed, perhaps dysfunctional individuals who could be rehabilitated; their dependence on social assistance could be corrected, just like it could be for anyone else. Tireless administration of public policy was required to help them become self-reliant and independent of the public purse. The assumption that Indian individuals were merely disengaged from the Canadian social and economic fabric led to the belief that making mirror images of Canadian social institutions in Indian communities could rectify Indian dependency. If the values and expectations inherent in these institutions were present on reserves, then they could be internalized. Self-reliance and employment would follow.

The committee concluded its hearings in May 1961 and presented its final report to the House of Commons on 8 July 1961. The text reflected – almost without qualification – the branch's philosophy and objectives. The preamble, which could almost have been written by Jones, emphasized the emergent view that Indians were members of Canada's pluralist society, an identity they had earned:

> The winds of change have been blowing through the ranks of Indian people, and ... there is also a growing awareness ... of their problems and needs amongst the non-Indian population. The time is ... fast approaching when the Indian people can assume the responsibility and accept the benefits of full participation as Canadian citizens ...
>
> It is the view of the Committee that the government should direct more authority and responsibility to Band Councils and individual Indians ... and that the Indians should be encouraged to accept and exercise such authority and responsibility.
>
> Your Committee believes that the advancement of the Indians towards full acceptance of the responsibilities and obligations of citizenship must be without prejudice to the retention of the cultural, historical and other economic benefits which they have inherited.[74]

To further the objective of full citizenship rights, the committee unequivocally accepted the branch policy of extending provincial welfare services onto reserves. It also iterated Jones's strategy to achieve it:

> Your Committee believes that wherever possible, existing provincial welfare legislation and services should be used for the benefit of the Indian population. Your Committee therefore recommends that this matter be placed on the agenda of a Dominion-Provincial Conference on Indian Affairs with a view to transferring the social welfare jurisdiction with respect to Indians to the provinces.[75]

The committee's lack of critical assessment of branch policy – indeed, its seeming reliance upon it for direction and assurance of Indian 'advancement' – indicated how dominant liberal consciousness and ideas about developmental humanism were in Canadian social thought. There was no disputing the assumption that Indians had been swept up by a civilization beyond their ken and that, though they had been innocent victims of progress, their destiny lay in participating in that same progress which had reduced them to wards of the state. The committee report confirmed the rightness of Canada and the liberal social order. This was especially reflected in its endorsement of the plan to extend provincial welfare services – in fact, any services – that would enhance Indians' transition into regular Canadian life. The market economy that had exploited and displaced Indians was now to be their lifeline.

Anger: The First Nations' Submissions and Responses to the Committee's Report

First Nations' testimony and briefs to the committee focused on three related themes: land claims and treaty rights, economic deprivation and poverty exacerbated by inadequate social assistance, and integration policy. At the urging of the National Commission on the Indian Canadian, many bands and organizations had submitted briefs directly to the committee clerk.[76] Other bands, however, submitted their concerns through the Indian Affairs Branch, where they were cast into a different context before being forwarded to the committee. The wording of the briefs was not changed, but the branch added explanatory comments or replies to assertions. For example, a brief from Chief Pelletier of the Fort William Band listed many problems and also vigorously opposed integration policy. Jones had made his final committee appearance before he received the letter. He addressed each concern in a reply to Pelletier, but ignored the chief's opposition to integration.[77]

The better route was to avoid the branch. This was the approach taken by the Sheshegwaning Band of Manitoulin Island, Ontario whose chief, Theodore Simon, wrote directly to the MP for Fort William that 'Mr. Jones and that crowd began to push their notions of integration and that's what wrecked the Reserve ... We were doing well enough on integrating ourselves with the white population of Canada without Mr. Jones and his hatchet men starting to push us around.'[78] Simon, who was alluding principally to the branch's education policies, was saying that his people were quite capable of deciding for themselves how and on what terms they wished to associate with the Euro-Canadian mainstream.

Several submissions from Maritime bands dwelt on their impoverishment, their living conditions, and the inadequacy of social assistance. One, from the Burnt Church Band in Burnt Church (Lagaceville), New Brunswick, complained about recent treatment by the local superintendent:

> My councillors and I held a very important meeting the Subject of this meeting was based on Relief, 'Higher Rate' we went as far as to Notify the Minister. The results were as far as we know was that our local Supt. was given the Authority to provide us with the fullest Benifits. The local Supt. then made an indication by raising the relief with a Sum, not worth while mintioning.
>
> The employment Situation in this vicinity is very grave each time we've approached this problem to the local Supt. we've been Simply ignored.[79]

Another New Brunswick band, the Oromocto Band, pointed to the dearth of employment for its members. 'As I pointed out earlier,' wrote Chief John Sacobie, 'there is hardly any work going on. We would be most grateful if some provision could be made for winter relief ... There are about thirteen families and most of them will require some assistance during the winter.'[80] The chief of the Chapel Island Band of Barra Head (St Peters), Nova Scotia, described the marginal position of his band with respect to Euro-Canadian society:

> Our Reserve for the past two years has witnessed serious unemployment and destitution. We have no timber resources whatsoever and cannot compete on the labour market with the non-Indian labour force, because ... our adult residents are without salable skills ...
>
> Our housing needs are very great, rooms are small and over crowded and many occupy small dilapidated structures which represent health haz-

ards many homes are in need of repairs because our ... income is insufficient to provide family needs ... We are unable to afford to repair their homes ... If a proper home environment is to be given our children while they attend school and also when mixing with white children substantial and physical structures should be provided.[81]

The Middle River (Wagmatcook) Band made similar complaints: 'There is much lacking in promoting employment on the Reserve, which is without wood or mineral resources. Our main source of employment has been derived from road construction and woodswork ... There is a great need for new houses as many family living in shacks unfit for human habitation ... People cannot acquire desirable social habits while the present situation exists.'[82]

In many respects, these and other submissions revealed that little had changed materially or socially since the 1946–8 joint committee hearings. Complaints of destitution, inadequate housing, and the lack of economic resources were paramount. Two things were, however, different. First, there was a change in the language; some bands now used the language of integration and referred, for example, to their position in the labour market and the dominant economy, or to the relationship of social assistance rates to family size. Second, an odious, damaging point of comparison with 'white society' had entered the submissions. With the continued application of integration policy, Indians – and especially Indian children – were being placed in mixed situations with the mainstream population, which was usually more affluent and, in the case of schooling, culturally advantaged as well. In some briefs, there was a hint of feelings of inferiority to whites and a negative, collective self-image.

Confusion and division about integration were also present. A prominent Indian, Dr Peter Kelly, who had testified before the 1946–8 committee, appeared on behalf of the Native Brotherhood of British Columbia.[83] He spoke in favour of integration, but he also pointedly urged the government to provide Indians with the resources necessary to achieve it: 'The economic position of the Indian must improve. He must be taught the value of systematic training in the broad fields of labour and education ... If this committee subscribes to the view that the native people should be integrated completely into the body politic in the foreseeable future, there should be definite assistance and action towards this end.'[84] Kelly's statement was not atypical. It was flavoured with the conformist optimism of the mid-twentieth century, the naive belief in developmental democracy and equal opportunity. But it was also tinged with historical shell shock – it was the response of a collaborator whose culture is under attack. According to Seal, a theorist and writer on the nature of British colonial oppression in India, collaborators are usually well-educated people from the oppressed group who outwardly reject the dominant order in favour of national aspirations, but who adopt the ways of the oppressor. They circulate among the elite class of the dominant order and are often admired by that order as reasonable representations of their people.[85]

The Experience of Integration at the Time of the Hearings

A more illuminating insight into Indian confusion and ambivalence was demonstrated, not before the committee, but in a television program aired during the hearings. In November 1960 the CBC television program *Close-Up* did a documentary investigation into the effects of Indian integration policy in Manitoba, both in the city (Winnipeg) and on a reserve (Peguis of the Sioux Nation). The program focused on racial discrimination and the effects of poverty on First Nations. The investigators tended to take a sympathetic view of integration and tried to show that its success depended on changed attitudes among non-Indians. They tried to show that Indians were just like non-Indians and only needed a fair chance.[86]

Not all Indians interviewed held this point of view. Walter Cochrane from the Peguis reserve worked in a Winnipeg furnace factory. He said that Indians 'should be given a chance the same as any body.'[87] The interviewer asked him if he would want to 'pass' – to represent himself as non-Indian:

COCHRANE: Most certainly not. I'm not ashamed that I'm an Indian – in fact, I'm proud to be an Indian. Lot of times I could have passed.
INTERVIEWER: So what is special about you being an Indian? You don't speak any special language, you don't dress any different from me ... You hold a job like another white man here in town. What's different about you, then?
COCHRANE: Well, I can say that I came from an Indian tribe that was here before the white man was here – that's quite a bit different. I'm from an Indian reserve – I make my home there.
INTERVIEWER: But you're going to stay in the city now, aren't you?
COCHRANE: Oh, no. I have good standing in the city, sure – but I'm going back to the reserve.

INTERVIEWER: Why?

COCHRANE: I like it better there. It's more freer ... I want to live here [Winnipeg] now because I have to. But the time will come when I won't have to and I'll have the choice: I can live here or the reserve. My choice will be the reserve.[88]

Marion Meadmore very poignantly expressed a deep attachment to her people and their traditions. It was in Meadmore that the camera and the interviewer uncovered a loneliness and pain deeper than perhaps even she had realized. Meadmore was a young Indian woman who had been a pre-med student at the University of Manitoba before she married her husband, a non-Indian. In the interview's opening sequence she described herself as a fully integrated Indian. Suddenly she remarked, 'Mind you, I'd like to reverse the situation and integrate into my own again ... I would like to feel at home again, on the reserve.'[89] The issue of her marriage to a white man was raised:

INTERVIEWER: But do some of your Indian friends and relatives object? Do they look down on you? Is this one reason you don't feel at home with them because they resent you having married a white man?

MEADMORE: This may be so. But I don't find this among my own relatives ... Perhaps I've noticed it more when I've been on other reserves and some of the people say, 'Oh! You're different, you've married a white man.' [She brushes away a tear and gives a quiet sigh].[90]

Later, the interviewer raised the topic of Indian betterment:

INTERVIEWER: Do you think that they [other urban Indians] are better off than they were on the reserve?

MEADMORE: Yes. Well, on the reserve they got the relief. In the city ... some ... get jobs some of the time. There is nevertheless the feeling that perhaps they're doing something for themselves for part of the time ... I think it's good that they have come into the city because it shows that they do want something better and they've tried to come to something better. Mind you, they haven't found it – but I think it's a good thing that they have come.

INTERVIEWER: I feel sympathy for the Indian ... and that his education and training on reserve have not fitted him to jump right into the hurly burly of life in Winnipeg. On the other hand, he's one of a very small minority coming in here and trying to make a go of it. Now, shouldn't he put up or shut up? This is our way. This is the way Winnipeg lives – shouldn't he adjust to that?

MEADMORE: Yes. [Pause] Well, uh, the Indian of course has to adjust and this is one of the problems of our people that they don't deal with. They don't owe anything to the world – it's just that the world owes everything to us – or the government because they've taken our country away. I think this is an old feeling that we have and I ...

INTERVIEWER: You don't have this feeling?

MEADMORE: Oh! Once in a while it comes back. Yes.[91]

Meadmore's comments tell us much about the effectiveness of government policy, Indians' historical resistance to it, and the interface between the Euro-Canadian and First Nations cultures at mid-century. She was confused about her place in the Indian world and ambivalent about the Western one: she was in psychological limbo. Still Meadmore clung stubbornly to her sense of identity, her Indian-ness. When she said it was good that Indians came to the city, she did not mean that they came to be a part of Canadian society, but that by coming they were demonstrating that they were not 'dirty and immoral' or 'useless, shiftless, no good.'[92] Her most powerful statement, however, came when the interviewer resorted to the image of the struggling minority, which arose from the experience of the immigrant and of mainstream pluralism. Meadmore seemed to reply instinctively from the pain of history and collective dispossession. Unmistakably she said, 'We are different.'

The First Nations' Response to the Committee's Report

The First Nations' initial response to the joint committee's report was hostile, so much so that the Indian Affairs Branch felt it necessary to solicit the opinion of Saskatchewan Indians for each of the report's recommendations. Other bands and organizations from other provinces wrote directly to Diefenbaker or to Senator James Gladstone, one of the committee's co-chairs and a Blood Indian from Alberta. In May 1962, Gladstone wrote to Diefenbaker to distance himself from the committee's recommendations. With some embarrassment, Gladstone admitted that the committee had done nothing more than endorse the master plan of Indian Affairs.

There is no doubt that the Indians ... are dissatisfied with the Report, and I do not blame them.

The main complaint is that the Final Report seems to be based upon the requests and suggestions of the Indian Affairs Branch, rather than Indians who gave evidence ... There is now a great fear that changes in the Indian Act might be made, based upon the Final Report ...

I can see that I could have served my people better if I could have been a member of the Joint Committee, rather than Co-Chairman ... I felt that I should send these observations to you, as the feelings of my people towards the Joint Committee report are quite pronounced.[93]

Also in 1962, the chief of the Gleichen Reserve in Alberta, C. McHugh, sent Diefenbaker a copy of the April minutes of his band council, in which the band firmly rejected all the committee's recommendations with respect to Health and Welfare.[94]

In October 1962, Hugh Dempsey of the Indian Association of Alberta wrote to R.A. Bell, the new Minister of Citizenship and Immigration, to explain the association's outright rejection of the joint committee's report, which had been conveyed to all senators, MPs and other Canadians in January of that year. In the letter, Dempsey attacked the recommendations concerning the individual ownership of reserve lands and noted that they would result in the destruction of the reserves and the band collective.[95] This letter made Gladstone's discomfort more understandable; at one time he had been the association's president.

The special report commissioned by the branch on the response of Saskatchewan Indians was released in December 1962. Known as *The Dreaver Report* after its author, Chief Joseph Dreaver, Sr, of the Mistawasis Band, Saskatchewan, it took a similar position to that of the Alberta association. After surveying sixty-seven bands in Saskatchewan, Dreaver wrote of the land management recommendations that 'their lands are band owned, therefore the management of their lands within their reservations is strictly their own affairs and should be administered with the guidance of their chief and councillors.'[96]

The sixty-seven bands represented Treaties 4, 6, and 10, comprising the Cree, Saulteaux, Assiniboine, and Chipewyan nations. In response to the report, L.L. Brown, head of the Agencies Division, wrote in defence of Euro-Canadian culture and Indian advancement: 'The opposition of Saskatchewan Indians to this recommendation of the Joint Committee was expected and is consistent with their long standing opposition to the idea of individual holdings. I can only comment that if they are ever to take their place in the Canadian society, Indian bands must recognize that a formal system of land holding is an essential part of our existence.'[97] In the context of the Cold War and the Cuban missile crisis, these words would have had considerable additional meaning. Earlier comments by Lloyd Landon, the director of the Indian-Métis Committee of the Winnipeg Welfare Council, perhaps placed this issue in its fullest ideological context. In *Close-Up*, he stated quite bluntly that Indians were not future oriented. They had no concern about deadlines, and to them time was more general. Saving was not important to them because they were used to living off natural resources. Habituation to routine work was not a part of Indian life, he said, nor did Indians have any ambition. It was just not important to them; they lived in a communistic society.[98]

The Consolidation of Welfare Administration, 1961–1963

Following the joint committee's final report, the adverse Indian reaction to it, and the Diefenbaker government's failure to promote good federal–provincial relations, the impetus to reform Indian welfare was significantly deflated. Recommendations for a Dominion–provincial conference on Indian Affairs received little or no consideration. The policy to extend services remained official, but its prominence waned as the division found itself consumed by the daily problems of administering a complex social assistance program.[99] Between 1959 and 1961 there had been serious efforts to refocus the activities of the Welfare Division; those efforts, for the time being, had stopped.

The focus on administrative themes actually began in May 1960, well before the conclusion of the joint parliamentary committee hearings. That year, largely influenced by the work of the project on public welfare statistics of the Canadian Welfare Council, the branch introduced a comprehensive means test application form, and Jones invited comment from the regions regarding its use. Then in March 1961 he wrote to all the regional supervisors about an especially positive report received from one superintendent. From the report, Jones had gleaned several themes.

First, he noted that the application form provided a clearer picture of Indian work habits, income, and attitudes. Second, its method of appraising need 'benefited those in real need and eliminated the professional "con" men.' Consequently it had 'proven to be the most equitable method of granting welfare assistance that we have yet found.' Third, because there were indications that Indian bands were resisting introduction of the form, Jones emphasized its 'careful interpretation ...

at Band meetings' and recommended a 'positive stand ... [because] the form is a "good break" for the Indian people.' Resistance to the form, Jones explained, had arisen because it was preventing band chiefs and councillors from dispensing patronage. In Jones's opinion, the form undermined what he thought was a prevalent belief among Indians – that social assistance was their right and compensatory due from the federal government. This belief had to be eradicated if the work ethic was ever to be properly understood. C.N.C. Roberts expressed the branch's position concerning Indian attitudes to assistance most clearly in 1963 correspondence to Walter Rudnicki, the new head of Welfare Division: 'Many Indians still consider that the government is obligated to provide the necessities of life and earnings are for items which are not provided through ... assistance. The fact that relief is ... for those who cannot maintain a decent standard of living by their own efforts is not fully accepted. There is a continuing need for interpretation of individual responsibility through interviews with relief applicants, band councils and other groups.'[100]

These themes recurred often over the next three years. They underscored the determination of the Indian Affairs Branch to promote Indian integration, despite Indian resistance to this form of political and cultural intrusion. Social assistance, in its increasingly bureaucratized form, sought to exert even firmer control over Indian behaviour. A case example from the Quebec region provided a good illustration of this management. A simple request for direction on the provision of relief fuel produced a lengthy, pedantic memorandum:

I think we were agreed upon the principle that aid ... is given only when need exists ...

Of ... significance is the ... practice adopted by many seasonal workers of spending their entire income during the period they are employed in the knowledge that they can turn to the Indian Affairs Branch for aid when they become unemployed.

A ... punitive administration of relief which would deny ... families assistance on the grounds that ... previous earnings should and could have been saved is unlikely ... to achieve any major change in attitude. The practice of saving and making ... provision for the future are characteristics of our culture ... One finds much the same indifference for the future amongst ... non-Indian society which is undereducated, and largely dependent upon poorly paid, seasonal labouring jobs.

We must ... tighten our practices and raise our expectations but not expect ... to apply immediately the regulations designed to meet such conditions in non-Indian communities. This process should be gradual and ample warning ... given.[101]

This pursuit of Indian acculturation to white society and focus on individual problem adjustment was typical of Ottawa's policy directives during this period. In case the Quebec supervisor had not grasped the branch's intention, Gordon concluded that 'the solution rests in such approaches as higher education, trades training and development of motivation by encouraging Indians to adopt a way of life which will react against the ... standard of living possible while "on relief." This problem will not be solved until the desire for an improved standard of living ... becomes important enough that people are willing to practice thrift ... and to accept all casual work available during "off seasons."'[102] Gordon was here revealing a somewhat duplicitous part of himself. His association with the Canadian Welfare Council had made him appear – to outside organizations at least – as if he favoured more generous and lenient relief policies. In practice this did not seem to be the case.

Shortly after this correspondence, an extensive report about the administration of welfare assistance was received from Saskatchewan region. This was the first substantial commentary from the field on welfare policy. Carl Latham, a degreed social worker, and his regional welfare superintendent had written the report for the acting regional supervisor of Saskatchewan, W.J. Brennan. Brennan forwarded the report to Ottawa for comment. Brennan's covering letter made the suggestion, based on Latham's remarks, that the branch was becoming too involved in direct welfare. This was contrary to its own policy, which was to devolve administration to provincial jurisdiction. The field offices, he noted, had no qualified social workers to administer welfare properly. Furthermore, the regional office was not adequately staffed to provide proper guidance, and complaints from Indians were many.[103]

Latham's analysis of social assistance in Saskatchewan mirrored, at a regional level, the array of administrative and jurisdictional issues confronting the branch nationally.[104] He first of all assessed the mishmash of relief and income support programs available to Indians in 1962. The branch, he noted, placed its policy emphasis on relief for employable recipients rather than on the disabled and the chronically unemployed. In doing so, he asserted, it was tacitly endorsing the principle of categorical assistance programs, by which those deemed less worthy received lesser benefits and were monitored more closely. He rejected this principle outright because it discriminated against individuals on the basis of age and/or employability. Instead, he argued, benefits should be based only on need:

> I cannot endorse the establishment of a categorical assistance programme. A comprehensive social assistance programme should be based on need rather than categories of persons in need. It would be possible to adhere to this principle and to introduce administrative procedures whereby persons perpetually in need of assistance can be isolated for administrative purposes. A common policy would obtain with respect to the determination of need and the issuance of assistance to long and short term recipients.[105]

A problem with this statement was that it failed to distinguish between those categorical programs already administered by the provinces and cost shared with the federal government (Old Age Assistance, Blind and Disabled Person's Allowances) and the basic social assistance administered by the branch to the employable unemployed and to families not receiving provincial Mothers' Allowances. Thus, it was unclear whether eligible Saskatchewan Indians were receiving any categorical assistance from the province. At any rate, Latham's solution to categorical assistance seemed, in the end, to be no solution at all. Even he could not resist placing recipients into short and long-term categories.

Latham also isolated the direct relationship between the availability of employment and the successful administration of social assistance programs. Social assistance for the employable only made sense, he implied, if one, employment was the normal channel for a person's welfare, and two, unemployment was unusual and temporary. Based on this position, he endorsed a proposal for a work program to 'relieve the need for direct relief assistance.' He cautioned against an 'Indian only' approach as paternalistic, and he recommended instead a work program integrated with those of other Saskatchewan communities.[106] He echoed the fear that Indians considered social assistance a right, and he urged agency staff to 'develop the concept that Indians are primarily responsible for meeting their own needs.'[107]

Latham next reported that few Indians were registered with the National Employment Service (NES). Pointing out that Indian Affairs was not an employment agency, he proposed that able-bodied Indians register with the NES as a condition of eligibility. This condition, he stated, should be made in conjunction with the NES, which could then make provisions for Indians' special employment needs. But Latham

opposed suggestions of 'work for welfare' and cited the liberal principles of freedom of choice: 'It is proposed that all able-bodied applicants
for relief assistance perform such jobs as necessary repair and painting
of their own buildings, tidying and cleaning their own yards, etc. *I object
strenuously to this proposal.* The requirements that relief recipients do
chores for themselves infringes on the rights of individuals to live in a
manner of their own choosing.'[108]

Latham's opinions on band responsibility for the administration of
social assistance and the future of provincial jurisdiction were interesting. On the one hand, he agreed with a branch proposal that bands be
encouraged to accept responsibility comparable to that of municipalities in the province in which they were situated. To that end, Ottawa
should establish a relationship between the branch and the bands similar to that which existed between the provincial and municipal governments in Saskatchewan.[109] On the other hand, he believed that the
branch social assistance program was rudimentary compared with those
in municipal and provincial jurisdictions: 'At this time, the Indian
Affairs Branch does not have a sufficiently clear statement of policies
and procedures for administering social assistance. Accordingly, it
would be difficult to transfer responsibility [to the bands].'[110] Consequently, before any paradigm of the municipal-provincial relationship
could be established, the social assistance program needed to be more
completely developed.

Latham viewed the paradigm as a transitional step, perhaps even an
unnecessary one. What would be the point, he mused, of developing
such a relationship between the branch and the bands if the real objective was to transfer jurisdiction to the provinces and not to the bands?
They 'should not be encouraged to accept responsibilities which they
have to relinquish in a year or two.'[111] Latham said. This transfer of
responsibility to the provinces was an objective he supported and that
he considered inevitable. In fact, he provided the branch with a suggested strategy for bringing about the transfer:

During the coming fiscal year the staff of the Indian Affairs Branch should
...
b) Structure the Indian Affairs Branch social assistance programme in such
a way as to facilitate its transfer to provincial auspices.
c) Continue negotiations with the provincial government for the extension
of welfare services to Indians living on reserves.
d) Develop appropriate means of keeping Indian Band Councils and mem-

bers informed of pertinent information with respect to the social assistance programme.[112]

Latham's recommendations, though sympathetic to Indian self-management, simply supported the principal objectives of branch policy. His document provided headquarters with field support and also with a rationale for continuing its initiatives. Of most importance was that he had identified a method for bringing about a transition to provincial services – that method being, develop national policy which for the time being would parallel the structure of provincial–municipal relations. This policy would maintain the principle of Indian integration while laying the groundwork for provincial take-over. Public works would foster employment skills and undermine the idea of social assistance as a right; at the same time, a requirement that employable Indians register with the NES would maintain a link – however tenuous – with the labour market.

Latham's report provided a critique of branch policy yet stayed on course. At headquarters, readers made frequent margin notes, check marks, and favourable comments. But not all field staff agreed that social assistance developed according to market society assumptions was an appropriate model for Indians. The superintendent of the Crooked Lake Indian Agency in Saskatchewan wrote in his quarterly report:

> Eighty percent of the twenty-five hundred Indians in this agency appear to be permanent relief recipients ... The over all picture of Welfare administration on the reserve is not good. Instructions and policies do not take into consideration the fact that Indian reserve economies are different and the organization of the reserve economy is different ... Welfare is an area of Administration, which ... needs to start over again.[113]

There were no positive comments or gold stars on his report.

Policy at an Impasse

By the middle of 1962 it was evident that the branch was more involved in welfare administration than it had ever intended. This was revealed in a survey of its regional welfare administrations conducted by Roberts in late 1961.[114] Typical of the responses was one made by F.B. McKinnon, the regional supervisor of the Maritime region:

> The fact we will spend close to fourteen million dollars next year to meet

the special welfare needs of less than 200,000 people ... is almost an indict-
ment against us as Canadians, for our treatment of our native people. I
don't think this should be so and ... we must strive to ... administer the ...
most constructive welfare program we can ... No matter what we come up
with, it will result in different treatment for Indians than for neighbouring
non-Indians. I wonder if we should not devote our energies to having the
provincial and municipal governments perform these services for us in
preference to our running a separate show for Indians. Everywhere there is
evidence that Canadians as a whole ... feel that Indians should become part
and parcel of the local picture.[115]

Two of the survey's conclusions were especially important. First, the
regions had clearly responded that the branch ought to purchase provincial or municipal services wherever possible. Second, in the current
pattern of administration the branch ought to adopt provincial scales of
assistance.[116] Despite the regions' support for pursuing the provincial
option, negotiations with the provinces had fallen flat. Only Ontario
had extended its services, and it had done so without any particular
encouragement from the branch. By 1963, the initiative was moribund
and the branch's social assistance program was on a treadmill. Worse,
the branch's work as a whole was at an impasse. The general welfare of
First Nations had reached its lowest point since the Depression.[117]

Three changes in 1963 gave new energy to the branch, especially to
Welfare Division. The first occurred in January when the national executive of the Imperial Order Daughters of the Empire urged the minister, Dick Bell, to commission an independent study to determine how
Indians could best achieve full parity with other Canadians. The branch
supported the idea, and the minister consequently authorized a three-
year, national survey of Indians under the direction of H.B. Hawthorn
from the University of British Columbia.[118] The activity surrounding the
study and the branch's involvement in gathering data energized Indian
Affairs.

The second change, in February, was more dramatic. The minority
Progressive Conservative government of John Diefenbaker fell and was
replaced by the Liberal government of Lester B. Pearson. The Conservative regime had been criticized for its indecisiveness,[119] a shortcoming
evident in its failure to address the provinces on the issue of Indian welfare services. Pearson's government proclaimed a new period of cooperative federal-provincial relations. The new Minister of Citizenship and
Immigration, Guy Favreau, lacked any special interest in or knowledge

of native matters, but quickly built a new senior administration in branch headquarters. In particular, it now had a new deputy minister, C.M. Isbister. Isbister was acquainted with community development ideas from his knowledge of similar programs in the United Nations, and during his stint as assistant deputy minister at the Department of Finance, he had built a reputation for being 'constructively-minded.' Isbister said of his appointment: 'I came into the department knowing little about Indians with the exception of the fact that one of my most illustrious, not quite ancestors but a sort of a cousin of grandparents was a very eminent Métis, was one of the founders of the University of Manitoba, A.K. Isbister.'[120] In keeping with the emphasis on cooperative federalism, a Federal–Provincial Relations Division was established within the branch to act as a funnel for policy initiatives involving the provinces. By the end of the year, two federal–provincial conferences – one in September, the other in November – had been convened. These conferences did not deal exclusively with Indian issues; nevertheless, those issues were on their agendas. By year's end, the climate for negotiating an extension of provincial services had improved markedly.

The third change in 1963 occurred within the branch: Colonel Jones retired. Gordon filled in for him as branch director until his own retirement in 1964. Jones's permanent successor was R.F. Battle, who had been regional supervisor in Alberta and, just before his appointment, head of the relatively new Economic Development Division in Ottawa. Walter Rudnicki, a professional social worker with an interest in community development, transferred over directly from the Arctic Division of Northern Administration to replace Gordon as the head of Welfare Division.[121] Finally, at about the same time, Jean H. Lagassé was appointed director of the Citizenship Branch. Lagassé had been a senior bureaucrat in the provincial government of Manitoba. There he had been highly respected as a progressive thinker on Indian issues and had instituted community-based projects on several Manitoba reserves.[122] His appointment signalled a closer relationship between Citizenship and Indian Affairs. Thus, by the summer of 1963 a dynamic leadership was in place, one that was determined to reform Indian Affairs and to initiate a new era for branch policy.

The Community Development Initiative[123]

Welfare Division was now led by Rudnicki, who was strongly supported by Battle and Isbister.[124] This division was going to be the spearhead of reform. Rudnicki quickly became the *enfant terrible* of Indian Affairs, so determined was he to ignite change in an organization that had been mired for so long in its own dismal operational culture. Rudnicki's memories of his first days in the branch and of the state of Indians in 1963 suggest why he wanted so badly to change things so quickly:

I came as head of what was then called the Welfare Division, which later became the Social Programs Division. Jones was still the head of the Indian Affairs Branch. I guess the rationale for having it in Citizenship and Immigration was that in effect Indians were aliens. So the big thrust in terms of program direction in the Branch was to make Indians fit for citizenship, enfranchisement being the exit from the Indian Act. Integration became a euphemism for assimilation or leadership training. Jones was great on leadership training. He kept pushing, 'We gotta have more leadership training!' So I walked into the situation, looked around and was appalled, really.

I guess the first image I had was sitting in Battle's office. He had an intercom system which when it buzzed sounded like a bloody fire alarm! You couldn't talk above the noise. I remember this thing going off. I didn't know what the hell it was! An ear-shattering sound. And Battle leaped to his feet, snapped to attention and marched out! He came back in a few minutes and I said, 'What was that?' He said, 'Oh! I was being summoned by Colonel Jones.' It was just a military environment. People were just scared to death of Jones. Indians used to come to the Department totally – well, you had to see it – submissive people, their hats in hand, heads bowed low and they'd be very deferential, very timid. They looked like terrorized people. So Jones retired. He got his stereo equipment and everything else as his parting gift from his admiring staff.

Well, then they got Claude Isbister in there as deputy minister and Guy Favreau came in as the minister and it was a new look. These guys came in with clearly the intent of bringing this branch up to scratch. So my timing, my arrival was just right. I was the only guy there who had a broader orientation to – well, as slender as that might have been 'cause back in the sixties I had very little knowledge about the history of Indians. So I just set about dealing with the basic issues. I wanted people there who weren't people who could be called the old guard in Indian Affairs. On my recommendation they sent over Vic Valentine from Northern Affairs and he took over ... I think it was called the Industrial Division. Davey stayed on in Education. D'Astous was head of administration.

So anyway, one of my first assignments was – well, Isbister who had some exposure to international concepts of community development, or had heard about them and read about them, asked John Gordon who was head of.the division – well, a directive came down – I suspect from Isbister who said 'Look, we want community development here.' And Gordon sent the word down to me as the guy who knew something about community development because he didn't have the faintest idea what it was, what the [deputy] minister was talking about! So I got the authority to prepare a submission to Cabinet on community development, which I did.[125]

Isbister also recalled that Indians in the mid-1960s were very different in their comportment from the politically active and astute leaders with whom Canadians would become familiar in the late twentieth century. As Isbister remembered, one of the primary objectives of the community development initiative was leadership training! Yet his description of it was quite different from Jones's ideas:

Well, we didn't have Indians talking about discontent. We had them in a very bad state. Well, anyway, one of the things we wanted to do was to develop Indian leadership. Well, *now* we've got Indian leadership! What sort of things could we do? One thing we could do was to have meetings ... to spot bright, young Indian youths on the reserves and bring them together from different reserves to get some intermingling of people and ideas among Indian people. You know, that kind of thing didn't exist and we were trying to bring it into existence.[126]

Isbister seemed unaware that in the interwar years and during the Second World War, Indians such as Loft, Paull, Sioui, and Tootoosis had provided dynamic and politically active leadership for their people. These men and other men and women like them were certainly remembered and emulated in First Nations communities. Under Jones, the branch had succeeded in stifling or ignoring them and damping the political fires that were burning among First Nations. The department's focus on community development would prove to be key to the evolution of branch policy and its approach to Indian peoples. It would also, eventually, have the unintended effect of allowing those fires to flame up.

The idea of community development was not, as Rudnicki suggested, entirely unknown to the branch, although its 'new' meaning certainly was. Since 1954, the branch had been referring to Indian leadership training and the creation of Indian Homemakers' Clubs as methods of community organization. This promotion of Indian leadership was equivalent to Lord Baden Powell's preparation of worthy young men and women to be responsible citizens who would lead others to be the same.[127]

In its annual report for 1960, the branch described community organization as band governments taking more responsibility for 'planning and development of measures to improve social and economic conditions on reserves.'[128] This phrase, however, had only one meaning, best revealed in the 1962 Indian Affairs pamphlet, *The Indian>In<Transition*, a propaganda piece aimed at explaining Indians to Euro-Canadians and at manipulating their opinion in favour of government policy:

> First there is the Indian's attitude towards his reserve. This is his 'home' – as the small town is to ... rural Canadians. Yet, the reserve is something more. It is also a 'retreat.' Many Indians still consider the European took away the land and in return gave them a poor bargain – a reserve, free education, a small annuity, sometimes weapons for hunting. Many Indians find it hard to understand the past as an historical fact ... This is one reason for the great reverence paid by the Indian to the treaties. In a world of flux, a treaty is a promise to cling to.
>
> ...
>
> The Indian's traditional attitude towards making a living is often different from the non-Indian. In the past – and still prevalent to some extent – is the idea of living only for today. The meat prepared for today is eaten today and shared with others; tomorrow someone else will have food to share. The non-Indian ideas of putting money in the bank for a rainy day, of saving today in order to buy desirable goods for tomorrow, seem confusing and somehow unacceptable.
>
> The Indian has also found it difficult to recover from the social disorganization of the tribal groups caused by the advent of European settlers. Thus many have acquired ... inhibitions vis-a-vis the non-Indian. They are hesitant about accepting the values and standards of a fast-paced, non-Indian civilization.[129]

Through contrasts – even the use of arrows in the title graphics was deliberate – and allusions to the superiority, excitement, and materialism of Euro-Canadian society, Indians were depicted as quaint and pitiable, even though Canadians were expected to treat them as equals. The idea of dispossession was dismissed; by implication, compensation was generous and grievances amounted to denials of historical fact. The failure to adapt could be understood in the familiar language of Freudian psychology: the Indian was an inhibited individual. Indeed, the use of the term 'the Indian' was a powerful tool, for it could simultaneously suggest collective (unacceptable) and individual (acceptable) images. Indians' stubborn reluctance to let go of the past could be overcome with help and encouragement. But how could the Indian best be helped?

The answer lay in identifying the problems faced by Indians in cities and on the reserves. Thus, loneliness in the city was a problem to be solved by Indian youth clubs and friendship centres. A 1962 study about friendship centres by Alex Sim of the Citizenship Branch suggested a bizarre plan to engineer Indians into the cities using methods akin to Britain's eighteenth- and nineteenth-century strategies for reducing surplus, working-class populations. The urbanization of Indians was to be part of a broader federal strategy to drain the population from northern reserves in order to reduce welfare costs; however, a manageable labour force would be left in place for northern development. Jones had thought this an excellent idea. In commenting on Sim's study to Jean Boucher, director of the Citizenship Branch, he emphasized that the branch's intention was to accelerate the movement of Indians to non-Indian communities.[130] Another problem was the Indian's lack of understanding of work and need to learn about 'promptness and regular attendance, employer-employee interviews, trade unions, salary deductions, income tax, unemployment insurance, pension schemes, workman's compensation, credit resources.'[131] A third problem of adaptation for the Indian was 'within himself, to learn to adjust to a new society.' In the cities this could be facilitated through professional counselling. On the reserves, however, it was branch policy to negotiate with provincial, municipal, and private agencies 'for the extension of the same services to meet similar needs of Indian peoples,' including rehabilitation services.[132] Where provincial programs were not available – which was nearly everywhere – services were provided through the local Indian agency in a manner 'comparable to that provided in neighbouring non-Indians [sic] communities.'

To facilitate Indian adaptation to Canadian social structures and institutions, the Indian Affairs Branch set as its long-range objective 'the development of Indian communities with adequate standards of housing, hygiene and essential services which will provide a base for the economic, educational, health and welfare aspects of a broad rehabilitation programme aimed at the eventual integration of Indians into the provincial and municipal organization of Canadian society.'[133] The amelioration of community standards was to be achieved through two methods. The first was the development of physical infrastructure, especially housing. The second was leadership training so that band councils would eventually behave like any Canadian municipal government.[134] In a parallel development, Indian Homemakers' Clubs were intended to train women in Euro-Canadian domestic life and community service. The pamphlet described these clubs as 'similar to Women's Institutes' and as places where women could gather 'to exchange ideas and talk over schemes for community betterment.'[135] These clubs reflected Euro-Canadian standards of charity and benevolence. The more privileged women of the community helped poorer Indian mothers by giving Christmas parties and summer picnics, providing scholarships for deserving students, and teaching crafts. Club members also listened to talks on homemaking, health, and education, and raised funds through socials and card parties.[136]

During the 1950s, 'helping others help themselves' became the branch's stock phrase to describe community development. As a notion, this was safe and controllable, and it had just the right appeal to bourgeois sensibilities in government and voluntary organizations. At a conference early in 1959, D.A. Green, a social worker for Indian Affairs in Regina presented a paper, 'On Human Relationships.' The paper dealt with issues of racism, paternalism, and the problems of 'developing' peoples. Green wrote: 'The main theme of this paper is the necessity of working with the Indian people and not for them, in order to help them to help themselves.'[137] Green equated development with advancement. Clearly, 'help' had a subtext, just as it was taken for granted who would be doing the helping.

Jones was so impressed by Green's paper that he made it recommended reading for all Indian Affairs staff and invited their comments from the field.[138] In July 1959 he wrote directly to Green to ask him for more information on community development practices that he thought 'could be used to advantage by the Branch' and to advise him that community development was being studied at headquarters as a method for 'accelerating the advancement of Indians.'[139] This was not an unusual approach by Jones. He often solicited mounds of information on various themes; but then, having received that information, he seemed unable or unwilling to apply it in forming progressive policy.

The Relationship with the National Commission on the Indian Canadian

An example of the branch's early flirtation with forms of community development is embodied in its relationship with the National Commission on the Indian Canadian. This commission was formed in January 1957 as a standing committee of the Canadian Association for Adult Education. Initially, its primary purpose was 'to study the problems of the Indian in the community off the reserve, thereby stimulating organizations to make surveys, conduct research, appoint specialists and provide services as needs arise.'[140] Essentially, the commission was a liberal, non-Indian friendship organization that promoted understanding of Indian peoples in Canada through community education.[141] It backed the policy of integration, and like the Canadian Welfare Council, it involved the Indian Affairs Branch in its committees. Stan Bailey from Welfare Division sat on the commission's first executive committee; then over the years both the Citizenship and Indian Affairs branches became members, as did the Arctic Division of the Department of Northern Affairs and National Resources.[142]

For some time, the Indian Affairs Branch maintained a close relationship with the commission and its independent successor, the Indian-Eskimo Association of Canada. This was possible because the commission did not interfere with the branch's work; rather, it complemented it. The commission's initial focus on the welfare of off-reserve Indians abetted Indian policy and provided positive publicity for the branch's objectives. For example, in October 1957 the CBC radio program *Trans-Canada Matinee* ran a two-week, daily special about Indians migrating to the cities. These programs featured Indians talking about themselves – about their hopes, achievements, and disappointments. The commission promoted the program and was consulted during its preparation.[143]

By April 1958 the commission was still without an executive director, a gap that hampered its work. Because it was committed to adult education and to helping Indians adapt to urban life, it was interested in finding someone with a background in community and adult group work. John Melling was such a person, and was courted. At the National Conference on Adult Education in Winnipeg in May 1958, he was presented to the commission's executive committee. Melling, a Quaker and a pacifist, had studied philosophy and politics at the University of Manchester and at Oxford. During the Second World War he had done relief work; from 1945 to 1947 he had worked as a community organizer and adult educator in Cornwall, England. Since then he had been at the University of Leeds in the Department of Adult Education and Extra-Mural Studies. At the time of the Winnipeg conference he was that department's deputy director. Melling became executive director of the commission in August 1958.[144]

Melling's appointment reflected the commission's intention to incorporate community education methods into its activities. Its initial goal was to wake up what it perceived to be an apathetic Euro-Canadian community, to educate it about the 'Indian problem' and to involve it in the solution. In January 1959, in the concluding statement to the commission's brief to the Human Rights Anniversary Committee for Canada, Melling wrote:

> The task of winning acceptance of Indians by Whites and for encouraging and securing their full participation as equal and responsible members of the Canadian community is not primarily a job for Government. It is a job for voluntary organizations, national, provincial, and local, including women's organizations, local agencies, employers' and trade union groups, and especially the Churches, which in Canada are actually and potentially very influential. The job is educational ... Government assistance at the Provincial and lower levels, indeed at every level, is needed, not least in helping supply the substantial funds necessary to an extensive programme of informing and transforming public opinion of Canada in this regard. NCIC and its many associated bodies are fully committed to this educational enterprize, and will see it through.[145]

On 21 December 1959, the commission formally broke from the Canadian Association for Adult Education and became the Indian-Eskimo Association of Canada (IEA).[146] From its beginnings as the commission to its new identity as the IEA, its relationship with the Indian Affairs Branch had been cordial and cooperative. The branch found nothing offensive in the work of the IEA, and it was content to let the IEA proceed so long as it felt supported by it, and so long as the association's efforts at community education never amounted to more than endless meetings, conferences, seminars, and pronouncements of good intentions.

This fully cooperative relationship lasted until late 1961. Melling's efforts to achieve a rapprochement of the Indian and non-Indian communities eventually brought him into contact with the reserves and Canada's northern communities. What he saw he did not like. In a speech to the Women's Canadian Historical Society, Melling was highly critical of government policy. Unfortunately for him, the *Globe and Mail* was present. His speech was quoted in part:

> Although those in Ottawa express belief in equality for ... native ... peoples by the time their policies reach new municipalities in the north they

appear as zoning regulations to keep Indian and Eskimo Canadians separate from white people; they find themselves underwriting policies of business firms in the north which forbid fraternizing; and, although Ottawa
officials believe housing for both Indian and Eskimo people is ... inadequate, the Government's own policies reflect established patterns based on
inequality.

...

Cultural contact with white people has meant, for Indians, that they have
become a completely subjugated people, firmly controlled politically, and
dependency and apathy have resulted ...

But there is a *new* feeling of nationalism amongst Indian Canadians and
new leaders are emerging among them. However troublesome this may be
for politicians, it is a necessary development ...

There is extreme bitterness behind every smiling Indian face and it is
justified.[147]

This report did not sit well with Ottawa. R. Gordon Robertson, the
deputy minister of the Department of Northern Affairs and National
Resources, wrote a four-page letter to Melling castigating him for his
remarks and practically accusing him of treachery. Robertson copied his
letter to Jones and to Clare Clark, president of the IEA.

Melling immediately wrote a letter of apology to Jones and compli-
mented him for his continually supportive and helpful attitude.[148] On
the same day, he wrote a long, rambling letter of explanation and apology to Robertson. His final words, however, made it clear that a collision
of philosophy, means, and objectives was inevitable:

Government and IEA are engaged in most difficult work. Their ways of
approach, though they should be complementary, cannot, in a number of
respects, be quite the same ... For the pain caused your Minister, yourself
and your senior colleagues, and for ... any damage done to your Department's work, I sincerely apologize. Can we blot out the infamy of this incident right away and get back to our very satisfactory cooperation?[149]

It was not to be. The pathos of Melling's plea fell on deaf ears. He
most probably felt like the Indians he so eloquently spoke for: humili-
ated for his ingratitude and for his audacity in speaking out of turn. As
for Jones, he never replied to Melling's letter, and the file correspondence stopped shortly thereafter.[150] Although the incident did not irre-
vocably damage the relationship between the branch and the IEA, it

likely confirmed in Jones's mind his sense that community development was potentially subversive and dangerous.

The 1964 Community Development Submission to Cabinet

Indian development and training were essentially dormant when Rudnicki and the new administration took over in 1963. Social and economic conditions in Indian communities were still a national disgrace. Welfare dependency was extremely high – a particular concern to the new government. The national rate of social assistance dependency in 1963 was 3.5 per cent; the Indian rate was over ten times that, at 36 per cent. As well, per capita welfare expenditures were widely disparate: ten dollars per non-Indian compared with seventy dollars per Indian.[151] In fact, in one fiscal year, from 1961–2 to 1962–3, total welfare expenditures had risen 5 per cent, even though the rates of assistance had not changed since April 1959.[152] These increases could be explained partly by additional costs related to child welfare and adult care, but for the most part they were directly attributable to reliance on social assistance. In addition, the average age at death for Indians was still nearly half that for non-Indians: 34 years compared with 62.3 years. These figures, the Hawthorn researchers had discovered, continued to be attributable to diseases, nearly all of which were preventable. Public health, housing, and sanitation were deplorable.[153]

When Rudnicki received his instructions from Isbister and Gordon to prepare a community development submission for Cabinet, he knew that any proposal he made would have to appeal to the fiscal objectives of reducing welfare dependency and promoting self-sufficiency. At the same time, it would have to entice the public by dwelling on the principles of Indian equality and citizenship. 'I had been long enough in government,' he recalled. 'I had enough battle experience from the Northern Affairs side trying to get things through Cabinet that I knew that if you didn't demonstrate – well, in other words I played the game. If I just came forth with a community development program I didn't think it would get very far.' He continued:

> If I linked it to the kinds of things I knew some of the ministers were concerned about like self-sufficiency and getting rid of the dependency problems they perceived, reducing welfare costs, and all that stuff ...
>
> Frankly, I didn't think it through in terms of today's concepts; it was the sixties concepts and the politics of the day. Something Sally Weaver never

quite understood, I don't think. But once you're in the big battle systems, sometimes you're up here going this way when you're actually trying to go this way. [He points in different directions] To get things through! To get things through! To get the mandate then to go *this* way![154]

The 'sixties concepts' of community development were largely influenced by two models. The first, the British model, was based on theories of adult education. It had been developed to assist former colonies in their social and economic development. It had also been applied in areas such as London's East End, notably Toynbee Hall. According to file evidence, this model heavily influenced Rudnicki. The model centred on the idea of developing and supporting indigenous leaders, who would organize the community around key issues, identify strategies for resolving those issues, and take constructive action based on those strategies. The second model was American and was less well developed. It focused on the idea of concerted community action in response to poverty, juvenile crime, and inequality in America's inner cities. By 1965 the community action model had become the central strategy of the American War on Poverty. When Rudnicki's submission to Cabinet appeared in final form in February 1964, its wording with respect to the meaning of community development was vague. The document mainly emphasized what would happen to Indians and to government expenditures as a result of community development.

In essence, community development was to be a cost-sharing initiative. Ottawa was going to encourage the provinces to accept more responsibility for Indian communities, especially in the broad areas of health and welfare. The submission began by stating the obvious facts to Cabinet. Indians were a rapidly increasing population; at the same time, they were a 'high-cost' and 'multi-problem' segment of the society. Urgent measures were required to bring them into the twentieth century. 'Experience in the under-developed areas of the world and current trends in Canadian public opinion,' the document asserted, 'support a community development approach as one effective way of achieving this aim.'[155]

In the proposal, the branch made it clear that a community development program would maximize the use of available material and human resources in Indian communities and in each province. The effect of this, the document continued, 'would be to step-up mobilization of Indian initiative and to further promote self-sufficiency. One of its end results would be to accelerate transfer to Indian communities of responsibility and authority for the management of their affairs.'[156] Thus, the program would provide a framework for coordinating existing health, education, welfare, and economic development services on the reserves and ultimately 'reduce costs in such palliative areas as welfare assistance payments.'[157] Just how or why this would occur was never explained to Cabinet. It seems that the argument rested on the idea that increased autonomy over their own affairs coupled with integral links to provincial infrastructures would lead First Nations to greater self-sufficiency and reduced welfare dependency.

Rudnicki opined in his interview that the principle being followed was really the beginning of devolution of authority to the band level. The problem was that no one at the time understood that devolution was

> a two-edged sword ... Devolution could be returning to people their sover-
> eignty if you like, as nations and so on. Or devolution could be working
> towards final termination. I didn't perceive it in those terms back in the six-
> ties, but that's what it turned out to be – devolution as a termination issue.
> Working towards what the government now calls self-government, which is
> actually like Sechelt – a termination, coming [ending up] under provincial
> jurisdiction.

When it was suggested to him that this was like a macro form of integration, he replied, 'Yeah, exactly.'[158]

The February 1964 submission continued with the statement that the effectiveness of the community development program could be best measured by the eventual reduction of per capita Indian welfare costs to the same levels as among non-Indians. The claim was that this had already occurred in selected pilot projects.[159] The proposal would have appealed to the Cabinet for its two promised outcomes: a projected long-term saving in welfare expenditure, and the integration of Indian and provincial welfare services. These surely would lead to the actual integration of Indians at the provincial and municipal levels of civil society. This latter point was crucial, because the research activities of the Hawthorn report – already underway at the time – also clearly pointed to this kind of desirable outcome.[160]

The involvement of the Department of Health and Welfare at this stage was also necessary. First, it was clear that Ottawa was gearing up to rationalize and broaden the sharing of welfare costs with the provinces. 'Experts' at the Department of National Health and Welfare were already working on formulas for Indian welfare cost sharing with the provinces; these would later be incorporated into Part II of the 1966 Canada Assistance Plan.[161] Judging from the Indian Affairs submission to Cabinet, however, it was apparently thought that with a formula in hand, cost sharing could perhaps start to happen as soon as possible following a scheduled federal–provincial conference in May 1964. Once this happened, the Welfare Division could wind down its direct involvement in social assistance – an involvement that was undesirable – and become the Social Programs Division, devoted primarily to community development.[162]

As early as January 1964, Rudnicki had been busy putting the proposed program's infrastructure in place. This included acquiring information from Dr T.R. Batten at the University of London,[163] and planning the number of projects and staffing required once approval had been obtained. A community development committee was established within the branch to oversee the program's planning and implementation. Richard Gilbert, a producer with the National Film Board of Canada, was contacted and asked to prepare a film about community development in Indian communities.[164] Although a full script was written, the film never went into production. On 28 May 1964, Cabinet approved the program, and the branch immediately began planning to launch it in the new year.[165] Preparations included hiring and training twenty-five community development officers and seven supervisors for the regions, as well as establishing criteria for selecting communities where the program would most likely be effective.[166] All that was needed now was Treasury Board's approval for the branch to make grants to provinces and to individual bands.[167] This came on 15 January 1965. The community development program was underway.[168]

The training of the new community development officers, their assistants (nearly all of whom were Indian), and Indian Affairs officials from the field began almost immediately. Initially, two-week training sessions were planned; these were to be provided in a vacated Catholic seminary in Ottawa and at other locations under the direction of Dr Farrell Toombs, a Rogerian psychologist from the University of Toronto. However, the intensity of the sessions, and the volatile mix of Indian leaders, youthful radicals, and Indian Affairs staff, soon meant that they were extended to three months. Rudnicki recalled that some of the new officers were Indians. One was George Manuel, who later led the National Indian Brotherhood, which much later – after his time – became the Assembly of First Nations. Manuel led much of the effective resistance to the 1969 White Paper on Indian Policy.[169]

Parallel Worlds: The Approval of Provincial Rates, 1964

In late 1963, as part of the community development initiative, Rudnicki asked Roberts to prepare a report projecting the potential added cost to the branch of providing social assistance at prevailing provincial rates and standards. This request was necessary so that the branch could begin to develop, in accordance with the submission to Cabinet, a standard measurement for the effectiveness of the community development program in each province. Roberts wrote to Rudnicki that an additional $3 million would be required if the branch continued to administer assistance directly. Roberts did not think Treasury Board would agree to such an expensive proposal.[170] Rudnicki replied that if, as anticipated, a federal–provincial cost-sharing agreement could be worked out under the normal terms for welfare services, the actual cost to the branch would be $1.5 million. (At this time, 'normal' meant the 50 per cent share by the federal government under the Unemployment Assistance Act.) Nevertheless, Rudnicki instructed Roberts to prepare a Treasury Board submission for the full amount. To soften the impact and to entice the board to accept, he suggested that Roberts mention the three provinces that had expressed some interest in cost sharing.[171]

Why did the branch want to change the basis of social assistance rates at this time? First, the community development proposal hinged on demonstrating a direct relationship between enhanced community autonomy and a reduction in per capita assistance. As part of the proposal, the provinces were to be encouraged to extend their welfare services on to the reserves to promote equality of citizenship and to 'normalize' Indians. The measure of effectiveness then was to be based on the implementation of provincial rates as demonstrating greater equality of treatment. Second, social assistance expenditures were rising, and in anticipation of the federal–provincial conference on the extension of services, it was strategic to have an authority in place that would, in effect, permit the branch to enter into a cost-sharing agreement with the provinces. To have an authority in place in advance of the conference would prepare Indians for the eventuality of provincial services by introducing provincial standards into branch administration. This was in keeping with branch thinking since the late 1950s. Nevertheless, these reasons alone did not explain the requirement for an immediate submission to Treasury Board.

Roberts prepared the draft submission to the board requesting authority to adopt provincial or local municipal welfare rates and regulations for Indians.[172] In his rationale, a third reason for the submission became evident – the rates of Indian assistance had not changed since 1959. Sometime in late 1962 or early 1963, the branch had distributed to all bands, through its field agencies, copies of the Canada Food Guide, *Good Food–Good Health*. Later in 1963, the branch conducted a survey, based on the guide, of food costs at the band level. The results were harrowing. Roberts wrote: 'It is evident from the survey that the ... scale of assistance is inadequate in over 150 Indian communities ... and must be revised.'[173] There was more. Roberts continued: 'The infant mortality rate amongst Indians is nearly four times the national rate. The preschool mortality rate amongst Indian children is more than eight times the national rate ... Indian mortality rates trended upwards during 1962 ... The Tuberculosis death rate amongst Indians in 1960, the latest year ... statistics are available, was 23.8 per 100,000 persons as compared with 4.6 ... nationally.'[174] Roberts balanced this moral appeal to the board with an assurance that the branch was pursuing cost sharing with the provinces and that the request to apply provincial rates directly was to be seen only as an interim measure.

Rudnicki commented on the draft on 31 December 1963. He advised Roberts that he and acting director Gordon had discussed the matter and had decided to delay the request. The reason he gave was that 'we have a number of things going that could affect this whole matter ... – particularly the Fed-Prov. Conference and the FORMULA [for cost-sharing]. If our C.D. proposal is accepted and the formula approved as a basis for negotiating we might tackle B.C. first.'[175] Rudnicki was referring to the conference planned for May 1964 and finally held in October 1964. The Rudnicki-Gordon decision suggested two things. One, it was probably not wise to alarm Treasury Board with these statistics and their linkages to branch administration. In the end, any political embarrassment to Treasury Board – an arm of Cabinet – could backfire on the branch. Two, the administration was gambling on a quick resolution to the community development proposals and on the instant cooperation of the provinces.

It was a politically reasonable gamble, if not a morally correct one. After all, a negotiated agreement with the provinces to extend their services would result in a treatment of Indians no better or worse than that of other Canadians. For the federal government, this was the preferred alternative. If negotiations failed, the branch could then seek Treasury Board's authority to allow it to adopt provincial and municipal rates. In the end, Indians would receive comparable benefits but at a greater cost to the branch. Either way, the principle of integration in the form of 'like treatment' would remain intact, although obviously not as effective.

Events now occurred rapidly. On 27 January 1964, E.R. Rickinson, deputy minister of Social Welfare in British Columbia, wrote to Isbister. Rickinson informed him that British Columbia provided social assistance to Indians living off reserve in the same manner as it did to non-Indians. Rickinson complained that this had created a situation where Indians left the reserve deliberately in order to qualify for his department's higher benefits. 'The purpose in writing to you,' he concluded, 'is to ask that in the interest of the Indians on reserves who are in need, that your department should take under consideration a revision of your schedule of allowances.'[176]

Rickinson's letter required a careful reply; the department did not want to reveal its hand or appear to accept any jurisdictional responsibility until the federal-provincial conference. Moreover, British Columbia was a candidate for cost sharing. If the branch raised its rates, as Rickinson suggested there would be no pressure on British Columbia to extend its services. Rudnicki and his new director, R.F. Battle, were well aware of this when they crafted their benign and seemingly neutral response for Isbister's signature.[177] Rickinson was invited to be part of a cooperative solution: 'This has been a matter of grave concern to us also. I am hopeful that the present structure of federal-provincial discussions will solve this and other comparable problems by an extension of provincial services to Indians. In line with discussions which we had this month, it is hoped that we will be able to offer some definite proposals ... soon and review some of the problems in detail.'[178]

The branch knew it was vulnerable. Over the years it had been unable to prevent the perception that it was responsible for providing welfare to Indians. The branch would be in a weak position if, in negotiations with the provinces, it appeared to be looking for a way to 'unload' a program it did not adequately fund. The objective of assuring Indians' equal right to services available to all Canadian citizens would be severely undermined if the branch itself was shown to be negligent. An unsigned memo on the file noted cryptically: 'We are going to have to face up to our responsibility here ... It will cost 3 million. Could begin Apr 1/64 (?)'[179]

The turning point came on 21 February 1964. A memorandum from the deputy minister's office relayed a question asked of the minister in the House of Commons: 'There appeared in the Calgary "Albertan" recently a statement made by a Blackfoot Chief of the Gleichen Reserve to the effect that the children are facing starvation, are badly clothed, and cannot attend school. Will the Minister check into that statement.'[180] This question touched a nerve in the branch and caused a review of the Rudnicki–Gordon decision made in December. On 26 February, the minister gave his answer to the House: 'The statement of the Blackfoot Chief ... has been ... investigated and I am assured that there is no starvation on this reserve ... The Indian children are adequately dressed and nourished.'[181] This partial truth obscured the whole picture. No mention was made of at least 150 other Indian bands where this question would have required an entirely different answer.

The branch had to take immediate initiatives to maintain its credibility on Indian integration. It had to be seen to be implementing policies that reflected this purpose. Consequently, on 28 February 1964 Rudnicki asked Battle to ask the deputy minister for permission to canvass all the regions for information on provincial rates, standards, and procedures.[182] Battle complied, and sent a memorandum adapted from Roberts's draft Treasury Board submission:

A survey of costs in relation to foods recommended by the Department of National Health and Welfare was conducted during the summer of 1963 ... It is evident from the survey that the Indian Affairs Branch scale of assistance is inadequate in over 150 Indian communities throughout Canada.

As you are aware, it is our hope that cost sharing agreements regarding provision of welfare services may be entered into with at least some of the provinces soon. It is unlikely, however, that agreement will be reached with all of the provinces at an early date ... It is necessary, therefore, that consideration be given to amending the Indian Affairs Branch scale of assistance ...

As an interim measure and as a means of rectifying the present inadequacy of the Indian Affairs Branch scale of assistance, adoption of provincial or local municipal rates is recommended.[183]

The memorandum outlined the entire situation and included the data on Indian mortality. There is, however, no evidence that Isbister responded or that the regions were canvassed. Isbister likely had decided to await Cabinet's decision on the branch submission. Presumably, he thought that the case for Treasury Board would be stronger if Cabinet approved the more comprehensive plan.

In the meantime, certain administrative procedures required change. The responsibility of solvent bands to pay up to 100 per cent of social assistance from their own trust funds was not in keeping with the principle of comparable treatment. Battle wrote to Isbister that 'bands with funds have been paying from a small percentage to the total cost. Indian bands who pay the total cost of welfare assistance from band funds are therefore the only segment of the Canadian population for whom a share of the cost is not paid from federal funds.'[184] For provincial services to be extended, or for the branch to adopt provincial rates and standards, the share of social assistance from the bands would have to be changed to no more than 50 per cent. This would require Treasury Board approval, which was requested in May 1964.[185]

Shortly after, on 1 June, Cabinet approved the branch's community development submission. It was now necessary, in order to implement the community development program, to secure Treasury Board approval to adopt provincial rates and standards for social assistance. In an April memorandum, Battle had alerted Isbister to this requirement: 'The next step would be to bring Indian Affairs Branch scales of assistance in line with provincial scales as an interim measure before master agreements are signed with the provinces. The ... submission ... now before Cabinet makes provision for this, and if approved will allow us to proceed with our program.'[186] Thus, on 16 June 1964 a Treasury Board submission was made requesting 'authority for adoption of provincial or local municipal welfare rates and regulations for Indians.'[187] Treasury Board approved the first request to limit band welfare expenditures in early July, and Battle so informed the regional and field agency offices. At the same time, he wrote: 'If, at some future date, provinces are able to participate in the provision of welfare services to Indians, the cost of assistance to bands could be reduced further.'[188]

It now remained for Treasury Board to approve the adoption of provincial rates and standards. This came on 20 July 1964 when, in a handwritten memo, Roberts advised Rudnicki: 'Walter: Bud Long [from Treasury Board] advised me this morning that our submission re: adoption of provincial rates was approved on July 16th (TB627879)'[189] (see Document 9.3).

The 'crisis of the rates' was used to advantage by the branch and strengthened its conviction that the future of Indians lay in their equal treatment as full participants in Canadian society. Indians themselves were still a part of the problem, and the inadequacy of social assistance did not preclude the danger of their dependency on it. The last words

Document 9.3 Representation of Treasury Board Minute No. 627879,
23 July 1964.

Mr. C. M. Isbister,
Deputy Minister of
Citizenship and Immigration,
Ottawa, Canada.

Dear Mr. Isbister:

At its meeting of July 16, 1964, the Treasury Board approved your Department's proposal to adopt provincial or local municipal standards and procedures for the administration of relief assistance for Indians, as being in line with the recent Cabinet decision on the extension of provincial services to Indians.

The Board understood that your Department will delay the implementation of these new standards and procedures until some time in the autumn, so that no further supplementary estimates will be necessary for this purpose during 1964-65.

Yours truly,

C. J. Mackenzie
Assistant Secretary.

Source: Canada, Indian and Northern Affairs Canada, Social Development Program, *Policy and Procedures Manual*, BC Region, Vancouver, 1992.

are left to C.N.C. Roberts. At the height of the activity surrounding Treasury Board and the new rates, his concern was that the attitude toward social assistance would have to improve if the new program were approved. In his comments to a colleague at headquarters relating to notes he had received from a conference of welfare superintendents held in British Columbia, he wrote: 'Notwithstanding the criticism received ... regarding the documentation required I think we must insist upon a review of employable applicants' circumstances at least once each month. If their skills, experience and the efforts which they have made to secure employment are not reviewed at least once a month, increasing dependency and the conviction that relief is a "right" is inevitable.'[190] The ghosts of Vankoughnet, Reed, Scott and McGill were ever present.

Concluding Discussion

Battle immediately advised the regions of the Treasury Board decision. He asked personnel to meet with provincial officials, to inform Indians of the new policy, and to hold local staff conferences for planning its early implementation. The regions were also asked to submit copies of provincial policies, procedures, and forms to headquarters for comment and revision.[191] Large packages of provincial documents soon began arriving at headquarters. Typical of these was one from British Columbia, which consisted of selections from the social welfare policy manual, some administrative forms, and the B.C. Social Assistance Act and Regulations. The branch adopted these for use with the concurrence of the province, and the new system became effective there on 1 January 1965.[192]

In the case of British Columbia, provincial policy was not entirely dissimilar from the intent and procedures of the April 1959 branch policy. That province's procedures, however, were more specific concerning rules of eligibility, assets, earned and unearned income, unmarried mothers, children living in the home of a relative, the treatment of fraudulent applications, and the right of appeal. Also, the rate structure was more complex and included an array of supplementary benefits.

Generally – though not necessarily – Indians received richer benefit packages than had been the case under the previous Indian Affairs rates. Yet they were now subject to far more complicated systems that equated welfare eligibility and dependence with individual need and unemployment. Provincial welfare systems all operated on the assumption that recipients had equal access to the labour market. This was what made the community development program so vital to the success of the introduction of provincial systems. If the provinces came on board and began delivering social assistance as well as community programs, Indian transition to the marketplace would come about more easily.

The adoption of provincial rates and standards had yet another impact on the goal of integration. By deciding to align with each provincial model, the branch had abdicated its direct control over social assistance policy and procedures. First Nations had been relegated *de facto* into the provincial sphere, and their possible direct influence on social assistance policy had been considerably minimized as a result. Except in Ontario, they were not direct recipients of provincial benefits, and what they thought about provincial policy was of little interest to the provinces. Of more concern was the implication for the final policy objective: if the provinces extended their services, the devolution process leading to the termination of the historical relationship between First Nations and Canada would be hastened.

The federal–provincial conference planned for May 1964 took place the following October. At the conference, agreements about the provinces' role in community development were reached, and an approach to extending services was developed. According to newspaper reports of the conference, the extension of welfare services would happen in two stages and on a province-by-province basis. In the first stage, regional Indian advisory committees, to be formed as part of the community development program, would be consulted about the extension of services. In the second stage, the extension of services would go ahead with the agreement of each band. Bands that wished to continue to receive federal services could do so. Thus, the *Globe and Mail* reported, provincial services would not be imposed on the bands, but federal services would continue to meet appropriate provincial standards.[193]

Only Ontario took advantage of the agreement. Although Ontario had already extended its services onto the reserves, the funding arrangements had not been satisfactory, and only a few bands had been able to take part. The new authority to fund bands on a more equitable basis with other responsible bodies provided the incentive for Ottawa and Ontario to reach an agreement on the full extension of welfare services. In 1965, Canada and Ontario signed the Memorandum of Agreement Respecting Welfare Programs for Indians. This bipartite agreement followed the guidelines set out by the 1964 conference, including the one that required the agreement of each participating band. In many respects it resembled the original ideas incorporated into the 1959 Memorandum to Cabinet and followed the lucrative funding formula developed by Health and Welfare referred to earlier in this chapter.[194]

The other provinces did not follow suit in extending their services, although some – including the three prairie provinces – became involved in community development. As Isbister described it, getting the provinces involved 'was like hammering sand.'[195] He recalled going to various meetings with the provinces and 'talking about it [the extension of services], listening to their hard luck stories about their budgets and their problems, and about federal responsibilities. You'd go to a lot of effort. The waves would come up and nothing to be seen the next morning!'[196] According to Isbister, the provinces resisted extending their services not only to the reserves, but to Indians off reserve as well.

This created a situation, he recalled, where the department had to set up off-reserve field offices in many cities. Roberts, who had not been a fan of Rudnicki's community development ideas, also offered insights into provincial resistance: 'I think they realized what a can of worms they would be getting into ... I think the ... people at the provincial level understood what a difficult thing the Indian administration was. Ottawa was sort of glossing over so much of it. And they realized ... to do it ... was going to cost an awful lot of money.'[197] Even after 1966, when the Indian funding formula had been made a part of the Canada Assistance Plan, the provinces simply did not take up the offer.

As for the First Nations, they were third-party onlookers. They had no direct role in the matter. As in the case of Ontario, they were consulted but were not signatories to any agreements. They could have agitated for direct provincial involvement in their affairs, but there was no evidence that very many did.[198] The recommendations of the 1959–61 joint committee showed only Saskatchewan Indians in favour of the extension of services. Overall, the language of First Nation submissions reflected a continuing desire to maintain an exclusive relationship with Ottawa in all matters. If there was to be an improvement in services, this was Ottawa's responsibility; and if not Ottawa's, then it was to be their own through some form of self-government.

The response of the Iroquois in Quebec following the 1964 conference conveyed this position well. Under a headline in the *Globe and Mail*, QUEBEC IROQUOIS FEAR TRANSFER TO OLD ENEMY, the chiefs said they would resist any transfer of services to provincial jurisdiction because they regarded Quebec as their historical enemy. The proper relationship, they maintained, lay between themselves and Ottawa.[199] The Iroquois had allied themselves principally with the British during the fur trade, and Canada was, principally, a British creation. As sovereign peoples, they wished to maintain the direct relationship with the government they considered their equal.

The First Nations' response returns the discussion to Rudnicki's critical point concerning community development, devolution, and termination. Clearly, Indian policy and welfare policy in particular had since the Second World War focused on termination. Every time the branch reformed its social assistance program, every time it associated with organizations like the Canadian Welfare Council, and every time it conferred with the provinces, it was attempting to move First Nations toward the termination of the constitutional relationship between them and Canada. The process culminated with the community development program, which had, Rudnicki realized in retrospect, released two conflicting forces.

The first was devolution leading to termination. Community development was intended to provide Indians with the necessary inner strength to reach out to Canada and become a part of it. This would come about as the First Nations accepted more responsibility for managing their own affairs. But this really meant the management of *Indian Affairs* on behalf of the government. Understood this way, community development and devolution would spawn a replica bureaucracy on the reserves, whether or not the provinces extended their services. The oppressed would become the oppressors.

Because of the emphasis placed on welfare administration as a method of integration – and thus, termination – it followed that social assistance would become one of the first branch programs to be devolved to band administrations. This was what occurred in Ontario and what followed through non-statutory measures in other regions in the 1960s and 1970s.[200] Indeed, the failure of the Liberal government's 1969 *White Paper on Indian Policy* simply prompted the government to overwhelm Indian communities with new programs and services that they were encouraged to administer. What could not be accomplished through legislative means could be accomplished through stealth.[201]

The second outcome of community development was that the process helped re-establish a more radical Indian leadership, which began to agitate consistently for Indian rights and sovereignty. The development of national and regional Indian advisory committees, the bringing together of young Indian leaders, the consultation process that took place around several stages of the *White Paper* – these and other processes contributed to a new, highly politicized relationship between Indian leaders and the federal government.[202] In this instance, the oppressed became the liberators.

As John Melling had astutely observed, there was anger behind the smiling faces, and it did not take long for someone like Rudnicki to find it and tap it. In the end, the community development program was perceived to have created too much unrest, adverse publicity, and division within the branch.[203] Rudnicki was transferred to another section of the branch but soon left to take a position with the Privy Council Office in 1966.[204] By then it was too late to return to former ways of bringing about Indian compliance to state domination.

10

Shooting an Elephant in Canada

Indian 'tribalism' seems to be foreign to our ... way of life. It seems to block individual development. We do not know how to deal with it. Consciously or unconsciously, we ignore it or try to eliminate it. Remove the tribe, rehabilitate the individual, and our problem is solved – so runs our instinctive thinking.

Circular by Indian Commissioner John Collier, U.S. Bureau of Indian Affairs,
15 November 1943

I realized that I should have to shoot the elephant after all ... And it was at this moment, as I stood there with the rifle in my hands, that I first grasped the hollowness, the futility of the white man's dominion in the East. Here was I, the white man with his gun, standing in front of the unarmed native crowd – seemingly the leading actor of the piece; but in reality I was only an absurd puppet pushed to and fro by the will of those yellow faces behind. I perceived in this moment that when the white man turns tyrant it is his own freedom that he destroys.

George Orwell, 'Shooting an Elephant'

In the first chapter I cited Bruce Trigger's assertion that the problem of dependency in Canada's native population would be understood only after intensive historical research into government Indian policies and their administration.[1] My task has been to describe the development and administration of federal Indian welfare policy in a way that would bring an analysis to bear on its ideology and objectives. Two questions still need to be asked about this venture. First, does the information support the analysis applied to the ideology and objectives of Indian welfare policy? Second, what does this study say about Indian welfare dependency?

My analysis proceeds from the premise that Canadian Indian policy must be understood as a continuation of the history of Indian–European encounter in Canada. In other words, the treatment of Indians by the Canadian state cannot be seen as a discrete segment of Canadian history or public policy; instead, it requires treatment as a phase in the unfolding relationship between natives and newcomers. The displacement of Indian economies and Indians' dispossession from their lands by Western capitalism caused a continuing struggle between First Nations and the colonial and Canadian states, which tried to impose hegemonic rule. After the Canadian state had gained physical dominance over Indian lands, the struggle shifted to issues of culture and First Nations' resistance to government efforts to assimilate them into civil society. Welfare dependency became a manifestation of First Nations' economic marginalization and of their resistance to the ideology of the liberal state.

The institutions and laws of liberal society were imposed through the administrations of federal and provincial governments. The administration of Indian policy by the federal department (later branch) of Indian Affairs was the identifiable locus of the struggle between First Nations and the Canadian state. Through that administration, state power was applied forcefully and translated into knowledge and disciplines that sustained the dominant culture. At Indian Affairs headquarters and in the field, a 'silent' war against the Indians was waged. In this war, Indians experienced acutely the dynamics of oppression and resistance.

This continuing war features a particular relationship between economic domination and cultural hegemony. Said describes this connection in his depiction of culture and imperialism:

> The force of, say, the British army in India was very minimal in a way, considering the vast amount of territory that they administered and held. What you have instead is a program of ideological pacification whereby, for example, in India the system of education which was promulgated in the 1830s, was really addressing the fact that the education of Indians under the British should teach the Indians the superiority of English culture over Indian culture. And of course when there was a revolt, as in the case of the famous so-called 'Indian Mutiny' in 1857, then it was dealt with force, mercilessly, brutally, definitively ... So it was force, but much more important ... than force, which was administered selectively, was the idea inculcated in the minds of the people being colonized that it was their destiny to be ruled by the West.[2]

Said's example is from the British Raj, but quite evidently it can be applied to the Euro-Canadian domination of First Nations. In Canada, force has been used selectively but ruthlessly at the first signs of trouble. The most dramatic instances were the quelling of the 1885 North-West Rebellion and of the 1990 uprising at Kanesatake (Oka), Quebec. The primary tool of First Nations' subjugation, however, was ideological pacification, which was accomplished through education as well as through measures, such as welfare, that reflected the expectations of liberal society.

How, then, was welfare used as a method of ideological pacification? The dominant culture legitimizes the economic system in which it participates. Those who are not *of* the culture but are dominated by it are consequently *defined* by it. In Euro-Canadian culture there was an ideological explanation for the economic domination of the First Nations. This explanation served two purposes. The first, a latent purpose, was to reinforce the macro-dependency that had resulted. The second, a manifest purpose, was to explain economic domination in terms that obscured the relations that made dominance possible.[3] This meant that dependency had to be explained, not in collective language, but rather in the individualistic terms of the dominant culture. Thus, attributions of individual welfare dependency and of a culture of dependency were not self-ascribed by the First Nations; instead, the ascription was made by the culture of the liberal, capitalist system that had rendered First Nations dependent. Dependency, in this sense, was a fabrication of the dominant culture and all solutions to it – which focussed on individual responsibility – remained within its dialectic, its discourse.

First Nations rejected the world view that made the individual the foundation of the economic and social order and that tied prosperity to the idea of the competitive, self-interested individual who was in the marketplace and in struggle with a hostile environment. First Nations' welfare dependency has been and still is key to their political subjugation. Generally, they do not accept the premise that they are Canadian first. Thus, their dependency is not a result of their failure as individuals to succeed in the marketplace, nor is it a result of the failure of the dominant Canadian society to make them more than 'marginal citizens.' Rather, their dependency is a complex form of resistance to a socio-economic order that Indian nations neither chose nor fundamentally accept.

The liberal state's explanation of and solution for Indian welfare dependency persists. For example, the 1994 *Report of the Auditor General of Canada* reflects such an explanation and demonstrates how firmly entrenched it remains, notwithstanding recent political events. Concerned about an Indian welfare dependency rate of 43 per cent, the auditor general opined that social assistance for First Nations should be closely integrated with proposed changes to the Canadian social security system.[4] Despite consistent evidence of Indians' wishes to the contrary, the report stated that Indian Affairs should make every effort with the provinces to utilize Part II of the then extant Canada Assistance Plan. Moreover, it singled out inadequate skills training, poor access to capital, weak community infrastructure, and remote community locations as the chief obstacles to reducing welfare dependency.[5] It seems that as a vision, the report was taking First Nations back to the future.

A Discussion of the Evidence

This book has covered two main periods – the post-Confederation period of subjugation, from 1873 to 1945, and the post–Second World War period of citizenship, from 1946 to 1965. The period of subjugation was characterized by the rapid westward expansion of the Canadian state, the marginalization of Indians in the fur trade, and the dispossession of Indians from their lands. It was further characterized by the decline of the fur trade's importance in the Canadian and European economies, the rise of southern industrialization and urbanization, and the beginnings of northern resource exploitation. Overarching these developments was the ecological destruction wrought by North American settlement. During the entire period of subjugation, fear of Indian dependence on the state underlay the administrative rationale for Indian relief.

Transition to Subjugation, 1867–1913

During Confederation's first fifty years, relief to Indians was granted sparingly and meanly as successive economic shock waves ended traditional modes of survival and replaced them with a new order. According to the data I have covered, although the general principles of relief policy were uniform throughout the country, the underlying objectives of relief administration differed somewhat from east to west and from north to south. These variations were based on the perceived advancement of the Indians and on the development of market structures in each region.

In south-central and eastern Canada, where market societies were firmly in place, government agents or their representatives issued relief as a means of acculturation to market principles and wage dependence. In southern Ontario especially, there were attempts to administer relief as though the bands were municipal entities responsible for relief from their own revenues. Sharp distinctions were made between 'pension' recipients – the elderly, the infirm, and widows with children – and 'periodic' recipients – the able bodied. Bands with sufficient funds could disburse a monthly amount to recipients in the former category; only time-limited issues were permitted for the able bodied. In contrast, the Montagnais along the remote north shore of the St Lawrence had been severely affected by ecological changes that had weakened their survival modes. Conservation laws further restricted their capacity to be self-sufficient. Relief to ease their starvation was provided slowly and reluctantly. The government was determined to make them settle on their reserves, learn agricultural methods, and maintain traditional subsistence. Thus, relief was granted to them on an *ad hoc* basis, and only in quantities sufficient to tide them over from one season to another. The same approach was taken for bands in similar straits.

In northwestern Ontario, changes in the fur trade, the building of the transcontinental railways, and the outbreak of disease all resulted in severe economic hardship for First Nations. The railways transformed native life by promoting resource extraction, the incursion of white fortune seekers, and more settlement. The Hudson's Bay Company found itself competing vigorously with other companies; similarly, Indians had to compete with other traders and trappers. In response, the company stopped issuing credit advances. In the meantime, the government did little to protect the First Nations' position in the trade; instead it admonished them to become farmers, gardeners, and wage-dependent labourers. Relief issue – again, usually from the bands' own revenues – was minimal and periodic. Adaptation to the rapidly expanding wage economy was to come about in a sink-or-swim manner. It was thought that generous relief would only act as a deterrent to Indian participation in the expanding marketplace.

In the western territories and northern British Columbia, the treatment of Indians was not entirely dissimilar to the treatment meted out to Indians in northern Ontario. Indians were to make way for capitalist development and expansion. In the West, where the territory had been unorganized for so long and Indians had remained sovereign over the land, the methods of subjugation had to be very firm and fast. As rapid settlement occurred – spurred on by Macdonald's National Policy – Indian policy amounted to a mopping up operation intended to ensure that Indians either took to reserves or dispersed. At first, relief was used to bribe Indians to take treaty and to entice them back to their reserves. Guided by the principle of less eligibility, relief soon became a means of overwhelming them with lessons on individual self-reliance by tying their relief to the performance of work. Work for relief also served as a cheap way to build roads, clear land, and fence private farms. Fuelling the meanness of Indian welfare policy in the West were continued fears of Indian uprisings, the precarious state of the federal treasury, and the consequent need to ensure the success of the National Policy. Indian assimilation was defined principally in terms of aversion to relief and rapid, individual absorption into the labour market.

Most relief during this transitional period was provided periodically, and only reactively, on an *ex post facto* basis each time need was established. This reactive administrative method began to raise questions about responsibility for Indian welfare. In the many remote areas of the country where the Department of Indian Affairs had not established a presence, the various missions or the Hudson's Bay Company acted as agents for Indian relief. In particular, the special relationship between the company and the First Nations created a situation that allowed the federal government to maintain that the company was wholly responsible for Indian relief.

Incidents of starvation at Ungava Bay provided a focus for the company to dispute this responsibility. It claimed that because it no longer had a trading monopoly, the government should shoulder the responsibility for Indian relief. Furthermore, the company – which was still willing to be an agent for relief distribution – urged the government to develop a system whereby relief could be furnished immediately once need was established. Eventually the company's position prevailed, and the Department of Indian Affairs authorized a system that permitted the company to distribute relief and then claim the costs.

This decision was important for several reasons. First, the company benefited greatly by being able to supply and distribute its own goods as relief. Although this was not the first example of a company having an exclusive contract to provide relief supplies, it reinforced the practice and entrenched patronage throughout the Indian agency system. Indian relief in this way became a boon to local commerce. Second, the decision provided the basis for a rationalized program of relief requiring methods of determining need, setting and allocating benefits, and establishing conditions of receipt. Third, the Reed–Chipman correspondence that had led to the decision demonstrated the linkage between the economic level of production in Canadian society and the political level. Finally, and perhaps most importantly, both the process of reaching the decision and the resulting system turned Indians more than ever into objects of government administration and bureaucratic power.

This formative period of Indian relief policy established two principles from which the government never departed, though it would reinvent them from time to time. The first was the idea that Indians in need should receive the same treatment as Euro-Canadians in need. Assimilation into the mainstream could be accomplished, it was thought, not by recognizing difference but by pursuing similarity. Actually, the persistent attribution of difference, of the idea of 'other,' made the task of assimilation impossible. When Indians 'failed' to assimilate, it was precisely their difference and lack of advancement that prevented them from 'elevation' to the status of the white 'race.' They could conveniently be blamed for their inability to rise above their condition.

The second principle that was established during this period concerned Indian poverty and its solution. Poverty among the First Nations was linked to their failure to assimilate. An unassimilated Indian was not a working Indian. Thus, Indian poverty – a general 'feature of the race' – was defined purely in terms of liberal values, which included a good dose of Puritan ideas about the moral deficiencies of those who were idle. The capacity and ability to labour were crucial concepts in late nineteenth and early twentieth century thought about the production of wealth, the importance of the working classes to its production, and the pride those classes could take in being self-reliant or, more accurately, wage dependent.

Indian relief and education policies were both concerned with turning Indians into moral, thrifty workers. Indians were perceived as lazy, idle, and intemperate, and this perception served to explain their dependence on the state and to justify the government's obsessive fear of that dependence. The task of turning Indian individuals into independent wage labourers became the focus of Indian welfare policy. Ironically, the repression of First Nations' autonomy and their subjugation to the state only exacerbated the dependence that the state was seeking to end and at the same time generated resistance to assimilation.

Consolidation of Subjugation, 1914–1945

The latter part of the period of subjugation – roughly from 1914 to 1945 – witnessed the state's relentless, dogmatic approach to effecting Indian assimilation. Relief policy and its administration were central to efforts to undermine Indian collectivity and to replace it with a culture of liberal individualism. During this period the state gradually rationalized a relief system and applied it relatively uniformly across the country. Consequently, general relief principles were articulated more clearly and were supported by administrative procedures to ensure their translation into practice.

The formation of these procedures and the delineation of the roles of various levels of the bureaucracy in the administration of relief further relegated Indians to the realm of subject objects. They were the administrative problem for which fiscally responsible solutions had to be found. The accomplishment of these bureaucratic tasks, both at headquarters and in the field, depended on civil servants who displayed unswerving devotion to duty and an unshakable belief in their mission to save the Indians from themselves. The end result of this sort of administration was the emergence of a harsh, faceless bureaucracy that was consumed by rules, accountability, and fiscal restraint and completely out of touch with Indians as human beings.

The deterioration of economic conditions, whether localized or widespread, only resulted in harsher relief measures. This was evident in the Maritimes, which did not share in the prosperity of the 1920s. There, able-bodied Indians were simply removed from the relief rolls during the summer and early autumn months. Similar patterns emerged in British Columbia, where at any sign of economic problems or excessive expenditures, the agencies were instructed to tighten their rules and reduce their numbers on relief. Indeed, during this period relief was generally available only to the elderly, the ill, and the infirm.

Relief policy also obscured darker problems created by the sale and lease of Indian lands and by the incursion of Euro-Canadians into traditional Indian economies. Admonitions to participate in the labour market diverted attention from issues of collective well-being toward those of individual survival. With few exceptions, able-bodied Indians were not eligible for assistance. For them, the lessons of the marketplace could only be imparted through the school of hard knocks. If the ability to labour was interrupted or not present, that was a problem not for the state but for the individual to resolve. Thus, following the purest of residual principles of charity, the able bodied had to rely on family, friends, or the church to meet the most basic of their needs. During the Depression, this mean-minded bullying directed at those deemed capable of supporting themselves continued with only minimal relaxation.

Relief – even for those considered worthiest – was kept to the bare minimum and issued as food rations. Clothing, initially issued twice a year, was eventually not considered a standard benefit. By the late 1920s, scales of food rations had become standardized. For a brief period, Class 2 and 3 rations took into minimal account the requirements of tubercular Indians and undernourished babies. These additional provisions did not last. During the Depression and the Second World War, relief was again reduced to one scale for basic food necessities. Indeed, for four years during the Depression, 1931 to 1934, per capita relief expenditure for Indians *declined* by 16.5 per cent while for Euro-Canadians it rose by 367 per cent. By 1934, Indian per capita relief expenditure was 36 per cent less than for Canada as a whole; by 1936 it was 44 per cent less.

During the interwar years, the Indian Affairs bureaucracy single-mindedly pursued a policy of reducing Indian dependence through increased fiscal restraint. The equation made was that reduction of expenditures would forcibly lessen Indian dependence. This thinking resulted in a duplicitous game whereby the Department of Indian Affairs could claim success in reaching government objectives by showing how little had been spent on programs of dependence, especially on relief. In fact, it was a hollow claim; it was rhetoric without results except that relief expenditures were minimized to the detriment of the impoverished victims. By 1945, Indian policy had reached an impasse; the department lacked the funds, the energy, and the will to carry out assimilation. Most reserve communities had become government-managed slums where meagre relief was given in exchange for labour.

In some ways, the period of subjugation ended as it had begun. The First Nations remained unassimilated into the mainstream society and resisted and expressed their displeasure at the Indian administration. Most lived in abject poverty, with their economies, their communities, and their health ruined by years of futile and often punitive attempts to 'civilize' them. The Second World War, however, proved to be an important catalyst in changing the dynamic of the state's actions toward them. The war effort aroused a new understanding of democratic citizenship in Canada, an understanding that was extended to include Indians. Riding a public opinion in favour of Indian equality, the government embarked on a new direction in Indian policy. The objective, assimilation, remained substantially the same, but the strategy and the resources brought to bear were transformed. The benevolent state was to become the next form of ideological pacification.

Citizenship, Knowledge, and the New Bureaucracy, 1946–1965

The period of citizenship is labelled so only to distinguish it from the more obvious repressive measures of the period of subjugation. Citizenship – or at least those policies which were meant to encourage what Bryan Turner referred to as the active status of citizenship, of *belonging* to the state – became its own form of subjugation and as such represented another drawn-out battle in the war against the Indians. The period of citizenship was characterized by the complete hegemony of the Canadian liberal state and market society. Social welfare policy, like other aspects of Indian policy, denied the possibility of political alternatives and acted on the assumption that modern, democratic capitalism was the best of all possible worlds and one to which any right-minded individual would wish to belong. The dominant class, having achieved the spontaneous consent of the civil society to its hegemony, utilized that consent to legitimize the state for Indians. The period of citizenship was characterized by the relationship developed between the political and civil levels of the state with the goal of engineering Indians' integration into the Canadian state.

During the interwar years the government had two major experiences of attempted partnership with outside agencies. One was with a voluntary organization, the Social Service Council of Canada; the other was with an external government agency, the Mothers' Allowances Commission of Ontario. These attempts met with mixed success. The administration was highly suspicious of the overtures made to it by the Social Service Council of Canada, but it also recognized the value of support from an influential national organization. Such support could help legitimize the department's objectives and the relationship between the state and First Nations in the public mind. Also, it was better to have a prominent national organization in well-meaning collaboration with the state rather than antagonistic to it and in alliance with the First Nations.

The extended relationship with the Ontario Mothers' Allowances Commission had initially been productive. Ontario had extended the allowances onto the reserves, and both levels of government as well as solvent Indian bands had shared in the costs. The Department of Indian Affairs had seen the extension of the allowances as a way of reducing its direct relief costs and as a vehicle for assimilating Indians into Ontario society. Complications about cost sharing eventually caused the department to cancel the arrangement; even so, it served as a model for Indian welfare in the postwar era.

After the war, the Indian Affairs Branch became far less isolated from outside influences. This is not to say that it was transformed by new interactions, but it learned how to incorporate other agencies' advice and to cooperate with them to its own advantage. It turned a cold shoulder if it believed an outside organization was working at cross-purposes with its own. During the postwar period, the branch attempted to develop a plan for Indian integration into Canadian society. Vital to the plan's success was the promotion of welfare services as a principle of citizenship. The branch tried to persuade the provinces to extend their services to all Indians on and off the reserves. In the interim, it was prepared to offer those services in as comparable a fashion as it thought possible.

To achieve these general objectives, the branch developed partnerships with academics in the social sciences. The social sciences, it was thought, could bring correct knowledge to bear on the Indian psyche, culture, and socioeconomic organization. An understanding of 'what made Indians tick' could generate programs that would motivate them to adapt to modern society. During this period the social sciences supplanted the church as the agent of the dominant culture and developed a fully secular interpretation of the Indian 'other' for Euro-Canadians. This reformulation of the 'other' further dehumanized First Nations by attempting to force their participation in their own oppression while leaving them as objects of administration. With the social sciences as an important background for its social welfare initiatives, the Indian Affairs Branch began to work closely, though not always harmoniously, with other government and non-government agencies.

There were three categories of working relationships: with other federal agencies, with provincial welfare departments, and with national voluntary organizations. During the 1950s the branch worked mainly with Indian Health Services of the Department of National Health and Welfare. This relationship was a difficult one, partly because Health and Welfare was a powerful department. In addition, Indian Health Services had become an important player in Indian matters and held strong opinions on solutions to Indian poverty and ill health. Despite the medical establishment's view that inadequate relief rations were a contributing factor to Indian malnutrition and infectious disease, it strongly opposed the branch's proposals to reform social assistance administration. This dispute was based on different problem-solving models. Indian Health Services operated from a well-developed medical model in which the doctor knew best and prescribed the medicine. Indian Health Services thus believed that Indian relief should continue to be distributed in the form of nutritionally balanced rations. Indeed, there was a strong, tacit suggestion that Indian Affairs should transfer relief administration to Indian Health.

Indian Affairs, on the other hand, operated from a less developed social model. The branch believed that Indian prosperity could best be achieved by promoting Euro-Canadian nuclear family patterns and the individual male's responsibility for his family's affairs. This could be achieved by reforming relief administration – more specifically, by replacing food rations with cheques and by permitting Indian recipients to shop for and purchase their own supplies. The Indian Affairs position prevailed, with some concessions to Health and Welfare concerning nutrition and the abuse of benefits. Indian Affairs' position was less paternalistic, but it contained its own assumptions about the political economy of the family and what was best for Indians. As a method of welfare administration, it necessitated an ever more complex, rationalized system for determining eligibility and issuing benefits. This system further undermined Indians' collective responsibility; it also treated them as individuals with problems.

Many of the branch's ideas about implementing modern welfare programs came from its association with the Canadian Welfare Council. The council's joint brief with the Canadian Association of Social Workers to the 1946 Joint Parliamentary Committee on the Indian Act neatly dovetailed with the government's new thinking about Indian matters. In the Canadian Welfare Council – a successor of sorts to the Social Service Council of Canada – the branch found a respectable and influential ally for its project of integrating Indians. The council commanded the respect of many of Canada's bourgeois and intellectual elites; it also served as a point of collaboration and information sharing among Canada's top welfare administrators. The Canadian Welfare Council was *the* guiding light of welfare reform in Canada immediately after the war.

The partnership proved fruitful for both. The council was able to work closely with a federal agency to implement ideas about Indian integration that were largely its own, and this strengthened its position nationally and added to its already impressive corporate résumé. For its part, the branch soaked up the council's ideas and information about welfare administration, as well as its culture generally, and all of this strongly influenced the development of its social assistance policy. Jones and especially Gordon were flattered by the prestige and professional hobnobbing that flowed from the partnership.

Indian social assistance policy was influenced in two ways by the branch's association with the council. The first was largely administrative. By coming to know other welfare administrators through workshops, information sharing, and so on, the branch learned more about systematic methods of administering assistance in an objective manner. Through the council, the branch began to absorb the culture of the postwar welfare state. Consequently, it developed its program more strongly around the responsibilities of the individual citizen in a market society. A more articulated policy with defined procedures reflected this turn toward an administratively efficient but supposedly just welfare program.

The council also indirectly influenced the branch's thinking about the appropriate role for the provinces in Indian welfare. The inclusion of Section 87 in the new Indian Act in part reflected the council's recommendations to the 1946 joint committee; the same section placed pressure on the Indian Affairs Branch to find ways to involve the provinces. The branch's relationship with the council was largely one of patterning. The branch was well aware of the council's attempts – through its lobbying for the Unemployment Assistance Act, for example – to promote citizenship through national standards of welfare administration. If national standards were to be set, then Indian welfare ought to reflect those standards and the standards of each band's province. This being so, it made even more sense for Indians to be included under provincial welfare programs and treated as full citizens subject to the same standards as any other provincial resident. The branch believed that since many prominent welfare administrators belonged to the council and presumably subscribed to its principles, through the council it could influence provincial and municipal administrations to subscribe to a logical extension of those principles.

The relationship between the Indian Affairs Branch and the Canadian Welfare Council reinforced the idea that Indians were a problem and thus objects requiring treatment and administration. The process that engaged Indian Affairs and the council and the solution of welfare citizenship that they proposed seemed so sensible to them as white, middle-class Canadians. In this scheme of things, Indians hardly counted except in terms of anticipated results. They remained bystanders to the machinations of the professional elites; they were simply raw material on a social policy assembly line.

During the late 1950s and into the 1960s, the branch began to seek a relationship with the provinces with the objective of having them extend their welfare services onto the reserves. The idea was that provincial services would forge a structural sense of citizenship within Indian communities. This rationale clearly emanated from influences such as the U.S. Meriam Report and the parliamentary hearings during and after the war. But except for the inclusion of Section 87 in the Indian Act, few federal initiatives with the provinces were actually taken.

The most important initiative came from Ontario, which passed the Indian Welfare Services Act in 1955. Under this act, Ontario extended onto the reserves the Mothers' Allowances as well as its categorical assistance programs and related welfare services. As well, the act established an Indian Advisory Committee to the Minister of Public Welfare.[6] The Canada-Ontario Child Welfare Agreement followed in 1956. This agreement – essentially a funding arrangement – enabled Children's Aid Societies and other Ontario provincial authorities to deliver protective and preventive child welfare services to Indian communities. In 1959 an amendment to the General Welfare Assistance Act accorded Indian bands municipal status for the purpose of administering social assistance under the act.[7] These changes in Ontario provided the Indian Affairs Branch with a blueprint for Indian integration into provincial welfare systems.

The Diefenbaker government's inept relations with the provinces, and the provinces' own intransigence, meant that little action resulted from the branch's further attempts to negotiate with provincial welfare departments. By the early 1960s the extension-of-services policy had reached an impasse, and the branch turned its attention back to an on-reserve welfare program administered in a manner similar to the provinces. In 1963, however, the new Liberal government of Lester Pearson vigorously renewed federal efforts to complete Indian integration into Canadian society.

It was thought that two obstacles were preventing integration. The first was Indian rejection and ambivalence; the second was a Canadian public that had again become prejudiced against Indians, whom they perceived as an unsuccessful ethnic minority in the same category as immigrants. From the Euro-Canadian perspective, these two obstacles were related. Indians' ambivalence to integration stemmed from the prejudice they experienced; the prejudice arose from a lack of understanding of Indians' heritage and of how opportunities were being denied them. The two worked together to keep Indians marginalized. A program was needed that would address both problems and provide a bridge between the dominant and Indian societies.

A new senior Indian administration in Ottawa seized on the idea of community development as a solution. In fact, a rudimentary, tightly controlled model of community development – referred to as leadership training – had already been toyed with for some time. In addition, another voluntary organization with which the Branch had worked closely, the National Commission on the Indian Canadian – later, the Indian-Eskimo Association of Canada – had already been working to educate the Canadian public about the problems with integration that Indians were facing. The principles underlying these initiatives – leadership and education – now had to be amalgamated under one program spearheaded by the federal government and supported by the provinces.

What was envisaged was something far more kinetic than the stultifying, conservative application of community development up till then. The new administration wanted a program that would transform the psychology of the First Nations and restore to them enough pride that they could look at Canada as a land of hope and opportunity. The provinces would assist by providing services to Indians on and off the reserves, by helping fund social programs, and by developing alternatives for greater self-sufficiency and self-determination. Also, the Indian bands would assume more responsibility for managing their own affairs by receiving grants to fund initiatives identified and planned by themselves. One of the key measures of the program's success would be the reduction of welfare dependence as Indian self-reliance, confidence, and participation – that is, their active citizenship – in Canadian society increased.

While this study has only briefly covered the program's early implementation in 1965, Rudnicki's personal recollections of its unforeseen consequences are extremely important. First, it is important to note that the program was planned as another aspect of integration policy. Community development, no matter how well intentioned, was simply another scheme to bring about the dispersal of Indians and turn them outward to Canadian society as fully participating, individual citizens. This process of devolution had a double edge. Conceptually, community development is about self-determination and the devolution of power to local levels. In the case of First Nations, however, devolution had two different possible outcomes. It could lead to self-government and sovereignty, but it could also be subverted toward the termination of the federal responsibility for First Nations and their abandonment to the dominant society.

It was this latter scenario that prevailed. Devolution became a method of managing Indians 'under the guise of Indian self-management'[8] and resulted in today's increased bureaucratization of Indian bands – particularly in their administration of government programs, including social assistance. Still, the rise of a more radical Indian leadership – which was only in part a result of the community development program – delayed the end of the process (i.e., termination) and permitted the emergence of a strong counter-voice to the state. By the late 1960s, this counter-voice of the First Nations had emerged as a significant force in Indian-Euro-Canadian relations and had begun to redefine the 'Indian problem' and the nature of Indian welfare dependence.

Welfare Dependence, the Language of Domination, and the Process of Emancipation

What then does this study say about Indian welfare dependency? First, there was a clear relationship between growing European economic hegemony and the marginalization of First Nations. As Fisher observed, when the European purpose in Canada changed from trade to exploitation of the land, so too, from the European perspective, viable native societies and economies became irrelevant and often obstructive. Yet by then native economies – though not their societies *per se* – had already been sucked into the engine of Western capitalism. Two distinct economic systems deriving mutual benefit from trade had intertwined as one. This had created by the time of colonization – and later Confederation – an *a priori* situation of sovereign dependencies. Indian societies remained relatively intact as collective, self-governing entities with a strong sense of their own historical past, but they were also largely dependent on their continuing role in the unfolding economy of the continent.

Liberal values, however, informed this economy, and were themselves rooted in an economic view of the individual and the existence of the individual prior to society or the community.[9] The settler society, which developed according to this view, considered the idea of First Nations as self-governing peoples sharing in the commonwealth incompatible with the principles of individualism enshrined in the constitutional framework of the liberal nation-state. Equally unacceptable was the thought of

Indians becoming dependent on the state. Consequently, the only solution for them in pre- and post-confederation Canada was to adopt the philosophy and acquire the skills necessary for assimilation into the liberal society as free, wage-dependent individuals.

To effect this transition, the political level of the state, supported by the civil level, was required to exert its hegemony over the First Nations and to dictate the conditions of existence in the dominant society. Hegemony could not be exerted in economic terms alone; it was also necessary to harness the language, laws, and behaviour of the dominant culture. That is, culture was the medium of oppression. It was through culture as the medium for the underlying economic order that the state sought to dominate First Nations in Canada. To achieve domination, the state needed to define First Nations in terms relative to its superior position and to ascribe this definition to them in such a way that both they and the state accepted it as the truth about their subordinate position. Noël refers to this as the process of abstraction:

> Having stripped his victims of any individuality of their own, summing them up in a few general characteristics, the oppressor has an even better claim to relegate them to intellectual confines if he believes that he has defined the boundaries of their essence. The definition of the dominated proposed by the dominator will always be simple and reductive. It is intended as an instrument of power as well as a means of knowledge. A too-complex victim risks escaping the oppressor's hold. Victims must be made to correspond to their imposed character sketch, whether they like it or not ...
>
> Thus it is through another's eyes that the dominated receive their identity and, therefore, their relative worth and place in society.[10]

The process of abstraction dehumanizes the oppressed and forces them to accept their new identity and to learn to define their collective existence in the oppressors' terms.

The outcome of this process of abstraction, of course, is the objectification of the oppressed and the dominator's control of the discourse in defining their identity, their problems, *and* the solutions to them. In the modern, liberal state, these problems became subjects of scientific measurement and the production of empirical knowledge. Empiricism, therefore, became the ultimate weapon of domination. Thus, the 'problem' of Indian welfare dependence was and is purely a construction of the dominant state, defined and measured within its lexicon and dealt with through the discourse of its institutional power arrangements.

Noël argues that in the process of abstraction, the oppressor exercises power through fabrications of higher moral purpose derived from the dominant state's strength and assumed superiority. The dominant society will seek to reinforce in the oppressed feelings of guilt and shame associated with victimization. Typically, this domination occurs through the administration of policies designed 'for the good' of the oppressed. Domination is thus interpreted as benevolent and protective.[11] In the case of dependence on welfare, Indians were instilled with a sense of shame and taught that it was disgraceful to be on assistance – to be dependent on the state or on the community in any way. Policies associated with their protection were ostensibly intended to civilize them and to include them so that they could then rid themselves of this shame.

Moreover, Noël states, once the oppressor has defined the problem and its solution, the burden of proof for being rid of the problem lies not with the oppressor but with the oppressed, because they are to blame for their own condition.[12] In this way, the dominant state was able historically to ascribe to First Nations characteristics such as laziness, idleness, backwardness, savagery, and any other attributes thought to be 'inherent in the race.' The oppressed had the job of demonstrating to the state that they were not dependent and that these characteristics did not exist. Yet it was impossible for them to do so, since the state had to maintain a dominant position and could not permit the oppressed to rise above the conditions of subordination. It has always been in the state's interests to keep Indians dependent on welfare and to falsify the reasons for their condition.

The emancipation of the oppressed can come about only through their challenge to the dominant discourse. Noël astutely observes that the oppressed are dependent on the oppressor for the production of the discourse of their oppression:

> Not only does the oppressor initially hold the monopoly on power, which sometimes must be snatched from him piece by piece, but the dominated depend on him for the production of discourse. The dominated thus are beholden to the dominator even in the need to give meaning to their condition. They may reject or accept this meaning, but for a long time they will continue to define themselves in its terms.[13]

Here Noël exposes the supreme irony of the method of oppression since it must be the source of destabilizing the relationship between the oppressor and the oppressed. Once the oppressed question the meaning of their condition, they must begin to develop a discourse that gives a different meaning to their condition and then act on that new meaning.[14] The process required to develop a new discourse is not easy. It begins with the search by the oppressed for a redefined identity and ends with their emancipation.

The oppressor is necessarily involved, for as new explanations are developed, the oppressor must surrender old ones and ultimately concede equality with the oppressed. Noël explains:

> As renewed by the dominated, the discourse will be based on such notions as diversity, complementarity, and flexibility rather than on the more exclusive concepts of superiority or totality. Not only did these concepts work to the disadvantage of the oppressed, even the oppressor could not live up to them. By basing his power on the supposed obviousness of his own wholeness, the oppressor denied himself the right to fail; by hoping to be the ideal Man, he condemned himself to eternal perfection ...
>
> Thus, there are limits to the oppressor's competence and power, and even to his morality. In short, after claiming to be perfect, the dominator will be shown to be just as human as the dominated who he had complained were too human ... or not human enough. In their growing doubts about the oppressor's intrinsic superiority, the oppressed have to reconsider the parallel principle of their own inferiority. Once the victim's alienation, hitherto maintained by stigmatization and the artful pedagogy of guilt, has been shattered, there is no longer any 'definitive' truth that cannot be retought [sic], nor any new frontiers that cannot be explored.[15]

This theme was much earlier articulated by George Orwell in his classic essay, 'Shooting an Elephant,' in which he recalled his own days as a subdivisional police officer in the British colony of Burma.[16] One day, the villagers called upon him to shoot a 'must' elephant, and he was suddenly struck by the absurdity and vulnerability of his colonial role and by the enormous assumptions inherent in the imperial relationship between the dominator and the dominated. That he was shooting an elephant normally valuable to their culture and performing a task that they – the dominated – had had to perform many times throughout their history, caused him to understand his equality with them. At that moment he understood how he had been set up to demonstrate that he could measure up to his self-proclaimed superiority.

Indian welfare dependence will only be solved when the political autonomy of First Nations is realized. In the dominant Canadian consciousness, the reserves symbolize Indian poverty and backwardness; for First Nations, they are symbols – often bitter – of survival and sovereignty. First Nations have resisted domination since before Confederation, but in modern Canada have been earnestly engaged in the process of emancipation since 1969, the year of the infamous White Paper. The term 'First Nations' – scarcely used twenty years ago – is now common within Indians' discourse; their identities and their futures are becoming clearer to themselves, and they are refusing to play the games of their Euro-Canadian oppressors.[17]

Despite their pride in being champions of human rights, liberal democratic states like Canada restrict these rights mainly to individual civil and political freedoms whose origins are in the rights to property and capital accumulation. Liberal democracies, Macpherson argues, do not generally recognize collective rights as human rights.[18] It was in the interests of the most powerful members of the United Nations to leave collective rights out of the Universal Declaration of Human Rights. Collective rights, according to the logic of the omission, are not a universal need, since they are limited to certain historically defined groups, including indigenous peoples. Macpherson argues that this precludes collective rights as human rights, which logically is not the case: 'Thus, the right to national self-determination may be humanly more important to its claimants than any of the individual rights.'[19] Macpherson concludes that 'the right of a subjected native people to its traditional way of life and to the resources necessary to maintain it may be the greater part of what it means to them to be human (as well as being, in the extreme case where genocide is threatened or is in process, prerequisite to any other rights).'[20] In his recent book, *Citizens Plus*, Alan Cairns calls for a re-examination of the recommendations of the 1966 Hawthorn report with a view to implementing a limited accommodation of collective rights while still promoting forms of integration.[21] Still, given the rise of political consciousness and political activism among First Nations since the 1969 White Paper, this view is neither sufficient nor desirable. Taiaiake Alfred, the noted First Nations scholar, rejects concepts of political sovereignty held by some First Nations as simply reflective of the dominant colonial and postcolonial discourse on what is meant by independence and autonomy. Native communities must reject the authority of the Canadian, liberal state. He advocates instead a return to more traditional forms of autonomy balanced by leaders who 'have the knowledge and skills required to bring traditional objectives forward as the basic agenda of the political and social institutions they work within.'[22] In my view, emancipation will not be realized, nor will the discourse of Indian welfare dependence substantially change, until the Canadian liberal state yields to the fundamental principle of full collective rights and restores political autonomy in a manner acceptable to the First Nations. Orwell, who understood the metaphor of the elephant as the imperial beast, shot it. Thus, as the agent of the state, he took the step necessary to end its domination:

> When I pulled the trigger I did not hear the bang or feel the kick – but I heard the devilish roar of glee that went up from the crowd. In that instant, in too short a time, one would have thought, even for the bullet to get there, a mysterious, terrible change had come over the elephant. He neither stirred nor fell, but every line of his body had altered. He looked suddenly stricken, shrunken, immensely old, as though the frightful impact of the bullet had paralysed him without knocking him down. At last, after what seemed a long time – it might have been five seconds, I dare say, – he sagged flabbily to his knees. His mouth slobbered. An enormous senility seemed to have settled upon him. One could have imagined him thousands of years old. I fired again into the same spot. At the second shot he did not collapse but climbed with desperate slowness to his feet and stood weakly upright, with legs sagging and head drooping. I fired a third time. That was the shot that did for him. You could see the agony of it jolt his whole body and knock the last remnant of strength from his legs. But in falling he seemed for a moment to rise, for as his hind legs collapsed beneath him he seemed to tower upwards like a huge rock toppling, his trunk reaching skyward like a tree. He trumpeted for the first and only time. And then down he came, his belly towards me, with a crash that seemed to shake the ground even where I lay.[23]

The Canadian elephant is ready to be shot. But who will shoot it, and when?

Notes

1 Themes and Issues

1 Tom Flanagan, *First Nations? Second Thoughts* (Montreal: McGill-Queen's University Press, 2000), esp. ch. 3, 27–47.

2 Alan D. McMillan, *Native Peoples and Cultures of Canada* (Toronto: Douglas and McIntyre, 1988), 1–3, 239–40, 273–5; Ontario, *First Nations' Project Team Report*, Principal Report on New Social Assistance Legislation for First Nations in Ontario, Marie Tincombe-Shaw and Audrey Hill, co-chairs (Toronto: Queen's Printer for Ontario, May 1992), 39. In the book, unless otherwise stated, I use the term 'European' to refer to the white, non-Indian peoples of Canada and more specifically to English cultural and political traditions. The term 'Indian' refers to persons registered under the Indian Act (RSC, 1988) and is a legal term. First Nation is a political term and refers to a political body authorized to represent a First Nation community. A First Nation community is a band of First Nation persons who reside together on a reserve as defined under the Indian Act. I will use 'Indian' and 'First Nation' somewhat interchangeably.

3 For an excellent discussion of this encounter, see Eric R. Wolf, *Europe and the People without History*, 2nd ed. (Berkeley: University of California Press, 1997), 158–94, and also Part 3.

4 Canada, Department of Indian Affairs and Northern Development, *Indian Social Welfare*, booklet extract from *Social Security, National Programs*, Vol. 7, 'Other Programs' (Ottawa: Indian and Northern Affairs Canada, 1982), 72, 74; *Basic Departmental Data*, 1999 (Ottawa: Indian And Northern Affairs Canada, 2000), 7, 44; National Council of Welfare, *Welfare Reform* (Ottawa: Supply and Services Canada, 1992), 3; National Council of Welfare, *Welfare Incomes 1997 and 1998* (Ottawa: Public Works and Government Services,

2000), Appendix; Paul Driben and Robert S. Trudeau, *When Freedom Is Lost: The Dark Side of the Relationship between Government and the Fort Hope Band* (Toronto: University of Toronto Press, 1983), 36–7; Hugh Shewell, 'The Use of Social Assistance for Employment Creation on Indian Reserves: An Appraisal,' in *Alternatives to Social Assistance in Indian Communities*, ed. Frank Cassidy and Shirley B. Seward (Halifax: Institute for Research on Public Policy, 1991), 20; Hugh Shewell and Annabella Spagnut, 'The First Nations of Canada: Social Welfare and the Quest for Self-Government,' in *Social Welfare with Indigenous Peoples*, ed. John Dixon and Robert P. Scheurell (London: Routledge, 1995), 41.

5 Bruce G. Trigger, 'The Historians' Indian: Native Americans in Canadian Historical Writing from Charlevoix to the Present,' in *Out of the Background: Readings on Canadian Native History*, ed. Robin Fisher and Kenneth Coates (Toronto: Copp Clark Pitman, 1988), 38.

6 Edward W. Said, *Culture and Imperialism* (New York: Alfred A. Knopf, 1993), 168.

7 Albert Memmi, *The Colonizer and the Colonized*, trans. Howard Greenfeld, (Boston: Beacon Press, 1967), 119–41.

8 Robin Fisher, *Contact and Conflict: Indian-European Relations in British Columbia, 1774–1890* (Vancouver: University of British Columbia Press, 1977), 48, 94.

9 Michael Asch, *Home and Native Land: Aboriginal Rights and the Canadian Constitution* (Toronto: Methuen, 1984), 46, 57–8.

10 See Michel Foucault, 'Two Lectures' and 'Truth and Power,' in *Power/Knowledge: Selected Interviews and Other Writings, 1972–1977*, ed. Colin Gordon (New York: Pantheon, 1980), 78–133. Also Patrick Brantlinger, *Crusoe's Footprints: Cultural Studies in Britain and America* (New York: Routledge, 1990), 102–4. Brantlinger discusses Foucault's abandonment of this schema and chastises him for it.

11 David T. McNab, 'Herman Merivale and Colonial Office Indian Policy in the Mid-Nineteenth Century,' in *As Long As The Sun Shines and Water Flows: A Reader in Canadian Native Studies*, ed. Ian A.L. Getty and Antoine S. Lussier (Vancouver: University of British Columbia Press, 1983).

12 Ibid., 87–99.

13 Olive Patricia Dickason, *Canada's First Nations: A History of Founding Peoples from Earliest Times* (Toronto: McClelland and Stewart, 1992), 190–1; J.R. Miller, *Skyscrapers Hide the Heavens: A History of Indian-White Relations in Canada*, 3rd ed. (Toronto: University of Toronto Press, 2000), 117–18, 132–3.

14 John L. Tobias, 'Protection, Civilization, Assimilation: An Outline History of Canada's Indian Policy,' *Western Canadian Journal of Anthropology* 6, no. 2 (1976).

15 E.J. Hobsbawm, *Nations and Nationalism since 1780: Programme, Myth, Reality* (Cambridge: Cambridge University Press, 1990), 38, 39.

16 Ibid., 40.

17 Herman Merivale, *Lectures on Colonization and the Colonies* (New York: A.M. Kelly 1967), quoted in David T. McNab, 'Herman Merivale and Colonial Office Indian Policy,' 88.

18 Ibid., 87–8.

19 Bernard McGrane, *Beyond Anthropology: Society and the Other* (New York: Columbia University Press, 1989), 94–9.

20 Fisher, *Contact and Conflict*, 73–94.

21 Ibid., 89, 165–6.

22 Ibid., 87–8.

23 Ibid., 84.

24 Ibid., 86; Tobias, 'Protection, Civilization, Assimilation,' 14.

25 J.E. Chamberlin, *The Harrowing of Eden: White Attitudes toward North American Natives* (Toronto: Fitzhenry & Whiteside, 1975), 83–99, 109–11; Tobias, 'Protection, Civilization, Assimilation,' 13–16.

26 Chamberlin, *The Harrowing of Eden*, 99.

27 Tobias, 'Protection, Civilization, Assimilation,' 17–18.

28 Joyce A. Green, 'Towards a Detente with History: Confronting Canada's Colonial Legacy,' *International Journal of Canadian Studies* 12 (Fall 1995): 91–2. The other three components of the National Policy, and those which were generally held to be the only ones, were the building of the transcontinental railway, the protective tariff, and settlement of the West.

29 E. Brian Titley, *A Narrow Vision: Duncan Campbell Scott and the Administration of Indian Affairs in Canada* (Vancouver: UBC Press, 1986), 13.

30 Tobias, 'Protection, Civilization, Assimilation,' 17–18.

31 Titley, *A Narrow Vision*, 13; Tobias, 'Protection, Civilization, Assimilation,' 17–19.

32 Harry B. Hawthorn, ed., *A Survey of Contemporary Indians of Canada*, Part 1, chapter 17, 'The Politics of Indian Affairs' (Ottawa: Queen's Printer, 1966), abridged in Getty and Lussier, eds., *As Long As the Sun Shines and Water Flows*, 172–3 (page references are to Getty and Lussier).

33 Titley, *A Narrow Vision*, 25.

34 Ibid., 33–4, 36.

35 James S. Frideres, *Native Peoples in Canada: Contemporary Conflicts*, 3rd ed. (Scarborough: Prentice-Hall, 1988), 150; Miller, *Skyscapers Hide the Heavens*, 255–61; Tobias, 'Protection, Civilization, Assimilation,' 19–21.

36 Miller, *Skyscapers Hide the Heavens*, 255–82; Titley, *A Narrow Vision*; Tobias, 'Protection, Civilization, Assimilation,' 21.

37 Miller, *Skyscrapers Hide the Heavens*, 281–2; Titley, *A Narrow Vision*, 104–7.

38 Chamberlin, *The Harrowing of Eden*, 99, 108–9; Tobias, 'Protection, Civilization, Assimilation,' 16.

39 Christopher J. Berry, *Human Nature* (Atlantic Highlands, NJ: Humanities Press International, 1986), 63–4; Adam B. Seligman, 'Towards a Reinterpretation of Modernity in an Age of Postmodernity,' in Bryan S. Turner, ed., *Theories of Modernity and Postmodernity* (Newbury Park, CA: Sage Publications, 1990), 122.

40 Seligman, 'Towards a Reinterpretation of Modernity in an Age of Postmodernity,' 123.

41 Tobias, 'Protection, Civilization, Assimilation,' 13–16.

42 Anthony Arblaster, *The Rise and Decline of Western Liberalism* (London: Basil Blackwell, 1986).

43 C.B. Macpherson, *The Real World of Democracy*, Massey Lectures, 4th ser. (Toronto: CBC Enterprises, 1965), 4.

44 C.B. Macpherson, *The Life and Times of Liberal Democracy* (Oxford: Oxford University Press, 1977), 23–92.

45 Ibid., 43.

46 Ibid., 49.

47 Ibid., 60.

48 Ibid., 61–2.

49 Vic George and Paul Wilding, *Ideology and Social Welfare*, revised and expanded (London: Routledge and Kegan Paul, 1985), 44–68.

50 Macpherson, *The Life and Times of Liberal Democracy*, 78–9.

51 C.B. Macpherson, *The Political Theory of Possessive Individualism* (Oxford: Clarendon Press, 1962; Oxford University Press Paperback, 1964), 226–7; Gertrude Himmelfarb, *The Idea of Poverty: England in the Early Industrial Age* (New York: Vintage Books, 1985); Samuel Mencher, *Poor Law to Poverty Program* (Pittsburgh: University of Pittsburgh Press, 1974).

52 Douglas Leighton, 'A Victorian Civil Servant at Work: Lawrence Vankoughnet and the Canadian Indian Department, 1874–1893,' in *As Long as the Sun Shines and Water Flows*, 113.

53 Arblaster, *The Rise and Decline*, 6, 8.

54 Noel Dyck, *What Is the Indian 'Problem': Tutelage and Resistance in Canadian Indian Administration* (St John's: Institute of Social and Economic Research, Memorial University of Newfoundland, 1991), 1.

55 Chamberlin, *The Harrowing of Eden*, 108.

56 Said, *Culture and Imperialism*, 164.

57 Dyck, *What Is the Indian 'Problem,'* 74–97; Miller, *Skyscrapers Hide the Heavens,* 254–82; Titley, *A Narrow Vision,* 1–22, 75–93, 162–83; Arthur J. Ray, *The Canadian Fur Trade in the Industrial Age* (Toronto: University of Toronto Press, 1990), 199–228.

58 Shewell and Spagnut, 'The First Nations of Canada,' 23, 44.

2 The Context of Relief Policy Development at the Time of Confederation

1 McNab, 'Herman Merivale and Colonial Office Indian Policy.'

2 Ibid., 93–6; William C. Wonders, 'Northwest Territories' and Shirlee Anne Smith, 'Rupert's Land' in *The Canadian Encyclopedia* (Edmonton: Hurtig, 1985); Arthur J. Ray, *Indians In the Fur Trade: Their Role as Hunters, Trappers and Middlemen in the Lands Southwest of Hudson Bay, 1660–1870,* 2nd ed. (Toronto: University of Toronto Press, 1998), 195.

3 Andrew J. Siggner, 'The Socio-Demographic Conditions of Registered Indians,' in *Arduous Journey: Canadian Indians and Decolonization,* ed. J. Rick Ponting (Toronto: McClelland and Stewart, 1986), 57–8.

4 *Census of Canada,* 1871 cited in Allan Moscovitch and Glenn Drover, 'Social Expenditures and the Welfare State: The Canadian Experience in Historical Perspective,' in *The 'Benevolent' State: The Growth of Welfare in Canada,* ed. Allan Moscovitch and Jim Albert (Toronto: Garamond Press, 1987), 16.

5 Henry F. Dobyns, 'Estimating Aboriginal Population: An Appraisal of Techniques with a New Hemispheric Estimate,' *Current Anthropology* 7 (1966), 114, cited in Francis Jennings, *The Invasion of America* (New York: W.W. Norton & Company Inc., 1976), 16, 30; Francis Jennings, *The Invasion of America,* 15–31; Alfred L. Kroeber, 'Cultural and Natural Areas of Native North America' (Berkeley: University of California Press, 1939), cited in Jennings, *The Invasion of America,* 17–20, and in Siggner, 'The Socio-Demographic Conditions,' 57; J.M. Mooney, *The Aboriginal Population of America North of Mexico,* ed. John R. Swanton, Smithsonian Miscellaneous Collections 80, no. 7 (Washington, DC, 1928), cited in Jennings, *The Invasion of America,* 16–18.

6 Miller, *Skyscrapers Hide the Heavens,* 58–9, 113–14, 312; R.T. Naylor, *Canada in the European Age 1453–1919* (Vancouver: New Star Books, 1987), 400–2; Ray, *Indians in the Fur Trade,* 182–92, 213, 217–28.

7 Frideres, *Native Peoples in Canada,* 44–68; McNab, 'Herman Merivale and Colonial Office Indian Policy,' 88–93; Miller, *Skyscrapers Hide the Heavens,* 131–2.

8 Miller, *Skyscrapers Hide the Heavens*, 254–6; Tobias, 'Protection, Civilization, Assimilation,' 18–19.

9 Miller, *Skyscrapers Hide the Heavens*, 206–11; Naylor, *Canada in the European Age*, 399–400; Titley, *A Narrow Vision*, 9–10.

10 Chamberlin, *The Harrowing of Eden*, 72, 162–81; Miller, *Skyscrapers Hide the Heavens*, 206–16; Tobias, 'Protection, Civilization, Assimilation,' 18–19.

11 Fisher, *Contact and Conflict*.

12 Ibid., 171, 176–7; Frideres, *Native Peoples in Canada*, 80; Titley, *A Narrow Vision*, 8.

13 See, Asch, *Home and Native Land*, 44; Emmerich de Vattel, *The Law of Nations; or Principles of the Law of Nature, Applied to the Conduct and Affairs of Nations and Sovereigns* (1760; published in Northampton, MA, 1820), quoted in Wilcomb E. Washburn, 'The Moral and Legal Justification for Dispossessing the Indians,' in *Seventeenth-Century America: Essays in Colonial History*, ed. J.M. Smith (Chapel Hill: University of North Carolina Press, 1959), 15–32; Macpherson, *The Political Theory of Possessive Individualism*, 200–1.

14 Asch, *Home and Native Land*, 45–6.

15 Fisher, *Contact and Conflict*, 66–8, 150–6, 160; Paul Tennant, *Aboriginal Peoples and Politics: The Indian Land Question in British Columbia, 1849–1989* (Vancouver: UBC Press, 1990), 26–38.

16 Tennant, *Aboriginal Peoples and Politics*, 35.

17 Fisher, *Contact and Conflict*, 162.

18 Ibid., 165, 176.

19 Ibid., 161–7; Tennant, *Aboriginal Peoples and Politics*, 39.

20 Fisher, *Contact and Conflict*, 176; Paul Tennant, *Aboriginal Peoples and Politics*, 43–4.

21 Fisher, *Contact and Conflict*, 188; Tennant, *Aboriginal Peoples and Politics*, 42–5.

22 Tennant, *Aboriginal Peoples and Politics*, 42–5

23 Ibid., 52.

24 Fisher, *Contact and Conflict*, 180–98; Paul Tennant, *Aboriginal Peoples and Politics*, 46–52.

25 Dickason, *Canada's First Nations*, 'The Many Fronts within Confederation,' 257–72.

26 Ray, *The Canadian Fur Trade*, 30–42.

27 Chamberlin, *The Harrowing of Eden*, 79–80.

28 Ibid., 5–6; Peter Carstens, *The Queen's People: A Study of Hegemony, Coercion, and Accomodation among the Okanagan of Canada* (Toronto: University of Toronto Press, 1991), 104–13, 166–80; Fisher, *Contact and Conflict*, 210; Miller, *Skyscrapers Hide the Heavens*, 138–46.

29 Peter S. Schmalz, *The Ojibwa of Southern Ontario* (Toronto: University of

Toronto Press, 1991), 174, 223–4. Agriculture was practised by those eastern Ojibwa who came in contact with the Huron. See McMillan, *Native Peoples and Cultures*, 96.

30 Miller, *Skyscrapers Hide the Heavens*, 125–46; E. Brian Titley, *A Narrow Vision*, 76–7.

31 Eric W. Kierans, *Globalism and the Nation-State*, CBC Massey Lecture Series, ed. Jonathan Kaplan (Toronto: CBC Enterprises, 1984), 67; Kenneth McNaught, *The Penguin History of Canada*, rev. ed. (London: Penguin Books, 1988), 172.

32 Kierans, *Globalism and the Nation-State*, 67.

33 Frances Abele and Daiva Stasiulis, 'Canada as a "White Settler Colony": What about Natives and Immigrants?' in *The New Canadian Political Economy*, ed. Wallace Clement and Glen Williams (Montreal: McGill-Queen's University Press, 1989), 252; McNaught, *The Penguin History of Canada*, 76–8, 175; Desmond Morton, *A Short History of Canada* (Edmonton: Hurtig, 1983), 43–4, 96–7, 121–3; Naylor, *Canada in the European Age*, 200–8, 408–16.

34 Abele and Stasiulis, 'Canada as a "White Settler Colony,"' 252; Peter J. Usher, 'Northern Development, Impact Assessment, and Social Change' in *Anthropology, Public Policy and Native Peoples in Canada*, ed. Noel Dyck and James B. Waldram (Montreal: McGill-Queen's University Press, 1993), 114–15.

35 Helen Buckley, *From Wooden Ploughs to Welfare: Why Indian Policy Failed in the Prairie Provinces* (Montreal: McGill-Queen's University Press, 1992), 45–58; Sarah Carter, *Lost Harvests: Prairie Indian Reserve Farmers and Government Policy* (Montreal: McGill-Queen's University Press, 1990); Miller, *Skyscrapers Hide the Heavens*, 269–76; Titley, *A Narrow Vision*, 18–19, 77.

36 Leighton, 'A Victorian Civil Servant at Work,' 113.

37 Chamberlin, *The Harrowing of Eden*; Dyck, *What Is the Indian 'Problem,'* 86–97.

38 Ray, *Indians in the Fur Trade*, 61–2.

39 Ibid., 62–3.

40 Ibid., 137–8.

41 Ibid., 203–4.

42 Chamberlin, *The Harrowing of Eden*, 81.

43 Ray, *Indians in the Fur Trade*, 220–1.

44 Ibid., 225.

45 Ibid., 228.

46 National Archives of Canada (NAC), RG-10, Red Series, Vol. 1995, File 6886, Memorandum Relative to the Policy of the Government of the Dominion in their administration of Indian Affairs, Ottawa, Ontario, 22 August, 1876. Draft Correspondence from Deputy Superintendent General, Lawrence Vankoughnet to W.P. Ross, editor, the *Indian Journal*, Muskogee Indian Territory, USA.

47 Dyck, *What Is the Indian 'Problem,'* 24, 25.
48 Chamberlin, *The Harrowing of Eden*, 55.
49 Bernard W. Sheehan, *Seeds of Extinction: Jeffersonian Philanthropy and the American Indian* (Chapel Hill: University of North Carolina Press, 1973), 153, cited in Chamberlin, *The Harrowing of Eden*, 162–3. McKenney's remarks are taken from a report delivered by him to the U.S. Senate, 27 December 1821. In his text, Chamberlin dates Mckenney's statement as 1821, but his reference refers to a report made to the Senate in 1871. The correct date is likely 1821.
50 Titley, *A Narrow Vision*, 4–5.
51 Ibid., 9.
52 Ibid., 10–11.
53 Frideres, *Native Peoples in Canada*, 32.
54 Titley, *A Narrow Vision*, 13.
55 Leighton, 'A Victorian Civil Servant at Work,' 105–7.
56 Ibid., 114.
57 Ibid., 109; Titley, *A Narrow Vision*, 13–15.

3 The Development of Rudimentary Relief Administration during the Initial Period of Subjugation, 1873–1912

1 Arblaster, *The Rise and Decline*, 237–53; Ray, *The Canadian Fur Trade*, 41.
2 Chamberlin, *The Harrowing of Eden*, 72–3, 79; Ray, *The Canadian Fur Trade*, 4–5, 40–1.
3 NAC, RG-10, Red Series, Vol. 1861, File 201. The fund was approved under the act, 14 and 15 Victoria, Chapter 106. While no date was found on the file, it was likely early 1872. This was the earliest reference found to the fund, which possibly had been created earlier.
4 NAC, RG-10, Red Series, Vol. 1903, File 2162, North Shore River St. Lawrence Superintendency – Mingan Reserve – Reports Concerning the death by starvation of several Indians in the winter, 1873. Memorandum to the minister of the Department of the Interior from W. Spragge, deputy superintendent general of Indian affairs, Ottawa, 13 August 1873.
5 Ibid., Letter to E.A. Meredith, deputy minister of the interior from W. Whitcher, aide to or deputy minister of marine and fisheries, Ottawa, Ontario, 10 July 1873.
6 Ibid., Memorandum to E.A. Meredith from W. Spragge, Ottawa, 19 July 1873.
7 Ibid., Letter to E.A. Meredith, deputy minister, Department of the Interior, Ottawa, from Jean, bishop of St-Germain-de-Rimouski, P.Q., 28 July 1873. Translator not named.

8 Ibid.

9 Ibid., Memorandum to the minister of the Department of the Interior from W. Spragge, Ottawa, 13 August 1873.

10 Ironically, Hudson's Bay Company agents, especially in western Canada, were often suspicious of the government's agents! See Ray, *The Canadian Fur Trade*, 4–5.

11 Ibid., 210.

12 Ken S. Coates, *Best Left as Indians: Native–White Relations in the Yukon Territory, 1840–1973* (Montreal: McGill-Queen's University Press, 1991), 169–70.

13 Ray, *The Canadian Fur Trade*, 46–7; Titley, *A Narrow Vision*, 52–5.

14 NAC, RG-10, Red Series, Vol. 2004, File 7646, Establishment by the Privy Council of a Fund for the Benefit of the Indians of Quebec, 1877–1878. See, for example, PAC, RG-10, Red Series, vol. 2445, File 93225, Grants To Different Tribes of the Province of Quebec for the Purchase of Seed Grain and Agricultural Implements and also for Aid to Destitute and Infirm Indians, 1889. Also, Vol. 2496, File 102,621, 9 January 1890; Vol. 2554, File 112,847, 9 January 1891.

15 Report to the Privy Council forwarded by David Mills, minister of the interior, Ottawa, 13 February 1877.

16 Memorandum to McNeill from E.A. Meredith, deputy minister of the Department of the Interior, Ottawa, 20 March 1877.

17 Correspondence to Captain John Holliday from McNeill, Ottawa, 21 March 1877.

18 Correspondence to James Bissett, officer of the Hudson's Bay Company, Montreal, Quebec, from McNeill, Ottawa, 21 March 1877.

19 Correspondence to McNeill, Department of Indian Affairs, Ottawa, from James Bissett, Hudson's Bay Company, Montreal, 22 March 1877.

20 Correspondence to the Department of the Interior, Ottawa, from the Rev. Father Boucher, Lorette, Quebec, 26 March 1877.

21 Leighton, 'A Victorian Civil Servant at Work,' 113; Ray, *The Canadian Fur Trade*, 48.

22 NAC, RG-10, Red Series, Vol. 2004, File 7646, Correspondence to the Department of the Interior, Ottawa, from the curé of the Gaspé, 17 June 1877.

23 NAC, RG-10, Red Series, Vol. 2071, File 10589, the Rev. E. Langevin on the extreme poverty of the Indians on the Coast from Nabaskowan to Bonne Espérance and asking that aid may be sent to them this fall, 1878, Letter to Lawrence Vankoughnet, deputy superintendent general of Indian affairs, Department of the Interior, Ottawa, from Bishop Langevin, St-Germain-de-Rimouski, Quebec, 27 October 1878. Translator not named. The file gave the bishop's initial as 'E.' This was probably incorrect. He was the same

Bishop Jean Langevin who had replied to Spragge's inquiries regarding the Montagnais in 1873.

24 Ibid., Letter to Bishop Langevin, St-Germain-de-Rimouski, from Lawrence Vankoughnet, Ottawa, 26 November 1878.

25 Ibid., information on file.

26 Ray, *The Canadian Fur Trade*, 3–29, 206–7.

27 D.J. Hall, 'Clifford Sifton and Canadian Indian Administration 1896–1905,' *Prairie Forum* 2, no. 2 (1977), reprinted in *As Long As the Sun Shines and Water Flows*, 129.

28 Robin Moore, *Paul Scott's Raj* (London: Heinemann, 1990), 93; Paul Scott, *The Towers of Silence* in *The Raj Quartet* (London: Heinemann, 1976), 269.

29 Moore, *Paul Scott's Raj*, 175.

30 NAC, R-G 10, Red Series, Vol. 3086, File 279,222-1, Ottawa – Correspondence and Circular from the Department of Indian Affairs to Indian Agents Across Canada Regarding All Agency Matters, Letter to Joseph Perillard, Esq., Indian agent, Oka, from the secretary of the department, Ottawa, 13 October 1890.

31 NAC, R-G 10, Red Series, Vol. 2671, File 134382, Circular No. 134382, To all Indian agents from L. Vankoughnet, deputy Sup. General of Indian Affairs, Ottawa, 10 January 1893.

32 NAC, R-G 10, Red Series, Vol. 2076, File 10,957, MANITOWANING AGENCY, Request by Superintendent Phipps For an Advance From the Funds of the French River Band (Ontario) for the Relief of Chief Edowekezis, who is ill. Correspondence to the department in Ottawa from Superintendent Phipps, 31 December 1878.

33 NAC, R-G 10, Red Series, Vol. 2445, File 93189, Grand River Superintendency, Six Nations Reserve – Resolution of the Six Nations Council to Place Christian Walker, Chief George Elliott, Susannah Powless and Sampson Fish on the Six Nations pension list at the rate of $25 per year, Letter to L. Vankoughnet, deputy superintendent general of Indian Affairs, Ottawa from A. Dingman, Indian agent, Indian Office, Brantford, Ontario, 8 February 1889.

34 Six Nations Reserve, Band Council Resolution passed at the Oshweken Council House, 17 January 1889.

35 NAC, R-G 10, Red Series, Vol. 2496, File 102615, Scugog Agency Recommends that $3.00 per month be allowed Edward Atthill and wife during winter months. 1890. Correspondence to Lawrence Vankoughnet, Ottawa from agent George B. McDermot, n.d.

36 Frideres, *Native Peoples in Canada*, 66.

37 Ibid., 66; Titley, *A Narrow Vision*, 53.

38 Ray, *The Canadian Fur Trade*, 50–95.

39 Chamberlin, *The Harrowing of Eden*, 171–5.

40 Leighton, 'A Victorian Civil Servant at Work,' 114–17.

41 Titley, *A Narrow Vision*, 14–16; PAC, RG-10, Black Series, Vol. 3755, File 30961, Letter to Indian Commissioner, Winnipeg, from Hayter Reed, Indian agent, Indian Office, Battleford, 18 June 1881.

42 NAC, RG-10, Red Series, Vol. 2496, File 102,521, Northern Superintendency, 4th Division – Port Arthur – The Chiefs of the Pic and Pays Plat Bands Are Sending Two Fine Stones As a Gift for the New Year to the Deputy Superintendent General, L. Vankoughnet, Letter to L. Vankoughnet from the four chiefs of the Pic and Pays Plat Bands, 2 January 1890.

43 Leighton, 'A Victorian Civil Servant at Work,' 113.

44 NAC, RG-10, Red Series, Vol. 2496, File 102,521, Draft Letter in reply to the Chiefs of the Pic and Pays Plat Bands from Lawrence Vankoughnet, Ottawa, 10 January 1890. In the draft, Vankoughnet had first written 'industrious people' but had crossed this out and replaced it with 'industrial,' a seemingly minor correction. Perhaps Vankoughnet was not ready to concede that the Pic and Pays Plat peoples were industrious. Industriousness was a trait of the Europeans and contributed to their undoubted superiority. Industriousness might be acquired by becoming industrial – that is, by learning and adapting to the culture and organization of Anglo-European society.

45 NAC, RG-10, Red Series, Vol. 2739, File 144,620-8, Correspondence Regarding Relief to Indians in the Port Arthur Agency 1895–1902, Letter to Hayter Reed, Deputy Superintendent General of Indian Affairs, Ottawa, from J.P. Donnelly, Indian agent, Port Arthur, 17 January 1894.

46 Letter to J.P. Donnelly, Port Arthur agency, from Hayter Reed, Ottawa, 20 January 1894.

47 Ibid., Letter to Reed from Donnelly, 9 February 1894.

48 Ibid., Letter to Donnelly from Reed, 20 February 1894.

49 Ibid., Letter to Reed from Donnelly, 11 April 1894.

50 Ibid., Fort William Band Council Resolution, 15 January 1894, sent to Hayter Reed with a covering letter from Indian agent J.P. Donnelly, 17 January 1894. The use of square brackets within the text indicates an illegible word or letter. The resolution appears to have been written by Donnelly but signed by the chiefs.

51 Ibid., Letter to Reed from Donnelly, 23 April 1894.

52 Ibid., Letter to Donnelly from Reed, 9 May 1894.

53 Ibid., Fort William Band, Band Council Resolution, 3 January 1895.

54 Ibid., Letter to Donnelly from Reed, 10 January 1895.

55 Chamberlin, *The Harrowing of Eden*, 170–8; Ray, *The Canadian Fur Trade*, 34–42.

56 Dennis Guest, *The Emergence of Social Security in Canada*, 3rd ed. (Vancouver: UBC Press, 1997), 29–33; Moscovitch and Drover, 'Social Expenditures and the Welfare State,' 20–2.

57 Himmelfarb, *The Idea of Poverty*, 163–4; *U.K. Report from His Majesty's Commissioners for Inquiring into the Administration and Practical Operation of the Poor Laws* (London, 1834), 144, 128, 147, 127, cited in Himmelfarb, *The Idea of Poverty*, 163–4.

58 Coates, *Best Left as Indians*.

59 NAC, RG-10, Red Series, Vol. 2739, File 144,620-8, Letter to Hayter Reed from J.P. Donnelly, 3 February 1896. The text of the letter and its spelling are copied as they appeared. This makes it difficult to assess the accuracy of Donnelly's arithmetic!

60 Ibid., compiled from general correspondence.

61 Ibid. See also Morton, *A Short History of Canada*, 143; Arthur J. Ray, 'Periodic Shortages, Native Welfare, and the Hudson's Bay Company, 1670–1930,' in *The Subarctic Fur Trade: Native Social and Economic Adaptations*, ed. Shepard Krech III (Vancouver: University of British Columbia Press, 1984), 12–14; Ray, *The Canadian Fur Trade*, 202–4; Hudson's Bay Company Archives, Provincial Archives of Manitoba, 'Report of Medical Service to Indians Located along the Line of the Canadian National Railways from Cochrane, Ontario to La Tuque,' October 1926. London Office Correspondence (General), A92/Corr/257/1, 21, quoted in Ray, *The Canadian Fur Trade*, 203.

62 Frideres, *Native Peoples in Canada*, 75; Ray, *The Canadian Fur Trade*, 40–1.

63 NAC, RG-10, Black Series, Vol. 3703, File 17680, Are Destitute Non-Treaty Indians to Receive Food, Letter to L. Vankoughnet, deputy superintendent general, Indian Affairs, Department of the Interior, Ottawa, from N.L. Orde, Indian agent, Battleford Agency, Treaty No.6, North West Territory, 14 November 1879.

64 Ibid., Letter to N.L. Orde, Battleford Agency, from Vankoughnet, Ottawa, 21 December 1879.

65 Jennifer S.H. Brown, 'Métis,' *The Canadian Encyclopedia*; Morton, *A Short History of Canada*, 80–4.

66 NAC, RG-10, Black Series, Vol.3703, File 17681, Letter to Vankoughnet from N.L. Orde, For instructions re: furnishing supplies to Half breed (Indian & French) women residing in Battleford, 15 November 1879. The particular reference to halfbreeds as Indian and French may have been essential in determining a more legitimate claim to federal attention than halfbreeds not of French – or perhaps Scottish – background. The Métis had had a long historical presence in the Northwest Territories by the time of Confederation, and this had been partly acknowledged in the Manitoba Act. It was not

until 1885 that Macdonald decided to reject absolutely their claim to distinct status. See Brown, 'Métis';' and Frideres, *Native Peoples in Canada*, 297.

67 NAC, RG-10, Black Series, Vol. 3703, File 17681, Letter to Orde from Vankoughnet, 21 January 1880.

68 It was not until after the First World War that women in Euro-Canadian society were able to campaign successfully for pension relief for widows, especially widowed mothers. See, Guest, *The Emergence of Social Security in Canada*, esp. ch. 5.

69 In the general population, the work test 'meant that an applicant for public assistance, unless he had a medical certificate excusing him from work, could be required to saw cordwood or break rock as a condition for receiving help.' See Guest, *The Emergence of Social Security in Canada*, 38.

70 In my research for this period, I was unable to locate the general instructions to agents. The earliest 'General instructions to newly appointed agents' were found for those in British Columbia in 1910.

71 Morton, *A Short History of Canada*, 97.

72 Chamberlin, *The Harrowing of Eden*, 172; Ray, *The Canadian Fur Trade*, 41.

73 *Commons Debates*, Sir John A. Macdonald, 11 March 1881, 1351, quoted in Ray, *The Canadian Fur Trade*, 41.

74 Ray, *The Canadian Fur Trade*, 41–2.

75 Carter, *Lost Harvests*, 72.

76 Ray, *The Canadian Fur Trade*, 41.

77 Chamberlin, *The Harrowing of Eden*, 172. Chamberlin uses this term. I have been unable to find its use in other literature and assume it to be either the superintendent or deputy superintendent general of Indian Affairs. Since the quotation following is from 1880, the person can only be either Sir John A. Macdonald or Lawrence Vankoughnet.

78 Canada, House of Commons, *Debates*, 15 April 1886, 724, quoted in Chamberlin, *The Harrowing of Eden*, 172. The words had been spoken in 1880, but were brought up again by the opposition in debate following the Riel Rebellion.

79 Carter, *Lost Harvests*, 79–129.

80 Ibid., 100.

81 Canada, House of Commons, *Sessional Papers*, Vol. 15, No. 6 (Ottawa, 1881), 75, and McCord Museum, McGill University, Hayter Reed Papers, 'Address' (n.d.), 65, quoted in Carter, *Lost Harvests*, 101, 144. Carter notes that Reed's address was given sometime in the 1890s.

82 Carter, *Lost Harvests*, 144, and McCord Museum, Reed Papers, 'Address,' 65, quoted in *Lost Harvests*, 144.

83 NAC, RG-10, Black Series, Vol. 3755, File 30961, Letter to Indian Commis-

sioner, Winnipeg, from Hayter Reed, Indian agent, Indian office, Battleford, 18 June 1881.

84 Carter, *Lost Harvests*, 144–5.

85 Ibid., 93.

86 Ibid., 145–9.

87 Canada, House of Commons, *Debates*, 15 April 1886, 741–2, quoted in Chamberlin, *The Harrowing of Eden*, 173.

88 T.H. Marshall, 'Changing Ideas about Poverty,' in *The Right to Welfare and Other Essays*, with an introduction by Robert Pinker (New York: Free Press, 1981), 33.

89 Hugh Brody, *Maps and Dreams: Indians and the British Columbia Frontier* (London: Pelican Books, 1983), 22–3; Harold A. Innis, *The Fur Trade In Canada: An Introduction to Canadian Economic History*, based on the revised edition prepared by S.D. Clark and W.T. Easterbrook, with a foreword by Robin W. Winks (Toronto: University of Toronto Press, 1962), 201–3; McMillan, *Native Peoples and Cultures*, 221.

90 NAC, RG-10, Black Series, Vol. 3708, File 19502, Pt.1, Letter to the Hon. D. Laird, Lieutenant-Governor of the Northwest Territories, from H.D. Moberly, Hudson's Bay Company officer, Fort Vermilion, 23 May 1880.

91 Ibid.

92 Ibid.

93 Ray, *The Canadian Fur Trade*, 41–3.

94 NAC, RG-10, Vol. 7094, File 1/10-3-0, Relief Food Policy 1888–1963, Letter to Sir Donald Smith, Hudson's Bay Company, Montreal, from T. Mayne Daly, superintendent general of Indian Affairs, Ottawa, 5 December 1892.

95 D.M.L. Farr, 'Smith, Donald Alexander, 1st Baron Strathcona and Mount Royal'; *The Canadian Encyclopedia*, Morton, *A Short History of Canada*, 87–8.

96 NAC, RG-10, Vol. 7094, File 1/10-3-0, Relief Food Policy 1888–1963, Letter to Daly from Vankoughnet, 2 December 1892.

97 Coates, *Best Left as Indians*.

98 Ray, *The Canadian Fur Trade*, 44, 206–7; London Correspondence Inward – Official Hudson's Bay Company, A11/119a, Letter to William Armit, Secretary of the company, from James Fortescue, chief factor, York Factory District, 1 December 1880, cited in Ray, *The Canadian Fur Trade*, 44.

99 NAC, RG-10, Red Series, Vol. 2710, File 143,423, Destitution In Labrador, Report from A.P. Low through Geological Survey re: starvation of Inds. near Fort Chimo in Labrador, 1893, Letter to T. Mayne Daly, minister of the interior, from George M. Dawson, Geological Survey of Canada, Ottawa, 9 November 1893.

100 Ibid., Extract from Preliminary Report of Mr. A.P. Low, Geol. Survey. Dated Fort Chimo 9.9.93.

101 Ibid.

102 Ibid., Letter to Daly from Dawson.

103 Ibid., Letter to D.C. Scott, chief clerk, Indian department, Ottawa, from P. McKenzie, an officer of the Hudson's Bay Company, Montreal, 11 November 1893.

104 Ibid., Memorandum to the governor general's secretary, Ottawa, from H.M. Embassy at Paris, 27 November 1893. Forwarded to the superintendent general of Indian Affairs, 15 December 1893.

105 Ibid., Letter to Arthur Gordon, secretary of the governor general of Canada from the acting deputy of the superintendent general of Indian Affairs, Ottawa, 21 December 1893. Since D.C. Scott was the chief clerk, it is probable that he was also the acting deputy.

106 Ibid.

107 Ibid., Letter to George M. Dawson from Hayter Reed, 6 June 1894.

108 Ibid., Letter to Hayter Reed from George M. Dawson, 7 June 1894.

109 Ibid.

110 Ibid., Letter to T. Mayne Daly from Hayter Reed, 9 June 1894.

111 Ibid., Note to Reed from Daly, n.d.

112 Ibid., Letter to C.C. Chipman, Esq., commissioner, Hudson's Bay Company, Winnipeg, Manitoba, from Hayter Reed, 13 June 1894.

113 Ibid., Letter to Reed from C.C. Chipman, Re: Destitute Indians, 19 June 1894.

114 Ibid.

115 Ibid., Letter to Chipman from Reed, 28 June 1894.

116 Ibid., Letter to Reed from Chipman, 4 July 1894.

117 Ibid., Letter to Chipman from Reed, 16 July 1894.

118 Titley, *A Narrow Vision*.

119 NAC, RG-10, Red Series, Vol. 2710, File 143,423, Memo to Hayter Reed from D.C. Scott, 11 July 1894.

120 Ibid., Letter to Reed from Chipman, Subject: Destitute Indians, 12 July 1894.

121 Ibid., Memorandum for the Superintendent General, from Hayter Reed, 24 July 1894.

122 Ibid.

123 Ibid., Memorandum to Department of Indian Affairs, Ottawa, from Duncan Matheson, Hudson's Bay Company, Fort Chimo, 26 August 1896. A.P. Low referred to him as 'Mathewson,' but he signed himself 'Matheson.'

124 Ibid., Internal Department memo, n.d.

125 Ray, *The Canadian Fur Trade*, 207–10.

126 PAC, RG-10, Red Series, Vol. 2710, File 143,423, Account of Supplies furnished to sick and destitute Indians at Moose Factory For year ending May 31st, 1896.

127 Ibid.

128 Ibid., Report from Rupert House.

129 There is some confusion in the literature over the date of Reed's forced retirement. Carter states that it was 1 July 1897. Ray cites correspondence from Reed to Chipman in the Hudson's Bay Company archives dated 23 September 1897. I accept Ray's more closely documented example. See Carter, *Lost Harvests*, 238, and Ray, *The Canadian Fur Trade*, 210nn21 and 22.

130 NAC, RG-10, Red Series, Vol. 2710, File 143,423, Letters to Hayter Reed from C.C. Chipman, 5 and 10 November 1896.

131 Ibid., Letter to Chipman from Reed, 18 December 1896.

132 Ibid., Letter to Reed from Chipman, 24 December 1896.

133 Ibid., Letter to Reed from Chipman, 27 January 1897.

134 Hudson's Bay Company Archives, London Fur Trade Subject Files, A12/FT, 49, Letter to Reed from Chipman, 23 September 1897. Copy included in letter from Chipman to Hudson's Bay Company Secretary Ware, 1 October 1897. Cited in Ray, *The Canadian Fur Trade*, 210.

135 NAC, RG-10, Red Series, Vol. 2710, File 143,423, Letter to Departmental Secretary, Re: Sick and Destitute Indians, from C.C. Chipman, 2 March 1905.

136 NAC, RG-10, Black Series, Vol. 3960, File, 143,423; Ray, *The Canadian Fur Trade*, 210, 221.

137 Macpherson, *The Real World of Democracy*, 8.

138 Arblaster, *The Rise and Decline*, 167, 203–23; Macpherson, *The Real World of Democracy* and *The Life and Times*.

139 Ray, *The Canadian Fur Trade*, 9, 88–9, 93–7.

140 NAC, RG-10, Red Series, Vol. 2102, File, 18,516, Part 1, Draft response to Memorandum from the under secretary of state, 3 February 1880, by Vankoughnet, n.d.

141 NAC, RG-10, Black Series, Vol. 4048, File 360,377, Copy of General Instructions to newly appointed Indian agents in British Columbia, 1910. Writer unknown, but likely J.D. McLean, the departmental secretary, with the authority of Frank Pedley, the deputy superintendent general.

142 NAC, RG-10, Red Series, Vol. 3086, File 279,222-1, Circulars on all Policy Matters 1904–1934, Circular on Relief, Ottawa, 28 October 1903, Issued by the deputy superintendent general. The deputy superintendent in 1903 was

Frank Pedley. The microfilm copy was very poor. Words in brackets [ ] are my own insertions based on what would seem to make the most sense. Empty brackets represent completely illegible words.

143 Ibid., Circular to all Indian Agents, Nova Scotia, from J.D. McLean, Department Secretary, Ottawa, 10 May 1905.

144 Ibid., Circular to all Agents in Manitoba, Saskatchewan and Alberta, from J.D. McLean, 17 December 1906; and to all Agents from J.D. McLean, 13 April 1908.

145 Hall, 'Clifford Sifton and Canadian Indian Administration,' 121, 126, 128, 130.

146 Macpherson, *The Political Theory,* 226–7.

147 Hall, 'Clifford Sifton and Canadian Indian Administration,' 122–3.

148 Alan Swingewood, *A Short History of Sociological Thought,* 2nd ed. (Houndmills, Hampshire: Macmillan, 1991), 191.

4 Relief Policy and the Consolidation of Subjugation, 1913–1944

1 Ramsay Cook, *The Regenerators: Social Criticism in Late Victorian English Canada* (Toronto: University of Toronto Press, 1985); Doug Owram, *The Government Generation: Canadian Intellectuals and the State 1900–1945* (Toronto: University of Toronto Press, 1986).

2 Titley, *A Narrow Vision,* 22.

3 Ibid., 23–30.

4 Derek Sayer, *Capitalism and Modernity: An Excursus on Marx and Weber* (London: Routledge, 1991), 129–40; Swingewood, *A Short History of Sociological Thought,* 190; Max Weber, *The Protestant Ethic and the Spirit of Capitalism,* trans. Talcott Parsons (New York: HarperCollins Academic, 1930; reprint, with an Introduction by Anthony Giddens [1976], London: Routledge, 992), 180–3; and Weber, *The Methodology of the Social Sciences,* trans. and ed. Edward A. Shils and Henry A. Finch, with a foreword by Edward A. Shils (New York: Free Press, 1949), 54–7.

5 Weber, *The Protestant Ethic,* 182.

6 J.L. Granatstein, *The Ottawa Men: The Civil Service Mandarins, 1935–1957* (Toronto: Oxford University Press, 1982), xi.

7 Titley, *A Narrow Vision,* 24.

8 John H. Taylor, *Ottawa: An Illustrated History* (Toronto: James Lorimer and the Canadian Museum of Civilization, National Museums of Canada, 1986), 64, 120; Titley, *A Narrow Vision,* 13, 37–8.

9 Alvin Finkel, 'Origins of the Welfare State in Canada,' in *The Canadian State: Political Economy and Political Power,* ed. Leo Panitch (Toronto: University

of Toronto Press, 1977), 345; Morton, *A Short History of Canada*, 158–60; Moscovitch and Drover, 'Social Expenditures and the Welfare State,' 20–4; Reg Whitaker, 'Images of the State in Canada,' in *The Canadian State*, 53–7.

10 Titley, *A Narrow Vision.*

11 Guest, *The Emergence of Social Security*, 49–50; Hobsbawm, *Nations and Nationalism since 1780*, 22–3; Owram, *The Government Generation*, 80–106.

12 NAC, RG-10, Red Series, Vol. 3086, File 279,222-1A, General Instructions to Indian Agents in Canada, Item 5, issued by Duncan Campbell Scott, Ottawa, 25 October 1913.

13 Ibid., Item 6.

14 The section (now section 88) is subject to federal-provincial wrangling and First Nation challenges. First Nations generally resent the section because they see it as infringing on their traditional claim as a third order of government and thus their right to deal directly with Ottawa.

15 NAC, RG-10, Red Series, Vol. 3086, File 279,222-1A, General Instructions to Indian Agents in Canada, Item 5.

16 Ibid.

17 Ibid.

18 NAC, RG-10, Red Series, Vol. 3086, File 279,222-1A, Circular sent to selected Indian Agents in addition to Scott's reissued instructions of October 1913, also signed by Scott, Ottawa, 21 September 1914.

19 Ray, *The Canadian Fur Trade*, 98, 212.

20 Ibid., 210.

21 NAC, RG-10, Red Series, Vol. 3086, File 279,222-1A, Circular to selected Indian Agents signed by Scott, Ottawa, 21 September 1914.

22 N.F.R. Crafts, 'Long-term Unemployment in Britain in the 1930s,' *Economic History Review*, 2nd ser., 40, no. 3 (1987): 418–32; Guest, *The Emergence of Social Security*, 84–6; Guest, 'Dealing with Unemployment: Full Employment and Income Security,' in *Unemployment and Welfare: Social Policy and the Work of Social Work*, eds. Graham Riches and Gordon Ternowetsky (Toronto: Garamond Press, 1990), 33–46; and Guest, *Histoire de la Sécurité sociale au Canada*, traduit de l'anglais par Hervé Juste en collaboration avec Patricia Juste (Montreal: Boréal, 1993), 353–4; Ernie Lightman, 'Conditionality and Social Assistance: Market Values and the Work Ethic,' in *Unemployment and Welfare*, 91–105; William Ryan, *Blaming the Victim*, rev. ed. (New York: Vintage Books, 1976).

23 Ray, *The Canadian Fur Trade*, 42–3, 227; C.N.C. Roberts, interview with the author, 5 May 1993, Ottawa.

24 NAC, RG-10, Red Series, Vol. 3086, File 279,222-1A, Additional Circular from Scott, Ottawa, 21 September 1914.

25 Ray, *The Canadian Fur Trade*, 210–11, 228.

26 NAC, RG-10, Red Series, Vol. 3086, File, 279,222-1A, Policy Circular sent to all Indian Agents in New Brunswick, Nova Scotia, and Prince Edward Island, from J.D. McLean, assistant deputy superintendent general and departmental secretary, Ottawa, 22 February 1915.

27 Ibid.

28 Carniol, *Case Critical: Challenging Social Work in Canada*, 4th ed. (Toronto: Between the Lines, 2000), 29–32.

29 Mary E. Richmond, *Social Diagnosis* (New York: Free Press, 1917) cited in Katherine A. Kendall, *Social Work Education: Its Origins in Europe* (Alexandria, VA: Council on Social Work Education, 2000), 100–1. Richmond's book is the classic early work on casework principles bringing to bear scientific method and knowledge. In addition, she shifted individuals' problems away from ideas about their immorality to their need to adjust to society. This theme later became explicit in Indian policy.

30 NAC, RG-10, Red Series, Vol. 3086, File 279,222-1A, Circular to Indian Agents from McLean, 22 February 1915.

31 See chapter 3, note 31.

32 Dyck, *What Is the Indian 'Problem,'* 77; Titley, *A Narrow Vision*, 39.

33 Dyck, *What Is the Indian 'Problem,'* 7.

34 Ibid., 77. Also, Peter Douglas Elias, *The Dakota of the Canadian Northwest: Lessons for Survival* (Winnipeg: University of Manitoba Press, 1988), 160, cited in Dyck, *What Is the Indian 'Problem,'* 77.

35 NAC, RG-10, Black Series, Vol. 4093, File 570,970, 'Civilizing Influences,' Excerpts from the proposed pamphlet by Thomas Deasy, Indian Agent. Scott, in a 20 December 1920 letter to Deasy, acknowledged his effort: 'I shall read this article with interest and give consideration to your proposal.' No further action was taken. Scott may have been sympathetic to the views expressed but he recognized foolishness when he encountered it.

36 NAC, RG-10, Red Series, Vol. 3086, File 279,222-1A, Letter with relief policy circular to the Paying Officer, Treaty 9, Indian office, Winnipeg, from J.D. McLean, secretary, Ottawa, 31 May 1917.

37 Ibid.

38 Titley, *A Narrow Vision*, 56.

39 Ibid., 58.

40 NAC, RG-10, Red Series, Vol. 3086, File 279,222-1A, Circular to all Indian Agents in British Columbia from J.D. McLean, departmental secretary, Ottawa, 23 November 1915.

41 *The Concise Oxford Dictionary of Current English*, ed. H.W. Fowler and F.G. Fowler, 4th ed., revised (1951), s.v. 'destitute.'

42 Macpherson, *The Real World*, 43.

43 Ibid.

44 Indian and Northern Affairs Canada, Indian and Inuit Affairs, Economic Development Program, B.C. Region, File E4545-13, Vol. 2, 'Employment/ General Reports and Statistics,' internal correspondence to Ottawa, 19 August 1983; cited in Shewell, 'The Use of Social Assistance for Employment Creation,' 31. See also chapter 2, note 30.

45 British Columbia, Guaranteed Available Income for Need Act, Revised Statutes of British Columbia, Chapter 158, 1979, as Amended to 1 January 1993; Ontario, Family Benefits Act, Revised Statutes of Ontario, Chapter 151, 1980, Regulations as amended to 30 January 1990. The General Welfare Assistance Act, Revised Statutes of Ontario, Chapter 188, 1980, Regulations as amended to 30 January 1990.

46 Arblaster, *The Rise and Decline*, 43–5. Arblaster analyses liberal principles of freedom and the value placed on family and privacy.

47 Carstens, *The Queen's People*, 126; McNaught, *The Penguin History of Canada*, 214; Naylor, *Canada in the European Age*, 505.

48 NAC, RG-10, Red Series, Vols. 3086 and 3087, Files 279,222-1A and 1B.

49 NAC, RG-10, Red Series, Vol. 3087, File 279,222-1B, Letter to all Indian Agents in New Brunswick and Nova Scotia from J.D. McLean, Ottawa, 4 April 1918.

50 Ibid., Letter to all Indian Agents of the Maritime Provinces from McLean, 1 June 1918.

51 McMillan, *Native Peoples and Cultures*, 51–2; McNaught, *The Penguin History of Canada*, 215.

52 NAC, RG-10, Red Series, Vol. 3087, File 279,222-1B, Directive to all Indian Agents in the Maritimes from McLean, 19 June 1919.

53 Titley, *A Narrow Vision*, esp. ch. 6, 94–109.

54 McNaught, *The Penguin History of Canada*, 237.

55 Moscovitch and Drover, 'Social Expenditures and the Welfare State,' 24.

56 NAC, RG-10, Red Series, Vol. 3087, File 279,222-1B, Circular to all Indian Agents in the Maritimes from McLean, 28 May 1924.

57 NAC, RG-10, Red Series, Vol. 3220, File 536,764-1, Correspondence Regarding the Amalgamation and Reorganization of Agencies in the Maritime Provinces, 1918–1937, Letter to H.S. Trefry, M.D., Tusket, Nova Scotia, from Scott, 3 February 1925.

58 NAC, RG-10, Red Series, Vol. 3220, File 536,764-1, Correspondence Regarding the Amalgamation and Reorganization of Agencies in the Maritime Provinces, 1918–37, Letter to the Department of Indian Affairs, Ottawa, from H.S. Trefry, M.D., Tusket, NS, 20 December 1924; and Scott's reply, 3 February 1925.

59 Warren E. Kalbach, 'Population,' *The Canadian Encyclopedia*; Frideres, *Native Peoples in Canada*, 140; Titley, *A Narrow Vision*, 57. See also chapter 2, notes 3 and 4.

60 Janice Dickin McGinnis, 'Influenza,' *The Canadian Encyclopedia*; Titley, *A Narrow Vision*, 57.

61 NAC, RG-10, Red Series, Vol. 3087, File 279,222-1B, Directive to Several Indian Agents in Manitoba, Kenora and Fort Frances, from McLean, 22 October 1919.

62 Ibid., Circular to All Indian Agents, British Columbia from McLean 24 February 1920.

63 Ibid., Circular to All Indian Agents in British Columbia from McLean 3 February 1920.

64 Ibid.

65 Ibid., Letter to All Indian Agents in British Columbia Advising Them of Relief Allocations for 1921–2, from J.D. McLean, 19 May 1921.

66 Ibid., Letter to Agents of British Columbia, 25 January 1922.

67 NAC, RG-10, Red Series, Vol. 3087, File 279,222-1B, Circular for Distribution to the Chiefs of British Columbia from J.D. McLean, 12 April 1922.

68 Ibid., Letters to Indian Agents in British Columbia from McLean, 19 March 1922 and 14 April 1923.

69 George Woodcock, *British Columbia: A History of the Province* (Vancouver: Douglas and McIntyre, 1994), 207–8.

70 NAC, RG-10, Red Series, Vol. 3087, File 279,222-1B, Letter to all Indian Agents, British Columbia from McLean, 23 September 1926.

71 Ibid., Circular to all Indian Agents in British Columbia, from McLean, 5 October 1927.

72 Ibid., Letter to All Indian Agents in B.C., Ontario, Québec, and the Maritimes and to Commissioner Ditchburn, Inspectors Parnell and Parker, from A.F. MacKenzie, acting assistant deputy and secretary, Ottawa, 20 January 1928.

73 Titley, *A Narrow Vision*, 56, 83–8.

74 P.H. Bryce, *The Story of a National Crime* (Ottawa: James Hope, 1922), cited in Titley, *A Narrow Vision*, 85–6.

75 NAC, RG-10, Red Series, Vol. 3087, File 279,222-1B, Circular to all Indian Agents in Ontario, Québec and the Maritimes from Scott, Ottawa, 23 April 1931.

76 Ibid., Correspondence to all Indian Agents from Scott, 1 May 1931.

77 Ibid., Schedule of Benefits Sent to All Indian Agents, 15 May 1931.

78 Guest, *The Emergence of Social Security*, 84.

79 Morton, *A Short History of Canada*, 178.

80 Ibid., 177.

81 James Struthers, 'Canadian Unemployment Policy in the 1930s,' in *Readings in Canadian History*, vol. 2, *Post-Confederation*, 4th ed., ed. R. Douglas Francis and Donald B. Smith (Toronto: Harcourt Brace, 1994), 375–89.

82 Ibid., 178; For an especially interesting discussion of the modern meaning of work in capitalist society and to make sense of this revulsion toward relief, see Sayer, *Capitalism and Modernity*, 130–3. See also Max Weber's *The Protestant Ethic*, 109, 157–9, 163, 174, 177.

83 Canada, Parliament, House of Commons, *Report of the Royal Commission on Dominion-Provincial Relations*, Appendix 6, A.E. Grauer, 'Public Assistance and Social Insurance,' (Ottawa, 1940), Table 3, p. 14, reproduced in Guest, *The Emergence of Social Security*, 86; Guest, *The Emergence of Social Security*, 86; Moscovitch and Drover, 'Social Expenditures and the Welfare State,' 21, 25.

84 McNaught, *The Penguin History of Canada*, 247–51; Morton, *A Short History of Canada*, 177–83.

85 Guest, *The Emergence of Social Security*, 93–5; Moscovitch and Drover, 'Social Expenditures and the Welfare State,' 25–8; Owram, *The Government Generation*, 219–20, 221–53.

86 NAC, RG-10, Red Series, Vol. 3087, File 279,222-1B, Circular to all Indian Agents from Scott, Ottawa, August 1, 1931.

87 Ibid., Letter to the Assistant Deputy Superintendent and Secretary, from C. Bourget, M.D., Indian Agent, Resolution, N.W.T., 22 August 1931.

88 Ibid.

89 Ibid., Circular to all Indian Agents from A.F. MacKenzie, Secretary, Ottawa, 10 September 1931.

90 Titley, *A Narrow Vision*, 198.

91 C.N.C. Roberts, interview.

92 Grauer, 'Public Assistance,' cited in Guest, *The Emergence of Social Security*, 86.

93 NAC, RG-10, Red Series, Vol. 3087, File 279,222-1C, Circular to all Indian Agents in Ontario and Québec, from A.F. MacKenzie, Secretary, Ottawa, 12 April 1932.

94 NAC, RG-10, Red Series, Vol. 3087, File 279,222-1C, Letter to the secretary, Department of Indian Affairs, Ottawa, from M. Christianson, Inspector of Indian Agencies, Alberta, 4 October 1932.

95 Ibid., Letter to All Indian Agents in Alberta, Saskatchewan and Manitoba, Maritimes, Ontario, Québec, British Columbia, from MacKenzie, 4 February 1933.

96 C.N.C. Roberts, interview.

97 NAC, RG-10, Red Series, Vol. 3087, File 279,222-1C, Letter to All Indian Agents from MacKenzie, 13 April 1933.

98 Ibid., Letter to All Indian Agents from MacKenzie, 26 June 1933.

99 Diamond Jenness, 'Canada's Indians Yesterday: What of Today?' *Canadian Journal of Economics and Political Science* 20, no. 1 (1954), 95–100; reprinted in *As Long as the Sun Shines*, 161–2.

100 NAC, RG-10, Red Series, Vol. 3087, File 279,222-1C, Memorandum to all Indian Agents, Re: Sick Relief, Special Relief for Sick Indians, from A.F. MacKenzie, Secretary, 20 September 1933.

101 Ibid.

102 Ibid.

103 When I came upon this directive I was reminded of my former career in administering public welfare in Vancouver. I recall a discussion with one of our ministry inspectors, who told me that he distinguished between 'fraud for need' and 'fraud for greed.' Those who defrauded welfare for greed could be as easily found committing similar acts of deception with banks or insurance companies. These persons were his particular concern. Fraud for need, however, constituted an insignificant percentage of caseloads and commonly resulted from someone struggling to make ends meet. In effect, this was a tacit admission that low welfare rates drove recipients to desperate measures.

104 See John A. Cormie, 'Forgotten Canadians,' *Social Welfare* (December 1937–March 1938), 74–6.

105 NAC, RG-10, Red Series, Vol. 3087, File 279,222-1C, Circular to all Indian Agents in Ontario and British Columbia, from A.F. MacKenzie, 10 February 1934.

106 NAC, RG-10, Red Series, Vol. 3087, File 279,222-1C, Directive to all Indian Agents in Ontario and Québec, from T.R.L. MacInnes, acting secretary, 3 Ottawa, March 1932.

107 Ibid., Circular to Indian Agents in Ontario and British Columbia, 10 February 1934.

108 Department of Mines and Resources, Indian Affairs Branch, *Annual Report, 1936–1937*, 189.

109 Owram, *The Government Generation*, 227–8.

110 Department of Mines and Resources, Indian Affairs Branch, *Annual Report, 1936–1937*, 194.

111 For an excellent account of this continued struggle and of the state rhetoric used in it, see Chamberlin, *The Harrowing of Eden*, esp. ch. 12, 182–204.

112 Department of Mines and Resources, Indian Affairs Branch, *Annual Report, 1936–1937*, 194.

113 Ibid.

114 NAC, RG-10, Red Series, Vol. 3087, File 279,222-1B, Circular to all Indian Agents in Ontario and Québec, from J.D. McLean, Ottawa, 15 June 1927.

McLean's circular revealed that in Ontario, relief was still paid from the annual interest that had accrued to the bands' trust accounts. Only amounts in excess of the total interest were to be included in the agents' annual estimates for additional parliamentary appropriations. Trust accounts had also been established for bands in Québec, thus eliminating the special legislation that had established one capital fund for all Indians in the province.

115 Ray, *The Canadian Fur Trade*, Figures 46–8, pp. 203–5.
116 Ibid., figure 52, p. 209.
117 Ibid.
118 Ibid., 211–18.
119 Ibid., 219.
120 Hudson's Bay Company Archives, Provincial Archives of Manitoba, London Office Correspondence-General, A92/Corr/257/1, Home Industries, enclosure to letter from Ralph Parsons to manager, Hudson's Bay Company, 10 July 1928; cited in Ray, *The Canadian Fur Trade*, 219.
121 Ibid., 220.
122 Hudson's Bay Company Archives, Provincial Archives of Manitoba, Development Department Dossiers, 1925–1931, Native Welfare, 1926–1928, A 95/52, Résumé of conference Held in Ottawa 23rd and 24th November, 1927, 1–2; cited in Ray, *The Canadian Fur Trade*, 219.
123 Department of Mines and Resources, Indian Affairs Branch, *Annual Report, 1936–1937*, 194.
124 Ray, *The Canadian Fur Trade*, 219–21, 227–8.
125 Miller, *Skyscrapers Hide the Heavens*, 323–5; PAC, RG-10, Central Registry, Vol. 8585, File 1/1-2-17, 'The Canadian Indian,' clipped article from *The Montreal Gazette*, 28 July 1944, reprinted from *The Economist* (London); and, 'The Indians' Need,' by B.T. Richardson, clipped article from the *Calgary Albertan*, 22 August 1944.
126 Guest, *The Emergence of Social Security*, 84; Struthers, 'Canadian Unemployment Policy,' 379.
127 NAC, RG-10, Central Registry, Vol. 7094, File 1/10-3-0, Relief Food Policy, 1888–1963, Circular C-118–1, to Inspectors and all Indian Agents from H.W. McGill, director, Indian Affairs Branch, Department of Mines and Resources, Ottawa, 22 May 1940.
128 Ibid., and Memorandum to Inspectors and Indian Agents from H.W. McGill, 15 June 1940.
129 Ibid., Memorandum from McGill, 15 June 1940.
130 Ibid.

131 Union of Ontario Indians Elder Ernie DeBassige, interview by Annabella Spagnut, 8 November 1991, Toronto, for Shewell and Spagnut, 'The First Nations of Canada.'

132 Shewell, 'The Use of Social Assistance for Employment Creation,' 40.

133 NAC, RG-10, Central Registry, Vol. 7094, File 1/100300, Memorandum from McGill, 15 June 1940.

134 C.N.C. Roberts, interview.

135 Canada, Department of Mines and Resources, Indian Affairs Branch, Annual Report, 1944–1945, 170; Frideres, Native Peoples in Canada, 140.

136 Ibid., 170. The term, 'the Indian' referred to First Nations collectively. As a term, it reflected the extent to which the state had stripped First Nations of social and cultural differences, and preferred to see them for policy and administrative purposes as indistinguishably one.

137 Leonard Marsh, Report on Social Security for Canada (Ottawa: King's Printer, 1943; reprint, Toronto: University of Toronto Press, 1975), Appendix VI, Table V(a), 316 (page references are to reprint edition); Paul Phillips and Stephen Watson, 'From Mobilization to Continentalism: The Canadian Economy in the Post-Depression Period,' in Modern Canada, 1930–1980's, ed. Michael S. Cross and Gregory S. Kealey (Toronto: McClelland and Stewart, 1984), 22, 28.

138 C.N.C. Roberts, interview.

139 Canada, Department of Citizenship and Immigration, Indian Affairs Branch, A Review of Activities, 1948–1958 (Ottawa: Queen's Printer, 1959), 14.

140 Guest, The Emergence of Social Security, 134–41.

141 Shewell, 'The Use of Social Assistance for Employment Creation,' 17, 19.

142 Andrew Armitage, 'Work and Welfare,' in Alternatives to Social Assistance in Indian Communities, 97–8, 105–6; Bain, 'Social Assistance Policy Alternatives,' 66–9; Canada, Canada Assistance Plan, 1966–7, c.45, s.1 (Ottawa: Queen's Printer, 1971), Section 2(a), 6(2); and Department of Indian Affairs and Northern Development, National Standards, Social Assistance Program (Ottawa 1982); Ontario, First Nations' Project Team Report, 32–5; David P. Ross and Peter J. Usher, From the Roots Up: Economic Development As If Community Mattered (New York: Bootstrap Press, 1986), 144; cited in Bain, 'Social Assistance Policy Alternatives,' 41; Shewell, 'The Use of Social Assistance,' 72–3; TAP Associates, A Starving Man Doesn't Argue, Report of the Tripartite Task Group on Social Services to Indians in Ontario, Phase 1, (Toronto: TAP Associates, 1979); and Community Care: Toward Indian Control of Social Services, Report of the Tripartite Task Group on Social Services to Indians in Ontario, Phase 2 (Toronto: TAP Associates, 1980).

5 Other Influences: The Transition to the Period of Citizenship, 1918–1944

1 Dyck, *What Is the Indian 'Problem,'* 31–2, 95; Hawthorn, ed., 'The Politics of Indian Affairs,' 172–3.
2 Dyck, *What Is the Indian 'Problem,'* 95.
3 Ibid., 86–97; See also James S. Frideres, with Lilianne Ernestine Krosenbrink-Gelissen, *Aboriginal Peoples in Canada: Contemporary Conflicts,* 5th ed. (Scarborough: Prentice-Hall Allyn & Bacon Canada, 1998), 257–64; Peter Kulchyski, '"A Considerable Unrest": F.O. Loft and the League of Indians,' *Native Studies Review* 4, nos. 1–2 (1988): 95–117; Miller, *Skyscrapers Hide the Heavens,* 318–22; Paul Tennant, 'Native Indian Political Organization in British Columbia, 1900–1969: A Response to Internal Colonialism,' *B.C. Studies* 55 (Autumn 1982): 3–49; and Titley, *A Narrow Vision,* ch. 6 and 8.
4 Cook, *The Regenerators.*
5 James L. Hughes, 'An Experiment in Altruism,' *Methodist Magazine and Review* 19 (January 1899): 23, quoted in Cook, *The Regenerators,* 195.
6 Cook, *The Regenerators,* 195; Thomas L. Haskell, *The Emergence of Professional Social Science: The American Social Science Association and the Mid-Nineteenth-Century Crisis of Authority* (Urbana: University of Illinois Press, 1977), cited in Cook, *The Regenerators,* 195; and United Church Archives, S.D. Chown Papers, 11, file 51, 'The Relation of Sociology to the Kingdom of Heaven,' cited in Cook, *The Regenerators,* 195.
7 Cook, *The Regenerators,* 195.
8 Guest, *The Emergence of Social Security,* 32.
9 Cook, *The Regenerators,* 196, note 2; Guest, *The Emergence of Social Security,* 32–4; Owram, *The Government Generation,* 31.
10 Allan Irving, 'The Scientific Imperative in Canadian Social Work: Social Work and Social Welfare Research in Canada, 1897–1945,' *Canadian Social Work Review* 9, no. 1 (1992): 15.
11 NAC, RG-10, Red Series, Vol. 3201, File 508,890, 'Reports by the Social Service Council of Canada on the Conditions of Indians, 1918–1923,' *Minutes of the Annual Meeting of the Social Service Council of Canada,* 9–10 January 1918.
12 Ibid., 24; Irving, 'The Scientific Imperative,' 15; *The Social Service Council of Canada, The Community Survey: A Basis for Social Action* (n.d., copy in the library of the McGill School of Social Work), 1, quoted in Irving, 'The Scientific Imperative,' 15.
13 Ibid., 24–5.
14 Ibid., 25; Titley, *A Narrow Vision,* 139–40, 155–7.
15 NAC, RG-10, Red Series, Vol. 3201, File 508,890, Letter to Duncan Campbell

Scott from Dr T. Albert Moore, General Secretary, The Social Service
Council of Canada, Toronto, 8 May 1918.

16 Ibid., Letter to Moore from Scott, 25 May 1918; Canada, An Act to amend
the Indian Act, Chapter 26, 8–9 George V (assented to 24 May 1918), cited in
Titley, *A Narrow Vision*, 48.

17 Ibid., Letter to Scott from Moore, 14 June 1918.

18 Ibid.

19 Canada, Department of Indian Affairs, Report of the Department of Indian
Affairs for the year ended 31 March 1919, 32, Titley, *A Narrow Vision*, 48.

20 NAC, RG-10, Red Series, Vol. 3201, File 508,890, Letter to Moore from Scott,
17 June 1918.

21 Titley, *A Narrow Vision*, 48–9.

22 Ibid., 49.

23 NAC, RG-10, Vol. 6810, File 470-2-3, Pt.7, Evidence of Scott before the
Committee of the House, Titley, *A Narrow Vision*, 50.

24 NAC, RG-10, Vol. 3201, File 508,890, Letter to Hon. Arthur Meighen, Minister of the Interior, from Jack Forster, Chairman, Indian Affairs Committee,
the Social Service Council of Canada, 16 April 1920.

25 Ibid., Letters to Jack Forster, The Social Service Council of Canada, and to
Scott, from the Private Secretary of Arthur Meighen, 28 April 1920.

26 Ibid., Letter to Meighen from Scott, 6 May 1920.

27 Titley, *A Narrow Vision*, 50–1.

28 John S. Moir, 'Shearer, John George,' *The Canadian Encyclopedia.*

29 NAC, RG-10, Red Series, Vol. 3201, File 508,890, The Social Service Council
of Canada, 'Report of the Indian Affairs Committee,' enclosure to Scott with
covering letter from J.G. Shearer, 22 February 1922.

30 Ibid., Letter to Shearer from Scott, 1 March 1922.

31 Ibid., 'Report of the Committee on Indian Affairs,' and covering letter to
Scott from Shearer, 6 February 1923.

32 Ralph Miliband, *The State in Capitalist Society: The Analysis of the Western System
of Power* (London: Quartet Books, 1973), 162–5; Talcott Parsons, '"Voting"
and the Equilibrium of the American Political System,' in *American Voting
Behavior,* ed. E. Burdick and A.J. Brodbeck (New York: Free Press, 1959), 101,
cited in Miliband, *The State in Capitalist Society,* 163; Swingewood, *A Short History of Sociological Thought,* 212–13.

33 Christopher Ham and Michael Hill, *The Policy Process in the Modern Capitalist
State* (Brighton, UK: Wheatsheaf, 1984), 63–6.

34 Gale Wills, 'Values of Community Practice: Legacy of the Radical Social
Gospel,' *Canadian Social Work Review* 9, no. 1 (1992), 30–1.

35 Moscovitch and Drover, 'Social Expenditures and the Welfare State,' 24.

36 Ibid.

37 Canada, Department of Indian Affairs and Northern Development, Indian and Inuit Affairs Program, *Welfare Programs for Indian People of Ontario before 1965*, Report prepared by W. Henry Rogers, Social Development Directorate, for the Intergovernmental Social Services Planning Committee (Ottawa, April 1983), 6.

38 NAC, RG-10, Red Series, Vol. 3224, File 549,421-1, Correspondence Regarding the Mothers' Allowance Commission As It Applies to Indian Women in Ontario, Letter to Duncan Campbell Scott, Deputy Superintendent General of Indian Affairs, from W.G. Frisby, Executive Secretary, Mothers' Allowances Commission of Ontario, Toronto, 19 October 1920.

39 Ibid., Letter to All Indian Agents in Ontario from Scott, 26 October 1920.

40 Ibid., Memorandum to A.S. Williams from Scott, 27 October 1920.

41 Ibid., Letter to Scott from A.S. Williams, legal clerk, 29 November 1920.

42 Under section 91(24) of the British North America Act (1867) – renamed the Constitution Act (1867) – the federal government was given jurisdiction over Indians and lands reserved for Indians. Sections 92(7), (8), and (16), in tandem with section 92(13) concerning property and civil rights, effectively gave the provinces exclusive jurisdiction over social welfare. Arguments related to jurisdictional responsibility for Indian social services arose in response to the increase in state activity in social welfare in the post–Second World War era.

43 NAC, RG-10, Red Series, Vol. 3224, File 549,421-1, Letter to Frisby from Scott, 23 March 1921.

44 Ibid., Letter to Scott from Frisby, 20 April 1921.

45 Ibid., Letter to Frisby from Scott, 25 April 1921.

46 Tobias, 'Protection, Civilization, Assimilation,' 19–20.

47 Canada, *Statutes of Canada*, An Act Respecting Indians, 43 Victoria, Chapter 28, ss. 69, 70, and 84.

48 NAC, RG-10, Red Series, Vol. 3224, File 549,421-1, Letter to Scott from Frisby, 3 May 1921.

49 NAC, RG-10, Vol. 3226, File 549,421-1D, Reports of the Department of Indian Affairs to Mothers' Allowances Commission, Toronto, Ontario.

50 Canada, *Welfare Programs for Indian People of Ontario*, 6–7.

51 Alison Prentice, Paula Bourne, Gail Cuthbert Brandt, Beth Light, Wendy Mitchinson, and Naomi Black, *Canadian Women: A History* (Toronto: Harcourt Brace Jovanovich, 1988), 259.

52 Canada, *Welfare Programs for Indian People of Ontario*, 7.

53 Guest, *The Emergence of Social Security*, 103–4, 108–14, 118–19; Marsh, *Report on Social Security for Canada*, xiii–xviii; Morton, *A Short History of Canada*, 204–6.

54 Marsh, *Report on Social Security*, xix.

55 See, for example, Noel Dyck and James B. Waldram, 'Anthropology, Public Policy and Native Peoples: An Introduction to the Issues,' in *Anthropology, Public Policy and Native Peoples*, 9; Hawthorn, 'The Politics of Indian Affairs,' 164; Miller, *Skyscrapers Hide the Heavens*, 324–5; Tobias, 'Protection, Civilization, Assimilation,' 24; Sally M. Weaver, *Making Canadian Indian Policy: The Hidden Agenda, 1968–1970* (Toronto: University of Toronto Press, 1981), 12.

56 NAC, RG-10, Central Registry Series, Vol. 8585, File 1/1-2-17, Special Committee on Postwar Reconstruction and Re-Establishment of Indian Population, 1944–1946, *Minutes of Proceedings and Evidence*, Appendix A, House of Commons, Ottawa, 18 May 1944, 263.

57 Canada, Department of Mines and Resources, Indian Affairs Branch, *Annual Report, 1936–1937*, 190; and, *Annual Report, 1948–1949*, 189; Ray, *The Canadian Fur Trade*, 204.

58 NAC, RG-10, CR Series, Vol. 8585, File 1/1-2-17, Special Committee, *Minutes of Proceedings and Evidence*, Testimony of D.J. Allan, Superintendent of Reserves and Trusts Services, 18 May 1944, 243.

59 Ibid., 18 May 1944, 259; May 24, 308, 309; and Letter to the Honourable T.A. Crerar, Minister of Mines and Resources, from George H. Ross, Member of Parliament, Calgary East, Ottawa, 19 May 1944; Prentice et al., *Canadian Women*, 303.

60 NAC, RG-10, CR Series, Vol. 8585, File 1/1-2-17, Special Committee, *Minutes of Proceedings and Evidence*, 24 May, 295.

61 Ibid., 295.

62 Ibid., 300–1.

63 Ibid., 302.

64 Ibid., 302.

65 Ibid., 302, 304.

66 Ibid., 305.

67 Ibid., 309.

68 Ibid., 310.

69 Ibid., 312.

70 Ibid., Special Committee, Memorandum to Dr H.W. McGill, Director of Indian Affairs Branch from Charles Camsell, deputy minister, Department of Mines and Resources, 1 June 1944.

71 Ibid., Letter to Camsell from McGill, 8 June 1944.

72 Ibid., Letter to McGill from Camsell, 12 June 1944.

73 Ibid., Letters placed on the file.

74 Ibid., *Minutes of Proceedings and Evidence*, 24 May 1944, 305.

75 Ibid., 326, 327–8.
76 I am referring here to the intensification of First Nations' political activity, especially since 1969, to their demands for constitutional self-government and, for many, to their assertions of sovereignty.
77 NAC, RG-10, Vol. 8585, File 1/1-2-17, Special Committee, *Minutes of Proceedings and Evidence*, 24 May 1944, 313–14, 321.
78 Ibid., 320.
79 Ibid., 314, 322.
80 Ibid., 'Report of the Nutritional Expeditionary Committee,' filed as evidence, 24 May 1944, 315.
81 Ibid., 320.
82 Ibid., 320–1. The term 'welfare officer' was usually synonymous with 'social worker.' It was certainly what Dr Moore intended.
83 NAC, RG-10, Central Registry, Vol. 8618, File 1/1-15-1, Psychological and Sociological Studies of Indians, October 1947 to January 1964.
84 A more complete treatment of this episode is in Hugh Shewell, 'Jules Sioui and Indian Political Radicalism in Canada, 1943–1944,' *Journal of Canadian Studies* 34 no. 3 (1999): 211–42.
85 Titley, *A Narrow Vision.*
86 Ibid.
87 Miller, *Skyscrapers Hide the Heavens*, 217; Titley, *A Narrow Vision*, 59.
88 NAC, RG-10, Red Series, Vol. 3087, File 279,222-1C, Correspondence to All Indian Agents from Harold W. McGill, Deputy Superintendent General, 15 March 1933.
89 Shewell, 'Jules Sioui,' 213; Titley, *A Narrow Vision*, 198.
90 Hawthorn, 'The Politics of Indian Affairs,' 169.
91 NAC, RG-10, Central Registry, Vol. 7141, File 1/3-7, Pt. 1, General Correspondence Regarding Indian Delegations and Deputations, 1898–1963, Memorandum to the Deputy Minister of Mines and Resources, from Dr H.W. McGill, director, Indian Affairs Branch, Ottawa, 4 April 1941.
92 Ibid., Letter to A.D. Moore, Indian Agent at Deseronto, Ontario for the Tyendinaga Reserve from McGill, 6 December 1941.
93 NAC, RG-10, Red Series, Vol. 3212, File 527,787-4, Indian Conventions Held in Ottawa Oct. 19–21, 1943 and June 5–7, 1944, Letter to G. Swartman, Indian Agent, Sioux Lookout, Ontario, from McGill, 23 September 1943. Similar letters were sent out across the country.
94 Shewell, 'Jules Sioui,' 225–6.
95 NAC, RG-10, Central Registry, Vol. 8585, File 1/1-2-17, Special Committee, *Minutes of Proceedings and Evidence*, 24 May 1944, 312.
96 Ibid.

97 NAC, RG-10, Central Registry, Vol. 7141, File 1/3-7, pt. 1, Circular letter to all Indian Agents, Inspectors, and the Indian Commissioner for British Columbia from acting director, Indian Affairs Branch, 25 May 1944.

98 Ibid.

99 Shewell, 'Jules Sioui,' 222. See also Norma Sluman and Jean Goodwill, *John Tootoosis: A Biography of a Cree Leader* (Ottawa: Golden Dog Press, 1982).

100 NAC, RG-10, Red Series, Volume 3212, File 527,787-4, Various memoranda, clippings, June 1944.

101 Ibid., Clipping from the *Journal*, Ottawa, 8 June 1944.

102 F.J.K. Griezic, 'Crerar, Thomas Alexander,' *The Canadian Encyclopedia*; J.E. Rea, *T.A. Crerar: A Political Life* (Montreal: McGill-Queen's University Press, 1997), 183.

103 NAC, RG-10, Red Series, Vol. 3212, File 527,787-4, Transcript of Speech Delivered by the Minister, T.A. Crerar, to the Convention of Indians, Ottawa, 7 June 1944.

104 Frideres, *Native Peoples in Canada*, 263; Titley, *A Narrow Vision*, 101–9.

105 Memmi, *The Colonizer and the Colonized*, 119–41.

106 Frideres, *Native Peoples in Canada*, 264, 270–1.

107 NAC, RG-10, Red Series, Vol. 3212, File 527,787-4, Letter to W.S. Arneil, c/o the Indian Agent, Christian Island, Ontario, from D.J. Allan, Superintendent of Reserves and Trusts, Ottawa, 10 June 1944.

108 C.N.C. Roberts, interview.

109 Jenness, 'Canada's Indians Yesterday,' 160.

110 Ibid.

111 Tobias, 'Protection, Civilization, Assimilation,' 17–18.

112 Cormie, 'Forgotten Canadians,' 74–6; Jenness, 'Canada's Indians Yesterday,' 160–1.

113 Tobias, 'Protection, Civilization, Assimilation,' 22.

114 Ray, *The Canadian Fur Trade*, 199–221.

115 Hawthorn, 'The Politics of Indian Affairs,' 166.

116 Bryan S. Turner, 'Contemporary Problems in the Theory of Citizenship,' in *Citizenship and Social Theory*, ed. Bryan S. Turner (Newbury Park, CA: Sage, 1993), 6.

117 Ibid., 6–7; Robert Pinker, 'Introduction,' in T.H. Marshall, *The Right to Welfare and Other Essays*, 10–12.

118 Turner, 'Contemporary Problems,' 2, 14–17.

119 Ibid., 2.

120 Ibid., 3.

121 Ibid., 5.

122 Ibid., 14.

6 Citizenship: The General Context of Postwar Indian Welfare Policy

1 See Richard Simeon and Ian Robinson, *State, Society, and the Development of Canadian Federalism*, Collected Research Studies for the Royal Commission on the Economic Union and Development Prospects for Canada, vol. 71 (Toronto: University of Toronto Press, 1990), 31–57, 107–15.

2 Dyck, *What Is the Indian 'Problem,'* 104–8.

3 C.N.C. Roberts, interview.

4 Canada, Parliament, Special Joint Committee of the Senate and the House of Commons, Appointed to Examine and Consider the Indian Act, *Minutes of Proceedings and Evidence* (Ottawa: Edmond Cloutier, Printer to the King's Most Excellent Majesty, 1946), No. 1, iii–iv; No. 9, 419–20; Tobias, 'Protection, Civilization, Assimilation,' 24.

5 Special Joint Committee, *Minutes of Proceedings and Evidence*, No. 1, 16 May 1946, iii.

6 Dickason, *Canada's First Nations*, 329; Dyck, *What Is the Indian 'Problem,'* 104–5; Miller, *Skyscrapers Hide the Heavens*, 221.

7 Special Joint Committee, *Minutes of Proceedings and Evidence*, No. 1, 30 May 1946, ix.

8 Ibid., 4 June 1946 52.

9 Ibid.

10 Ibid., 21 June 1946, 268.

11 Ibid.

12 Ibid., 269.

13 Ibid.

14 Ibid., 270.

15 Ibid., 27 June 1946, 415.

16 Ibid., 416–17.

17 Ibid., Statement of Mr MacNicol, MP, 9 July 1946, 490.

18 Ibid., 489–91.

19 Ibid., 493.

20 Canada, Special Joint Committee on the Indian Act, *Minutes of Proceedings and Evidence*, 27 June 1946, 440.

21 Ibid., 441.

22 Ibid., 9 July 1946, 494.

23 Ibid., 494.

24 Canadian Press, 'Defeat Move to Let Indians Give Opinion,' *Toronto Star*, 9 July 1946, quoted in Canada, Special Joint Committee on the Indian Act, *Minutes of Proceedings and Evidence*, 11 July 1946, 512.

25 Special Joint Committee on the Indian Act, *Minutes of Proceedings and Evidence*, 11 July 1946, 511.

26 Ibid., 514–15.

27 Ibid., 516.

28 Ibid.

29 C.B. Macpherson, 'Problems of Human Rights in the Late Twentieth Century,' in *The Rise and Fall of Economic Justice and Other Essays* (Oxford: Oxford University Press, 1987), 22–3.

30 Canada, Special Joint Committee, *Minutes of Proceedings and Evidence*, 30 May 1946, 4–5.

31 Ibid., 16.

32 Ibid., 16–17.

33 Ibid., 17.

34 Ibid., 23.

35 Commissioner Burke, 'Foreword' to *The Red Man in the United States* (no author or date) quoted by R.A. Hoey, in Canada, Special Joint Committee on the Indian Act, *Minutes of Proceedings and Evidence*, No. 1, 30 May 1946, 24.

36 Chamberlin, *The Harrowing of Eden*, 93.

37 United States, Institute for Government Research, *The Problem of Indian Administration*, report prepared by Lewis Meriam for the Department of the Interior (Washington, DC, 1928); quoted in Canada, Special Joint Committee on the Indian Act, *Minutes of Proceedings and Evidence*, No. 1, 30 May 1946, 25.

38 Chamberlin, *The Harrowing of Eden*, 93–4.

39 Canada, Special Joint Committee on the Indian Act, *Minutes of Proceedings and Evidence*, 30 May 1946, 28.

40 Ibid., 27–8.

41 Chamberlin, *The Harrowing of Eden*, 94–5.

42 Frideres, *Native Peoples in Canada*, 33.

43 Canada, Special Joint Committee on the Indian Act, *Minutes of Proceedings and Evidence*, submission by the Honourable Brooke Claxton, K.C., minister of National Health and Welfare, Part 7, item 54, 6 June 1946, 75.

44 Chamberlin, *The Harrowing of Eden*, 93.

45 Canada, Special Joint Committee on the Indian Act, *Minutes of Proceedings and Evidence*, Appendix HS, Danforth Avenue United Church Women's Association, Toronto, Ontario, n.d., 1947, 2090; Appendix GP, Creston Valley Hospital Association, British Columbia, 18 June 1947, 2033.

46 Ibid., Appendix BP, the Canadian Legion of the British Empire Service League, University Branch No. 72, Vancouver, B.C., n.d., 1947, 162.

47 Ibid., Appendix AF, Society for the Futherance of B.C. Indian Arts and Crafts, n.d., June 1946, 846.

48 Canada, Special Joint Committee on the Indian Act, *Minutes of Proceedings and Evidence*, Appendix GO, Brief Submitted by the Vancouver Branch of the Canadian Civil Liberties Union, 28 June 1947, 2020–1.

49 Ibid., 2022.

50 Ibid., 2029.

51 Guest, *The Emergence of Social Security*, 108–14; Irving, 'The Scientific Imperative,' 24; Owram, *The Government Generation*, 309–10.

52 Guest, *The Emergence of Social Security*, 114, 123. Guest notes that the council's approval of the Marsh report was, however, 'restrained.'

53 Canada, Special Joint Committee on the Indian Act, *Minutes of Proceedings and Evidence*, Appendix BO, Joint Submission by the Canadian Welfare Council and the Canadian Association of Social Workers, Ottawa, January 1947, 155–8.

54 Ibid., 157.

55 See Tobias, 'Protection, Civilization, Assimilation,' 16.

56 Canada, Special Joint Committee on the Indian Act, *Minutes of Proceedings and Evidence*, Appendix BO, January 1947, 159.

57 Ibid., 159.

58 Ibid., 160.

59 Ibid., 160.

60 Ibid., 161.

61 Ibid., Appendix BN, Submission of the Dog-Ribs Indians of Fort Rae, N.W.T. to the Indian Affairs Branch, 8 January 1947, 153; Appendix BQ, Resolutions of the Ohamil Indian Reserve, Laidlaw, B.C., n.d., 1947, 162; Appendix HT, Letter to Norman E. Lickers, Liaison Officer, Joint Committee on Indian Affairs, from John Cowie, Chief, Fort Chipewyan Cree, Alberta, 16 June 1947, 2090–1.

62 Ibid., Appendix AC(1), Supplementary Brief of the Indian Association of Alberta, n.d., 1946; Submission by the Union of Saskatchewan Indians, 8 May 1947.

63 Ibid., Appendix ID, Written statement to the Joint Committee to Investigate the Indian Act, from the Mohawk Nation, St-Regis Reserve, 11 May 1948, 209.

64 Ibid.

65 Ibid., Appendices BN, 153; BQ, 163; CQ, Submission of the Fort Alexander Reserve, Pine Falls, Manitoba, 8 December 1946, 232; HT, 2092; Testimony of Chief William Meawasige, 22 May 1947, 1295.

66 Ibid., Appendix BQ, 163.

67 Ibid., Testimony of William Meawasige, 22 May 1947, 1295.

68 Ibid., Appendix CQ, 232; Appendix HT, 2092.

69 Ibid., Appendix HT, 16 June 1947, 2092–3.

70 Ibid., 2093.

71 Ibid., Appendix BQ, 163.

72 Ibid., Testimony of Chief William Meawasige, 22 May 1947, 1295.

73 Ibid., 1295–6.

74 Ibid., Appendix CQ, 233.

75 Ibid., Statement of Mr Norman Lickers, liaison officer for the Joint Committee, 27 June 1946, 428.

76 Ibid., Testimony of Chief Andrew Paull, president, North American Indian Brotherhood, 27 June 1946, 420–2.

77 Ibid.

78 Ibid., 424.

79 Ibid., 427.

80 Ibid.

81 Ibid., 449.

82 Ibid., Appendix AC (1), Supplementary Brief of the Indian Association of Alberta, n.d., 1946, 807.

83 Ibid.

84 See, for example, Augie Fleras and Jean Leonard Elliott, *The 'Nations Within': Aboriginal-State Relations in Canada, the United States and New Zealand* (Toronto: Oxford University Press, 1992), 56–8; and Ian G. Scott and J.T.S. McCabe, 'The Role of the Provinces in the Elucidation of Rights,' in *Governments in Conflict? Provinces and Indian Nations in Canada*, ed. J. Anthony Long and Menno Boldt, in association with Leroy Little Bear (Toronto: University of Toronto Press, 1988), 62–4.

85 Canada, Joint Committee on Indian Affairs, *Minutes of Proceedings and Evidence*, Submission of the Union of Saskatchewan Indians, 8 May 1947, 984.

86 Ibid.

87 Ibid., Appendix GY, Submission of the Catholic Indian Institute of B.C., Lillooet, B.C., 1 May 1947, 2048.

88 Ibid., 2048–9.

89 Ibid.

90 Ibid., *Minutes of Proceedings and Evidence*, Chief Tom Jones, Cape Croker Reserve, Ontario, and Treasurer of the North American Indian Brotherhood, 27 June 1946, 430.

91 The reference was to the pension provided under the Old Age Pensions Act of 1927, which remained in effect until 1952. See Guest, *The Emergence of Social Security*, 74–9.

92 Canada, Special Joint Committee on the Indian Act, *Minutes of Proceedings and Evidence*, Appendix AC(1), Supplementary Brief of the Indian Association of Alberta, n.d., 1946, 808.

93 Ibid., 808.

94 Ibid., Appendix AB, Submission prepared by Berry Richards, MLA, The Pas, Manitoba, in consultation with the Chief and Council of The Pas Indian Band, n.d., 1946, 668.

95 Canada, *Report of the Commission on Indian Affairs*, J. Fred Johnston and Don F. Brown, Joint Chairmen, Ottawa, 8 July 1947, 1–2. See also Canada, Joint Committee on the Indian Act, *Minutes of Proceedings and Evidence*, Appendix GN, 8 July 1947.

96 Canada, *Report of the Commission on Indian Affairs*, 5.

97 Ibid.

98 Ibid, 10.

99 Ibid., 10–11.

100 Ibid., 13.

101 Ibid., 11, 13.

102 Ibid., 12.

103 Ibid., 14–15.

104 Ibid., 15.

105 Canada, Special Joint Committee on the Indian Act, *Minutes of Proceedings and Evidence*, Fourth Report, 22 June 1948, 187.

106 Ibid., items (c) and (e), 187.

107 Ibid., item (h), 187.

108 Ibid., item 8, 188.

109 Ibid., item 12, 189–90.

110 For a similar discussion of this and other joint committee recommendations, see Dyck, *What Is the Indian 'Problem,'* 104–5; Tobias, 'Protection, Civilization, Assimilation,' 24–5.

111 *Statutes of Canada*, 1951, 15 Geo. VI, c. 29.

112 Chamberlin, *The Harrowing of Eden*, 97.

113 Ibid.

7 The Influence of the Social Sciences: The Secular Understanding of the 'Other'

1 For a more complete discussion of this topic, see Hugh Shewell, '"What Makes the Indian Tick?" The Influence of Social Sciences on Canada's Indian Policy, 1947–1964,' *Histoire sociale/Social History* 34, no. 67 (May 2001): 134–67.

2 Frank G. Vallee, 'Social Science,' *The Canadian Encyclopedia*; Fleras and

Leonard Elliott, *The Nations Within*, 76–83; Frideres, *Native Peoples in Canada*, 230–59; Driben and Trudeau, *When Freedom Is Lost*, 33–7.

3 John J. Honigmann, 'The Logic of the James Bay Survey,' *Dalhousie Review* 30, no. 4 (1951): 378–9. In PAC, RG-10, Central Registry Series, Vol. 8618, File 1/1-15-1, Psychological and Sociological Studies of Indians, October 1947 to January 1964.

4 Ibid., 378–9, 381.

5 Ibid., 378.

6 Ibid., 378.

7 Peter Kulchyski, 'Anthropology in the Service of the State: Diamond Jenness and Canadian Indian Policy,' *Journal of Canadian Studies* 28, no. 2 (1993): 37–8.

8 Ibid.

9 NAC, RG-10, CR Series, Vol. 8618, File 1/1-15-1, Letter to Herbert Marshall, Dominion statistician, Dominion Bureau of Statistics, Ottawa, from Forrest E. LaViolette, McGill University, Montreal, 26 October 1947.

10 Ibid., Memorandum to Dr Hugh Keenleyside, Deputy Minister, Department of Mines and Resources, from R.A. Hoey, Director, Indian Affairs Branch, 15 December 1947.

11 Coates, *Best Left as Indians* Miller; *Skyscrapers Hide the Heavens*, 327–8; Morton, *A Short History of Canada*, 215–6; Phillips and Watson, 'From Mobilization to Continentalism,' 32–3, 38–43; David Wolfe, 'The Rise and Demise of the Keynesian Era in Canada: Economic Policy, 1930–1982' in *Modern Canada, 1930–1980s*, 60.

12 Legitimization of state policy, as argued in the previous chapter, was one of the principle objectives of the Joint Parliamentary Committee on the Indian Act.

13 NAC, RG-10, CR Series, Vol. 8618, File 1/1-15-1, Letter to Dr Hugh Keenleyside, Deputy Minister, Department of Mines and Resources, from C.J. Mackenzie, President, Canadian Social Science Research Council, 23 January 1948.

14 Ibid., Letter to Indian Affairs Branch, Department of Mines and Resources, from G. Swartman, Superintendent of Sioux Lookout Agency, 10 September 1948. In his letter Swartman referred to Moore's article in the *C.M.A. Journal* but gave no date. However, the second article, which had just appeared, was clearly an early report on the James Bay Survey initiated in 1947. See R.P. Vivian, MD, Charles McMillan, MD, E. Chant Robertson, MD, W.H. Sebrell, MD, F.F. Tisdall, MD, and W.G. McIntosh, DDS, 'The Nutrition and Health of the James Bay Indian,' *Canadian Medical Association Journal* 59 (1948): 505–18.

15 Ibid., Letter to G. Swartman from Dr L.C. Bartlett, quoted by Swartman in his letter to branch headquarters.
16 Ibid.
17 Canada, Indian and Northern Affairs Canada, Child and Family Services Task Force, *Indian Child and Family Services in Canada: Final Report* (Ottawa: 1987), 3–4; Patrick Johnston, *Native Children and the Child Welfare System* (Ottawa: Canadian Council on Social Development, 1983); Brian Wharf, *Toward First Nation Control of Child Welfare: A Review of Emerging Developments in B.C.* (Victoria: University of Victoria, 1987), 9–10.
18 NAC, RG-10, CR Series, Vol. 8616, File 1/1-15, Part 1, Anthropological Research, Correspondence to D.M. McKay, Director, Indian Affairs Branch, Department of Citizenship and Immigration, from F.J. Alcock, Chief Curator, National Museum of Canada, Ottawa, 21 November 1949.
19 Ibid., Letter to the Hon. Ross Macdonald, K.C., Speaker of the House of Commons, from Mrs R.A. Farmer, Brantford Local Council of Women, Brantford, Ontario, 17 May 1950.
20 Ibid., Letter to Mrs R.A. Farmer from F.J. Alcock, 23 May 1950.
21 See NAC, RG-10, CR Series, Vol. 8617, Parts 8 to 10 and Vol. 8618, File 1/1-15.
22 NAC, RG-10, CR Series, Vol. 8618, File 1/1-15-1, Memorandum to members of the Advisory Panel on Indian Research, from T.F. McIlwraith, University of Toronto, Department of Anthropology, n.d., but probably February 1951.
23 Ibid.
24 Ibid.
25 Ibid., Minutes of the Panel on Indian Research, 21 September 1951. 'Advisory' had been dropped from the panel's official title.
26 Ibid.
27 Ibid., Results of IQ Tests of Indians at the Caradoc Reserve, Ontario, conducted by D.J. Penfold under the direction of G.H. Turner, University of Western Ontario. Reported by N.W. Morton to the Panel on Indian Research, Ottawa, 14 October 1951.
28 Ibid.
29 NAC, RG-10, CR Series, Vol. 8616, File 1/1-15, Part 1, Letter and research proposal to Major S.D. MacKay, Director of Indian Affairs, from Dorothy Woodward, University of Toronto, 11 March 1952.
30 Ibid.
31 NAC, RG-10, CR Series, Vol. 8616, File 1/1-15, Part 3, Correspondence re: Citizenship Project with Indians, to Colonel E. Acland, Senior Administrative Officer, Indian Affairs Branch, from R.F. Davey, Acting Superintendent of Education, 4 March 1954.
32 Ibid., Memorandum to Colonel H.M. Jones, Director, Indian Affairs Branch, from J.P.B. Ostrander, Superintendent, Welfare Service, 3 March 1954.

33 Ibid., Letter to Col. Laval Fortier, Deputy Minister, Department of Citizenship and Immigration, from H.M. Jones, Director, Indian Affairs Branch, 1 April 1954.

34 NAC, RG-10, CR Series, Vol. 8618, File 1/1-15-1, 'Social Problems of the Ojibwa Indians in the Collins Area in Northwestern Ontario,' Received by the Department of Citizenship and Immigration, 12 May 1958; and Correspondence from Laval Fortier, Deputy Minister, Department of Citizenship and Immigration, to William Baldwin, 14 May 1958.

35 Ibid., Correspondence between Dr Frank Vallee, Citizenship Branch, and F.H. Tyler, J.H. Gordon, and Col. H.M. Jones, Indian Affairs Branch, 15, 27 March, 17, 23, and 24 April, 1957; and between Jones and R.F. Battle, Regional Supervisor of Indian Agencies, Alberta, 30 April, 9 May, and 5 September, 1957. Vallee went on to a distinguished academic career at Carleton University, Ottawa.

36 NAC, RG-10, CR Series, Vol. 8617, File 1/1-15, Part 8, Correspondence to Various Regional officials concerning the visit of Professor Lisabeth Welskopf-Henrich of East Berlin, German Democratic Republic, Summer 1963. Professor Welskopf-Henrich visited various Indian bands throughout the country collecting information for a chidren's book on Indian myths and legends. Officials were instructed not to discuss Indian policy with her for fear of adverse foreign publicity.

37 H.B. Hawthorn, C.S. Belshaw, and S.M. Jamieson, *The Indians of British Columbia* (Toronto: University of Toronto Press, 1958), cited in Weaver, *Making Canadian Indian Policy*, 21.

38 NAC, RG-10, CR Series, Vol. 8616, File 1/1-15, Part 3, Copy of correspondence to Dr H.B. Hawthorn, Museum of Anthropology, University of British Columbia, Vancouver, attached to a copy of his proposal for a survey of the social and economic situation of the Indians of British Columbia, from Jean Boucher, Assistant to the Deputy Minister, Department of Citizenship and Immigration, 30 March 1954.

39 Ibid. Explanatory correspondence in support of Dr Hawthorn's proposal to the Secretary, The Treasury Board, from Laval Fortier, Deputy Minister, Department of Citizenship and Immigration, 16 March 1954.

40 Ibid., Part 4, Research proposal of Professor W.J. Morris, Department of Anthropology, University of Toronto, appended to correspondence to Colonel H. M. Jones, Director, Indian Affairs Branch, from Morris, 30 November 1959.

41 John J. Honigmann, 'The Logic of the James Bay Survey,' 377, in NAC, RG-10, Vol. 8618, File 1/1-15-1.

42 Ibid., 378.

43 Ibid.

44 Ibid.
45 Ibid., 378–9.
46 Ibid., 379.
47 See Vivian et al., 'The Nutrition and Health of the James Bay Indian.'
48 Honigmann, 'The Logic of the James Bay Survey,' 379–80.
49 Ibid.
50 Ibid.
51 Ibid., 381.
52 Ibid., 382.
53 Ibid.
54 Ibid., 383.
55 Ibid., 384.
56 Ibid.
57 Ibid.
58 Ibid., 385.
59 Ibid.
60 Ibid.
61 Ibid., 385–6.
62 NAC, RG-10, CR Series, Vol. 8618, File 1/1-15-1, Memorandum to Colonel
    B.F. Neary, Superintendent of Education, Indian Affairs Branch, Depart-
    ment of Mines and Resources, from Major C.A.F. Clark, Educational Survey
    Officer, Welfare and Training Service, Ottawa, 14 September 1948.

8 The Emergence of Indian Welfare Bureaucracy, 1945–1960

1 Canada, Special Joint Committee, *Minutes of Proceedings and Evidence*, 30 May
   1946, 16.
2 Wolfe, 'The Rise and Demise of the Keynesian Era in Canada,' 51.
3 Canada, *Indian Social Welfare*, 72, 74.
4 Siggner, 'The Socio-Demographic Conditions of Registered Indians,' 71–2.
   Siggner says that a problem in determining Indian unemployment and
   labour force participation rates is that traditional subsistence occupations
   such as hunting and trapping are not defined as jobs. Frideres, *Aboriginal
   Peoples in Canada: Contemporary Conflicts*, 144.
5 Hawthorn, ed., *A Survey of the Contemporary Indians of Canada*, 317.
6 Special Joint Committee, *Minutes of Proceedings and Evidence*, 1947, 367, 369;
   cited in Hawthorn, ed., *A Survey of the Contemporary Indians*, 318.
7 Guest, *The Emergence of Social Security*, 117–20, 128–31, 134–7; Ronald Manzer,
   Public Policies and Political Development in Canada (Toronto: University of
   Toronto Press, 1985), 50, 62.

8 Hawthorn, *A Survey of the Contemporary Indians*, 318.

9 Internal report of the Indian Affairs Branch, title and author not named, 1947; quoted in Hawthorn, *A Survey of the Contemporary Indians*, 318.

10 Hawthorn, *A Survey of the Contemporary Indians*, 318.

11 Canada, Special Joint Committee, *Minutes of Proceedings and Evidence*, 30 May 1946, 16.

12 Guest, *The Emergence of Social Security*, 121–2; Prentice et al., *Canadian Women*, 262.

13 Canada, Special Joint Committee, *Minutes of Proceedings and Evidence*, 30 May 1946, 21–2.

14 Guest, *The Emergence of Social Security*, 122–3.

15 Canada, Department of Citizenship and Immigration, Indian Affairs Branch, *A Review of Activities, 1948–1958* (Ottawa: Queen's Printer, 1959), 12.

16 Canada, Department of Mines and Resources, Indian Affairs Branch, *Annual Report, 1948–1949*, 200.

17 C.N.C. Roberts, interview.

18 Canada, Department of Mines and Resources, Indian Affairs Branch, *Annual Report, 1948–1949*, 200.

19 Ibid., 189.

20 Ibid., 190–5.

21 Canada, *Welfare Programs for Indian People of Ontario*, 8; Guest, *The Emergence of Social Security*, 75–7.

22 Canada, *Welfare Programs for Indian People of Ontario*, 8; Guest, *The Emergence of Social Security*, 137.

23 Hawthorn, *A Survey of the Contemporary Indians*, 315.

24 Canada, *Welfare Programs for Indian People of Ontario*, 8–9; Guest, *The Emergence of Social Security*, 137–8.

25 Hawthorn, *A Survey of the Contemporary Indians*, 317.

26 Robert Bothwell, Ian Drummond, and John English, *Canada since 1945: Power, Politics, and Provincialism*, rev. ed. (Toronto: University of Toronto Press, 1989), 320–1, 324–5; Eugene Forsey, *A Life on the Fringe: The Memoirs of Eugene Forsey* (Toronto: Oxford University Press, 1991), 121; Granatstein, *The Ottawa Men*; C.N.C. Roberts, interview; Weaver, *Making Canadian Indian Policy*, 46. The highly formalized 'mandarin network' of running the civil service did not change substantially until first, civil servants won the right to unionize during the Pearson years, and second, Trudeau and Michael Pitfield embarked on changing the entire size and culture of the federal administration.

27 NAC, RG-10, CR Series, Vol. 7094, File 1/10-3-0, Relief Food Policy 1888–1963, 'Welfare and Relief Assistance for Indians,' and covering correspon-

dence to all Indian Superintendents, Regional Supervisors of Indian Agencies and the Indian Commissioner for British Columbia, from H.M. Jones, Superintendent, Welfare Service, Indian Affairs Branch, Department of Citizenship and Immigration, Ottawa, 4 March 1952.

28 NAC, RG-10, CR Series, Vol. 7094, File 1/10-3-0, 'Welfare And Relief Assistance,' General Policy, 1.

29 Ibid., Relief Food, 1.

30 Ibid., 2.

31 Dennis Guest, 'World War II and the Welfare State in Canada,' in *The 'Benevolent State,'* 214–15; Brigitte Kitchen, 'The Introduction of Family Allowances in Canada,' in *The 'Benevolent State,'* 237–8; Marsh, *Report on Social Security,* 196, 199–200; Moscovitch and Drover, 'Social Expenditures and the Welfare State,' 34–6.

32 NAC, RG-10, CR Series, Vol. 7094, File 1/10-3-0, 'Welfare and Relief Assistance,' Relief Food, 2.

33 Ibid., Authorities, 5.

34 Ibid., Relief Food, 1.

35 Ibid., Tubercular Indians, 3.

36 Hawthorn, ed., *A Survey of the Contemporary Indians,* 320.

37 NAC, RG-10, CR Series, Vol. 7094, File 1/10-3-0, 'Welfare and Relief Assistance,' 2.

38 Canada, Department of Indian Affairs and Northern Development, Indian and Inuit Affairs Program, 'Interpretation of the Legal Mandate and Responsibilities of Federal, Provincial, Municipal and Indian Band Governments for Social Services to Indian People with Special Reference to the Canada-Ontario Welfare Services Agreement of 1965,' Draft Document prepared by the Social Development Directorate, Ottawa-Hull, 24 July 1984, 4–7.

39 NAC, RG-10, CR Series, Vol. 7094, File 1/10-3-0, 'Welfare and Relief Assistance,' 1.

40 Dickason, *Canada's First Nations,* 329, 331; Donna Lea Hawley, *The Indian Act Annotated* 2nd ed. (Toronto: Carswell, 1986), 40–2; Tobias, 'Protection, Civilization, Assimilation,' 25.

41 Frideres, *Native Peoples in Canada,* 145.

42 NAC, RG-10, CR Series, Vol. 7094, File 1/10-3-0, Correspondence to Dr P.E. Moore, Director, Indian Health Services, Department of National Health and Welfare, Ottawa, from H.M. Jones, Director, Indian Affairs Branch, Department of Citizenship and Immigration, Ottawa, 5 January 1955.

43 Bothwell et al., *Canada since 1945,* 169–70.

44 NAC, RG-10, CR Series, Vol. 7094, File 1/10-3-0, Correspondence to Dr P.E. Moore from H.M. Jones, 5 January 1955.

45 Ibid.

46 Ibid., Correspondence to Moore from Jones, January 27, 1955.

47 Ibid.

48 For an excellent discussion of Inuit health and relief measures and the operation of the Department of Northern Affairs and National Resources during
this period, see Frank James Tester and Peter Kulchyski, *Tammarniit (Mistakes):
Inuit Relocation in the Eastern Arctic, 1939–1963* (Vancouver: UBC Press, 1994).

49 NAC, RG-10, CR Series, Vol. 7094, File 1/10-3-0, Minutes of the Meeting of
the Interdepartmental Committee on Relief and Tuberculosis Rehabilitation
Rations, Ottawa, 13 July 1956, Prepared by Mr R.J. Orange, Secretary.

50 Ibid.

51 Ibid., Letter to all Indian Superintendents, Regional Supervisors of Indian
Agencies and the Indian Commissioner for British Columbia, from H.M.
Jones, Director, Indian Affairs Branch, Ottawa, 7 August 1956.

52 For a discussion of the whole issue of the administration of Family Allowances to the Inuit, see Tester and Kulchyski, *Tammarniit*, 339–42.

53 NAC, RG-10, CR Series, Vol. 7094, File 1/10-3-0, Letter to All Superintendents, Regional Supervisors, and the Indian Commissioner for B.C., from
H.M. Jones, Director, Indian Affairs Branch, 3 December 1956.

54 NAC, RG-10, CR Series, Vol. 7094, File 1/10-3-0, Treasury Board Minute No.
508331, Letter to Colonel Laval Fortier, Deputy Minister, Department of
Citizenship and Immigration, from D.M. Watters, Secretary to the Treasury
Board, Ottawa, 20 December 1956.

55 Ibid.

56 Ibid., Relief Assistance By Agency Cheque, Policy document sent to the field
from H.M. Jones, Director, Indian Affairs Branch, 25 April 1957, 1.

57 Ibid.

58 Alison M. Jaggar and Paula Rothenberg Struhl, eds., *Feminist Frameworks:
Alternative Theoretical Accounts of the Relations between Men and Women*, 2nd ed.
(New York: McGraw-Hill, 1984), 71.

59 An example of the Welfare Division's attempts to foster gendered role divisions was the creation of the Indian Homemakers' Clubs, initiated before the
Second World War. C.N.C. Roberts described the postwar clubs as 'like the
Women's Auxiliary in the Anglican Church. They would sort of go around
and organize these things and help the women select someone they would
like as a leader.' C.N.C. Roberts, interview.

60 NAC, RG-10, CR Series, Vol. 7094, File 1/10-3-0, Relief Assistance By Agency
Cheque, 25 April 1957, 3.

61 Ibid., 1.

62 Ibid., 1–2.

63 Ibid., 3.

64 Ibid., Relief Administration – Dollar Value Orders, Document issued to agency and regional field administration by the Acting Director, Indian Affairs Branch, Ottawa, 29 July 1957.

65 Ibid., Minutes of a Meeting to Discuss Relief Rations for Indians Including Special Relief Rations for Indian Infants, Ottawa, 17 September 1958, Prepared by Dr John S. Willis, Indian and Northern Health Services, Department of National Health and Welfare, item 2 a., 2.

66 Ibid., Minutes of a Meeting to Discuss Relief Rations, 1.

67 C.N.C. Roberts, interview.

68 NAC, RG-10, CR Series, Vol. 7094, File 1/10-3-0, Memorandum to the Director, Indian Affairs Branch, from J.H. Gordon, Chief, Welfare Division, Discussion with Indian Health Services and the Nutrition Division Regarding Relief Administration, Ottawa, 18 September 1958, 1.

69 Ibid., and Minutes of Meeting to Discuss Relief Rations, 17 September 1958, 1–2.

70 Ibid., Minutes of a Meeting to Discuss Relief Rations, 2–3.

71 Ibid., Memorandum to Jones from Gordon, 1–2.

72 Ibid., 2.

73 Ibid., Minutes of a Meeting to Discuss Relief Rations, item 2, f., p.4.

74 Ibid., Memorandum to Jones from Gordon, 2.

75 Ibid., Minutes of a Meeting to Discuss Relief Rations, items 4 and 5, p. 4.

76 Ibid., Memorandum to Jones from Gordon, 2.

77 Ibid., 2.

78 Ibid., Minutes of a Meeting to Discuss Relief Rations, items 6 and 8, pp. 5–6.

79 Ibid., items 10–12, pp. 6–7.

80 NAC, RG-10, CR Series, Vol. 8590, File 1/1-10-14, Part 1, 'Liaison With the Canadian Welfare Council,' Memorandum to W. [i.e., J.P.B. Ostrander, Superintendent of Welfare Division], Re: Canadian Welfare Council, from S.J. Bailey, Rehabilitation Officer, 11 February 1955.

81 Ibid.

82 Ibid.

83 Ibid., *A Policy Statement on Unemployment Assistance*, Pamphlet prepared by the Canadian Welfare Council, Ottawa, 1953; and *A Public Assistance Program for the Employable Unemployed: A Recommendation for Action to Canadian Governments from the Canadian Welfare Council*, Ottawa, January 1955; Guest, *The Emergence of Social Security*, 128–30, 138–9; Wolfe, 'The Rise and Demise of the Keynesian Era,' 51.

84 NAC, RG-10, CR Series, Vol. 8590, File 1/1-10-14, Part 1, Letter to J.P.B.

Ostrander, Superintendent of Welfare, Department of Citizenship and Immigration, Indian Affairs Branch, from C.A. Patrick, Secretary, Public Welfare Division, Canadian Welfare Council, Ottawa, 10 February 1955.

85 Ibid.

86 Ibid., Letter to C.A. Patrick, Public Welfare Division, Canadian Welfare Council, from J.P.B. Ostrander, Ottawa, 16 February 1955.

87 NAC, RG-10, CR Series, Vol. 8590, File 1/1-10-14, Part 1, Memorandum to W. (Ostrander) from W.6, S.J. Bailey, 23 March 1955.

88 Ibid.

89 Ibid.

90 Ibid., Parts 1–3, 1954–62.

91 Ibid., Part 1, Memorandum to W. from W.6, S.J. Bailey, 23 March 1955.

92 Ibid., Memorandum to the Deputy Minister from H.M. Jones, 22 August 1955 with attached blurb on Branch welfare activities; 'Draft Memorandum Re Services for Indians Leaving Reserves' to J.P.B. Ostrander from Phyllis Burns, n.d. but about October 1955; Letter to Phyllis Burns from Ostrander, 8 November 1955; Part 2, 'Memorandum Re Services for Indians Leaving Reserves' with covering letter to Ostrander from Burns, 16 November 1955; Memorandum to Jones from Ostrander, 4 January 1956 with attached article by Stan Bailey, 'The Indian Affairs Branch Conducts an Interesting Experiment in Edmonton.'

93 Ibid, Draft memorandum re: 'Services for Indians Leaving Reserves' to J.B.P. Ostrander from Phyllis Burns, n.d. but about October, 1955; Ostrander to Burns, 8 November 1955; Part 2, Burns to Ostrander, 16 November 1955.

94 Ibid, Part 2, Canadian Welfare Council, *Annual Report of the Public Welfare Division, 1955*, prepared by the Chairman, Ottawa, 19 June 1956.

95 Ibid., Part 2, Memorandum to H.M. Jones from J. H. Gordon, A/Superintendent of Welfare, 13 September 1956.

96 Ibid., Part 3, Memorandum to Jones from Gordon, 6 May 1957.

97 Ibid., Questionnaire for a proposed conference, 'Certain Issues In Social Security,' prepared by the Canadian Welfare Council, 15 November 1957; and Letter to Eric I. Smit, Executive Secretary, Family and Child Welfare Division, Canadian Welfare Council, from H.M. Jones, 5 December 1957.

98 Ibid., Letter to Smit from Jones.

99 Ibid., Letter to R.E.G. Davis, Executive Director, Canadian Welfare Council, together with the article, 'Major Revision in Social Assistance for Indians,' from H.M. Jones, Director, Indian Affairs Branch, 7 April 1959.

100 Ibid., 1–3.

101 Ibid., Transcript of 'The Future – What Lies Ahead for Our Native People,' address probably prepared and delivered by A.G. Leslie, Regional Supervisor of Indian Agencies for Manitoba, n.d. but likely early 1959.
102 Ibid., 2.
103 Ibid., 2.
104 Ibid., 2–6.
105 Ibid., 6.
106 Ibid., Letter to Col. H.M. Jones, Director of Indian Affairs, from Norman F. Cragg, Executive Secretary, Public Welfare Division, Canadian Welfare Council, 22 April 1959.
107 Ibid., Confirmation of Meeting of the Public Welfare Division, National Committee, sent to Indian Affairs Branch, 10 September 1959.
108 Ibid., Letter to Norman F. Cragg, Public Welfare Division, Canadian Welfare Council, from J.H. Gordon, Chief, Welfare Division, Indian Affairs Branch, 1 November 1960; and extract from *Canadian Welfare* 36, no. 1 (1960): 126, and covering memorandum to Fur, from SPO, 4 August 1960.

9 The Indian in Transition: Social Welfare and Provincial Services, 1959–1965

1 Canada, Indian Affairs Branch, *A Review of Activities, 1948–1958*, 2–5.
2 Ibid., 1–3.
3 Ibid., 12.
4 Ibid., 12–13; and Canada, Department of Citizenship and Immigration, Indian Affairs Branch, *Annual Report, 1957–1958*, 54–5.
5 Canada, *A Review of Activities*, 13–16. A good discussion of this and similar programs is found in Jessa Chupik-Hall, '"Good Families Do Not Just Happen": Indigenous People and Child Welfare Services in Canada, 1950–1965,' MA thesis, Trent University, 2001, 53–5.
6 Ibid., 14.
7 Canada, Indian Affairs Branch, *Annual Report, 1957–1958*, 56; NAC, RG-10, CR Series, Vol. 6924, File 1/29-1, Correspondence and Reports Regarding the Welfare Services Offered to Indians, Part 5, Memorandum to George F. Davidson, Deputy Minister, Department of Citizenship and Immigration, from H.M. Jones, 30 November 1960.
8 Leo Panitch, 'The Role and Nature of the Canadian state,' in *The Canadian State*, 5–9.
9 Canada, Indian Affairs Branch, *Annual Report, 1957–1958*, 56.
10 Canada, Indian Affairs Branch, *A Review of Activities*, 15.
11 David Reisman, *Richard Titmuss: Welfare and Society* (London: Heinemann Educational Books, 1977), 9–42.

12 NAC, RG-10, CR Series, Vol. 7094, File 1/10-3-0, Circular No. 97 to the
   Indian Commissioner for B.C., Regional Supervisors, Superintendents of
   Indian Agencies, Re: Relief Administration, Dollar Value Orders and Agency
   Cheque, with accompanying chapter 13.01 for the Indian Affairs Branch
   Field Manual, from H.M. Jones, Director, Ottawa, 27 February 1959.
13 Ibid., Chapter 13.01, 'Relief Administration by Dollar Value Orders and
   Agency Cheque,' 1.
14 Ibid.
15 Ibid., 7.
16 Ibid., 8.
17 Ibid.
18 Ibid., 6–7. The term *overage* is common in social assistance language and
   refers to amounts approved in excess of the regulated rate or allowance.
19 Ibid., 2.
20 Ibid., 1–2.
21 NAC, RG-10, Vol. 8590, File 1/1-10-14, Part 3, Correspondence to F. [*sic*]
   Cragg, Executive Secretary, Public Welfare Division, Canadian Welfare Council, from J.H. Gordon, Chief, Welfare Division, Indian Affairs Branch, 5 May
   1961.
22 NAC, RG-10, CR Series, Vol. 7094, File 1/10-3-0, Circular No. 97, Chapter
   13.01, Indian Affairs Branch *Field Manual*, 4–6, 8–9.
23 Ibid., 1.
24 Department of Indian Affairs and Northern Development, 'Interpretation
   of the Legal Mandate,' 17, 22–4. Ontario, Department of Public Welfare,
   Annual Report of the Department of Public Welfare, 1956/1957 (Toronto:
   Queen's Printer, 1957); and *Annual Report of the Department of Public Welfare
   1958/1959*, 6.
25 NAC, RG-10, Vol. 6923, File 1/29-1, Part 4. Letter from Laval M. Fortier,
   Deputy Minister, Citizenship and Immigration, to Dr G.F. Davidson, Deputy
   Minister of Welfare, Department of Health and Welfare, 24 February 1959.
26 Ibid., Memorandum to Laval Fortier, Deputy Minister, Department of
   Citizenship and Immigration, from H.M. Jones, Director, Indian Affairs
   Branch, 24 February 1959.
27 Ibid.
28 Ibid., Letter to Dr G.F. Davidson, Deputy Minister of Welfare, Department
   of National Health and Welfare, from Laval Fortier, Deputy Minister of
   Citizenship and Immigration, 24 February 1959.
29 Ibid., Correspondence to H.M. Jones, Re: General Welfare Assistance Act
   (Ontario, 1958) and its application to Indian bands, from J.H. Gordon,
   Chief, Welfare Division, 13 November 1959.

30 Ibid., Correspondence to M.S. Payne, Supervisor of Social Workers, Indian Affairs Branch, from W.W. Struthers, Deputy Commissioner, Direct Relief and Social Service Department, City of Ottawa, 6 April 1959; and, Memorandum to Fortier from Jones, 16 April 1959.

31 Ibid., Memorandum Re: Sharing of Relief Costs By the Provinces For Indians, to Laval Fortier, Deputy Minister, from Colonel H.M. Jones, Director, Indian Affairs Branch, 16 April 1959.

32 Ibid.

33 Ibid., Correspondence to H.M. Jones from J.H. Gordon, 13 November 1959.

34 Ibid., Memorandum to Cabinet from the Hon. Ellen Fairclough, Minister of Citizenship and Immigration, Re: Application and Extension of Provincial Welfare Services to Indians, Ottawa, 10 August 1959.

35 NAC, RG-10, CR Series, Vol. 6923, File 1/29-1, Part 4, Memorandum to Cabinet, 10 August 1959.

36 Ibid.

37 NAC, RG-10, Vol. 6923, File 1/29-1, Part 4, Memorandum to Cabinet, 10 August 1959.

38 Dickason, *Canada's First Nations*, 333–8.

39 NAC, RG-10, Vol. 8616, File 1/1-15, Part 5, Memorandum Re: Enfranchisement to Senior Administrative Officer, Reserves and Trusts, from L.L. Brown, Special Assistant, Reserves and Trusts, Indian Affairs Branch, Department of Citizenship and Immigration, Ottawa, 7 January 1958 [*sic*].

40 Canada, Indian Affairs Branch, *Annual Report, 1959–1960* (Ottawa: Queen's Printer, 1960), 52.

41 NAC, RG-10, Vol. 6923, File 1/29-1, Part 4. Correspondence to Jones from Gordon, 5 January 1960.

42 Ibid. Section 68 (1) is now 69 (1) of the Indian Act amended to 1985.

43 Ibid., Memorandum to Cabinet, 10 August 1959.

44 See Weaver, *Making Canadian Indian Policy*.

45 NAC, RG-10, Vol. 6924, File 1/29-1, Part 5, Clipping from the *Montreal Gazette* datelined Ottawa, 9 April 1960; and Part 6, Memorandum from Jones to the Deputy Minister, Re: Extension of Provincial Welfare Services to Indians, 19 January 1961.

46 Richard Daniel, *A History of Native Claims Processes in Canada, 1867–1979* (Ottawa: Department of Indian and Northern Affairs, 1980), 136, cited in Rob Cunningham, 'Community Development at the Department of Indian Affairs in the 1960s: Much Ado about Nothing,' (MA thesis, University of Saskatchewan, 1997), 44–5; Weaver, *Making Canadian Indian Policy*, 37, 44.

47 Interview with Dr George F. Davidson, Vancouver, BC, 12 December 1992.

48 Ibid.; and Canada, Twenty-Fourth Parliament, Second Session, Joint Committee of the Senate and the House of Commons on Indian Affairs, *Minutes of Proceedings and Evidence* (Ottawa: Queen's Printer, 1959); and, Third Session, Joint Committee of the Senate and House of Commons on Indian Affairs, *Minutes of Proceedings and Evidence* (Ottawa: Queen's Printer, 1960); and, Fourth Session, Joint Committee of the Senate and the House of Commons on Indian Affairs, *Minutes of Proceedings and Evidence* (Ottawa: Queen's Printer, 1961).

49 NAC, RG-10, CR Series, Vol. 6924, File 1/29-1, Part 5. Memorandum to George F. Davidson, Deputy Minister, Department of Citizenship and Immigration, from Colonel H.M. Jones, Re: Changing Economic Conditions and the Programs of the Indian Affairs Branch, 30 November 1960.

50 Ibid., Memorandum to Davidson from Jones, 30 November 1964.

51 Dr George F. Davidson, interview.

52 See Dyck, *What Is the Indian 'Problem'*; James B. Waldram, 'Canada's "Indian Problem" and the Indian's "Canada Problem,"' in Les Samuelson, ed., *Power and Resistance: Critical Thinking about Canadian Social Issues* (Halifax: Fernwood Publishing, 1994), 61–2. Prior to the Second World War the phrases 'the Indian problem' and 'the Indian question' were used somewhat interchangeably. After the war 'the Indian problem' was the more common usage and seemed to reflect a more secular, social scientific approach to Indian policy.

53 NAC, RG-10, Vol. 6924, File 1/29-1, Part 5. Memorandum to Davidson from Jones, 30 November 1960.

54 Ibid.

55 Ibid.

56 Canada, Indian Affairs Branch, *Annual Report, 1959–1960*, 52.

57 NAC, RG-10, Vol. 6924, File 1/29-1, Part 5, Memorandum to Davidson from Jones, 30 November 1960.

58 Ibid. Canadian Association for Adult Education, *Social Security Leads to Dependency?* Pamphlet No. 14, March 1960, placed on file, 20 June 1960.

59 Ibid., *Social Security Leads to Dependency?*

60 Ibid. Part 6. Memorandum to the Deputy Minister, G.F. Davidson, Re: Extension of Provincial Welfare Services to Indians, from Jones, 19 January 1961.

61 Ibid.

62 Ibid. By special legislation Jones meant that the federal government would enact legislation with respect to Indian social assistance and child welfare. Some Indian organizations today would prefer this alternative or to be given outright their own jurisdiction over social assistance and child welfare.

Special federal legislation would have affirmed federal responsibility – something the federal government was (and is) not prepared to acknowledge.

63 Canada, Joint Committee of the Senate and the House of Commons on Indian Affairs, *Minutes of Proceedings and Evidence*, No. 3, 12 May 1960, 247.

64 NAC, RG-10, Vol. 6924, File 1/29-1, Part 6, Memorandum to Davidson from Jones, 19 January 1961.

65 Ibid.

66 Ibid.

67 Canada, Joint Committee of the Senate and the House of Commons on Indian Affairs, *Minutes of Proceedings and Evidence*, No. 8, 2 May 1961, 278–9.

68 Ibid., 353.

69 Ibid., No. 10, 353–4.

70 Ibid., 354–5.

71 Ibid., 355.

72 Ibid., 355.

73 Ibid., 356.

74 Ibid., No. 16, 605.

75 Ibid., 612.

76 NAC, RG-10, CR Series, Vol. 8591, File 1/1-10-18, Liaison With the National Commission on the Indian Canadian, Copy of Letter to Indian Band Councils from Mrs W.H. Clark, Chairman, and John Melling, Executive Director, National Commission on the Indian Canadian of the Canadian Association for Adult Education, Toronto, Ontario, June 1959; and Memorandum to Jones from Gordon Re: NCIC Meeting, 30 October 1959, with attached meeting document, Appendix D.

77 NAC, RG-10, CR Series, Vol. 8584, File 1/1-2-16, Part 7, Examination of the Indian Act by a Joint Committee of the Senate and the House of Commons, 1959–61, Brief from Chief Pelletier, Fort William Band, Ontario sent to Indian Affairs, 28 May 1961; and Letter to Pelletier from Jones, 13 June 1961.

78 Ibid., Copy of letter to Mr Hubert Badanai, MP, Fort William, Ontario, from Chief Theodore Simon, Sheshegwaning Band, Manitoulin Island, Ontario, 22 June 1961.

79 Canada, Special Joint Committee on Indian Affairs, *Minutes of Proceedings and Evidence*, Appendix 'F5,' Submission to Mr E.W. Innes, Committee Clerk, Joint Parliamentary Committee on Indian Affairs, Ottawa, from Chief Edmund Francis and Councillors, Raymond Narvey, Basil Joe, Burnt Church Band, Burnt Church, NB, 15 November 1959, 434.

80 Ibid., Appendix 'F6,' Submission to E.W. Innes, Committee Clerk, from Chief John Sacobie, Oromocto Band, Oromocto, NB, 3 November 1959, 435.

81 Ibid., Appendix 'F2,' Submission to E.W. Innes, Committee Clerk, from Chief John [name illegible from copy], 23 December 1959, 430.

82 Ibid., Appendix 'F4,' Submission to E.W. Innes, Committee Clerk, from Chief Frank Bernard, Middle River Reserve, Baddeck, NS, 23 December 1959, 433.

83 Ibid., testimony of Dr Peter Kelly, 2 July 1959, 141.

84 Ibid.

85 Anil Seal, *The Emergence of Indian Nationalism: Competition and Collaboration in the Later Nineteenth Century* (Cambridge: Cambridge University Press, 1968), cited in Robin Moore, *Paul Scott's Raj*, 166.

86 NAC, Sound and Film Division, Ottawa, CBC Toronto Kine Collection, *Close-Up*, Canadian Broadcasting Corporation, #1360 T/C, 'The One in a Hundred,' Host, J. Frank Willis, 29 November 1960.

87 Ibid.

88 Ibid.

89 Ibid. Shortly after, in 1961, Meadmore became involved in the establishment of the National Indian Council. See Miller, *Skyscrapers Hide the Heavens*, 330.

90 Ibid.

91 Ibid.

92 Ibid., From interviews with Fraser Earle (organization not known) and the Rev. Ian Harvey of the United Church. Each man was identifying common Canadian stereotypes of the Indian.

93 NAC, RG-10, CR Series, Vol. 8584, File 1/1-2-16, Part 8, Letter to the Prime Minister, John G. Diefenbaker, from Senator James Gladstone, Ottawa, 15 May 1962.

94 Ibid., Minutes of the Gleichen [Blackfoot] Band Council Meeting held at Crowfoot Community Hall, Thursday, 26 April 1962, copy sent to Prime Minister John Diefenbaker from Chief C. McHugh, Gleichen, Alberta, n.d.

95 Ibid., Letter to the Hon. R.A. Bell, Minister of Citizenship and Immigration, with attached correspondence to Members of Parliament, Senators and other Canadians, 18 January 1962, from Hugh Dempsey, Honorary Secretary, Indian Association of Alberta, 12 October 1962.

96 Ibid., Report of Chief Joseph Dreaver, Sr, to the Indian Affairs Branch, 6 December 1962.

97 Ibid., Letter to the Executive Assistant to the Minister of Citizenship and Immigration, Re: The Dreaver Report, from L.L. Brown, Chief, Agencies Division, Indian Affairs Branch, 3 January 1963.

98 NAC, Sound and Film Division, *Close-Up*, 'The One in a Hundred,' 29 November 1960.

99 NAC, RG-10, Vol. 6924, File 1/29-1, Part 7, Letter prepared for signature of

G.F. Davidson, Deputy Minister, Department of Citizenship and Immigration, to Joe Willard, Deputy Minister of Welfare, Department of National Health and Welfare, 7 June 1962.

100 Ibid., Part 6. Correspondence from Jones to all Regional Supervisors and the A/Indian Commissioner, British Columbia, 13 March 1961; and, Vol. 6925, Part 9. Roberts to Rudnicki, 28 October 1963.

101 Ibid., Part 7. Memorandum from J.H. Gordon, Chief, Welfare Division to the Regional Supervisor, Quebec Region, 27 February 1962.

102 Ibid.

103 Ibid., Correspondence from W.J. Brennan, Acting Regional Supervisor, Saskatchewan Region, to J.H. Gordon, 15 March 1962.

104 Ibid., Correspondence from C.R. Latham, Regional Welfare Supervisor, Saskatchewan Region to W.J. Brennan, 9 March 1962. Correspondence appended to Brennan's letter to Gordon. See previous note.

105 Ibid.

106 This was in keeping with the Saskatchewan Indians' acceptance of the joint committee's recommendation to integrate Indians into the provincial welfare system. See NAC, RG-10, CR Series, Vol. 8584, File 1/1-2-16, Part 8, Report of Chief Joseph Dreaver Sr to the Indian Affairs Branch, 6 December 1962.

107 NAC, RG-10, Vol. 6924, File 1/29-1, Part 7, Latham to Brennan, 9 March 1962.

108 Ibid.

109 Ibid.

110 Ibid.

111 Ibid.

112 Ibid.

113 Ibid., Part 8, Quarterly Report of the Superintendent of the Crooked Lake Indian Agency, Extract: Welfare, 12 July 1962.

114 Ibid., Part 6, Departmental Survey of all Regional Offices Re: Administration of Direct Welfare Assistance, prepared by C.N.C. Roberts, Welfare Division, Ottawa, 8 November 1961.

115 Ibid., Part 8, Correspondence from F.B. McKinnon, Regional Supervisor, Maritime Region, re: Departmental Survey of Administration of Direct Welfare Assistance, 8 November 1961, to Branch headquarters, 10 September 1962.

116 Ibid., C.N.C. Roberts to R.D. Ragan, Acting Chief, Welfare Division, 18 October 1962.

117 Sally M. Weaver, *Making Canadian Indian Policy*, 20.

118 Ibid., 20–1. Hawthorn had already conducted a study of the Indians of

British Columbia during the 1950s. That study had drawn much praise from the Indian Affairs branch and it welcomed this second initiative. See H.B. Hawthorn, C.S. Belshaw, and S.M. Jamieson, *The Indians of British Columbia: A Study of Contemporary Social Adjustment* (Toronto: University of Toronto Press, 1958).

119 Bothwell et al., *Canada since 1945*, 222–8, 238–40; McNaught, *The Penguin History of Canada*, 302; Morton, *A Short History*, 222–33.

120 John English, 'Favreau, Guy,' *The Canadian Encyclopaedia*; Tom Kent, *A Public Purpose* (Montreal: McGill-Queen's University Press, 1988), 238; author's interview with Claude M. Isbister, Toronto, Ontario, 29 April 1993.

121 Author's interview with Walter Rudnicki, former chief, Welfare (Social Programs) Division, Indian Affairs Branch, Ottawa, 10 May 1993.

122 Weaver, *Making Canadian Indian Policy*, 28.

123 For a fuller treatment of the community development initiative, see Hugh Shewell, '"Bitterness behind Every Smiling Face": Community Development and Canada's First Nations, 1954–1968,' *Canadian Historical Review*, 83, no. 1 (2002): 58–84.

124 C.M. Isbister, interview.

125 Walter Rudnicki, interview. Valentine, an anthropologist, is now a professor at Carleton University in Ottawa.

126 C.M. Isbister, interview.

127 Canada, Department of Citizenship and Immigration, Indian Affairs Branch, *Annual Report, 1959–1960*, 52. See also Jessa Chupik-Hall, 'Good Families Do Not Just Happen,' 53–5.

128 Canada, Department of Citizenship and Immigration, Indian Affairs Branch, *Annual Report, 1959–1960*, 52.

129 Canada, Department of Citizenship and Immigration, Indian Affairs Branch, *The Indian>in<Transition: The Indian Today* (Ottawa: Queen's Printer, 1962), 5–7.

130 NAC, RG-10, CR Series, Vol. 6924, File 1/29-1, Part 7, 'A Study on Friendship Centres,' prepared by Alex Sim, Citizenship Branch, for both the Citizenship and Indian Affairs Branches of the Department of Citizenship and Immigration, Ottawa, 17 May 1962.

131 Canada, *The Indian>in<Transition*, 12.

132 Ibid., 21.

133 Ibid., 22–3.

134 Ibid., 25.

135 Ibid., 24.

136 Ibid., 24.

137 NAC, RG-10, CR Series, Vol. 6923, File 1/29-1, Part 4, 'On Human Relation-

ships,' by D.A. Green, paper presented to a conference of Welfare Superintendents, Indian Affairs Branch, n.d., but early 1959.

138 Ibid., Circular No. 111, to all Indian Affairs Branch staff, from H.M. Jones, 8 April 1959.

139 Ibid., Correspondence to D.A. Green from Jones, 9 July 1959.

140 NAC, RG-10, CR Series, Vol. 8591, File 1/1-10-18, Part 1, *Bulletin*, National Commission of the Indian Canadian, n.d., about February 1957.

141 Ibid., Parts 1, 2, 4.

142 Ibid., Part 4, Letter to Mrs Harold W. Clark, President, Indian-Eskimo Association of Canada, from George F. Davidson, Deputy Minister, Department of Citizenship and Immigration, 25 October 1960.

143 Ibid., Part 1, correspondence on file.

144 Ibid., Part 2, various correspondence; letter to Jones from Mrs W.H. Clark, Chairman, National Commission on the Indian Canadian, Toronto, 28 April 1958; Memorandum to J.H. Gordon from D.L. Jackson, 22 May 1958; Canada, Department of Citizenship and Immigration, Citizenship Branch, *Citizenship Projects among Indians* (Ottawa: Roger Duhamel, Queen's Printer, 1965), 4.

145 Ibid., Part 3, National Commission on the Indian Canadian, Unofficial Brief to the Human Rights Anniversary Committee for Canada, Prepared by John Melling, 10 January 1959.

146 Canada, Citizenship Branch, *Citizenship Projects among Indians*, 4.

147 NAC, RG-10, CR Series, Vol. 8591, File 1/1-10-18, Part 5, 'Attacks Lack of Equality,' Clipping from the *Globe and Mail*, 17 October 1961.

148 Ibid., Letter to Jones from Melling, Toronto, 23 October 1961.

149 Ibid., Letter to F.G. Robertson from John Melling, 23 October 1961.

150 It is likely that flooding in Ottawa destroyed some of the files dealing with the relationship with the IEA. The Citizenship Branch maintained an active relationship with the IEA and, in 1965, assisted in the publication of a book-let on its activities with native peoples.

151 Walter Rudnicki, 'The Big Picture,' Indian Affairs Branch Statement for Federal-Provincial Conference on Poverty, November 1965, cited in Weaver, *Making Canadian Indian Policy*, Table 4, 'Statistical profile of Indian poverty 1963.' and accompanying comments, 26–7.

152 NAC, RG-10, CR Series, Vol. 6924 and Vol. 6925, File 1/29-1, Parts 5 and 9, Memorandum to Davidson from Jones, 30 November 1960; and C.N.C. Roberts, document to file, Consolidation Sheet, 10 June 1963.

153 Walter Rudnicki, 'The Big Picture,' in Weaver, *Making Canadian Indian Policy*, and related comments, 26.

154 Walter Rudnicki, interview.

155 NAC, RG-10, CR Series, Vol. 8194, File 1/29-6, Part 3, Memorandum to Cabinet, 'Community Development, Indian Affairs Branch,' February 1964, with covering memorandum to the Deputy Minister, C.M. Isbister from R.F. Battle, Director, Indian Affairs Branch, Ottawa, n.d., presumably February 1964, items 2 and 3; and, Manitoba, Department of Welfare, *Annual Report 1963–64, Community Development Services,* copy to file, 26 May 1965, 10.

156 Ibid., Vol. 8194, File 1/29-6, Part 3, Memorandum to Cabinet, 'Community Development, Indian Affairs Branch,' item 4.

157 Ibid., item 5.

158 Rudnicki interview. Rudnicki was referring to the 1985 Sechelt Indian Band Self Government Act that conferred the equivalent of municipal status on the band.

159 NAC, RG-10, Vol. 8194, File 1/29-6, Part 3, Memorandum to Cabinet, 'Community Development,' item 7.

160 Ibid., items 8 and 9. Rudnicki and Jerry Gambill, interview, Ottawa, 10 May 1993. Gambill was a former community development officer. See also, Hawthorn, *A Survey of the Contemporary Indians,* in particular volume I and the discussion of legal, constitutional, and provincial issues.

161 R.B. Splane, former Assistant Deputy of Welfare, Department of National Health and Welfare, copy of personal correspondence from Splanc to Ms Joyce Timson, 11 January 1989.

162 NAC, RG-10, CR Series, Vol. 8194, File 1/29-6, Memorandum to Cabinet, 'Community Development,' item 9 (c).

163 Ibid., Vol. 8193, File 1/29-6, Part 1, Correspondence to Dr T.R. Batten, University of London Institute of Education, from Rudnicki, 29 January 1964.

164 Ibid., Minutes of Community Development Committee, Liaison meeting, Re: NFB Community Development Film Script, 25 March 1964, and attached film outline, *Community Development for Citizenship and Immigration* by Jack Ofield, 10 March 1964.

165 Ibid., Vol. 8194, File 1/29-6, Part 3, Details of Request to the Honourable the Treasury Board, 12 January 1965. NAC, RG-10, Vol. 6925, File 1/29-1, Part 10, Details of Request to the Honourable the Treasury Board, 16 June 1964; Weaver, *Making Canadian Indian Policy,* 27, footnote 15.

166 Ibid., Vol. 8193, File 1/29-6, Part 1, Letter to R.G. McNeill, Chairman, Civil Service Commission, from C.M. Isbister, 1 June 1964; Vol. 8194, File 1/29-6, Part 2, Letter to Rudnicki from Charles E. 'Chick' Hendry, Director, School of Social Work, University of Toronto, 16 October 1964; Part 3, Circular No. 117 to Indian Commissioner for B.C., Regional Supervisors, Re: Introduction of Community Development Program, from R.F. Battle, Assistant Dep-

uty Minister (Indian Affairs), 8 January 1965; Letter to Rudnicki from
Hendry, 19 March 1965; Walter Rudnicki, interview.

167 Ibid., Report on Grants to Band Councils, 1 April 1965.

168 Ibid., Letters to C.M. Isbister from C.J. Mackenzie, Assistant Secretary to the
Treasury Board, 18 and 19 January 1965; Treasury Board Minute No.
635419, 19 January 1965; and Treasury Board Minute No. 635420, 4 February 1965.

169 Rudnicki, interview. Also, see Cunningham, 'Community Development at
the Department of Indian Affairs,' 63–7; George Manuel and Michael
Posluns, *The Fourth World: An Indian Reality* (Don Mills, ON: Collier-
Macmillan, 1974), 130–3; Peter McFarlane, *Brotherhood to Nationhood: George
Manuel and the Making of the Modern Indian Movement* (Toronto: Between the
Lines, 1993); Brian Thorne, *Carl Rogers* (London: Sage, 1992). According to
Thorne, Rogers (1902–87) is considered the founder of a humanist, 'per-
son-centred' approach to psychotherapy in which the individual's sense of
trust is deepened once her or his 'subjective experience is respected and
progressively understood.' Rogerian techniques were incorporated into
encounter groups for training the community development officers.

170 NAC, RG-10, Vol. 6925, File 1/29-1, Part 9. Memorandum to Rudnicki from
Roberts, 16 December 1963.

171 Ibid., Memorandum to Roberts from Rudnicki, 17 December 1963.

172 NAC, RG-10, Vol. 6925, File 1/29-1, Part 9, Roberts, draft document to file,
request to Treasury Board for Adoption of provincial or local municipal
welfare rates and regulations for Indians, no date, but logically after 17
December 1963.

173 Ibid.

174 Ibid.

175 Ibid., Memorandum to Roberts from Rudnicki, 31 December 1963.

176 Ibid., Correspondence to C.M. Isbister, Deputy Minister, Department of
Citizenship and Immigration, from E.R. Rickinson, Deputy Minister,
Department of Social Welfare, Victoria, British Columbia, 27 January 1964.

177 Ibid., Rudnicki to R.F. Battle, Director, Indian Affairs Branch, 12 February
1964.

178 Ibid., Claude M. Isbister to E.R. Rickinson, 20 February 1964.

179 Ibid., Unsigned, handwritten memo to file, no date.

180 Ibid., Memorandum to the Director of Indian Affairs from the office of the
Deputy Minister, Citizenship and Immigration, 21 February 1964.

181 Ibid., Copy of statement prepared for the Hon. Rene Tremblay, Minister of
Citizenship and Immigration, and read to the House of Commons in reply
to the question of Mr Eldon Wooliams, MP, 26 February 1964.

182 Ibid., Memorandum to Battle from Rudnicki, 28 February 1964.

183 Ibid., Memorandum Re: Scale of Welfare Assistance, to Isbister from Battle, 28 February 1964.

184 Ibid., Memorandum to C.M. Isbister, Deputy Minister, from R.F. Battle, 16 April 1964.

185 Ibid., Part 10. Copy of Submission to Treasury Board requesting authority to 'reimburse Indian Bands which pay relief from Band Funds to the extent of 50% of such expenditures,' 25 May 1964.

186 Ibid., Part 9. Memorandum to Isbister from Battle, 16 April 1964.

187 Ibid., Part 10, Notation to file of submission to Treasury Board, 16 June 1964.

188 Ibid., Memorandum to all Regional Supervisors, Superintendents of Indian Agencies and the Indian Commissioner for B.C., from R.F. Battle, 8 July 1964.

189 Ibid., Roberts to Rudnicki, 20 July 1964.

190 Ibid., Memorandum to R.D. Ragan, from C.N.C. Roberts, 10 April 1964.

191 Ibid., Circular No. 107 to the Indian Commissioner for B.C. and Regional Supervisors, from R.F. Battle, Director, Indian Affairs Branch, Ottawa, 20 July 1964.

192 NAC, RG-10, CR Series, Vol. 6933, File 901/29-1, Part 3, Correspondence to Walter Rudnicki, Chief, Social Programs Division, from J.V. Boys, Indian Commissioner for B.C., 15 September and 16 December 1964.

193 'Indian Bands Will Get Choice of Federal, Provincial Welfare,' *Globe and Mail*, 31 October 1964; *Ottawa Citizen*, 30 October 1964.

194 Ontario, *Transitions: Report of the Social Assistance Review Committee*, Prepared for the Ministry of Community and Social Services (Toronto: Queen's Printer for Ontario, 1988), 438–9; and *First Nations Project Team Report*, 13–20; Splane to Timson, 11 January 1989.

195 C.M. Isbister, interview.

196 Ibid.

197 C.N.C. Roberts, interview.

198 Hawthorn later commented on this fact in his discussion of provincial issues affecting native peoples. Nevertheless, he believed that Indians ought to be induced to demand provincial services. Hawthorn, *A Survey of the Contemporary Indians*, 1: 338–9.

199 'Quebec Iroquois Fear Transfer to Old Enemy,' *Globe and Mail*, 31 October 1964.

200 Canada, Department of Indian Affairs and Northern Development, 'Indian Social Services Within a Self-Government Framework: Issues to Consider,' Paper prepared by Margaret Kovach for Policy Directorate, Self-Govern-

ment Sector, Ottawa, October 1990, 6; Shewell and Spagnut, 'The First Nations of Canada,' 5–6, 38.

201 Shewell and Spagnut, 'The First Nations of Canada,' 6.

202 For a fuller discussion of the uproar caused by and the outcomes of the community development program, see Cunningham, 'Community Development at the Department of Indian Affairs,' 73–5; Manuel and Posluns, *The Fourth World*; McFarlane, *Brotherhood to Nationhood*; Weaver, *Making Canadian Indian Policy.*

203 Buckley, *From Wooden Ploughs to Welfare*, 102–3.

204 Jerry Gambill and Walter Rudnicki, interview; Weaver, *Making Canadian Indian Policy*, 29.

10 Shooting an Elephant in Canada

1 Trigger, 'The Historians' Indian,' 38.

2 Edward W. Said, in conversation with David Barsamian, *The Pen and the Sword* (Toronto: Between the Lines, 1994), 67–8.

3 See Robert K. Merton, *Social Theory and Social Structure* (New York: Free Press, 1957). Essentially, by 'manifest' function Merton meant 'intended result,' whereas latent function meant the opposite.

4 Canada, *Report of the Auditor General of Canada to the House of Commons*, Volume 14, ch. 23, Assistant Auditor General, Don Young, Responsible Auditor, Nancy Cheng (Ottawa: Minister of Supply and Services, 1994), 5, 12–13.

5 Ibid., 12–14; Frank Cassidy, 'Approaches to Welfare Reform in Indian Communities,' in Frank Cassidy and Shirley B. Seward, ed., *Alternatives to Social Assistance*; Shewell and Spagnut, 'The First Nations of Canada,' 6–8.

6 Ontario, *Annual Report of the Department of Public Welfare, 1956/1957*; James Struthers, *The Limits of Affluence: Welfare in Ontario, 1920–1970* (Toronto: University of Toronto Press, 1994), 227.

7 Department of Indian Affairs and Northern Development, 'Interpretation of the Legal Mandate,' 25; Ontario, *Annual Report of the Department of Public Welfare, 1958/1959.*

8 Cassidy, 'Approaches to Welfare Reform,' 9.

9 Macpherson, 'Problems of Human Rights in the Late Twentieth Century,' 33.

10 Lise Noël, *Intolerance: A General Survey*, trans. Arnold Bennett (Montreal: McGill-Queen's University Press, 1994), 109–10.

11 Ibid., 125.

12 Ibid., 129.

13 Ibid., 147–8.
14 Ibid.
15 Ibid., 150, 151.
16 George Orwell, 'Shooting an Elephant.' The essay first appeared in *New Writing*, no. 2 (Autumn 1936).
17 Mel Watkins, 'Noughts and Crosses: The Games Whites Play,' in *Madness and Ruin: Politics and the Economy in the Neoconservative Age* (Toronto: Between the Lines, 1992), 133.
18 Macpherson, 'Problems of Human Rights,' 22–3.
19 Ibid., 23.
20 Ibid.
21 Alan C. Cairns, *Citizens Plus: Aboriginal Peoples and the Canadian State* (Vancouver: UBC Press, 2000). See especially chapter 5, 161–213.
22 Taiaiake Alfred, *Peace, Power, Righteousness: An Indigenous Manifesto* (Don Mills, ON: Oxford University Press, 1999), 137.
23 Orwell, 'Shooting an Elephant,' 271.

Bibliography

Primary Sources

National Archives of Canada

1. Record Group No. 10, 'Indian Affairs'

Red Series. Volume (years): 1861 (1872); 1903 (1873); 1995 (1876); 2004
  (1877–8); 2071 (1878); 2076 (1878); 2102 (1880); 2445 (1889); 2496 (1890);
  2554 (1891); 2671 (1893); 2710 (1893–1905); 2739 (1894–6); 3086 (1890–
  1917); 3087 (1918–34); 3201 (1918–23); 3209 (1943); 3212 (1943–4); 3220
  (1924–5); 3224 (1920–1); 3226 (1921–36).
Black Series. Volume (years): 3703 (1879–80); 3708 (1880); 3755 (1881); 3960
  (n.d.); 4048 (1910); 4093 (1920).
Central Registry. Volume (years): 6923 (1959–60); 6924 (1960–3); 6925 (1963–
  4); 7094 (1888–1963); 7141 (1898–1944); 8193 (1964); 8194 (1964–5); 8584
  (1959–62); 8585 (1944); 8589 (1947–66); 8590 (1955–62); 8591 (1957–60);
  8616 (1952–9); 8617 (1961–6); 8618 (1947–64);

2. Sound and Film Division

CBC Toronto Kine Collection. *Close-Up.* Canadian Broadcasting Corporation,
  #1360 T/C. 'The One in a Hundred.' Host, J. Frank Willis, 29 November 1960.

Government Documents

Canada. Department of Indian Affairs and Northern Development. Indian and
  Inuit Affairs Program. *Welfare Programs For Indian People of Ontario Before 1965.*

Report prepared by W. Henry Rogers, Social Development Directorate for the Intergovernmental Social Services Planning Committee. Ottawa, April 1983.

– 'Interpretation of the Legal Mandate and Responsibilities of Federal, Provincial, Municipal and Band Governments for Social Services to Indian People with Special Reference to the Canada-Ontario Welfare Services Agreement of 1965.' Draft document prepared by the Social Development Directorate. Ottawa-Hull, 24 July 1984.

– Indian and Northern Affairs Canada. Child and Family Services Task Force. *Indian Child and Family Services in Canada: Final Report.* Ottawa, 1987.

– Policy Directorate, Self-Government Sector. *Indian Social Services within a Self-Government Framework: Issues to Consider.* Prepared by Margaret Kovach. Ottawa, October 1990.

Interviews and Correspondence

Davidson, Dr George F. Interview by author, Vancouver, British Columbia, 12 December 1992.

Gambill, Jerry. Interview by author, Ottawa, Ontario, 10 May 1993.

Isbister, Claude M. Interview by author, Toronto, Ontario, 29 April 1993.

Roberts, C.N.C. Interview by author, Ottawa, Ontario, 5 May 1993.

Rudnicki, Walter. Interview by author, Ottawa, Ontario, 10 May 1993.

Splane, R.B. Copy of letter to Ms Joyce Timson, 11 January 1989.

Government Publications

Canada. Department of Citizenship and Immigration. Citizenship Branch. *Citizenship Projects among Indians.* Ottawa: Roger Duhamel, Queen's Printer, 1965.

– Indian Affairs Branch. *Annual Report, 1957–1958.* Ottawa: Queen's Printer, 1958.

– Indian Affairs Branch. *Annual Report, 1959–1960.* Ottawa: Queen's Printer, 1960.

– Indian Affairs Branch. *A Review of Activities 1948–1958.* Ottawa: Queen's Printer, 1959.

– Indian Affairs Branch. *The Indian>in<Transition: The Indian Today.* Ottawa: Queen's Printer, 1962.

– Department of Mines and Resources. Indian Affairs Branch. *Annual Report, 1936–1937.* Ottawa: The King's Printer.

– Indian Affairs Branch. *Annual Report, 1944–1945.* Ottawa: The King's Printer.

– Indian Affairs Branch. *Annual Report, 1948–1949.* Ottawa: The King's Printer.

– Indian and Northern Affairs Canada. *Indian Social Welfare.* Extract from *Social Security*, National Programs, Vol. 7, 'Other Programs,' 53–97. Ottawa, 1982.
– Joint Committee of the Senate and the House of Commons on Indian Affairs. *Minutes of Proceedings and Evidence.* Ottawa: Queen's Printer, 1959–61.
– National Council of Welfare. *Welfare Reform.* Ottawa: Supply and Services Canada, 1992.
– *Report of the Auditor General of Canada to the House of Commons.* vol. 14, ch. 23. Ottawa: Minister of Supply and Services, 1994.
– *Report of the Commission on Indian Affairs.* J. Fred Johnston and Don F. Brown, Joint Chairmen. Ottawa, 8 July 1947.
– Special Joint Committee of the Senate and the House of Commons Appointed to Examine and Consider the Indian Act. *Minutes of Proceedings and Evidence.* Ottawa: Edmond Cloutier, Printer to the King's Most Excellent Majesty, 1946–1948.
Ontario. Department of Public Welfare. *Annual Report of the Department of Public Welfare, 1956/1957.* Toronto: Queen's Printer, 1957.
– *Annual Report of the Department of Public Welfare, 1958/1959.* Toronto: Queen's Printer, 1959.
– Ministry of Community and Social Services. *Transitions: Report of the Social Assistance Review Committee.* Toronto: Queen's Printer for Ontario, 1988.
– *First Nations Project Team Report.* Principal Report on New Social Assistance Legislation for First Nations in Ontario, Co-Chairs, Marie Tincombe-Shaw and Audrey Hill. Toronto: Queen's Printer, May, 1992.

Secondary Sources

Books, Articles and Periodicals

Abele, Frances and Daiva Stasiulis. 'Canada as a "White Settler Colony": What about Natives and Immigrants?' In *The New Canadian Political Economy*, ed. Wallace Clement and Glen Williams, 240–77. Montreal: McGill-Queen's University Press, 1989.
Alfred, Taiaiake. *Peace, Power, Righteousness: An Indigenous Manifesto.* Don Mills, ON: Oxford University Press, 1999.
Arblaster, Anthony. *The Rise and Decline of Western Liberalism.* London: Basil Blackwell, 1984; reprint, paperback, 1986.
Armitage, Andrew. 'Work and Welfare.' In *Alternatives to Social Assistance in Indian Communities*, ed. Frank Cassidy and Shirley B. Seward, 83–111. Halifax: Institute for Research on Public Policy, 1991.

Asch, Michael. *Home and Native Land: Aboriginal Rights and the Canadian Constitution*. Toronto: Methuen, 1984.

Bain, Lesley J. 'Social Assistance Policy Alternatives: Issues and Options as Identified by Bands and Tribal Councils of B.C.' MSW Thesis, University of British Columbia, 1985.

Berry, Christopher J. *Human Nature*. Atlantic Highlands, NJ: Humanities Press International, 1986.

Bothwell, Robert, Ian Drummond, and John English. *Canada since 1945: Power, Politics, and Provincialism*. Rev. ed. Toronto: University of Toronto Press, 1989.

Brantlinger, Patrick. *Crusoe's Footprints: Cultural Studies in Britain and America*. New York: Routledge, 1990.

Brody, Hugh. *Maps and Dreams: Indians and the British Columbia Frontier*. London: Pelican Books, 1983.

Bryce, P.H. *The Story of a National Crime*. Ottawa: James Hope, 1922.

Buckley, Helen. *From Wooden Ploughs to Welfare: Why Indian Policy Failed in the Prairie Provinces*. Montreal: McGill-Queen's University Press, 1992.

Cairns, Alan C. *Citizens Plus: Aboriginal Peoples and the Canadian State*. Vancouver: UBC Press, 2000.

Carniol, Ben. *Case Critical: Challenging Social Services Canada*. 4th ed. Toronto: Between the Lines, 2000.

Carstens, Peter. *The Queen's People: A Study of Hegemony, Coercion, and Accommodation among the Okanagan of Canada*. Toronto: University of Toronto Press, 1991.

Carter, Sarah. *Lost Harvests: Prairie Indian Reserve Farmers and Government Policy*. Montreal: McGill-Queen's University Press, 1990.

Cassidy, Frank. 'Approaches to Welfare Reform in Indian Communities.' In *Alternatives to Social Assistance in Indian Communities*, ed. Frank Cassidy and Shirley B. Seward, 3–14. Halifax: Institute for Research on Public Policy, 1991.

Chamberlin, J.E. *The Harrowing of Eden: White Attitudes toward North American Natives*. Toronto: Fitzhenry and Whiteside, 1975.

Chupik-Hall, Jessa. '"Good Families Do Not Just Happen": Indigenous People and Child Welfare Services in Canada, 1950–1965.' M.A. thesis, Trent University, 2001.

Coates, Ken S. *Best Left as Indians: Native–White Relations in the Yukon Territory, 1840–1973*. Montreal: McGill-Queen's University Press, 1991.

Cook, Ramsay. *The Regenerators: Social Criticism in Late Victorian English Canada*. Toronto: University of Toronto Press, 1985.

Cormie, John A. 'Forgotten Canadians.' *Social Welfare*, December 1937–March 1938, 74–6.

Crafts, N.F.R. 'Long-term Unemployment in Britain in the 1930s.' *Economic History Review* 2nd. ser., 40, no. 3 (1987): 418–32.

Cunningham, Rob. 'Community Development at the Department of Indian Affairs in the 1960s: Much Ado about Nothing.' MA thesis, University of Saskatchewan.

Daniel, Richard. *A History of Native Claims Processes in Canada: 1867–1979.* Ottawa: Department of Indian and Northern Affairs, 1980.

de Vattel, Emmerich. *The Law of Nations; or Principles of the Law of Nature, Applied to the Conduct and Affairs of Nations and Sovereigns.* 1760. Northampton, Mass., 1820.

Dickason, Olive Patricia. *Canada's First Nations: A History of Founding Peoples from Earliest Times.* Toronto: McClelland and Stewart, 1992.

Dobyns, Henry F. 'Estimating Aboriginal Population: An Appraisal of Techniques with a New Hemispheric Estimate.' *Current Anthropology* 7 (1966): 395–416.

Driben, Paul and Robert S. Trudeau. *When Freedom Is Lost: The Dark Side of the Relationship between Government and the Fort Hope Band.* Toronto: University of Toronto Press, 1983.

Dyck, Noel. *What Is the Indian Indian 'Problem': Tutelage and Resistance in Canadian Indian Administration.* Social and Economic Studies, No. 46. St John's: Institute of Economic and Social Research, Memorial University of Newfoundland, 1991.

Dyck, Noel, and James B. Waldram. 'Anthropology, Public Policy and Native Peoples: An Introduction to the Issues.' In *Anthropology, Public Policy and Native Peoples in Canada*, ed. Noel Dyck and James B. Waldram, 3–38. Montreal: McGill-Queen's University Press, 1993.

Elias, Peter Douglas. *The Dakota of the Canadian Northwest: Lessons for Survival.* Winnipeg: University of Manitoba Press, 1988.

Finkel, Alvin. 'Origins of the Welfare State in Canada.' In *The Canadian State: Political Economy and Political Power,* ed. Leo Panitch, 344–70. Toronto: University of Toronto Press, 1977.

Fisher, Robin. *Contact and Conflict: Indian-European Relations in British Columbia, 1774–1890.* Vancouver: University of British Columbia Press, 1977.

Flanagan, Tom. *First Nations? Second Thoughts?* Montreal: McGill-Queen's University Press, 2000.

Fleras, Augie, and Jean Leonard Elliott. *The 'Nations Within': Aboriginal-State Relations in Canada, the United States, and New Zealand.* Toronto: Oxford University Press, 1992.

Forsey, Eugene. *A Life on the Fringe: The Memoirs of Eugene Forsey.* Toronto: Oxford University Press, 1991.

Forster, E.M. 'The Challenge of Our Time.' In E.M. Forster, *Two Cheers for Democracy.* New York: Harcourt Brace Jovanovich, 1951.

Foucault, Michel. 'Truth and Power.' In *Power/Knowledge: Selected Interviews and Other Writings, 1972–1977*, ed. Colin Gordon, 109–33. New York: Pantheon Books, 1980.

– 'Two Lectures.' In *Power/Knowledge: Selected Interviews and Other Writings, 1972–1977*, ed. Colin Gordon, 78–108. New York: Pantheon Books, 1980.

Freire, Paulo. *Pedagogy of the Oppressed*. New York: Continuum Publishing, 1970.

Frideres, James S. *Native Peoples in Canada: Contemporary Conflicts*. 3rd ed. Scarborough: Prentice-Hall, 1988.

– with Lilianne Ernestine Krosenbrink-Gelissen. *Aboriginal Peoples in Canada: Contemporary Conflicts*. 5th ed. Scarborough: Prentice-Hall Allyn & Bacon, 1998.

George, Vic, and Paul Wilding. *Ideology and Social Welfare*. Rev. ed. London: Routledge and Kegan Paul, 1985.

Granatstein, J.L. *The Ottawa Men: The Civil Service Mandarins, 1935–1957*. Toronto: Oxford University Press, 1982.

Gray, Grattan. 'Social Policy by Stealth.' *Policy Options* (March 1990): 17–29.

Green, Joyce A. 'Towards a Detente with History: Confronting Canada's Colonial Legacy.' *International Journal of Canadian Studies* 12 (Fall 1995): 85–105.

Guest, Dennis. 'Dealing with Unemployment: Full Employment and Income Security.' In *Unemployment and Welfare: Social Policy and the Work of Social Work*, ed. Graham Riches and Gordon Ternowetsky, 33–46. Toronto: Garamond Press, 1990.

– *The Emergence of Social Security in Canada*. 3rd ed. Vancouver: UBC Press, 1997.

– *Histoire de la Sécurité sociale au Canada*. Traduit de l'anglais par Hervé Juste en collaboration avec Patricia Juste. Montreal: Boréal, 1993.

– 'World War II and the Welfare State in Canada.' In *The 'Benevolent' State: The Growth of Welfare in Canada*, ed. Allan Moscovitch and Jim Albert, 205–21. Toronto: Garamond Press, 1987.

Hall, D.J. 'Clifford Sifton and Canadian Indian Administration 1896–1905.' *Prairie Forum* 2, no. 2 (1977). Reprinted in *As Long as the Sun Shines and Water Flows*, ed. Ian A.L. Getty and Antoine S. Lussier, 120–44. Nakoda Institute Occasional Paper No. 1. Vancouver: University of British Columbia Press, 1983.

Ham, Christopher, and Michael Hill. *The Policy Process in the Modern Capitalist State*. Brighton: Wheatsheaf, 1984.

Haskell, Thomas L. *The Emergence of Professional Social Science: The American Social Science Association and the Mid-Nineteenth-Century Crisis of Authority*. Urbana: University of Illinois Press, 1977.

Hawley, Donna Lea. *The Indian Act Annotated*. 2nd ed. Toronto: Carswell, 1986.

Hawthorn, H.B., C.S. Belshaw, and S.M. Jameson. *The Indians of British Columbia.* Toronto: University of Toronto Press, 1958.

– ed. 'The Politics of Indian Affairs.' In *A Survey of the Contemporary Indians of Canada.* Pt I, ch. 17. Ottawa: Queen's Printer, 1966; abridged and reprinted in *As Long as the Sun Shines and Water Flows: A Reader in Canadian Native Studies,* ed. Ian A.L. Getty and Antoine S. Lussier, 164–87. Nakoda Institute Occasional Paper No. 1. Vancouver: University of British Columbia Press, 1983.

– ed. *A Survey of the Contemporary Indians of Canada: A Report on Economic, Political, Educational Needs and Policies.* Volume 1. Ottawa: Queen's Printer, 1966.

Himmelfarb, Gertrude. *The Idea of Poverty: England in the Early Industrial Age.* New York: Vintage Books, 1985.

Hobsbawm, E.J. *Nations and Nationalism since 1780: Programme, Myth, Reality.* Cambridge: Cambridge University Press, 1990.

Honigmann, John J. 'The Logic of the James Bay Survey.' *Dalhousie Review* 30, no. 4 (1951), 377–86.

Hughes, James L. 'An Experiment in Altruism.' *Methodist Magazine and Review* 19 (January 1899).

Innis, Harold A. *The Fur Trade in Canada: An Introduction to Canadian Economic History.* Toronto: Canadian University Paperbacks, University of Toronto Press, 1962.

Irving, Allan. 'Federal-Provincial Issues in Social Policy.' In *Canadian Social Policy,* ed. Shankar A. Yelaja, 326–49. Rev. ed. Waterloo: Wilfrid Laurier University Press, 1987.

– 'The Scientific Imperative in Canadian Social Work: Social Work and Social Welfare Research in Canada, 1897–1945.' *Canadian Social Work Review* 9, no. 1 (1992): 9–27.

Jaggar, Alison M., and Paula Rothenberg Struhl, eds. *Feminist Frameworks: Alternative Theoretical Accounts of the Relations between Men and Women.* 2nd ed. New York: McGraw-Hill, 1984.

Jenness, Diamond. 'Canada's Indians Yesterday: What of Today?' *Canadian Journal of Economics and Political Science* 20(1) (February 1954): 95–100. Reprinted in *As Long as the Sun Shines and Water Flows,* ed. Ian A.L. Getty and Antoine S. Lussier, 158–63. Nakoda Institute Occasional Paper No. 1. Vancouver: University of British Columbia Press, 1983.

Jennings, Francis. *The Invasion of America.* New York: W.W. Norton & Company, 1976.

Johnston, Patrick. *Native Children and the Child Welfare System.* Ottawa: Canadian Council on Social Development, 1983.

Kendall, Katherine A. *Social Work Education: Its Origins in Europe.* Alexandria, VA: Council on Social Work Education, 2000.

Kent, Tom. *A Public Purpose.* Montreal: McGill-Queen's University Press, 1988.

Kierans, Eric W. *Globalism and the Nation-State.* CBC Massey Lecture Series, ed. Jonathan Kaplan. Toronto: CBC Enterprises, 1984.

Kitchen, Brigitte. 'The Introduction of Family Allowances in Canada.' In *The 'Benevolent' State: The Growth of Welfare in Canada*, ed. Allan Moscovitch and Jim Albert, 222–41. Toronto: Garamond Press, 1987.

Kroeber, Alfred L. 'Cultural and Natural Areas of Native North America.' *University of California Publications in American Archaeology and Ethnology* 38. Berkeley: University of California Press, 1939.

Kulchyski, Peter. '"A Considerable Unrest": F.O. Loft and the League of Indians.' *Native Studies Review* 4, nos. 1–2 (1988): 95–117.

– 'Anthropology in the Service of the State: Diamond Jenness and Canadian Indian Policy.' *Journal of Canadian Studies* 28, no. 2 (1993): 21–50.

Leighton, Douglas. 'A Victorian Civil Servant at Work: Lawrence Vankoughnet and the Canadian Indian Department, 1874–1893.' In *As Long as the Sun Shines and Water Flows*, ed. Ian A.L. Getty and Antoine S. Lussier, 104–19. Nakoda Institute Occasional Paper No. 1. Vancouver: University of British Columbia Press, 1983.

Lightman, Ernie. 'Conditionality and Social Assistance: Market Values and the Work Ethic.' In *Unemployment and Welfare: Social Policy and the Work of Social Work*, ed. Graham Riches and Gordon Ternowetsky, 91–105. Toronto: Garamond Press, 1990.

Macpherson, C.B. *The Life and Times of Liberal Democracy.* Oxford: Oxford University Press, 1977.

– *The Political Theory of Possessive Individualism: Hobbes to Locke.* Oxford: Clarendon Press, 1962; Oxford University Press Paperback, 1964.

– 'Problems of Human Rights in the Late Twentieth Century.' In C.B. Macpherson, *The Rise and Fall of Economic Justice and Other Essays.* Oxford: Oxford University Press, 1987.

– *The Real World of Democracy.* The Massey Lectures, 4th ser. Toronto: CBC Enterprises, 1965.

Manuel, George, and Michael Posluns. *The Fourth World: An Indian Reality.* Don Mills, ON: Collier Macmillan, 1974.

Manzer, Ronald. *Public Policies and Political Development in Canada.* Toronto: University of Toronto Press, 1985.

Marsh, Leonard. *Report on Social Security for Canada.* Toronto: University of Toronto Press, 1975.

Marshall, T.H. 'Changing Ideas about Poverty.' In T.H. Marshall, *The Right to Welfare and Other Essays.* New York: Free Press, 1981.

McFarlane, Peter. *Brotherhood to Nationhood: George Manuel and the Making of the Modern Indian Movement.* Toronto: Between the Lines, 1993.

McGrane, Bernard. *Beyond Anthropology: Society and the Other.* New York: Columbia University Press, 1989.

McMillan, Alan D. *Native Peoples and Cultures of Canada.* Toronto: Douglas and McIntyre, 1988.

McNab, David T. 'Herman Merivale and Colonial Office Indian Policy in the Mid-Nineteenth Century.' *Canadian Journal of Native Studies* 1, no. 2 (1981). Reprinted in *As Long as the Sun Shines and Water Flows: A Reader in Canadian Native Studies,* ed. Ian A.L. Getty and Antoine S. Lussier, 85–103. Vancouver: University of British Columbia Press, 1983.

McNaught, Kenneth. *The Penguin History of Canada.* Rev. ed. London: Penguin Books, 1988.

Memmi, Albert. *The Colonizer and the Colonized.* Trans. Howard Greenfeld. Boston: Beacon Press, 1967.

Mencher, Samuel. *Poor Law to Poverty Program.* Pittsburgh: University of Pittsburgh Press, 1974.

Merivale, Herman. *Lectures on Colonization and the Colonies.* New York: A.M. Kelly, 1967.

Merton, Robert K. *Social Theory and Social Structure.* New York: Free Press, 1957.

Miliband, Ralph. *The State in Capitalist Society: The Analysis of the Western System of Power.* London: Quartet Books, 1973.

Miller, J.R. *Skyscrapers Hide the Heavens: A History of Indian-White Relations in Canada.* 3rd ed. Toronto: University of Toronto Press, 2000.

Mooney, J.M. *The Aboriginal Population of America North of Mexico,* ed. John R. Swanton. Washington, DC: 1928.

Moore, Robin. *Paul Scott's Raj.* London: Heinemann, 1990.

Morton, Desmond. *A Short History of Canada.* Edmonton: Hurtig, 1983.

Moscovitch, Allan, and Glenn Drover. 'Social Expenditures and the Welfare State: The Canadian Experience in Historical Perspective.' In *The 'Benevolent' State: The Growth of Welfare in Canada,* ed. Allan Moscovitch and Jim Albert, 13–43. Toronto: Garamond Press, 1987.

Naylor, R.T. *Canada in the European Age, 1453–1919.* Vancouver: New Star Books, 1987.

Noël, Lise. *Intolerance: A General Survey.* Trans. Arnold Bennett. Montreal: McGill-Queen's University Press, 1994.

Orwell, George. 'Shooting an Elephant.' In *The Collected Essays, Journalism and Letters of George Orwell.* Vol. 1. *An Age Like This, 1920–1940.* Ed. Sonia Orwell and Ian Angus. London: Penguin Books, 1970.

Owram, Doug. *The Government Generation: Canadian Intellectuals and the State, 1900–1945.* Toronto: University of Toronto Press, 1986.

Panitch, Leo. 'The Role and Nature of the Canadian state.' In *The Canadian*

State: Political Economy and Political Power, ed. Leo Panitch, 3–27. Toronto: University of Toronto Press, 1977.

Parsons, Talcott. '"Voting" and the Equilibrium of the American Political System.' In *American Voting Behavior*, ed. E. Burdick and A.J. Brodbeck. New York: Free Press, 1959.

Phillips, Paul, and Stephen Watson. 'From Mobilization to Continentalism: The Canadian Economy in the Post-Depression Period.' In *Modern Canada, 1930–1980s*, ed. Michael S. Cross and Gregory S. Kealey, 20–45. Toronto: McClelland & Stewart, 1984.

Pinker, Robert. 'Introduction.' In T.H. Marshall, *The Right to Welfare and Other Essays*, 1–28. New York: Free Press, 1981.

Prentice, Alison, Paula Bourne, Gail Cuthbert Brandt, Beth Light, Wendy Mitchinson, and Naomi Black. *Canadian Women: A History.* Toronto: Harcourt Brace Jovanovich, 1988.

Ray, Arthur J. *The Canadian Fur Trade in the Industrial Age.* Toronto: University of Toronto Press, 1990.

– *Indians in the Fur Trade: Their Role as Hunters, Trappers and Middlemen in the Lands Southwest of Hudson Bay 1660–1870.* 2nd ed. Toronto: University of Toronto Press, 1998.

– 'Periodic Shortages, Native Welfare, and the Hudson's Bay Company 1670–1930.' In *The Subarctic Fur Trade: Native Social and Economic Adaptations*, ed. Shepherd Krech III, 1–20. Vancouver: University of British Columbia Press, 1984.

Rea, J.E. *T.A. Crerar: A Political Life.* Montreal: McGill-Queen's University Press, 1997.

Reisman, David. *Richard Titmuss: Welfare and Society.* London: Heinemann Educational Books, 1977.

Richmond, Mary. *Social Diagnosis.* New York: Free Press, 1917.

Ross, David P., and Peter J. Usher. *From the Roots Up: Economic Development As If Community Mattered.* New York: The Bootstrap Press, 1986.

Rushdie, Salman. *Midnight's Children.* London: Pan Books, Picador Paperback, 1982.

Ryan, William. *Blaming the Victim.* Rev. ed. New York: Vintage Books, 1976.

Said, Edward W. *Culture and Imperialism.* New York: Alfred A. Knopf, 1993.

– *The Pen and the Sword.* Toronto: Between the Lines, 1994.

Sayer, Derek. *Capitalism and Modernity: An Excursus on Marx and Weber.* London: Routledge, 1991.

Schmalz, Peter S. *The Ojibwa of Southern Ontario.* Toronto: University of Toronto Press, 1991.

Scott, Ian G., and J.T.S. McCabe. 'The Role of the Provinces in the Elucidation of Rights.' In *Governments in Conflict? Provinces and Indian Nations in Canada*, ed. J. Anthony Long and Menno Boldt, in association with Leroy Little Bear, 59–71. Toronto: University of Toronto Press, 1988.

Scott, Paul. *The Raj Quartet*. London: Heinemann, 1976.

Seal, Anil. *The Emergence of Indian Nationalism: Competition and Collaboration in the Later Nineteenth Century*. Cambridge: Cambridge University Press, 1968.

Seligman, Adam B. 'Towards a Reinterpretation of Modernity in an Age of Post-modernity.' In *Theories of Modernity and Postmodernity*, ed. Bryan S. Turner, 117–35. Newbury Park, CA: Sage, 1990.

Sheehan, Bernard W. *Seeds of Extinction: Jeffersonian Philanthropy and the American Indian*. Chapel Hill: University of North Carolina Press, 1973.

Shewell, Hugh. '"Bitterness behind Every Smiling Face": Community Development and Canada's First Nations, 1954–1968.' *Canadian Historical Review* 83, no. 1 (2002): 58–84.

– 'Jules Sioui and Indian Political Radicalism in Canada, 1943–1944.' *Journal of Canadian Studies* 34, no. 3 (1999): 211–42.

– 'The Use of Social Assistance for Employment Creation on Indian Reserves: An Appraisal.' In *Alternatives to Social Assistance in Indian Communities*, ed. Frank Cassidy and Shirley B. Seward, 17–81. Halifax: Institute for Research on Public Policy, 1991.

– '"What Makes the Indian Tick?" The Influence of Social Sciences on Canada's Indian Policy, 1947–1964.' *Histoire sociale/Social History* 34 (67) (2001): 133–67.

Shewell, Hugh, and Annabella Spagnut. 'The First Nations of Canada: Social Welfare and the Quest for Self-Government.' In *Social Welfare with Indigenous Peoples*, ed. John Dixon and Robert P. Scheurell, 1–53. London: Routledge, 1995.

Siggner, Andrew J. 'The Socio-Demographic Conditions of Registered Indians.' In *Arduous Journey: Canadian Indians and Decolonization*, ed. J. Rick Ponting, 57–83. Toronto: McClelland and Stewart, 1986.

Simeon, Richard, and Ian Robinson. *State, Society, and the Development of Canadian Federalism*. The Collected Research Studies for the Royal Commission on the Economic Union and Development Prospects for Canada. Volume 71. Toronto: University of Toronto Press, 1990.

Sluman, Norma and Jean Goodwill. *John Tootoosis: A Biography of a Cree Leader*. Ottawa: Golden Dog Press, 1982.

Struthers, James. 'Canadian Unemployment Policy in the 1930s.' In *Readings in Canadian History*, ed. R. Douglas Francis and Donald B. Smith. Vol. 2. *Post-Confederation*, 375–89. Toronto: Harcourt Brace, 1994.

– *The Limits of Affluence: Welfare in Ontario, 1920–1970*. Toronto: University of Toronto Press, 1994.

Swingewood, Alan. *A Short History of Sociological Thought.* 2nd ed. Houndmills, U.K.: Macmillan, 1991.

TAP Associates. *Community Care: Toward Indian Control of Social Services.* Report of the Tripartite Task Group on Social Services to Indians in Ontario, Phase 2. Toronto: TAP Associates, 1980.

– *A Starving Man Doesn't Argue.* Report of the Tripartite Task Group on Social Services to Indians in Ontario, Phase 1. Toronto: TAP Associates, 1979.

Taylor, John H. *Ottawa: An Illustrated History.* Toronto: James Lorimer and Canadian Museum of Civilization, National Museums of Canada, 1986.

Tennant, Paul. *Aboriginal Peoples and Politics: The Indian Land Question in British Columbia, 1849–1989.* Vancouver: UBC Press, 1990.

– 'Native Indian Political Organization in British Columbia, 1900–1969: A Response to Internal Colonialism.' *B.C. Studies* 55 (Autumn 1982): 3–49.

Tester, Frank James, and Peter Kulchyski. *Tammarniit (Mistakes): Inuit Relocation in the Eastern Arctic, 1939–1963.* Vancouver: UBC Press, 1994.

Thorne, Brian. *Carl Rogers.* London: Sage, 1992.

Titley, E. Brian. *A Narrow Vision: Duncan Campbell Scott and the Administration of Indian Affairs in Canada.* Vancouver: UBC Press, 1986.

Tobias, John L. 'Protection, Civilization, Assimilation: An Outline History of Canada's Indian Policy.' *Western Canadian Journal of Anthropology* 6, no. 2 (1976): 13–30.

Trigger, Bruce G. 'The Historians' Indian: Native Americans in Canadian Historical Writing from Charlevoix to the Present.' In *Out of the Background: Readings on Canadian Native History,* ed. Robin Fisher and Kenneth Coates, 19–44. Toronto: Copp Clark Pitman, 1988.

Turner, Bryan S. 'Contemporary Problems in the Theory of Citizenship.' In *Citizenship and Social Theory,* ed. Bryan S. Turner, 1–18. Newbury Park, CA: Sage, 1993.

– 'Periodization and Politics in the Postmodern.' In *Theories of Modernity and Postmodernity,* ed. Bryan S. Turner, 1–13. Newbury Park, CA: Sage, 1990.

Usher, Peter J. 'Northern Development, Impact Assessment, and Social Change.' In *Anthropology, Public Policy and Native Peoples in Canada,* ed. Noel Dyck and James B. Waldram, 98–130. Montreal: McGill-Queen's University Press, 1993.

Vivian, R.P., C. McMillan, E. Robertson, W.H. Sebrell, F.F. Tisdall, and W.G. McIntosh, 'The Nutrition and Health of the James Bay Indian,' *Canadian Medical Association Journal* 59 (1948): 505–18.

Waldram, James B. 'Canada's "Indian Problem" and the Indian's "Canada Problem."' In *Power and Resistance: Critical Thinking about Canadian Social Issues,* ed. Les Samuelson, 53–70. Halifax: Fernwood Publishing, 1994.

Watkins, Mel. 'Noughts and Crosses: The Games Whites Play.' In *Madness and Ruin: Politics and the Economy in the Neoconservative Age*. Toronto: Between the Lines, 1992.

Weaver, Sally M. *Making Canadian Indian Policy: The Hidden Agenda, 1968–1970*. Toronto: University of Toronto Press, 1981.

Weber, Max. *The Protestant Ethic and the Spirit of Capitalism*. Trans. Talcott Parsons. London: Routledge, 1992.

– *The Methodology of the Social Sciences*. Trans. and ed. Edward A. Shils and Henry A. Finch. New York: Free Press, 1949.

Wharf, Brian. *Toward First Nation Control of Child Welfare: A Review of Emerging Developments in B.C.* Victoria: University of Victoria, 1987.

Whitaker, Reg. 'Images of the State in Canada.' In *The Canadian State: Political Economy and Political Power*, ed. Leo Panitch, 28–68. Toronto: University of Toronto Press, 1977.

Wills, Gale. 'Values of Community Practice: Legacy of the Radical Social Gospel.' *Canadian Social Work Review* 9, no. 1 (1992): 28–40.

Wolf, Eric R. *Europe and the People without History*. 2nd ed. Berkeley: University of California Press, 1997.

Wolfe, David. 'The Rise and Demise of the Keynesian Era in Canada: Economic Policy, 1930–1982.' In *Modern Canada, 1930–1980s*, ed. Michael S. Cross and Gregory S. Kealey, 46–78. Toronto: McClelland and Stewart, 1984.

Woodcock, George. *British Columbia: A History of the Province*. Vancouver: Douglas and McIntyre, 1990; Paperback edition, 1994.

Index